THEOLOGY FOR THE TWENTY-FIRST CENTURY

CENTER OF THEOLOGICAL INQUIRY

Theology for the Twenty-first Century is a series sponsored by the Center of Theological Inquiry (CTI), an institute, located in Princeton, New Jersey, dedicated to the advanced study of theology. This series is one of its many initiatives and projects.

The goal of the series is to publish inquiries of contemporary scholars into the nature of the Christian faith and its witness and practice in the church, society, and culture. The series will include investigations into the uniqueness of the Christian faith. But it will also offer studies that relate the Christian faith to the major cultural, social, and practical issues of our time.

Monographs and symposia will result from research by scholars in residence at the Center of Theological Inquiry or otherwise associated with it. In some cases, publications will come from group research projects sponsored by CTI. It is our intention that the books selected for this series will constitute a major contribution to renewing theology in its service to church and society.

WALLACE M. ALSTON, JR., ROBERT JENSON,
and DON S. BROWNING
Series Editors

FOUNDATIONS OF
SYSTEMATIC
THEOLOGY

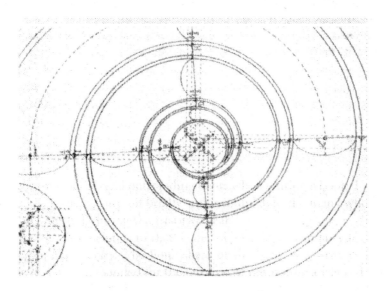

Thomas G. Guarino

t&t clark

NEW YORK • LONDON

Copyright © 2005 by Thomas G. Guarino

T&T CLARK INTERNATIONAL
80 Maiden Lane, Suite 704, New York, NY 10038

T&T CLARK INTERNATIONAL
The Tower Building, 11 York Road, London SE1 7NX

T&T Clark International is a Continuum imprint.

Cover design: Jim Booth

Library of Congress Cataloging-in-Publication Data

Guarino, Thomas G.
  Foundations of systematic theology / Thomas G. Guarino.
    p. cm. — (Theology for the twenty-first century)
  Includes bibliographical references and index.
  ISBN 0-567-02980-8 — ISBN 0-567-02751-1 (pbk.)
  1. Theology—Methodology. 2. Catholic Church—Doctrines. 3. Catholic Church and philosophy. 4. First philosophy. I. Title. II. Series.
  BX1751.3.G83 2005
  230'.01—dc22
                    2004029701

Printed in the United States of America

06 07 08 09 10   10 9 8 7 6 5 4 3 2

CONTENTS

ACKNOWLEDGMENTS

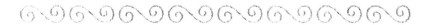

One accumulates several outstanding debts when writing a book. I would like to acknowledge, even if briefly and incompletely, the many who have aided my research during the past two years.

Pride of place belongs to the Center of Theological Inquiry (CTI) at Princeton, New Jersey. The lion's share of the book was written at this unique institution, founded for the purpose of promoting advanced theological research. I would not likely have completed the manuscript without the benefit of residency at CTI, nor would I have been the beneficiary of so many colleagues who graced me with their insights and friendship. I would like to thank Wallace Alston, director of CTI, for kindly inviting me; Robert Jenson, senior scholar for research, for his penetrating theological observations and his gracious advice; and Kathi Morley, CTI administrator, for her constant solicitude and good nature in the face of endless demands.

I would also like to thank Princeton Theological Seminary for the hospitality it extends to members of CTI. In particular, the Speer and Luce Libraries constituted valuable resources for research. I would add to these the libraries of my home institution, Seton Hall University, as well as the Firestone Library of Princeton University.

Robert Jenson of CTI and Avery Dulles, SJ, of Fordham University kindly dedicated their valuable time to reading and commenting upon the manuscript. I incorporated many of their keen insights into the book. For the great generosity of these scholars, I am deeply indebted.

I would like to acknowledge as well the help and friendship of David Lotz, formerly of Union Theological Seminary, and Edward Oakes, SJ, of Mundelein Seminary.

I am grateful to the administration, faculty, and staff of the School of Theology of Seton Hall University, who have been entirely supportive of my work. Cathy Trajer, in particular, has always been kindly available to me for printing and various editorial tasks.

Finally, I would like to thank Henry Carrigan of T&T Clark International for both his professional and personal support.

INTRODUCTION

There has rarely been much doubt among Christians that the content of their faith radiates a certain beauty. In broad outline, salvation history speaks of a just and compassionate God who guides and accompanies the people of Israel and who, in the fullness of time, sends his only begotten Son both to save a sinful humanity and to further share with them his own inner life. This narrative of salvation may be read as a love story, of a God who not only redeems his creatures from sin, but who, through the cross and resurrection of Christ, triumphs entirely over the hectoring effects of evil: suffering, tragedy, humiliation, and death.

Over the course of centuries, this salvific dialogue has become crystallized, precisely for the sake of its own truth, in determinate doctrinal and creedal forms. Statements such as those issued by the Councils of Nicea and Constantinople, for example, are judgments by the church about the meaning and truth of salvation history, about the actuality of God's gratuitous manifestation to us. They serve as unfailing guideposts in the human attempt at understanding God's action on our behalf. They constitute the particular form or vessel understood as one essential way of maintaining and enshrining the church's faith. Traditional characteristics of this doctrinal form, at least in its essential judgments, include its unity and organic continuity, its material identity and constancy. Such characteristics, in fact, help to constitute what may be called the "beauty" of doctrine; it is a beauty of balance and clarity, of intelligibility and aesthetic proportion. It is a form meant to mediate the splendor of revelation, the immanent and economic life of the Father, the Incarnate Word, and the Holy Spirit. Etienne Gilson, relying on Aquinas, helps us to appreciate the precise nature of doctrinal form: In what does Beauty consist? It consists of integrity, proportion, harmony, brightness and clarity. "Indeed, everything is beautiful as having a form . . . and this form is a sort of participation of the divine clarity."[1] To this we may add Balthasar's comment that a form appears beautiful because the delight it arouses in us is founded on the truth and goodness manifested in it.[2]

The argument of this book is that the doctrinal form of the Christian faith, in its essential characteristics, calls for certain theoretical exigencies. This is to say that the proportion and beauty of the form is not served or illuminated by simply any presuppositions. Rather, a determinate understanding of philosophy, of the nature of truth, of hermeneutical theory, of the predication of language, and of mutual correlation is required if Christian faith and doctrine are to maintain a recognizable and suitably mediative form. Failing to adduce specific principles will lead either to a simple assertion of Christian truth, absent philosophical warrants, in which case the form of Christianity becomes less intelligible and attractive, or to the substitution of a radically changed form, itself inappropriate for displaying the fundamental revelatory narrative of faith. Referring to the development of Christianity as "the drawing up of our faith, the foundation of our building," Irenaeus offers the apt image of the house of faith.[3] The house of Christian faith possesses a certain proportion or structure; the form will badly sag if one removes an undergirding beam, or if one beam is replaced with another of variable size or shape. The form's beauty will either be obscured, or the form will become something quite different, no longer architectonically related to what was originally the case. This book will discuss those doctrinal characteristics considered foundational to the Christian faith, as protective of its revelatory form and, concomitantly, will examine the theoretical principles required if such form is to remain both intelligible and beautiful.

I write as a Roman Catholic theologian (with serious ecumenical interests), committed to the truth of the Christian faith, asking to what extent this faith, given its own proportional structure, requires certain fundamental exigencies.

Notes

1. Etienne Gilson, *Elements of Christian Philosophy* (Garden City, N.Y.: Doubleday, 1960), 162–63, commenting on *ST*, I-II, q. 27, a. 1 ad 3.

2. Hans Urs von Balthasar, *The Glory of the Lord* (vol. 1; trans. Erasmo Leiva-Merikakis et al.; Edinburgh: T&T Clark, 1982), 118.

3. Irenaeus, *Proof of the Apostolic Preaching* (trans. Joseph P. Smith; Ancient Christian Writers 16; Westminster, Md.: Newman Press, 1952), 51.

CHAPTER 1

Christian Doctrine and Contemporary Challenges

Revelation and Doctrine

Revelation

Christian tradition has generally understood "revelation" to be, both in its fundamental linguistic and philological sense as well as in the sense that has developed both historically and theologically, nothing less than God's unveiledness, his free, gratuitous self-manifestation to us. While it is certainly true that this manifestation is always filtered, by necessity, through human concepts, symbols, linguistic conventions, and historically and culturally conditioned perspectives, this does not detract from the fundamental Christian conviction that it is God himself who has entered into a loving relationship with his creation and freely manifested something of his own inner life.

From the viewpoint of Christian theology, this self-manifestation of God is humanly, and therefore linguistically, articulated as teaching, as doctrine. Jesus himself, of course, was a teacher, and part of his commission charges his followers to teach others, thereby making disciples of all nations (Matt 28:19–20). Paul, too, was clearly a teacher, one who not infrequently reminded his listeners that the teachings he laid down were to be neither altered nor contradicted.[1]

This intrinsic conjunction between divine revelation and Christian teaching is found throughout the early church. Origen's great work, *On*

First Principles, embodies significant elements belonging to the early doctrinal catechesis of the school at Alexandria. This same catechesis is found in Augustine's *De doctrina christiana* and in the theological works of the great Cappadocians. The early councils of the church—Nicea, Constantinople, and Chalcedon—themselves self-consciously offered further, definitive teachings, that is, authoritative explanations of the biblical text, in light of the church's worship, understanding, and spiritual experience. One element that the Scriptures, the early doctors, and the ancient councils have in common is this: The teaching tendered is not offered as a transitory or evanescent solution. It is proposed, rather, as God's word, or as a ratification of God's word, a word communicated personally to men and women for their salvation, for the sake of leading them to eternal life.

It is precisely this sense of teaching, as the scripturally and ecclesially articulated presence of the self-manifestation of the triune God, that continued with the Schoolmen in the Middle Ages and with the great teachers of the Reformation.[2] To teach with authority is to offer nothing less than the truth of the gospel of Jesus Christ, a Word that offers to all people the healing and saving message of God's own action and life. This self-understanding, characteristic of virtually the entire Christian tradition—that the mission of the church is to teach the truth of the gospel of Jesus Christ—has led to the defining characteristics of faith and doctrine.[3]

Characteristics of Christian Doctrine

Christianity has staked a great deal on the notion of revelation as the enduring, saving truth about Jesus Christ. Today's church proclaims, in essence, what the church of yesterday (and the two are intrinsically linked) held and believed about the triune God, about Christ as true God and true man, about the Lord and Giver of Life, about the church, the body of which Jesus is the head. This is not to say that such convictions are held without nuance. On the contrary, most Christians hold this belief with the concomitant recognition that over the course of time there has been organic development and genetic progress. Sometimes there is even a more generic reinterpretation. But in general contours and in fundamental principles, it is clearly a conviction of the church at large that teachings, once defined, especially those considered authoritative by the early church, are reflective of Scripture and continue, substantially intact, what the church has believed and continues to believe.[4]

Selected Documents

One may peruse just a few statements of the Roman Catholic Church, for instance, to see this conviction clearly stated. A glance at the dogmatic constitution on revelation promulgated at Vatican II, *Dei Verbum*, indicates that there is something in revelation that Christians consider to be universal, normative, self-same, and eternal. For example, God chose to reveal himself and to make known to us the hidden purpose of his will (art. 2). The Christian dispensation, as the new and definitive covenant, will never pass away (art. 4). Through revelation, God chose to manifest and to communicate himself and the eternal decisions of his will (art. 6). God has seen to it that what he has revealed will abide perpetually in its full integrity and be handed on to all generations (art. 7).

More recently, one may read similarly apposite sentences in the (certainly less authoritative) Declaration of the Congregation for the Doctrine of the Faith, *Dominus Iesus*.[5] There, Cardinal Joseph Ratzinger seeks to defend the "irreversible" doctrines that some have called into question, such as "the definitive and complete character of the revelation of Jesus Christ[,] . . . the inspired nature of the books of Sacred Scripture, the personal unity between the Eternal Word and Jesus of Nazareth, the unity of the economy of the incarnate Word and the Holy Spirit, [and] the unicity and salvific universality of the mystery of Jesus Christ" (art. 4). Similarly, the International Theological Commission observes that "the truth of revelation . . . is universally valid and unchangeable in substance" (art. I, 4). And again: "Dogma in a stricter sense . . . is a teaching in which the church proclaims a truth of revelation definitively and in a way that is binding for the universal church, with the result that denial of that teaching is rejected as heresy and anathematized" (art. III, 3).[6]

These few sentences from Vatican II, a recent magisterial document, and a body of theologians are only a few from among many other possible sources echoing the same theme. They clearly place the theological emphasis on the presence of God to his people, and the continuing importance of doctrine as one way of mediating that presence. One may also see from such statements the significant investment the Christian church has staked on its own ability to know God's self-manifestation with a certain dimension of clarity, objectivity, and perpetuity.[7] These watchwords are not recent inventions in the church; they characterize a long tradition of reflection upon the meaning of Christianity and the very nature of the affirmation that God has "revealed" himself.[8]

Theologians

What the church has stated in official documents is clearly affirmed by a variety of theologians as well. Wolfhart Pannenberg, for example, points out that in the days of early Christianity, dogma was often set in antithesis to competing theories since "it did not come from humans but was 'spoken and taught by God.'"[9] Origen described Christian doctrines as *dogmata theou* (*Comm. Matt.* 12.23), while for Aquinas, the articles of faith were an essential presupposition to theological reflection (*ST* I, q. 1, a. 2). In fact, for Aquinas, the assent of faith is the most certain of all the intellectual virtues, even though lacking in evidence, because its source is God himself (*ST* II-II q. 4, a. 3). Linking this explicitly with dogma's claim to universality, Pannenberg says, "Dogmatics has always accepted this task [i.e., confirming the truth of doctrine] in connection with the *divinely grounded universality of its content* which embraces the reality of the world from its creation to its eschatological consummation." Similarly, "Theology deals with the universality of the truth of revelation and therefore with the truth of revelation and of God himself." Ultimately, "the truth in its *binding universality* precedes our subjective judgment."[10]

This same emphasis on the church's ability to know God's self-manifestation objectively and with universal force is recently defended by Robert Jenson, who says, "We may press theology's claim very bluntly by noting that theology . . . claims to know the one God of all and so to know the one decisive fact about all things, so that theology must be either a *universal and founding discipline* or a delusion."[11] This accent on universality is complemented by Jenson's recognition that some elements of church teaching are irreversible: "Dogmas are the irreversible communal decisions made so far in that effort" [i.e., of the church to think through its mission of speaking the gospel]. Therefore, all theology is subject to the authority of dogma and may in turn contribute to dogma yet to be formulated."[12] The same point is made by Gerhard Sauter, who states, "Dogmatics . . . says what must be said as credible unconditionally and under all circumstances. God has revealed to us who he is." He later adds, "Dogma states that which has unassailable validity."[13]

This is not to say that dogma itself cannot in some sense be made the object of theological inquiry. Theology certainly adds to dogma's intelligibility, uncovers new dimensions previously unseen, and allows dogma, at times, to undergo further development. In a certain sense, then, one may speak of dogma as providing *both* presupposition of theology and material for theological inquiry. This is what Pannenberg has in mind when he notes that dogmatics does not expressly make the truth claims of Christian doctrine one of its questions, but must nevertheless do so or dogmatic theses will "not make contact with worldly reality but will hover above it and will not, therefore, be true." Theology, he argues, must "present, test and if possible confirm" the claims of the doctrinal tradition.[14] Pannenberg here sounds very much like Maurice Blondel and especially Karl Rahner, with the latter's constant and well-founded concern, in the face of the extrinsicism of the Catholic neo-Scholastic account of revelation, that theology should manifest, if possible, the congruency of the doctrinal tradition with human experience.[15] To claim that the dogmatic assertions of the church may have some resonance in human experience, or that theologians should seek to show an "immanent" element "reaching" correlatively for the truth of the doctrine—to, in other words, provide at least something of an apologetical element for systematic theology properly so called lest it sink into extrinsic mummification—is hardly to call into question the characteristics of doctrine. Indeed, as we shall see, it is to further confirm their necessity.

What is already clear is that both ecclesial documents and theologians affirm that revelation is given to us as a gift; it is articulated linguistically in Christian teaching, that is, doctrine, which at times, especially in its most formal statements, may be considered irrevocable, continuous, universal, materially identical, and objectively true.[16]

The problem, however, is that these traditionally denominated characteristics carry with them an undeniable philosophical freight. Terms such as "continuity," "perpetuity," and "universality" smack, for many, of the "metaphysics of presence," of the "ontotheology" characteristic of the classical philosophical tradition. It is, of course, such characteristics that have come under unremitting philosophical fire for being associated not only with the priority of "presence," but presence encased in a totalizing narrative, a *grand récit*, a normative truth, an enveloping *Ganzheit*.

Today's philosophical climate, on the contrary, is distinguished not by words such as "objectivity," "presence," "identity," and "continuity," but by terms such as "incommensurability," "historicity," "fissure," "otherness," and "difference." As John Caputo says, "The incoming of the 'same' [as opposed to the impossible, *l'autre*] . . . would simply further confirm the present, already familiar horizon, would be more of the dreary pedestrian, humdrum sameness of the possible—a mediocre fellow, Climacus said—and what Lyotard would call merely a new move in an old and familiar game."[17] Perhaps even more illustrative is the late Jacques Derrida who, also wishing the incoming of the impossible, frames it within specifically religious terms, holding for a deconstruction (a *sans*) which is developed "*without* reference to religion as institutional dogma, *without* getting involved in some 'article of faith' . . . while proposing a non-dogmatic doublet of dogma . . . a *thinking* that 'repeats' the possibility of religion *without* religion."[18]

Given this *mise en scène*, can the Christian notion of doctrine and contemporary philosophical accents be reconciled? Are they at absolute loggerheads? This book will examine those questions, and, in the process, will speak about the fundamental impulses of contemporary philosophy and the extent to which these may be incorporated within Christian theology.

Contemporary Challenges: Nonfoundationalist and Postmodern Thought

One dimension of the challenge to Christian doctrine, and the traditional characteristics accompanying it, is the calling into question of univocal thinking and *Identitätsphilosophie* that marks large swaths of contemporary thought.[19] Often enough this challenge goes by the controverted name of postmodernism. For some thinkers, such as William Everdell, postmodernism is really "ultramodernism," not significantly different from modernity itself.[20] The fact remains, nonetheless, that postmodernism and postmodernity have entrenched themselves as "movements" in scholarly literature, inspiring continuing debates about the "cult of theory" across the arts and sciences.[21]

In essence, postmodernism is a type of thinking that rebels against any totalizing understanding of reality, against any "grand metanarrative." It is opposed to universalization, rationalization, systematization, and the establishment of consistent criteria for the evaluation of truth-claims.[22] It is characterized by an abiding concern for the radicalness of historicity, the pervasiveness of ideology, the decentered subject, and the rejection of transcendentalism. Postmodernism resists, therefore, what has been called the "theoretical coronation of the whole" and the "tyranny of globalizing presence." It rejects all teleological, protological-eschatological narratives, and it rebels against all epistemic totalizations and *grand récits* of history, against overarching systems such as the "dialectics of the Spirit" or the "emancipation of the rational."

Postmodernism also rejects logocentric presence (the world truly mediated by language), entitative reasoning, and various attempts to "stop the show," "freeze the flux," and "release the truth-police."[23] The movement accuses its predecessor, modernity, of having sacralized human rationality. In the Enlightenment quest to uncover the essential structures of human life, thought, and discourse, modernity leveled and homogenized the irreducible multiformity and polysemy of life itself. Further, the Enlightenment concern with methodology as the path to truth caused it to veil the encompassing nature of historicity and, by necessity, to ignore the nuances, complexities, and ambiguities of being and knowing. This is the basis for the frequent cry that Descartes, Kant, and even Husserl must be deconstructed.[24] This truncated notion of humanity that postmodernism condemns has led, in science, to an excessive Baconism that ignores the historical-hermeneutical elements of thought and inappropriately canonizes the foundationalisms of positivism and empiricism.[25]

Particular postmodern invective is reserved for the kind of rationalism that deified algorithmic positivism, leading ineluctably to technocracy and even totalitarianism. This is the meaning of Adorno's suggestive and provocative phrase that modernity is the primitive "belly turned mind."[26] It is the mind of modernity that now represents the atavistic rage of instrumental reason against the Other. As Richard Bernstein says:

> Reason has been under attack from a variety of sources. There has been a prevailing suspicion that the appeal to reason functions as a deceptive mask for ruthless power; that all appeals to universality are disguises for violently suppressing cultural, ethnic and religious differences; that reason is to be identified exclusively with technocratic reason.[27]

Postmodernism, on the other hand, seeks to put an end to the manipulatable domination of instrumental reason, of the reificatory thinking of positivism and rationalism. It strives to overcome the pathology of the identity principle with its nostalgia for presence and its romance with totalities. It exhumes from the obsequies of the Enlightenment alterity, *différe(a)nce*, rupture, and breach.[28] In place of pallid universalism and homogeneity, postmodernism celebrates the opacity and sovereignty of the "other," the "apologetics of the accidental" and the deracinated and anamorphous nature of thought. By "presencing" horizons rooted in our factical situatedness—social location, ideological determination, cultural embeddedness, paradigm-bound rationality, and contextualized knowledge—postmodernity has frequently become a protest and a call to arms against universalizing tendencies of any type whatsoever.

As has been amply documented, Heidegger and Wittgenstein constitute the dual-headed Zeus from whom nonfoundationalist and postmodern thought ultimately springs.[29] The works of these thinkers have given rise (and taken new directions) in the insights of Derrida, Foucault, Lyotard, Kristeva, Baudrillard, Irigaray, and Rorty. Although each of these differs from the others in important and even essential ways, their fundamental goal and task has been to "present the absent," to uncover the world that *Dasein* has epistemologically buried, to put an end to ontologically inappropriate norms and standards, to, as Heidegger says, restore the *lēthē* to *alētheia*. Postmodern and nonfoundationalist thinkers argue that the newly presenced horizons of finitude, sociocultural embeddedness, and contextualized reason offer a conclusive and destructive argument against first philosophy of any kind. "Foundations," whether of the classical type, more recent transcendental ontologies, or empirical-positivistic approaches, have all been exposed as inappropriate and untenable.[30] Any attempt to establish a *prima philosophia*, a *philosophia perennis* or an *Ursprungsphilosophie* seeks to veil historicity and its ontologically productive effects.

Postmodern and nonfoundationalist thinkers reject metaphysics and first philosophies of all types because these philosophies seek to "close down" effective history, to end historical consciousness (*Bewusstsein*). What postmodernity has shown, however, is that historicity is not merely a casing for transcendental subjectivity or for any of the classical or modern attempts to "nail down" or finally "name" Being—to establish a totalizing view of reality.[31] Philosophy can give us no final answers, nor can it outline ultimate structures be they metaphysical, transcendental, or empirical. The postmodern philosopher's task, rather, is to foster civilized discourse, to "keep the conversation going."[32] This fostering of civilized speech serves as the legitimate replacement for philosophy's former goal: determining the deepest structure of reality and, in certain cases, the transcendental conditions allowing for knowledge of them. The radical temporality saturating every aspect of being and thought has forced the ancient discipline to rethink its object and task.

Given this fresh understanding of philosophy's goal, it is logical that postmodern and nonfoundationalist thinkers subject to particular invective ontological mainstays such as a common human nature or a universal notion of rationality. Such ideas seek to establish and embed a solid rock, an immovable object within the river of historicity. Richard Campbell, for example, is representative of current trends when he says, "In assuming the timelessness of truth, the traditional view assumed a human capacity to know that truth and thus a human nature that, if only in virtue of that decisive capacity, is unchanging."[33] Rebecca Chopp also observes, "Prophetic transformism opposes any 'essence' approach, including the 'essence of human being' approach in liberal equalitarianism and the 'essence of woman' approach of romantic expressivism. Rather, prophetic transformism assumes that gender identity, what it is to be a man or woman, is a matter of social construct."[34] Pierre Manent adds, "In the past man defined himself as rational animal, according to his specific difference in terms of genus and species, but modern man determines himself in an altogether different way."[35] He cites Heidegger in support of this thesis: "Dasein is never to be taken ontologically as an instance or special case of some genus of entities, as things that are present-at-hand."[36]

Rather than speaking of a stable and universal human nature, postmodern thinkers are much more likely to refer to a culturally constituted human rationality emerging from the tight web of history, society, and language. Precisely as *post*modernity, this represents a new moment in the history of thought.[37]

While the move to nonfoundationalism is presaged in the work of American pragmatic thinkers such as Dewey and James (later developed in Quine and Sellars), it is Heidegger, in fact, who is the most significant figure in the rise of nonfoundationalist and postmodern thought and, therefore, in the contemporary challenge to the traditional claims and characteristics of Christian doctrine. While Heidegger has at times been considered insufficiently postmodern, and while his thought remains within the horizon of Being-language, it is clear that he adumbrated many of the themes subsequently celebrated by postmodernity.

The crux of Heidegger's argument, of course, is that traditional Western philosophy represents a theory of form, substance, essence, and nature inherited from Plato, Aristotle, and the Stoics. The central defect in this thought was its virtually complete neglect of historicity and its productive ontological effects. The various philosophical epochs, from Plato onward, have illegitimately masked the factical and historical horizons encompassing life, thought, and reality. This is the basis of Heidegger's claim that metaphysics must be overcome and, likewise, for his interest in the pre-Socratics such as Anaximander and Heraclitus; they represent a time when Being was thought in a more primordial fashion, before it was "encased" as idea, substance, or essence.[38] The subsequent history of thinking, Heidegger claims, is dominated by "ontotheology," that is, by thinking about being in relation to God, a God who is Being itself, and who, therefore, dominates and controls all further thinking about being and appearance.[39] But ontotheology is nothing more that an unrestrained "metaphysics of presence" that has overlooked the essential interplay of presence and absence, of revealing and concealing, of *alethēia* and *lēthē*; it has lost sight of the fact that human life is shot through with historicity and finitude, with the facticity of life and world. Over the course of time, this kind of thinking degenerated into a technocratic rationalism and algorithmic positivism with little concern for dimensions of truth other than those that were strictly quantifiable.[40]

Heidegger was convinced, then, that he was establishing a new moment in the history of philosophy, one breaking even with Nietzsche and with his own teacher in phenomenology, Husserl. Nietzsche was still reacting to the parameters set by Plato while Husserl was, for all of his phenomenological insight, enthralled with the transcendental ego and the primacy of the theoretical. Heidegger, in fact, told Husserl that the pure ego, the foundation of his work, was derived only from the repression of historicity and concretion.[41] The fundamental thrust of *Being and Time*, and its philosophical advance over Husserl, is the "disclosure" of the world that *Dasein* epistemologically buries. This is the point of the book's famous examples such as the "slipping in and out of moods" and the "living with projects." They indicate the world that "seeps through" *Dasein*, that reveals our philosophical obsession with "presence" and our inattention to the "world" that saturates life and thought, leading inexorably to *Seinsvergessenheit*, the forgetfulness of Being itself.[42]

Heidegger's point here is a central one of all contemporary philosophy: A proper understanding of reality must allow the tears, the breaches, and the concealment that challenges presence to be itself unveiled. Philosophy must examine the enveloping world of historicity, finitude, and facticity that Western thought has continually masked. This is at the root of Heidegger's theoretical break with Catholicism in 1919, when he wrote, "Epistemological insights, extending as far as the theory of theoretical knowledge, have made the *system* of Catholicism problematic and unacceptable to me—but not Christianity and metaphysics" (the latter, to be sure, in a new sense).[43] Heidegger's claim here is that Catholic systematic theology is inextricably intertwined with a notion of philosophy that is itself captive to all of the ontotheological excesses of classical thought, to an ultimately discredited notion of Being. This does not invalidate Christianity itself, Heidegger thinks, but it does invalidate certain forms of it, one form being its encapsulation in the kind of dogmatic system characteristic of Roman Catholicism. For Heidegger, as will be discussed below, only a kind of Christianity that reflects on "faith-filled" life, avoiding questions of absolute ultimacy, of first philosophy, will be henceforth suitable.

With his desire to overcome the essentialism of the metaphysical tradition, with his deconstruction of transcendental thought, and with his championing of a metaontological philosophy creatively recovering the "forgotten" dimensions of "absence," "historicity," and "facticity," it is certainly possible to speak of Heidegger as a significant forerunner of postmodernity. This postmodern status is perhaps sealed by Richard Rorty's celebration of Heidegger's thought in virtually all of his works.[44] As Rorty asserted in his groundbreaking book on foundations, the three most important philosophers, whom he calls "edifying" and "therapeutic" thinkers, are Heidegger, Wittgenstein, and Dewey, since each abandoned any attempt at finding an ultimate "foundation" for thought.[45] He gives these thinkers pride of place, along with W. Sellars, whose critique of the "myth of the given" he takes as having deconstructed one of the pillars of contemporary analytical philosophy.[46]

Rorty makes it clear at the outset that his goal is to overturn the ideas of truth and objectivity that have dominated traditional philosophy. He admits frankly that "the True and the Right are matters of social practice," adding that this "may seem to condemn us to a relativism which all by itself is a *reductio* of a behaviorist approach."[47] More recently, in response to Habermas, he asserts, "When Habermas says that I am advocating a view according to which we should emancipate our culture from the whole philosophical vocabulary clustering around reason, truth, and knowledge, this seems to me exactly right."[48] Seeking to proleptically disarm the charge of relativism, he adds that one can only level that charge if one thinks there is a "permanent neutral matrix for all inquiry and all history," and it is precisely this kind of foundation which must be dispensed with, a foundation that does not exist.[49]

In his famous review of *Philosophy and the Mirror of Nature*, Richard Bernstein observes that Rorty's critique is aimed at all philosophers, continental as well as analytical: "The differences between Russell and Husserl are insignificant when compared with what they have in common."[50] Both men are foundationalists in the sense that both think that philosophy has identifiable foundations, even if they define these quite differently. Rorty's claim, on the other hand, is that "foundations" of any kind are illusory; his enemy is all systematic philosophy which "shares the conviction that there are real foundations that philosophy must discover."[51] For Rorty, one must oppose the idea that a person's "essence is to be a knower of essences." This kind of foundationalist thinking fails to recognize the socially constructed and historical nature of reality. It has failed to make the necessary *Kehre*: "The historical turn has helped free us, gradually but steadily, *from theology and metaphysics*—from the attempt to look for an escape from time and chance."[52] Rorty too, then, along with postmodernism generally, has little use for the kind of universal and perduring claims that adhere to the Christian notions of revelation and doctrine, and even less use for any attempt to explicate these claims philosophically. Such positions assume that they trump the notion that the "the True and the Right are matters of social practice." They pretend to norm social and cultural practice rather than be normed by them; they fail to recognize that historicity and culture are in dialectical opposition to nature and identity.

But what then becomes of any attempt to buttress philosophically, to illumine more fully, the truth-claims of Christian doctrine? Is not some kind of theological ontology necessary, one that, nonetheless, incorporates the legitimate concerns of historicity and culture in order to sustain rationally the characteristics associated with Christian truth? Is not some kind of metaphysics essential if the claims of Christian theology and doctrine are to have a logically intelligible foundation? A metaphysics deaf to the concerns of historicity and culture is certainly untenable, but is any first philosophy possible at all? Before answering these questions, let us, for the moment, look at some other points of view that present their own challenges.

If Rorty is telling us that metaphysics and first philosophy have no role in philosophical thinking, and *a fortiori* in theology, then what is the cognitive "yield" of philosophy? If "the True and the Right" are simply socially constructed, born from and encompassed by the tight nexus of history, culture, and language that envelops us, then toward what goal are we to think and live? Is Rorty leading us simply toward relativism, skepticism, historicism, nihilism, or some other philosophical aporia? Richard Bernstein points out that Rorty is trying to cure us of a philosophical disease, the search for foundations, for ultimate and lasting truth. If we truly recognized that we are historically and culturally determined, labels such as "relativism" and "skepticism" would not be applied because we would have already been liberated from our "Cartesian anxiety," an anxiety that, despite the label, applies to the entire ancient-medieval-modern nexus. Can any goal for philosophy be offered that recognizes our sociocultural determination but that does not thereby reduce the philosopher's role to what Rorty calls "useful kibbutzing," or continuing, communal conversation? Examining such philosophical goals in light of emerging constructions of rationality will be discussed later. The point now is simply that Rorty's thought has little use for the kind of universally veridical and transcultural claims that Christian doctrine, or any similarly comprehensive point of view, makes. Rorty sees such attempts as philosophically unsubstantiated, merely the result of unbridled and overweening hubris.

Bernstein, although departing from Rorty on several crucial points, is similarly pessimistic about any attempt at overarching, totalizing systems. In his celebrated book *Beyond Objectivism and Relativism*, Bernstein scores "objectivism," which he equates with foundationalism and metaphysics of different kinds.[53] This type of thinking, he avers, searches out permanent, ahistorical matrices; it seeks Archimedean points to which we can appeal for the sake of determining the ultimate nature of human life and thought. Objectivist thinking develops universal standards of rationality and truth in order to rigorously ground knowledge and language and to avoid the perils of relativism, skepticism, and nihilism. Bernstein coined the term "Cartesian anxiety" to describe the search for that which is "certain and indubitable" as first mentioned in the *Second Meditation*. Such "anxiety," Bernstein claims, is behind the ontological and transcendental foundations for philosophy that have been adduced over the course of history. Seeking to oppose, and to heal, such "anxiety," Bernstein, to the contrary, celebrates the thought of Kuhn, Gadamer, Wittgenstein, and Habermas sanctioning, in the process, an erasure of ontological or transcendental foundations in favor of a socially constructed understanding of nature and rationality.[54] The *theological* impact of such a position is perhaps best displayed by Bernstein's own recent analysis of the encyclical by Pope John Paul II on faith and reason.[55]

In this essay, Bernstein begins with a *captatio benevolentiae*, applauding the letter's defense of philosophy and human rationality. Very quickly, however, he launches his criticisms, objections clearly illustrating his fundamental viewpoint. He observes, for example, that the pope praises philosophy as a "search" and "journey" but that he equally makes "some very substantial claims about reason, truth and philosophy that are, at the very least, rationally contestable." For example, the pope speaks of the person as a "free and intelligent subject with the capacity to know God, truth and goodness." He similarly claims that "certain fundamental moral norms are shared by all." These assertions, Bernstein argues, are, at best, "disingenuous." Bernstein is also disconcerted by the encyclical's declaration that all persons seek an absolute truth, a final explanation, a certitude that is no longer open to doubt. The pope mentions this, of course, in the context of reviewing the age-old human search for the ultimate ground, purpose, and meaning of life. Bernstein counters, however, no doubt thinking of Peirce and others, that the best philosophy of the last century has questioned the very idea of a final and absolute truth. It seeks, on the contrary, to develop a fallibilistic spirit, one that recognizes that all knowledge claims are "open to further rational criticism and revision."[56]

Bernstein concludes that although the letter ostensibly stresses the journey toward truth, "it contains a substantial and extremely controversial conception of what constitutes human knowledge. This can be summed up in a single word: foundationalism." For Bernstein, the pope has committed capital sins against a nonfoundationalist understanding of philosophy. Not only has he proposed certain universal norms; he has further asserted that there is an "absolute and universal truth" that serves as the foundation for all knowledge. Bernstein counters that appeals to "absolute epistemological, metaphysical or ontological foundations" are unwarranted and should be avoided. If the contemporary critique of foundationalism and objectivism is to be challenged, then it should be, Bernstein continues, on philosophical grounds and not by "ex cathedra assertions."

This last statement underscores Bernstein's misunderstanding of the encyclical's primary intention. The pope is not, in the first instance, philosophically defending metaphysics and related theoretical dimensions; he is saying, however, that some such *prima philosophia* is needed if we are to undergird philosophically the church's indefeasible claims about revelation and doctrine, if we are to speak logically and appropriately about the universality, normativity, and perduring nature of Christian truth. Bernstein again objects that if one "questions the very idea of absolute foundations, if one questions whether we can ever achieve final certitude, if one has any doubts about metaphysical realism[,] . . . if one questions . . . whether there are indeed 'first universal principles of being,'" the encyclical seems to respond only with the claim that such a one is, presumably, "misguided." Once again, however, I think some of the confusion on Bernstein's part results from his not quite seeing what is involved in the proper theological task of the *fides quaerens intellectum*. Only someone thinking purely as a philosopher, unfamiliar with theological method, would claim, as Bernstein does, that in the search for truth "one cannot dictate from the outside what must be the results of this journey."

At the same time, Bernstein does raise some legitimate questions. He correctly points out, for example, that the encyclical tends to caricature postmodern and pragmatic thought. In fact, I would claim that the document fails to deal seriously with the chief adversary to the "renewed metaphysics" it champions, namely, a historicized, hermeneutical philosophy that accents historicity as the ultimate horizon of thought and being. Bernstein is also right—ironically, in language reminiscent of his earlier critique of Richard Rorty—when he says that the encyclical tends toward reinforcing the discredited "either/or" distinction, that is, either foundationalism or relativism, either objectivism or skepticism, as if there were no philosophers seeking a via media between these positions. He also brings to the fore an important issue when he notes that on two occasions the encyclical calls for the autonomy of philosophy without fully explaining what such autonomy entails. With regard to the encyclical, I have already examined several of these issues.[57] A protracted discussion of others, especially the issue of the autonomy of philosophy vis-à-vis revelation, will be left for the conclusions. The point here is simply that Bernstein, along with Heidegger, Rorty, and postmodernism generally, has little use for the kind of theologically disciplined first philosophy, or its allied correlates, that the understanding of revelation, ultimately issuing forth in Christian doctrine, seemingly calls for.

Another contemporary thinker who offers significant challenges to the traditional understanding of Christian doctrine and the characteristics classically attributed to it is Roman Catholic philosopher John Caputo. In a spate of books and articles, Caputo has argued over the course of some years for a philosophy, and thereby a theology, less committed to "presence" and more committed to historicity, absence, and "difference." In his earlier work, Caputo markedly emphasized the encompassing dimensions of radical historicity. He argued, along with Hans-Georg Gadamer, that even Husserl's phenomenological intuitionism was nothing more than disguised transcendentalism seeking "ontological neutrality" and encouraging a "flight from the flux."[58] Caputo found in Heidegger's radical *Abbau* of metaphysics a meta-ontotheology and metahermeneutics decidedly antifoundationalist in character.[59] Any proper philosophical or hermeneutical theory will recognize that the diverse *archai* or foundations proposed within the history of philosophy, whether *eidos, ousia, esse, res cogitans, Geist* or *Wille zur Macht* represent simply "names" of the "coming to be" within the flux (177). What Heidegger properly understood is that "being" and the differing "grounds" proposed throughout history are nothing more than a series of epochs of varying foundations that manifest themselves from a deep-set *lēthē*. The later Heidegger, especially, recognized that one should not waste time seeking "truth" or "*principia*"; one should simply recognize the *Seinsgeschicke*, the "play of the sendings" (204). To become lost in a particular idea of being, a *quod*, a specific message from Hermes, is to misunderstand the radical nature of the enveloping flux (258).

In two recent essays, Caputo continues this emphasis on historicity and the lethic nature of reality. He has gradually moved away from Heidegger, however, as insufficiently postmodern, seeing greater precision in the work of Jacques Derrida.[60] So, for example, Caputo now argues that what is needed is a premodern and postmodern dialogue, between the truth of religion and the truth of postmodernity, in service to the destabilization of Enlightenment modernity, which understands little of either religion or the nature of truth.[61] Borrowing from Derrida, Caputo argues for less "presence" and more of *l'autre*, the other, the impossible that cannot be anticipated or expected. What is needed is a prophetic postmodernism, a turn toward Derrida's phenomenology of the impossible. The problem with Heidegger was that he placed all his emphasis on the

Greeks, and then the Greco-Germans, but in the process he missed the prophetic witness of Israel and the passion for God witnessed there.

Caputo wants to use the prophetic theological witness of Israel to draw us away from theology's philosophical and metaphysical traditions, to nudge us toward Derrida's passionate overcoming of philosophy, toward the space of the "Jewgreek," a space which is not just philosophy and not just prophecy but prophetic postmodernism.[62] To this end, Caputo expands on Derridean themes: Unlike modernity, which expended its time on exploring the transcendental conditions for the possibility of knowing, Derrida explores the "conditions of the impossible," that is, the way in which the impossible is possible. The possible is the foreseeable and planned future, a future bordered by the horizon of expectation. When it comes, it was something we were waiting for all along. The absolute future, however, is that which we do not see coming, that shatters our horizon of expectation.[63] Caputo then issues a plea for a Christian postmodernity, a deconstruction that is really a neo-Augustinian recovery of the soul that is impenetrable to itself, the Augustine of the *inquietum est cor nostrum*, the *quid ergo amo cum deum meum amo*, and the *quaestio mihi factus sum*. The result will be a theological synthesis that leaves behind the metaphysical roots of the tradition and recovers the Jewgreek of Levinas as well as Derrida's phenomenology of the impossible. Caputo is not concerned with providing intelligible foundations for Christian doctrine and its classical characteristics. In fact, in the last analysis, one wonders if Caputo's notion of faith has any significantly cognitive dimension at all. Faith for him, it appears, has to do with dreaming, with weeping, with praying, with waiting, with nonappearing, with unfulfilled intentions.[64] Of course, Caputo clearly recognizes that within the tradition, especially the one shaped by Aquinas, faith is also a kind of knowing, one that is, in some ways, convergent with the knowing proper to the natural light of reason. Perhaps in recognition of this fact, he says, "When you look for resonances and correlations in the Catholic Christian tradition with this more Derridean deconstructive postmodern religion that I am describing, I must say that you find yourself back on the doorsteps of Augustine not Aquinas. . . . In my view, recent Continental thought asks Catholics to come back and reconsider Augustine."[65]

Caputo, with postmodernity generally, finds metaphysics and first philosophy of any kind to be an inappropriate way of understanding life and thought given the "presenced" horizons of absence and the impossible, of history and linguisticality, of socially and culturally constituted existence. Caputo argues that these elements, properly understood, are antithetical to the traditional characteristics constitutive of Christian doctrine as well as to the attempts to undergird such distinctive dimensions logically.

One other philosopher has, much like some of these other thinkers, strong and explicitly elaborated theological interests. Like them, he appears to be clearly wedded to at least certain postmodern themes. Can his work provide theology with any philosophical defense of doctrine's traditional characteristics?

This philosopher is Jean-Luc Marion, who, with the publication of his well-known book, *God without Being*, has become a significant force in both the philosophical and theological worlds. Under the penetrating influence of Heidegger and then Derrida, Marion too has sought to deconstruct theological ontology. In his magnum opus, Marion seeks even to out-*Differenz* Heidegger's ontological difference, thereby freeing God from his imprisonment in the language and horizon of being.[66] He argues that only the dismantling of traditional, ontotheological thought, represented preeminently by Aquinas, will allow an apposite notion of the Christian God to emerge, for the idolic imagination to be replaced by the truly iconic vision. Marion's project, then, is to establish the limits of the *Seinsfrage*, discarding in the process the classical and transcendental baggage that has led to a distorted image of divine life.[67]

In *God without Being*, Marion argues that being-language has no place whatsoever in the question of God. The celebrated Heideggerian distinction between Being and beings serves simply as a negative propaedeutic to thinking about divine life. In service to protecting divine Otherness, the language of being must be entirely jettisoned; its enclosing dimensions must be subverted. Marion illustrates the problem by invoking the difference between the idol and the icon. Borrowing from Husserl's intentionality analysis, Marion argues that the idol fills the breadth of our gaze, offering us pure presence without the transparency of absence. The icon, however, masks and obscures as well as "presences"; it challenges the viewer but is never exhausted by the viewer's subjectivity.[68] For Marion, it is precisely being-language that serves an idolic rather than an iconic purpose. As he says, quite bluntly, "conceptual idolatry" has a site (metaphysics); a function (theology in ontotheology); and a definition (*causa sui*).[69]

Marion has slowly and cautiously emended his original position, conceding that Aquinas's understanding of divine *Esse* remains at a transcendent distance from the *ens commune* of metaphysics. He has also argued that if ontotheology means that God is part of the matter of metaphysics, if it means that he is simply *causa sui*, then Aquinas does not fall within the purview of ontotheology.[70] This is the case because God is the cause and principle of metaphysics rather than its proper subject, thereby releasing him from the bounds of common being. God, conceived merely as the capstone of a grand ontotheological, metaphysical understanding is, for the later Marion, clearly not within the scope of Aquinas's own, original thought. As might be expected, even while exonerating Aquinas, Marion tends to interpret him through the lenses of an intense apophaticism, something akin to the "indiscreet" marriage between Dionysius and postmodernity mentioned earlier. Further, Marion has continued to ask questions in a manner reminiscent of Heidegger: Does *causa sui* or sufficient reason or *actus purus* "offer a name divine enough to make God appear?" Can God function as the "ultimate Ground" or "last Reason"?[71] He further claims that since metaphysics is the philosophy of presence par excellence, it is incapable of thinking about possibility, the very possibility of givenness and donation, in the last analysis, the possibility of what theology calls "revelation."[72]

At first glance, then, the imminent danger of Marion's thought, in his abjuration of any kind of metaphysics, is that there is nothing in his philosophy that can logically illuminate the assertions of Christian doctrine or the characteristics traditionally and consistently associated with it. It is not surprising, then, that he turns to Pseudo-Dionysius, Meister Eckhart, and the mystical tradition in order to explain the type of intelligibility proper to theology. The alleged inadequacy of being-language logically forces a doxological turn, somewhat reminiscent of Heidegger, and even Adorno, to negative theology and to more poetic and aesthetic forms of agapic love. Such a shift, Marion argues, successfully subverts the enclosing dimensions of ontology, turning our attention to the God who is ungraspable and unknowable. One wonders, nonetheless, if Marion does not finally move in the direction of a fideistic assertion of faith's truth severed from any ultimate philosophical intelligibility. Despite reservations, the newer, more nuanced Marion, who has turned his attention to the Derridean themes of the "impossible" and the "gift" may offer, even with all his protestations, new opportunities for a renewed metaphysics. We will explore this possibility below.

The point of this brief review of Marion, conjoined with several other thinkers, is clear: There are significant contemporary challenges to "first philosophy" in any form and thereby to the rational intelligibility of the church's understanding of doctrine, in particular to the classical characteristics of Christian teaching such as its universality, its continuity, and its material identity over the course of varying cultures and generations. Traditionally, some categories of metaphysics, in a commodious sense, purified of extraneous elements, are used in order to provide a logical substructure for such affirmations. But Rorty, Bernstein, Caputo, and Marion—and there are others[73]—have argued that such attempts are philosophically inappropriate and ontologically untenable.

What is the effect of these thinkers on theology? And how should these challenges be regarded? The danger to theology from such thinkers is twofold. In terms of understanding Christian doctrine, theology may now support either a historicized and socially constructed understanding of truth or, conversely, it may simply assert the truth of Christianity, but now severing ties with an infrastructure of rational intelligibility. In the first instance, all truth is not only born in history (which is certainly true), it is also thoroughly historical itself, and, therefore, highly protean and flexible in nature. Christian doctrine, no less than other statements, simply emerges from, and remains enmeshed within, the tight web of language, culture, and ideology. It is difficult, then, if not impossible, to sustain an understanding of doctrine claiming to be universally, transculturally, and abidingly true, even while, simultaneously, recognizing the legitimately positive and productive effects of historicity.

In a second option, one may turn to a kind of agapic mysticism that does place emphasis on the universal and normative truth of doctrine, but in a desire to cut all ties with attempts to explicate such characteristics through the use of first philosophy, courts the danger of simply fideistically asserting Christianity as true, thereby allowing it to remain at the level of "appearance" but never seeking to ground logically the continuity of appearance over time. This is the danger, I believe, of a Marionesque renunciation of metaphysics of any kind.

In my judgment, these particular options do full justice neither to what the church has understood as constitutively forming the *depositum fidei*, nor to the rational intelligibility for such understanding that is an exigency of theology properly called. In the following sections, I shall argue that theology has the resources to incorporate much that contemporary philosophy properly champions about otherness, difference, absence, and historicity. Consequently, I will argue that a renewed understanding of the fundamental dimensions of Christian doctrine may be developed that incorporates many of these legitimate concerns while concomitantly adhering to the consistent logic and principles constitutive of Christian thought. Can a theological *Aufhebung*, synthesizing both classical as well as contemporary approaches, be achieved?

Before answering that question, I would like to offer a tentative and hypothetical word on the Reformation. This hypothesis explores whether some Reformation theologies exhibit an innate connaturality and congruity with postmodern thought that is, perhaps, not intrinsically, although certainly concretely, present within Roman Catholicism.

A Hypothetical Word on the Reformation

Withering challenges have been issued to the classical characteristics of Christian doctrine, as well as to attempts to undergird such dimensions philosophically. In a bid to discern the roots of these challenges, one may legitimately ask if some currents in contemporary thought display a certain confluence with elements of traditional Reformation theology.[74]

At the root of this apparently inner congruence is the well-known difference between Roman Catholic and Protestant theology in their *classical* ways of understanding the nature/grace or creation/salvation distinction. For Catholics, the two orders, ontological and soteriological, are distinct (at least notionally) but in fundamental continuity. For traditional Protestantism, on the other hand, a wedge has been driven between fallen and corrupted nature and the work of the Redeemer. Logically, although speaking broadly, the gateway to evangelical theology has been either the authority of Scripture or the interior experience of the individual believer, not nature's own intelligibility. It would not be surprising, therefore, if some quarters of Protestantism find the call of contemporary thought for a meta-ontotheology legitimate and useful precisely because sectors of Reformation theology have resisted the notion of the form of the cosmos and the logos structure of reality as intelligible in itself, even apart (again, notionally) from Jesus Christ and the gospel of grace. Certain Protestant thinkers find in postmodernity's deconstruction of ontology a connatural convergence with their own suspicion about the inner intelligibility of nature and being.

Of course, the roots of the Protestant concern about theological ontology are anchored to a legitimate issue. The logos structure of reality that Christianity adopted from the ancient world, an idea further fueled by the late medieval rebirth of pagan learning, gave rise to the suspicion that the glory of the world was now confused with the glory of God. The Reformation protest was precisely against a semi-Pelagian analogizing imagination that tended to overlook God's judgment on the world rendered dramatically in the cross of Christ. This movement, *crux probat omnia*, challenged a too easy medieval and Renaissance elision of the majesty of nature with the ineffable grandeur of the revealed God.[75] This evangelical objection was aimed at every attempt to collapse the unique and undeducible form of the crucified God into the form of inner-worldly or subjective beauty. The Reformation philippics were against a metanarrative of cosmic glory that unconsciously reduced the cross, the central moment in salvation history, to an essential footnote. The starkness of Calvary became secondary to a prior unity and beauty given with creation.

This necessary Reformation defense of the cross may also be understood as a remonstrance against theological ontologies in all forms, finding theoretical expression in the dialectic of the *theologia crucis* against the *theologia gloriae* and in the classical apophatic Reformation axioms: *Quod supra nos, nihil ad nos*, and *Cognoscere Christum est cognoscere beneficia eius*. Even apart from the influence of postmodernity, then, the Reformation tradition has strongly lethic elements and decentering currents born of its understanding of the gospel of Jesus Christ.[76]

One possible, or at least perceived, indication of the theoretical confluence between Reformation thought and elements of nonfoundationalist and postmodern philosophy may be seen in the exchange between Hans-Georg Gadamer and Leo Strauss on the publication of *Wahrheit und Methode*. In one part of the dialogue, Strauss protests against Gadamer's hermeneutical theory, especially its overthrow of the stability of textual meaning. Gadamer responds, "What I believe to have understood through Heidegger (and what I can testify to from my Protestant background) is, above all, that philosophy must learn to do without the idea of an infinite intellect. I have attempted to draw up a corresponding hermeneutics."[77] For Gadamer, both hermeneutical phenomenology and the Reformation teach humanity primarily about finitude, about humanity's epistemological limitations.[78] While this certainly may be understood in a correct sense, it may also be taken to mean, by coupling an intense apophaticism with an emphasis on the eschatological, that fixed meanings and dogmas are ill-suited formulations in light of human limitations.

Gadamer's reflections on this issue closely follow those of Heidegger—and Heidegger's own inspiration by and interpretation of Luther—for developing his understanding of Being. As Heidegger's aforementioned comment of 1919 makes clear, his new emphasis on the hermeneutics of facticity and finitude could not be congruent with a dogmatic system.[79] He later claims, "Faith does not need the thought of Being. When faith has recourse to this thought, it is no longer faith. This is what Luther understood."[80] Heidegger uses this claim in service to his own thesis that philosophy is the true *ontological* discipline, reflecting on the whole of reality, while theology is, like chemistry, an ontic, regional science that examines and reflects on only one aspect of being, in this case on "faith-filled *Dasein*."[81] For Heidegger, the destruction of theological ontology by

Luther is, in one sense, a harbinger of his own project of rethinking the fundamental meaning of being. Of course, the very nature of theology is here reconceived. No longer is the formal object of the discipline God in his very being, but rather, Christian existence as faith-filled life. Of course, this overturns the traditional notion that theology is the highest discipline precisely because it gives us knowledge of the *creator* of being itself, while all other disciplines deal with one or another aspect of created *esse*.[82] Theology is not now afforded cognitive penetration of the triune Godhead; it is necessarily remanded to the predicamental level to examine the factical demands of Christian existence.[83]

Postmodernism, then, with its suspicion of first philosophy of any kind, approximates some themes already present, such as the protest against "fixity of meaning" and "totalizing intelligibility," in certain strands of Protestantism. But if Reformation thought displays a certain connaturality with postmodern and nonfoundationalist themes, it is now clearly the case that this type of thinking has spread into all areas of theology. David Tracy, for example, argues that in light of our newly presenced situation, theology must honestly evaluate its classical self-understanding.[84] The traditional assessment, notably with regard to doctrine, seeks to freeze the flux, to deaden historical *Bewusstsein*, to finish the conversation. By so doing, theology leaves itself open to Jürgen Habermas's charge that it must be sealed off from the ideal-speech situation and from the communicative praxis of egalitarian society. Theology is already committed a priori; it is fully "open" neither to effective history nor to the serious rethinking demanded by the horizons of temporality and finitude. In this understanding, theology is entirely teleological rather than historical in nature. But if this is indeed the case, theology must be necessarily relegated to the private and devotional sphere. The discipline must be excluded from any attempt to establish public norms through communicative discourse because it seeks to establish limits and finalities that are inappropriate to our lived, historical situation.

Tracy, of course, has long argued against a subjectless, contextless, and ahistorical theology.[85] And one must willingly endorse a significant measure of his emphasis. No thinking or speaking occurs outside of a sociocultural matrix or in an ahistorical vacuum. No objective knowing is devoid of a correlative and constitutive subjectivity. But how far may historical contingency be pushed? If pushed as far as Heidegger, does one end with a fully historicized notion of doctrine wherein doctrine's perduring nature and transcultural cognitive claims are difficult if not impossible to sustain? What kind of truth does Christian doctrine then mediate? We will consider this last question more fully in the next chapter. For the moment, it is enough to say that Tracy, in his most recent work, which is concerned with displaying the "fragmentary" nature of knowledge, is again seeking to overcome the totalizations of the tradition, especially that of modernity. Fragments, Tracy avers, are the clearest and most dominant metaphor for contemporary Western thought. They represent, beginning with Kierkegaard, the first deconstructor of reified rationalist systems, our existing spiritual (and intellectual) situation because they indicate the "collapse of the religious certainties of all modern totality systems."[86]

Tracy rightly shows how religion remains the "other" of modernity's rationalistic architectonics, how excessive and transgressive religious forms—those of the Kabalists, the Sufis, Dionysius, and Eckhart—are sought out by some postmodern thinkers because they represent fragments that refuse to yield to systematization, that continue to teach us about God's incomprehensibility.[87] But questions nonetheless persist: Does Tracy follow Marion, so warmly endorsed for his examination of saturated religious phenomena, into distaste for metaphysics of any kind, even one disciplined by faith? It appears he does, insofar as he encourages us to "let go of the hope for any totality system whatsoever."[88] And if this is the case, on what basis does one defend the rational intelligibility of doctrine's assertions and the traditional characteristics associated with it? Phenomenology alone? And is this enough? It is one thing to be wary of Hegelian systems, of a priori totalizations that "reduce" reality by subterfuge and seek, like algorithmic modernity, either to dismiss or ignore revelation as an aspect of life and thought resistant to systematization. It is another matter to call into question the ability of first philosophy to lay hold of reality, to lend theoretical support to Christian faith and teaching, thereby offering another dimension of intelligibility to theology's universal claims. One may still hold for the uniqueness of saturated religious phenomena, as Marion does, without thereby abandoning philosophies with genuine metaphysical tendencies, themselves ultimately supportive of revelation and the constitutive dimensions of Christian faith.

Summary

Several of the thinkers discussed to this point have a decided preference for claiming that "foundations," whether classical, metaphysical, transcendental, or empirical, are philosophically inappropriate. Such attempts at metaphysics and first philosophy fail to understand adequately the decided effects of historicity, linguisticality and sociocultural specificity, of the *lēthē*, absence and otherness that traditional foundations, with their emphasis on "presence" and "finality," overlook and ignore. It is clear that theology must now, as Heidegger first indicated, be rather dramatically rethought. Theology can no longer speak of perduring dogmas, or of doctrines that mediate transgenerational and transcultural truth, much less of a first philosophy that would serve as a logically articulated infrastructure for such assertions. For certain thinkers—while surely not following Nietzsche's dictum, "The truth is that there is no truth"—the truth is known only, as Bernstein, Gadamer, Habermas and others have argued, in fully historicized circumstances. We may make judgments as to what is the best at any point in time, as to what is better and what is worse. But we are unable to claim more than that. Such an approach, it appears, is only with difficulty reconciled to an understanding of Christian doctrine that is, in some significant measure, enduring, universal, and normative.

Nonfoundationalist thinkers contend that we must adopt the insights pulsating through the work of Heidegger, Wittgenstein, Kuhn, Quine, and Sellars. They argue that the church has allowed one form of ontology and one form of epistemology—that is, some form of metaphysical realism—to dominate its theology of revelation. This has had the effect of privileging one reception of the gospel, a Hellenistic or quasi-Hellenistic one, thereby making a particular philosophy normative. But, nonfoundationalist thinkers argue, such normativity is illusory and inappropriate because, as much contemporary philosophy has shown, the fundamental horizons of this ontology have been deconstructed. Theology has not taken seriously—that is, as truly constitutive of being and knowing—the horizons of facticity and historicity that indefeasibly saturate and envelope life and thought. As an antidote, theology must now give proper ontological and epistemological weight to the cultural and linguistic determinacy of forms of life, to the priority of the flux, and to the encompassing horizons of finitude and temporality.

Heidegger has taught us that the truth of being has been given differently over the course of centuries—that there is no "final" or "winning" name for truth. There are only different messages, *Seinsgeschicke*, emerging from the *Ereignis*, brought to us since the time of Anaximander. Given the primordial and overarching dimensions of history, one *appearance* of being can never be properly equated with being itself. Marion and Derrida have sought to go beyond Heidegger, showing in the process that even the horizon of being is limiting and deterministic. One must never try to enclose that which "appears" in a horizon of any sort. This is Heidegger's mistake, and to follow it is to remain trapped in the ontological-theological tradition.

We must learn, rather, to think the impossible from which possibility springs. Our gaze must be trained on what appears, whether it is nothing at all or a nonreductive saturating phenomenon.

I will argue in the next section that while we have much to learn from the thinkers discussed, theology cannot simply ratify these points of view without reservation. On the contrary, I will argue that Christian doctrine needs some kind of (commodious) metaphysical approach in order to support logically its claim to be universal, perduring, self-same, and normative. I hope it is unnecessary to add that this does not presage a simple return to the metaphysics of neo-Scholasticism, to an artless reassertion of the *philosophia perennis*. On the contrary, contemporary thinkers have developed several new directions that preserve the intelligibility needed to substantiate the claims of Christian doctrine, while simultaneously incorporating the legitimate elements brought to the fore by contemporary thought.

Notes

1. For more on "teaching" in Scripture, see *didaskalia* and *didachē* in *Theological Dictionary of the New Testament*, vol. 2 (ed. G. Kittel; trans. G. Bromiley; Grand Rapids: Eerdmans, 1964), 160–65. See also *didaskalia*, *didachē*, and *didaskalos*, in *Exegetical Dictionary of the New Testament*, vol. 1 (ed. H. Balz and G. Schneider; Grand Rapids: Eerdmans, 1990), 316–20.

2. It is clear, no doubt, that I am speaking of doctrinal and dogmatic teaching rather than theological speculation. The latter, of course, harbors an essential place in Christian life and often helps the church sharpen, develop, and advance its understanding of doctrine. This point has been clarified by, among others, Wolfhart Pannenberg, *Systematic Theology*, vol. 1 (trans. Geoffrey Bromiley; Grand Rapids: Eerdmans, 1988), 1–26. As Pannenberg says, theology has a constitutive relationship with revelation: "The knowledge of God that is made possible by God, and therefore by revelation, is one of the basic conditions of the concept of theology as such."

3. The emphasis in this study will be on the doctrinal and dogmatic tradition of the Christian church and how such teaching is buttressed by (even while it molds and shapes) varying philosophical ideas. It must be salubriously remembered, of course, that doctrine and dogma are only one element of Christian life—an essential element, to be sure, but one that lives within the manifestation of the Holy Trinity in a myriad of ways: in the church's prayer, ritual, preaching, action, and entire life. This point always constitutes the wider and essential context for the particular theme of this book. It should be said clearly, then, that doctrines are not the primary form of revelation, even if they are an essential form. I agree here with Avery Dulles, who states, "Christian doctrines are never so literal that they cease to participate in the symbolic. They live off the power of revelatory symbols." It is just these more basic elements of worship and mystery that doctrine intends to inadequately but actually express. Dulles, *Models of Revelation* (Garden City, N.Y.: Doubleday, 1983), 143. Along similar lines, Dulles rightly points out, "The symbolic language of primary religious discourse can never be left behind if the dogmas and theologi-

cal formulations of Christian faith are to be rightly appreciated." Dulles, *The Craft of Theology* (New York: Crossroad, 1992), 19. Gerhard Sauter recently notes that doctrine is sometimes given a bad reputation as nothing more than a collection of lifeless propositions, but this is only the case if they are misunderstood. Sauter, *Gateways to Dogmatics* (trans. Geoffrey Bromiley; Grand Rapids: Eerdmans, 2002), 71.

4. The International Theological Commission of the Roman Catholic Church stated that "the living character of tradition gives rise to a great variety of doctrinal statements, differing in import and degree of binding force." On dogmas in a strict sense, see article III, 3 of the International Theological Commission (ITC), "On the Interpretation of Dogmas," *Origins* 20 (May 17, 1990): 9. Of course, it should be pointed out that when speaking of Christian doctrine, several distinctions need to be made regarding, for example, theological weight, the possibility of reversals, and so on. I have treated many of these themes in Thomas Guarino, *Revelation and Truth* (Scranton, Pa.: University of Scranton Press, 1993), ch. 5. The chief point here is simply that there are certain fundamental teachings that the Christian church regards as permanent and irreversible.

In this study, I am prescinding from the question of what particular doctrines are viewed as irreversibly true, as well as what persons or bodies may make such a judgment. These questions, of course, have riven Christianity for centuries. It is enough to say that all Christians believe that certain fundamental elements of the faith are irreversibly true, and it is from this widespread ecclesial affirmation that this study proceeds. For excellent summaries on the meaning and nature of authoritative confessions and dogmas, see Jaroslav Pelikan, *Credo* (New Haven, Conn.: Yale University Press, 2003), esp. 88–92.

5. The authoritative text may be found in *Acta apostolicae sedis* 92 (2000): 742–65. An English translation may be found in *Origins* 30 (June 9, 2000): 6–8. Although this document is clearly set in a Roman Catholic context, the sections on the uniqueness and unicity of Christ are virtually coincidental with the historic faith of all Christians. This statement, for a variety of reasons, was subject to a storm of international criticism. In my judgment, some of this criticism was unjustified and ill-informed. The declaration was, however, unquestionably remiss in failing to make clear the notable and continuing progress in ecumenical and interreligious dialogue that has taken place since Vatican II and the way in which this progress, too, is reflective of the gospel. From that point of view, the declaration's omissions, both unfortunate and, in the last analysis, theologically unintelligible, enervate the statement's force.

6. ITC, "On the Interpretation of Dogmas," 9. The International Theological Commission of the Roman Catholic Church is composed of theologians from many nations, nominated by particular episcopal conferences, for the sake of deliberating upon and offering greater intelligibility to the mysteries of the faith. The Prefect of the Congregation of the Doctrine of the Faith is, ipso facto, the chairman of the commission. For more information on the ITC and its governing statutes, see Francis Sullivan, *Magisterium* (New York: Paulist Press, 1983), 174–75. Some have claimed that the ITC represents nothing more than a "house organ" and so its judgments are theologically suspect. See, for example, the "Statement of the CTSA," *Origins* 20 (December 27, 1990): 464. Although it is true that the statements of the ITC are of unequal value, some of them, for example "On the Interpretation of Dogmas," are nothing less than exemplary.

7. For example, in a recent encyclical by John Paul II, *Fides et ratio*, issued in September 1998, the pope invokes certain ideas as central to Christian revelation, for example, the document speaks of the necessity of neither obscuring nor denying the "universal validity" of the contents of faith (no. 84) and of the "universal and transcendent value of revealed truth" (no. 83). With regard to continuity and perpetuity, the encyclical says, "To every culture Christians bring the unchanging truth of God [*immutabilem Dei veritatem*]"

(no. 71) and notes that "certain and unchangeable doctrine" must be more profoundly understood. Equally important in this regard is the letter's criticism of historicism whereby "the enduring validity of truth is denied. What was true in one period . . . may not be true in another" (no. 87). With regard to objectivity, the encyclical inveighs against the nihilistic "denial of all foundations and the negation of all objective truth" (no. 90). In the same section the document notes that, philosophically speaking, "the neglect of being inevitably leads to losing touch with objective truth and therefore to the very ground of human dignity." Since the issue of truth will be discussed at length in chapter 3, I will only touch on it briefly in this chapter.

8. Of course, all theologians are aware that the church's knowledge of God is tempered and limited by a variety of elements, both those belonging to the social location of the knower, and those inherent in the "nature" of the God who reveals himself to us. Theologians fully recognize, therefore, that doctrinal statements are by necessity limited formulations rather than exhaustive ones. This does not, however, jeopardize their status as mediating some dimension of truth. Even disregarding the sociocultural dimensions limiting the cognitive penetration of humanity, it is important to note that, as Aquinas rightly says, theology's formal object, God, is in his essence, quidditatively, beyond the mind's scope, even when enlightened by faith and grace (*ST* 1. q. 2, ad. 2; *SCG* I, 30). This theme will be treated more fully in chapter eight.

9. Pannenberg, *Systematic Theology*, 1:9, citing Athenagoras, *Leg.* 11, 1.

10. Ibid., 48–52 (emphasis added).

11. Robert Jenson, *Systematic Theology*, vol. 1 (New York: Oxford University Press, 1997), 20 (emphasis added). This is of a piece with Jenson's claim that theology, because it is concerned both with God and universal truth, must be "what the logical positivists derided as 'metaphysical'" (20).

12. Ibid., 22. Jenson roots the difference between doctrine and dogma in the latter's irreversibility: "A dogmatic choice is one by which the Church so decisively determines her own future that if the choice is wrongly made, the community determined by that choice is no longer the community of the Gospel; thus no church thereafter exists to reverse the decision" (17). He sees the Niceanum as one such decision. The essential point for our purposes is not necessarily the terminology used but that certain ecclesial beliefs do in fact mediate the truth properly and are considered by the church as irreversible. Nicea is, as Jenson notes, one such truth. It constitutes a constitutive moment for the church's own understanding of revelation.

13. Sauter, *Gateways to Dogmatics*, 6, 36. Explaining this thesis, he notes, "But it [dogmatics] tells us what must be said as coming from God rather than giving expression to our concern. In this way dogmatics differs from mere reflection on religious experience or the inward supervising of a religious worldview" (9). He continues, "No dogma is formulated for all time or for eternity. It if could be, it would be a definite, i.e., final statement of truth, but that would anticipate the conclusive judgment of God" (41). This sentence should not be seen as contradictory to Sauter's other affirmations. He points out with these comments that no dogma is exhaustive. There is an eschatological element to every dogma indicating that its conclusive and final intelligibility will only be revealed in the heavenly Jerusalem. And even then, one may wonder, as some Scholastics did, if the glorified human intellect will be able to penetrate fully the divine mysteries.

14. Pannenberg, *Systematic Theology*, 1:49–50. Along much the same lines, Pannenberg notes that Christians "who do theology trust already by faith in the truth of the message even before commencing their theological investigation. . . . But theological ascertainment of the truth is not made superfluous by the certainty of faith" (50).

15. Although Rahner has at times been criticized for what is taken as a Schleiermachian attempt to accent human experience over and against doctrine, that position is, I think, finally unsustainable. What Rahner and others seek to do is to show that the Enlightenment understanding of autonomous "nature" as divorced from "revelation/grace" is untenable from a Christian point of view and, therefore, human experience's "congruency" with church teaching is not to be disdained.

16. As Geoffrey Wainwright has recently said, indicating convergences between Catholics and Protestants on the nature of dogmatic statements: "For classical Protestants at least, the Apostles' Creed and the conciliar Creed of Nicea, Constantinople and Chalcedon—precisely, of course, in their fidelity to Scripture—have always been taken as the irreversible deliverances and continuing guides of the Tradition." Wainwright, *Is the Reformation Over?* (Milwaukee: Marquette University Press, 2000), 39.

17. John Caputo and Michael Scanlon, introduction to *God, the Gift, and Postmodernism* (ed. John Caputo and Michael Scanlon; Bloomington: Indiana University Press, 1999), 3.

18. Jacques Derrida, *The Gift of Death* (trans. David Wills; Chicago: University of Chicago Press, 1995), 49; as cited in Caputo and Scanlon, introduction to *God, the Gift, and Postmodernism*, 4 (emphasis added by the editors). Derrida also speaks of "faith without dogma" in his essay "Faith and Knowledge" in Derrida, *Acts of Religion* (ed. Gil Anidjar; New York: Routledge, 2002), 57.

19. It is necessary at this point to distinguish postmodern philosophers from moderate, nonfoundationalist thinkers. While similarities exist between them, the essential difference between the two is that those adopting a moderate position, despite their deep reservations about first philosophy or metaphysics of any kind, will certainly not reject rationality, nor will they, in most cases, renounce the political and intellectual achievements of modernity. Richard Bernstein's *Beyond Objectivism and Relativism* (Philadelphia: University of Pennsylvania Press, 1983) is a clear example of this position. Another such thinker, Terry Eagleton, who wishes to preserve aspects of critical theory, calls the deconstructive type of postmodernism, a "jejune branch of anti-totalizing thought." For Eagleton, such attempts at postpolitical discourse are wrong because they conflate all attempts at social change "in Nietzschean fashion with a craven conformity." See Eagleton, *The Ideology of the Aesthetic* (Cambridge, Mass.: Blackwell, 1990), 354. Similarly, Albrecht Wellmer argues that while the pathologies of the Enlightenment must be opposed, many of its accomplishments, such as liberal democracy and critical consciousness, should be positively redeemed. Postmodernity, then, rightly resists transcendental deductions, but it must likewise avoid the temptation to demonize reason. See Wellmer, *The Persistence of Modernity* (trans. David Midgley; Cambridge, Mass.: MIT Press, 1991). Gadamer and Habermas, too, who will be discussed later in this work, are nonfoundationalist in their thought and critical of metaphysics of any kind, but they are certainly not postmodernists in the "classical" sense. It is the more moderate position, interesting in clearly adjusting rather than abandoning our notions of truth and rationality, that has had the greatest influence on theology.

20. William Everdell, *The First Moderns* (Chicago: University of Chicago Press, 1997). The same thesis is argued by Louis Dupré, "Postmodernity or Late Modernity," *Review of Metaphysics* 47 (1993): 277–95. There is something of this also in Pierre Manent's *The City of Man* (trans. Marc A. LePain; Princeton, N.J.: Princeton University Press, 1998). As Manent says, the Age of Enlightenment reverberates with the words "Reason" and "Nature"; in reality, however, the Enlightenment "deals a decisive deathblow to both" (6). For Manent, what chiefly characterizes the Enlightenment is neither rationalization nor systematization, but enchantment with "the new." Given this alleged continuity between

modernity and "postmodernity," it is perhaps not surprising that Jacques Derrida avoids the word "postmodernism" for, as Caputo and Scanlon note, he considers himself a "man of the Enlightenment," although without letting the spirit of the Enlightenment "freeze over into dogma." See Caputo and Scanlon, introduction to *God, the Gift and Postmodernism*, 2.

21. Literature dealing with postmodernism has now reached voluminous proportions. Among the more helpful books are: David Lyon, *Postmodernity* (Minneapolis: University of Minnesota Press, 1994); James Marsh, John Caputo, and Merold Westphal, eds., *Modernity and Its Discontents* (New York: Fordham University Press, 1992); Paul Lakeland, *Postmodernity: Christian Identity in a Fragmented Age* (Minneapolis: Fortress Press, 1997); Terry Eagleton, *The Illusions of Postmodernism* (Oxford: Blackwell, 1997); Hugo Meynell, *Postmodernism and the New Enlightenment* (Washington: Catholic University of America Press, 1999); Kevin Vanhoozer, ed., *The Cambridge Companion to Postmodern Theology* (Cambridge: Cambridge University Press, 2003); Steven Connor, ed., *The Cambridge Companion to Postmodernism* (Cambridge: Cambridge University Press, 2004).

22. See Victor E. Taylor and Charles E. Winquist, eds., *The Encyclopedia of Postmodernism* (London: Routledge, 2001), 304ff. As Terry Eagleton says, "Postmodernism is skeptical of truth, unity, and progress, opposes what it sees as elitism in culture, tends toward cultural relativism, and celebrates pluralism, discontinuity, and heterogeneity." See *After Theory* (New York: Basic Books, 2003), 13 n. 1.

23. These phrases may be found in various works of John Caputo. See, for example, *Radical Hermeneutics* (Bloomington: University of Indiana Press, 1987); and *More Radical Hermeneutics* (Bloomington: University of Indiana Press, 2000).

24. Richard Rorty, for example, sees Husserl as trying to establish an unconditional apodicticity for philosophy, which belongs properly only to mathematics. See Rorty, "Emancipating Our Culture," in *Debating the State of Philosophy: Habermas, Rorty, and Kolakowski* (ed. Jósef Niznik and John T. Sanders; Westport, Conn.: Praeger, 1996), 27. Hans-Georg Gadamer, although quite different from Rorty philosophically, nonetheless accuses Husserl of remaining captive to the transcendental ego and so sees him as final defender of the Enlightenment-Cartesian-modern tradition. See Gadamer, *Philosophical Hermeneutics* (trans. David Linge; Berkeley: University of California Press, 1976), 166–73. Attempting to establish a unique view of Husserl is John Drummond, *Husserlian Intentionality and Non-Foundational Realism* (Dordrecht: Kluwer Academic Publishers, 1990). Defending Husserl's foundationalist project is Kathleen Haney, *Intersubjectivity Revisited: Phenomenology and the Other* (Athens, Ohio: Ohio University Press, 1994).

25. One can understand Thomas Kuhn's postpositivist manifesto, *The Structure of Scientific Revolutions* (Chicago: University of Chicago Press, 1970), as having initiated the postmodern turn in the philosophy of science. For Kuhn's relationship to postmodernity, see Tian Yu Cao, "The Kuhnian Revolution and the Postmodernist Turn in the History of Science," *Physis* 30 (1993): 476–504.

26. Theodor Adorno, *Negative Dialectics* (trans. E. B. Ashton; New York: Seabury, 1973), 23. With his "negative dialectics," Adorno attempted to redeem the excesses of the Enlightenment aesthetically. Art is here a glimmer of messianic light avoiding dominative reason and the conceptual truncation of reality. With similar intentions, see Helmut Peukert, "Enlightenment and Theology as Unfinished Projects," in *Habermas, Modernity, and Public Theology* (ed. Don. S. Browning and Francis Schüssler Fiorenza; New York: Crossroad, 1992), 43–65.

27. Richard Bernstein, "Faith and Reason," *Books and Culture* (Philosophers Respond to *Fides et ratio*) 5 (July/August 1999): 30–32.

28. As Philipp Rosemann says, "This search for an irreducible alterity has become the leitmotiv of this elusive movement of contemporary thinkers and artists that is qualified occasionally as 'postmodernism.'" See Rosemann, "Penser l'Autre: théologie negative et 'postmodernité,'" *Revue philosophique de Louvain* 91 (1993): 299. Joseph Grünfeld adds, "Postmodernism calls attention to the vagueness of foundationalism, the myth of the given, the limits of representation, the elusiveness of apodicticity, the indeterminacy of meaning and the inscrutability of reference." Grünfeld, "Heidegger's Hermeneutics," *Science et esprit* 47 (1995): 141.

29. As Habermas says, Heidegger's "conclusions unexpectedly overlapped with those of the later Wittgenstein. In spite of different backgrounds and rather opposite styles of reasoning, the convergence of Heidegger's and Wittgenstein's approaches . . . set the stakes for the present debate on rationality." Habermas, "Coping with Contingencies," in Niznik and Sanders, *Debating the State of Philosophy*, 13. Recent works on these thinkers, vis-à-vis foundationalism generally and metaphysics in particular, include: Gertrude Conway, *Wittgenstein on Foundations* (Atlantic Highlands, N.J.: Humanities Press, 1989); Fergus Kerr, *Theology after Wittgenstein* (2nd ed.; London: SPCK, 1997); Jürgen Habermas, *The Philosophical Discourse of Modernity* (trans. Fredrick Lawrence; Cambridge, Mass.: MIT Press, 1987); Jacques Taminiaux, *Heidegger and the Project of Fundamental Theology* (trans. and ed. M. Gendre; Albany, N.Y.: SUNY Press, 1991); Fred Dallmayr, *Between Freiburg and Frankfurt: Toward a Critical Ontology* (Amherst: University of Massachusetts Press, 1991); Brice Wachterhauser, ed., *Hermeneutics and Truth* (Evanston, Ill.: Northwestern University Press, 1994); Susan Brill, *Wittgenstein and Critical Theory* (Athens, Ohio: Ohio University Press, 1995); Daniel Hutto, *Wittgenstein and the End of Philosophy* (New York: Macmillan, 2003); Anthony Rudd, *Expressing the World: Skepticism, Wittgenstein and Heidegger* (Chicago: Open Court, 2003).

30. It may be helpful at this point to clear up a terminological issue, one that will be discussed further later in this chapter. For the moment, it suffices to say that for many authors "foundationalism" is connected uniquely with the Cartesian view of adherence to a rigorous epistemic standard. A belief is justified only if it is certain or logically grounded in beliefs that are themselves certain. Evidential warrants must be adduced for a belief to qualify as apodictically "foundational." Other contemporary thinkers, such as Richard Rorty, condemn the entire classical, medieval, and modern axis with the "foundationalist" label (including Plato, Aristotle, Aquinas, Kant, Hegel, and Husserl), widening the original epistemic critique to an ontological one as well. See, for example, Rorty, *Philosophy and the Mirror of Nature* (Princeton, N.J.: Princeton University Press, 1979). Recently, one sees this same, wider usage in Richard Bernstein's essay on *Fides et ratio*, which directly accuses the encyclical of falling victim to foundationalism because of its defense of metaphysics. Bernstein, "Faith and Reason." It is important to note that when the term "foundations" is used here, it is intended to refer to metaphysics or some other first philosophy, with the argument that such philosophizing cannot simply be ruled out of court as illegitimate. Given this usage of the term "foundationalism," one can oppose the isolated ego of Descartes—and the notion that one achieves rational justification only through evidential certainty—evidential empiricism as an ultimate epistemological standard, and the imperialistic pretensions of certain philosophies vis-à-vis the revelatory narrative, without opposing foundationalism, or the importance of "first philosophy"—itself. The usage here does not imply that, theologically speaking, metaphysical and transcendental foundations are developed independently of Christian faith. On the contrary, the claim here is that the a posteriori use of first philosophy is demanded by the *prior* claims of Christian faith itself.

Conversely, "nonfoundationalism" refers here not simply to the epistemological position that rational justification is not limited to evidential certainty, to warranted basic belief. It refers, rather, to the claim found, inter alia, in philosophers such as Rorty, Bernstein, and Vattimo, that metaphysical or transcendental philosophy of any kind (i.e., "foundationalism") calcifies reality and betrays the encompassing horizons of historicity and cultural-linguistic determinacy. This kind of nonfoundationalism will be discussed at greater length below. Useful works on nonfoundationalism include John Thiel, *Nonfoundationalism* (Minneapolis: Fortress, 1994), which examines the postpositivist empiricism of Sellars and Quine, and Tom Rockmore and Beth Singer, eds., *Antifoundationalism Old and New* (Philadelphia: Temple University Press, 1992), which examines various attempts at "foundations" in the history of philosophy.

31. One cannot, in the words of John Caputo, "freeze the flux" with *eidos, ousia, esse, essentia, res cogitans,* the transcendental Ego, or any other foundation. The event character of Being is such that it is given differently in each epoch. The Heideggerian *es gibt* confounds every attempt to "outflux the flux."

32. In Heidegger's wake, this is the task of philosophy envisioned by, among others, Rorty, Bernstein, and Caputo. Rorty's position is outlined, inter alia, in *Philosophy and the Mirror of Nature*, 389–94; and *Contingency, Irony, and Solidarity* (Cambridge: Cambridge University Press, 1989); Bernstein's in *Beyond Objectivism and Relativism* (Philadelphia: University of Pennsylvania Press, 1983), 223–31; and Caputo's in *Radical Hermeneutics*, 257–64; and in *The Prayers and Tears of Jacques Derrida* (Bloomington: Indiana University Press, 1997), esp. 331–39. Besides keeping conversation alive, another goal, as Rorty says, is "to put social hope in the place that knowledge has traditionally occupied." Rorty sees this position reflected in the works of Derrida who, Rorty avers, holds something like this: "If we stop thinking of truth as the name of the thing that gives human life its meaning . . . then we can replace the search for truth with the messianic hope for justice." Rorty, "Emancipating Our Culture," in Niznik and Sanders, *Debating the State of Philosophy,* 27. Rorty's intention to fashion a kind of religion out of "social hope," substituting it for any traditional notion of "truth," may also be found in *Achieving Our Country* (Cambridge: Harvard University Press, 1998) and in "Wild Orchids and Trotsky" in *Wild Orchids and Trotsky* (ed. Mark Edmundson; New York: Penguin, 1993), 29–50.

33. Richard Campbell, *Truth and Historicity* (Oxford: Clarendon, 1992), 398. He continues, "But what if there is no permanent human nature? What if . . . man's very being is historical? These suggestions encapsulate the concept of historicity." Thomas Anderson identifies Sartre as one of the sources of the contemporary denial of a common human nature: "One obvious way in which Jean-Paul Sartre's thought differs significantly from that of most classical philosophers is in his denial of a human nature or essence common to all human beings." Anderson notes that for Sartre, the idea of a human nature "similar in all times and places" is a "theory of bourgeois universality which he rejects." Anderson, "Sartre and Human Nature," *American Catholic Philosophical Quarterly* 70 (1996): 585–95.

34. Rebecca S. Chopp, "Situating the Structure: Prophetic Feminism and Theological Education," in *Shifting Boundaries* (ed. Barbara Wheeler and Edward Farley; Louisville, Ky.: Westminster/John Knox, 1991), 76. Gordon Kaufman claims that with our recognition that we are "thoroughly historical beings," there is no place for the idea of an unchanging and universal human nature. See Kaufman, *In the Face of Mystery: A Constructive Theology* (Cambridge, Mass.: Harvard University Press, 1993), 21.

35. Martin Heidegger, *Being and Time* (trans. John Macquarrie and Edward Robinson; New York: Harper & Row, 1962), 67–68; cited in Manent, *City of Man,* 207 n. 2. Although there is much truth in Heidegger's passage, it has as a subtext a salvo against the notion of nature.

36. Manent, *City of Man,* 207 n. 2.

37. Louis Dupré makes much of the rise of medieval nominalism in the passage to modernity. For the ancient realists, nature was communicative of reality; truth was mediated by the cosmos. Dupré argues that the ancients were constructivists only to the extent that culture represented a further molding of a given nature. For the nominalists, on the contrary, form belongs not to nature but to the mind. With Descartes and Kant, the form-giving principle of the subject is intensified. There is a gradual loss of cosmic intelligibility, of the truth mediated by *physis* and *nomos*, of the link between God and creatures. For post-Kantian voluntarism, nature is an enemy of freedom precisely because it tries to mold the subject a priori. But only the idealizing synthesis of the person is truly meditative of meaning. See Dupré, *Passage to Modernity: An Essay in the Hermeneutics of Nature and Culture* (New Haven, Conn.: Yale University Press, 1993). Both the classical tradition and modernity, in different ways, sought to preserve the notion of form, one by means of nature, the other by synthetic interiority. Postmodernity seeks to overcome any ontology of cosmos, substance, or subject. This is very close to Pierre Manent's claim that "modern philosophy . . . is forever concerned to reveal an ever more radical historicity." Manent, *City of Man*, 49.

A more moderate position, characteristic of, for example, the hermeneutical approach of Gadamer or the late-Enlightenment approach of Habermas, does not reject form per se but only the classical "foundationalist" form of nature and substance and the "foundationalist" subject of modern transcendental thought. For example, Gadamer and Habermas defend form, but now in a highly protean manner: in the case of Gadamer, tradition and history; for Habermas, the discourse community.

38. For Heidegger's thought on "overcoming" the tradition, see his essay "Overcoming Metaphysics," in *The Heidegger Controversy: A Critical Reader* (ed. Richard Wolin; Cambridge, Mass.: MIT Press, 1993), 67–90. Also see Heidegger, "The End of Philosophy and the Task of Thinking," in *Basic Writings* (ed. David Farrell Krell; San Francisco: HarperSanFrancisco, 1993), 427–49. On the other hand, one should take note of Paul Ricoeur's caution: "The unity of 'the' metaphysical is an after-the-fact construction of Heideggerian thought, intended to vindicate his own labour of thinking and to justify the renunciation of any kind of thinking that is not a genuine overcoming of metaphysics. . . . It seems to me time to deny oneself the convenience, which has become a laziness in thinking, of lumping the whole of Western thought together under a single word, metaphysics." See Ricoeur, *The Rule of Metaphor* (trans. R. Czerny et al.; Toronto: University of Toronto Press, 1977), 311; cited in David B. Hart, *The Beauty of the Infinite* (Grand Rapids: Eerdmans, 2003), 8–9.

39. As Merold Westphal recently noted, ontotheology can simply mean that there is a highest being who is key to the whole of being and this is something held by every Christian theology. See Westphal, "Overcoming Onto-theology," in Caputo and Scanlon, *God, the Gift, and Postmodernism*, 146–69. Also see Westphal, "Postmodernism and the Gospel: Onto-theology, Metanarratives, and Perspectivism," *Perspectives: A Journal of Reformed Thought* 15 (April 2000): 6–10.

40. Of course, Heidegger is primarily trying to overturn a conception of reason and rationality predominant from the time of Descartes and the Enlightenment. At the same time, Heidegger is not just condemning the transcendental subject of speculative idealism; he is calling into question the entire classical and medieval tradition as well, at least as he understands them. Of course, the rationalism characteristic of the Enlightenment is far different from that of classical or medieval thought. Charles Taylor, for example, sees in thinkers such as Descartes and Locke what he calls an "ontologizing of rational procedure," and it is against this that Heidegger fundamentally reacts. The Enlightenment's emphasis on objectivity, which ultimately became knowing "without a world," ignored all

of the horizons and prejudices, the *Vorverständnis*, that necessarily saturates cognitive acts. Taylor says it is not wrong, of course, to remove prejudices that are distortive. But the danger is the "ontologizing of the disengaged perspective." This leads to claiming an untenable "neutrality" of the knowing subject. Taylor, "Engaged Agency and Background in Heidegger," in *The Cambridge Companion to Heidegger* (ed. C. Guignon; Cambridge: Cambridge University Press, 1993), 317.

41. Thomas Sheehan, "Reading a Life: Heidegger and Hard Times," in Guignon, *Cambridge Companion to Heidegger*, 80. T. Kisiel notes that in Heidegger's Marburg course in 1923–1924, Heidegger was criticizing Husserl for being infected with Cartesianism. Husserl's reduction was, for Heidegger, simply another attempt at establishing the "worldless transcendental ego." See Lester Embree et al., eds., *The Encyclopedia of Phenomenology* (Dordrecht: Kluwer Academic Publishers, 1997), 333–39.

42. For Heidegger on *Seinsvergessenheit* and concealment, see, for example, Heidegger, *Nietzsche*, vol. 1, *The Will to Power as Art* (trans. David Farrell Krell; San Francisco: Harper & Row, 1979), 193–95.

43. Cited by John Caputo, "Heidegger and Theology," in Guignon, *Cambridge Companion to Heidegger*, 272.

44. Such tributes may be found, for example, in Richard Rorty, *Philosophy and the Mirror of Nature*; *Contingency, Irony, and Solidarity* (Cambridge: Cambridge University Press, 1989); and *Essays on Heidegger and Others* (Cambridge: Cambridge University Press, 1991). Rorty names Heidegger, along with Gadamer, Derrida, James, Dewey, and Kuhn, among others, as the great anti-Platonists or antimetaphysicians of modern thought. See Rorty, "The Challenge of Relativism," in Niznik and Sanders, *Debating the State of Philosophy*, 35.

45. Rorty, *Philosophy and the Mirror of Nature*, 5.

46. In his recent critique of Thomas Kuhn's work, Steve Fuller rightly says that Rorty has turned Sellars's critique of the "myth of the given" into a "mantra of postmodernism." See Fuller, *Thomas Kuhn: A Philosophical History for Our Times* (Chicago: University of Chicago Press, 2000), 268.

47. Rorty, *Philosophy and the Mirror of Nature*, 178.

48. Richard Rorty, "Emancipating Our Culture," in Niznik and Sanders, *Debating the State of Philosophy*, 27.

49. Rorty, *Philosophy and the Mirror of Nature*, 179. One may see immediately the strong resonances between Rorty and Kuhn's philosophy of science. The latter thought it impossible to establish any independent or objective standards of rationality precisely because, as observers, we too are entirely enmeshed in historicity. This is why Kuhn always spoke of two worlds, the Kantian world in itself (unknowable by us) and the constructed world of the theory-laden scientist. For this point in Kuhn, see Paul Hoyningen-Huene, *Reconstructing Scientific Revolutions* (Chicago: University of Chicago Press, 1993), 31–42.

50. Richard Bernstein, "Philosophy in the Conversation of Mankind," *Review of Metaphysics* 33 (1979–1980): 760.

51. Ibid., 760.

52. Rorty, *Contingency, Irony, and Solidarity*, xiii (emphasis added).

53. Bernstein, *Beyond Objectivism and Relativism*, 5.

54. Bernstein, while holding that "foundations" for rationality have been discredited, does not, of course, want to demonize reason itself. As such, he seeks to develop new forms of rationality and truth that help to distinguish good from bad, right from wrong. In this he is similar to Gadamer, Habermas, Kuhn, et al., whose thought will be more fully examined in the next chapter.

55. Bernstein, "*Faith and Reason*." The following citations are from this article.

56. Of course, Bernstein's claim here is open to several interpretations. It is one thing to say that all truth-claims are open to new perspectives and further calibration. All theologians will admit that such is necessarily the case. It is another matter, however, to call into question the possibility of any abiding and irrevocable truth, which Bernstein seemingly does.

57. Thomas Guarino, "*Fides et ratio*: Theology and Contemporary Pluralism," *Theological Studies* 62 (December 2001): 675–700.

58. Caputo, *Radical Hermeneutics*, 54. Page numbers from this work are cited in the text.

59. Caputo distanced himself, however, from Gadamer's interpretation of Heidegger, claiming that Gadamer "constrained and domesticated" Heidegger's radicalism by turning to the *Horizontverschmelzung*, which is simply an eleventh-hour attempt to find some ultimate unity within history, a last gasp effort to ward off the death rattle of metaphysics (113). But, Caputo holds, this Hegelian ontologization of history betrays Heidegger's own deepest instincts.

60. For Caputo's judgment on Heideggerian insufficiencies, see Caputo, *Demythologizing Heidegger* (Bloomington: University of Indiana Press, 1993). For his turn to Derrida, see Caputo, *Prayers and Tears of Jacques Derrida*.

61. Caputo's call for such a dialogue echoes that of Thomas Carlson's recent work, *Indiscretion: Finitude and the Naming of God* (Chicago: University of Chicago Press, 1999). Carlson claims we need an "indiscreet" marriage between premodern and postmodern thought, in this case between Pseudo-Dionysius and Heidegger.

62. John D. Caputo, "Philosophy and Prophetic Postmodernism: Toward a Catholic Postmodernity," *American Catholic Philosophical Quarterly* 74 (2000): 549–67.

63. A theologian may hear resonances of the debate between Rahner and von Balthasar on something like these grounds. Balthasar's objection to Rahner was that the latter, strongly influenced by transcendental philosophy, was, in fact, always working within the horizon of expectation, never the "impossible." So, Balthasar, somewhat unfairly, argues, At the time of Jesus' resurrection, Christians could say something like, after all, on the basis of my own transcendental constitution, I have been expecting this all along. Balthasar, on the other hand, always held up as models Kierkegaard and Pascal, two thinkers who looked the bloodied Christ in the face and recognized in him the "impossible" that had been accomplished for humanity. The revelation of the paschal mystery far surpassed any horizon of human anticipation. For Balthasar, the German idealism that Rahner incorporated into his thought devalued history in favor of an a priori reduction, thereby curtailing the gift and beauty of God's revelation and love.

64. "What Do I Love When I Love My God? An Interview with John Caputo," in *Religion with/out Religion* (ed. James Olthuis; London: Routledge, 2002), 176. Anthony Godzieba rightly says of Caputo's work, *The Prayers and Tears of Jacques Derrida*, "The desire for any sort of determinate image of God is dismissed as the remnant of an 'excessively Hellenistic frame of mind.'" Godzieba, "Prolegomena to a Catholic Theology of God between Heidegger and Postmodernity," *Heythrop Journal* 40 (1999): 326. Taken a step further, a determinate image of God, one with cognitive content, will ultimately be equated with the violence of the particular.

65. "What Do I Love When I Love My God? An Interview with John Caputo," 176. Whether Augustine supports these Derridean moves, however, is itself debatable, as Caputo surely knows. One can certainly find more of conflict, doubt, uncertainty—indeed, even Derridean undecideability—in Augustine's introspective writings, such as the *Confessions*, than in Aquinas's purely formal theology. But is the belief that divine truth is effectively, continuously, and universally mediated by faith and grace ever seriously questioned by Augustine the pastor, bishop, and theologian? Further, although not "Continental,"

John Milbank sees his position as neo-Augustinian in identity and purpose (certainly that was the clear tendency of de Lubac and the *nouvelle théologie* whom Milbank acknowledges as his inspiration). The same can be said of Radical Orthodoxy generally. Presumably Milbank's brand is not the "uncertain" Derridean Augustinianism Caputo has in mind.

66. Jean-Luc Marion, *God without Being* (trans. Thomas Carlson; Chicago: University of Chicago Press, 1991). See also Marion, *The Idol and Distance: Five Studies* (trans. Thomas Carlson; New York: Fordham University Press, 2001).

67. As is well known, Marion's interpretation of Aquinas was severely criticized for following a truncated reading of the metaphysical tradition. See, for example, J.-H. Nicolas, "La supreme logique de l'amour et la théologie," *Revue thomiste* 83 (1983): 639–59; and R. Virgoulay, "Dieu ou l'Etre," *Recherches de science religieuse* 72 (1984): 163–98. See also David Burrell, "Reflections on 'Negative Theology' in the Light of a Recent Venture to Speak of 'God without Being,'" in *Postmodernism and Christian Philosophy* (ed. Roman T. Ciapalo; Mishawaka, Ind.: American Maritain Association, 1997), 58–67.

68. Marion, *God without Being*, 17, 27.

69. Ibid., 36.

70. See Jean-Luc Marion, "Saint Thomas et l'onto-théologie," *Revue thomiste* 95 (1995): 31–66. For a good account of Marion's development in his reading of Aquinas, see Brian Shanley, *The Thomist Tradition* (Dordrecht: Kluwer Academic Publishers, 2002) 62–66.

71. Jean-Luc Marion, "Metaphysics and Phenomenology: A Summary for Theologians," in *The Postmodern God* (ed. Graham Ward; Oxford: Blackwell, 1997), 284 and 288.

72. Ibid., 293.

73. One may also include here Richard Kearney, *The God Who May Be* (Bloomington: Indiana University Press, 2001) and Gianni Vattimo, *Belief* (trans. Luca D'Isanto and David Webb (Stanford University Press, 2000) and *After Christianity* (New York: Columbia University Press, 2002).

74. I leave it to my Protestant confreres, who know more about the fundamental impulses of the Reformation than I, to decide if this limited comparison between postmodernism/nonfoundationalism and Protestant thought has any merit. This entire section, then, should be understood more as a hypothesis, an extended reflection, rather than a declarative thesis. I also wish to be clear that I am not saying that contemporary Protestant theologians display more postmodern tendencies than Roman Catholic ones. In fact, the opposite seems often to be the case, perhaps because of what Habermas called Catholicism's "less troubled relationship with the *lumen naturale.*" But, as Habermas also pointed out, this "less" can be indicative of theology losing its identity in a series of "takeover" attempts by theology's "partners." I am asking, rather, if, in its origins, postmodernism harbors ideas that bear a closer resemblance to certain proto-Reformation themes.

75. Balthasar has pointed out that the protest of "Luther (and in our times Barth) remains important because it keeps the transcendental beauty of revelation from slipping back into equality with an inner-worldly natural beauty." Hans Urs von Balthasar, *The Glory of the Lord*, vol. 1 (trans. E. Leiva-Merikakis; San Francisco: Ignatius, 1982), 41. It will not enter into the discussion here, but it should be said that the philosophy against which Luther was reacting was often a bastardized Scholasticism that had lost the primacy of the personal and the existential. Since many of the criticisms he lodged against its lifelessness were clearly justified, Luther's theology may be understood as an attempt to rethink Christian truth within a new conceptual framework.

The concern that revelation not be equated with created beauty is found today preeminently in the work of E. Jüngel. For Jüngel, Luther's chief philosophical point is that metaphysics fails to understand the cross; it is, indeed, the cross that negates metaphysical thinking about God as well as the alleged divine attributes of immutability and impassibility. See Jüngel, *God as the Mystery of the World* (Grand Rapids: Eerdmans, 1983), 373. For a clear analysis of Jüngel on this point, see Ivor Davidson, "*Crux probat omnia*: Eberhard Jüngel and the Theology of the Crucified One," *Scottish Journal of Theology* 50 (1997): 157–90. Davidson says that for Jüngel, metaphysical theism conceives of God's essence without reference to the event of Christ on the cross (169).

76. Ghislain Lafont notes that some, in postmodernity's wake, seek to replace ontotheology with some form of staurotheology. This move, at least traditionally associated with the Reformation, serves as a kind of negative dialectic with the themes of disjunction and disharmony now challenging any totalizing vision of reality. See Lafont, *God, Time, and Being* (trans. Leonard Maluf; Petersham, Mass.: St. Bede's Publications, 1992).

77. Hans-Georg Gadamer, "Correspondence concerning *Wahrheit und Methode*," *Independent Journal of Philosophy* 2 (1978): 10.

78. "What a man has to learn through suffering is not this or that particular thing, but insight into the limitations of humanity, into the absoluteness of the barrier that separates man from the divine." More to the epistemological point: "This experience is the experience of finitude. The truly experienced person is the one who has taken this to heart, who knows that he is master neither of time nor the future." Hans-Georg Gadamer, *Truth and Method* (trans. J. Weinsheimer and D. G. Marshall; New York: Continuum, 1993), 357. This point, at least seemingly, is not so different from the claim of Tillich, who says, in a specifically religious context, "I deny the possibility of a vow because of the finitude of the finite. A vow, if it is an absolute commitment, would make the moment in which we make it infinite or absolute. Other moments may come which reveal the relativity of the moment in which this decision was once made." Paul Tillich, *Ultimate Concern: Tillich in Dialogue* (ed. D. Mackenzie Brown; New York: Harper & Row, 1965), 195–96.

79. As Gadamer says, "All of his [Heidegger's] efforts to sort things out with himself and with his questions were motivated by a desire to free himself from the dominating theology in which he had been raised—so that he could be a Christian." Hans-Georg Gadamer, *Heidegger's Ways* (Albany, N.Y.: SUNY Press, 1994), 170.

80. "Der Glaube hat das Denken des Seins nicht nötig. Wenn er das braucht, ist er schon nicht mehr Glaube. Das hat Luther verstanden." "Séminaire de Zurich," trans. F. Fédier in *Poesie* 13 (1980): 52–63; cited in Marion, *God without Being*, 61.

81. "Our thesis, then, is that *theology is a positive science, and as such, therefore, is absolutely different from philosophy*. . . . It is immediately clear from this thesis that theology, as a positive science, is in principle closer to chemistry and mathematics than to philosophy." Martin Heidegger, *The Piety of Thinking* (trans. J. Hart and J. Maraldo; Bloomington: Indiana University Press, 1976), 6. The same comments may also be found in Martin Heidegger, *Pathmarks* (ed. William McNeill; Cambridge: Cambridge University Press, 1998), 41. As an ontic discipline, theology is not suited to handle the primordial ontological questions. In fact, Heidegger argues, the "foundation" on which the system of dogma rests is a misguided attempt by theology to be a "first philosophy," inadequately understanding Luther's insight into the primacy of faith. See Heidegger, *Being and Time*, 30–31. Early on, as the letter of 1919 makes clear, Heidegger recognized that this position, along with his emphasis on temporality and finitude, would place him at odds with Catholicism's understanding of the universal and perduring truth-claims of theology. He believed a *certain* understanding of Protestantism, primarily that mediated by Bultmann, was amenable to his own thinking.

Husserl, for his part, applauded Heidegger for "free[ing] himself from dogmatic

Catholicism" and for "cut[ting] himself off . . . from the sure and easy career of a 'philosopher of the Catholic worldview.'" Thomas Sheehan, "Reading a Life: Heidegger and Hard Times," in Guignon, *Cambridge Companion to Heidegger*, 76.

82. Thomas Aquinas, *Commentary on Aristotle's Metaphysics* I, lectio 3, chs. 64–68 (trans. John P. Rowan; Chicago: Regnery, 1961). Heidegger thinks of philosophy as asking the primordial, fundamental questions, while theology reflects on human existence as determined by Christian faith: "Anyone for whom the Bible is divine revelation and truth has the answer to the question 'Why are there beings rather than nothing?' even before it is asked. There is, to be sure, a thinking and questioning elaboration of the world of Christian experience, i.e., of faith. That is theology." See Martin Heidegger, *An Introduction to Metaphysics* (trans. R. Manheim; Garden City, N.Y.: Doubleday, 1961), 6. Robert Sokolowski notes in passing that while Husserl had many disciples who were converts to Christianity (somewhat to Husserl's embarrassment), Heidegger had very few. This is likely a reflection of the fact that while Husserl's philosophy gave rise to reflection on wide-ranging domains of human experience, Heidegger presented his philosophy as a "resolution of the religious problem." See Sokolowski, "Phenomenology in the Last Hundred Years," in *One Hundred Years of Philosophy* (ed. Brian J. Shanley; Washington, D.C.: Catholic University of America Press, 2001), 206. Matthew Daigler is right, then, when he says, "The cosmos is truly divine for Heidegger, a *theios kosmos*, but not in the sense of a manifestation of a deity who transcends and towers over the world. In the end, for Heidegger, Being rules over both God and man." Daigler, "Heidegger and von Balthasar: A Lovers' Quarrel over Beauty and Divinity," *American Catholic Philosophical Quarterly* 69 (1995): 386.

83. It should be noted that Karl Barth clearly resisted Heidegger's attempts to dragoon Luther and Christianity at large for his own philosophical ends. At the same time, Barth's failure to see that, often enough, philosophy (and even the *analogia entis*) was used at the *service* of revelation may have unwittingly played into Heidegger's hands by granting him the philosophical "field." This will be discussed at greater length in chapter seven.

84. I have treated aspects of Tracy's reception of hermeneutical and nonfoundationalist themes in Thomas Guarino, *Revelation and Truth: Unity and Plurality in Contemporary Theology* (Scranton, Pa.: University of Scranton Press, 1993), 68–71, 77–78.

85. See, for example, David Tracy, *The Analogical Imagination* (New York: Crossroad, 1981), 100.

86. David Tracy, "Fragments: The Spiritual Situation of Our Times," in Caputo and Scanlon, *God, the Gift, and Postmodernism*, 173.

87. Ibid., 177.

88. Ibid., 179.

CHAPTER 2

Christian Doctrine and a Renewed First Philosophy

Metaphysical Themes and Theology

Contemporary Attempts

In order to fulfill its task, theology needs some kind of metaphysical structure or "foundation" that undergirds logically the assertions of Christian doctrine. What kind "foundation" or "foundationalism" is envisioned? It is important at the outset to define exactly what is meant by "foundationalism" in order to preclude misunderstandings. There are two broadly identifiable uses of the term foundationalism. On the one hand, philosophers and theologians rooted in the empirical-analytical tradition of philosophy tend to equate foundationalism with the Cartesian view of adherence to a rigorous epistemic standard. So, for example, Sally Haslanger observes, "By foundationalism, I mean here the philosophical view that a belief is justified only if it is itself certain, or is derivable from premises that are certain."[1] Along the same lines, Bruce Marshall describes foundationalism as demanding that "justified beliefs (including Christian ones) must either be tied . . . to self-evident or incorrigible data, or logically grounded in beliefs which are."[2] When criticized theologically, this type of foundationalism is normally scored for giving the impression that some standard *external to theology* is now proposed as the final criterion for truth and certainty. Theology is now called upon to justify itself before the bar of secular foundations (often some form of empiricism or logically derivable proposition) in order to attain validity. Normative epistemic primacy is now accorded to nontheological criteria.[3]

Alvin Plantinga decries precisely this kind of thinking that he calls "classical foundationalism," which holds that "at least in principle, any properly functioning human beings who think together about a disputed question with care and good will, can be expected to come to agreement."[4] For this type of thinking, some propositions are properly basic or foundational and clearly accepted by all, while other propositions are not. Those propositions that are not foundational must be traceable, on the basis of evidence, back to properly foundational statements. As a Christian philosopher, Plantinga is concerned because "the existence of God . . . is not among the propositions that are properly basic; hence a person is rational in accepting theistic belief [according to classical foundationalism] only if he has evidence for it."[5] Plantinga, for a variety of reasons, thinks that classical foundationalism is rooted in an unacceptable evidentialism seeking to marginalize theism as a warranted basic belief. But this kind of foundationalism, which allows philosophy to erect nontheological criteria that theology itself must answer to, or that forces theology into an evidentialist Procrustean bed, is hardly the kind of foundationalist thinking that theology can sanction.[6]

On the other hand, the term foundationalism is also used in a wider, more general, and less restrictive sense. In this usage, any type of *prima philosophia*, whether of the ontological, transcendental, or empirical variety, is regarded as foundationalist in kind. Here the entire axis of Western thought, whether Aristotelian, Thomistic, Kantian, or Husserlian, is understood as trying to establish some kind of "foundation" for philosophy, not specifically epistemological or Cartesian, to be sure, but nonetheless given to isolating a first principle, a metaphysical or transcendental foundation for thought and reality. Nonfoundationalist critics claim that this type of thinking both calcifies reality and betrays ignorance of the wider cultural and historical horizons displayed by Heidegger, Wittgenstein, and contemporary thought generally. Heidegger's primordial notion of temporality, Wittgenstein's cultural-linguistic web of experience, Derrida's destabilization of textual meaning, Gadamer's *phronēsis*-based rationality, and Habermas's postmetaphysical, neopragmatic communicative theory all serve to deconstruct foundationalist metaphysics and transcendental gnoseologies as legitimate philosophical options. Among contemporary philosophers, Rorty, Bernstein, Vattimo, and Caputo are several thinkers who oppose attempts at universalizing metaphysical systems that serve only to "freeze the flux" of historical thought.[7]

In fact, theology can endorse neither the kind of foundationalism demanded by evidentialism nor the notion that epistemic primacy may be accorded to some criterion or secular epistemological or ontological warrant other than revelation itself. This would be, indeed, to place revelation in a predetermined Procrustean bed, tailoring its dimensions *from the beginning* to a preconceived philosophical horizon. At the same time, theology must endorse, for the sake of its own intelligibility but precisely *within the prior parameters established by revelation itself*, philosophical warrants undergirding the rational structure of Christian faith. Consequently, the "foundationalism" here defended is the position that revelation requires a certain metaphysical range or structure in order to support logically doctrinal teaching, as well as the traditional hallmarks associated with this teaching such as its universality, normativity, and historical identity.[8] This is why the recent encyclical *Fides et ratio* properly points out that only a philosophy with some kind of metaphysical horizon is able to fulfill what it called philosophy's *officium congruum*: to provide suitably logical warrants for the *depositum fidei*.[9] Failing to seek such warrants will lead in the direction of a flaccid historicism or an assertive fideism, neither of which can offer the kind of philosophical linchpins that doctrine needs if it is to be logically intelligible. From this point of view, clearly, attempts to establish some kind of "first philosophy" are demanded by revelation, never done apart from it, and are ultimately subjected to theological criteria. The type of "foundationalism" here sanctioned, then, should always be understood as an exercise in the *fides quaerens intellectum*, as the "second moment" within the *auditus fidei-intellectus fidei* synthesis.[10]

Defending some kind of *prima philosophia*, some philosophy with a metaphysical "range" or "horizon," does not necessarily imply the endorsement of any particular one. Philosophical pluralism is here countenanced, although obviously within the boundaries set by revelation itself. This is not a simple return, then, to the *philosophia perennis*. It is, on the contrary, the recognition that many philosophies can rationally support Christian revelation and doctrine. As *Fides et ratio* properly points out, even while it partially subverts the prior teaching of the nineteenth-century encyclical *Aeterni Patris*, "The church has no philosophy of her own nor does she canonize any one particular philosophy in preference to others" (no. 49).[11] The document also states that "no historical form of philosophy can legitimately claim to embrace the totality of truth" (no. 51) and that "there are many paths which lead to truth . . . [and] any one of these paths may be taken as long as it leads . . . to the Revelation of Jesus Christ" (no. 38). The encyclical also proffers a variety of possible models, indicating by example the plurality of philosophical approaches sanctioned by the church. At different times, one finds cited favorably the expected classical thinkers such as Augustine, Dionysius, the Cappadocians, Anselm, and Aquinas, as well as modern theologians and philosophers such as Newman, Rosmini, Soloviev, Florensky, Lossky, and Stein. Even Pascal and Kierkegaard receive favorable mention for their epistemological humility in the face of rationalism. Of course, the thinkers adduced here are representative rather than exhaustive examples of those whose philosophy and theology is in "organic continuity with the great tradition" while developing "an original, new and constructive mode of thinking" (no. 85).[12]

What is clear is that the philosophies properly undergirding Christian doctrine are hardly identical with Thomism or Scholasticism.[13] All philosophies are to do what Thomism did, namely, provide what may be called a revelationally appropriate philosophy, capable of fulfilling the *officium congruum*, of providing a view of reality, of presence, and capable of sustaining Christian faith and teaching. This is why the letter speaks not simply of "metaphysics" but rather of philosophies with a "genuine metaphysical range." The encyclical, then, properly in my judgment, shows little ultimate sympathy for either the Heideggerian "overcoming of metaphysics," the postmodern "end of philosophy," or for an unqualified and blanket demise of ontotheology. On the contrary, it seeks ways of understanding reality, varying philosophical styles that, while not betraying the autonomy proper to philosophy itself, nonetheless offer logical support for revelation's own claims.[14]

Within this theological concern for philosophies "possessing a genuine metaphysical range" lie persistent systemic issues, especially the question of how the continuity, identity, and universality of the *depositum fidei* is intelligibly established. How are such characteristics protected when one turns toward postmodernism and nonfoundationalism? It appears undeniable that a move toward other approaches signifies either a turn toward significant mutability and flexibility in fundamental Christian teaching, or conversely, a fideistic assertion of the enduring truth of the gospel, prescinding from any attempt to undergird such perdurance on the basis of theoretical warrants. Without a "foundationalist" ontology of some sort, there is no possibility for logically sustaining the universality and continuity of doctrine, not to mention the stability of textual meaning and the referential notion of truth, essential principles, seemingly, for any recognizable understanding of Christian teaching.

Given the claims of postmodernity and of nonfoundationalism at large, and given the importance of not tailoring revelation to predetermined schemata, is it possible, nonetheless, to develop philosophies sensitive to legitimate contemporary demands yet able to serve as rational infrastructures for Christian life and thought? Certainly some thinkers have recognized precisely this issue. Bernard Lonergan, for example, has been one of the most balanced theologians on this matter, again and again seeking to show the extent to which historical consciousness and its attendant horizons have overturned the traditional understanding. Lonergan argues, for example, that classical culture was right in assuming there was a universal human nature but misunderstood the extent to which this essential nature was open.[15] In conjunction with this premise, Lonergan develops a transcendental philosophy outlining the invariant structures of human consciousness while concomitantly championing, against neo-Scholasticism, cultural mutability and so the necessary flexibility of conceptual constructs.[16] For Lonergan, historicity and cultural particularity are inextricably intertwined with human understanding. This recognition leads him to assert that while dogmas are permanent, the classical culture in which they were first formulated is not.[17] Expressions may change given varying cultural contexts, but meaning, in particular dogmatic meanings, are stable. He cites Vatican I favorably in this regard: "There is ever to be retained that meaning of the sacred dogmas that once was declared by the Church" (DH 3020). He argues that this meaning is continuous and permanent because "it conveys the doctrine of faith revealed by God." Again, "the meaning of dogmas is permanent because that meaning is not a datum but a truth and that truth is not human but divine."[18]

Lonergan recognizes that to warrant the permanence of meaning, a meaning both transcultural and transgenerational, and to avoid its being swallowed by cultural particularity, he needs some stable notion of human nature. This he offers with his universal cognitive structure, the open but universally invariable elements of experience, understanding, judgment, and decision that constitute human cognitional acts. So, for example, at the outset of his greatest work, *Insight*, Lonergan states, "Thoroughly understand what it is to understand and not only will you understand the broad lines of all there is to be understood but also you will possess a fixed base, an invariant pattern opening upon all further developments of understanding."[19] Further: "Knowing is a recurrent structure that can be investigated sufficiently in a series of strategically chosen instances."[20] Whether Lonergan's "foundationalist" philosophy is finally adequate is not here the crucial issue.[21] The point is that he has sought to establish a philosophy able to take account of cultural and historical mutability while still offering some kind of metaphysics logically accounting for the possibility of the transcultural and transgenerational meaning of Christian doctrine.

Karl Rahner too, even while defending his transcendental gnoseology, has ceaselessly sought to show the extent to which historical and hermeneutical consciousness has had a deep and lasting effect on meaning and interpretation. Like many theologians, Rahner defends the universal, normative, and perduring dimensions of revelation and Christian doctrine. His well-documented controversy with Hans Küng in the early 1970s was an attempt to maintain the material integrity and universal truth of doctrine while, at the same time, recognizing the indefeasible horizons of historicity and embeddedness that necessarily attend doctrinal formulations.[22] Even in his early work, Rahner observes, for example, that doctrines undergo a history: "The historically conditioned, limited terminology lends historical finiteness, concreteness and contingence to the statement of faith itself, particularly in its theological form."[23] At the same time, "this is not, of course, to maintain that the assertion does not remain the same."[24]

As his thought progressed, Rahner argued with increasing vigor for the effect of sociocultural particularity on the understanding and formulation of doctrine.[25] He also placed increasing emphasis on God as Holy Mystery, whose infinite and mysterious holiness should offer another reason for the church's cognitive humility even with regard to creedal and dogmatic statements.[26]

At the same time, Rahner never abandoned the theological ontology he had elaborated in his early works, *Spirit in the World* and *Hearers of the Word*, with their consistent attempts to defend some universally applicable notion of human nature (the *Vorgriff* toward Infinite Being), while simultaneously seeking to overcome an Enlightenment naturalism that saw this human nature as a self-enclosed entity unrelated to God. This latter understanding had been developed theologically in an Aristotelian key by Catholic neo-Scholastics, leading to the notion of a "natural end" of humanity, apart from the graced, supernaturally "elevated" one that caused countless confusions and aporias, which came to a head first with Maurice Blondel's *L'Action* and then, conclusively, with the publication of Henri de Lubac's *Surnaturel*, a book arguing the Christian tradition itself bears witness to the fact that any notion of "nature" must be drawn from the one and only lived supernatural order.[27]

The crucial point here is that, even as he increasingly defended otherness, historicity, absence, and mystery in theological knowing, Rahner continued to maintain his invariant transcendental ground, which served as a foundation both for understanding humanity's intrinsic relationship to God and for explaining the transcultural and transgenerational unity, identity, and meaning of Christian doctrine.[28] In a 1981 article, for example, Rahner argued that the question of a "metaphysical theology" occurs when the "knowing subject . . . asks itself, in a total return to itself, about the conditions of the possibility of the subject and of a knowledge and a freedom which have a reflexive knowledge of themselves. . . . In this transcendental reflection on oneself there is contained a metaphysical anthropology."[29] As with Lonergan, it is not a matter of deciding on the adequacy of Rahner's philosophical theology; it is matter of recognizing that he saw clearly only such a foundation would allow for the permanency and universality of the church's doctrine to be intelligibly and logically defended.[30]

A recent phenomenological defense of a broadly "foundational" viewpoint is offered by Robert Sokolowski, who justifies both the possibility of philosophically knowing "essentials" and the constructive dimension of noetic acts intrinsically connected with temporality. Seeking to illumine the complementarity rather than opposition between nature and culture, he says, "We never have sheer nature without convention or sheer convention without nature; the two are always tangled. Nature is displayed to us only as refracted through custom and custom always mixes with the natural. The interweaving of the two is what makes it so apparently plausible to say that there is no nature, but only convention."[31] Explaining the Husserlian notion of eidetic intuition, wherein the *eidos* or form is grasped by intentionality, Sokolowski claims that "a perceived object's being an identity in a manifold of sides, aspects and profiles is universal and necessary, and we can see that it is so. Essences are evidenced to us."[32] To grasp an essence is to grasp an identity within the manifold of appearances; it is to "reach a feature that it would be inconceivable for a thing to be without." Although Sokolowski, like many phenomenologists, often avoids the language of "being" and "metaphysics," he affirms many of the same truths using the Husserlian language of "eidetic intuition," and "identity synthesis," such as that "essentials" are graspable in and through historical flux and cultural convention by human intuition and intending.

Sokolowski is not a theologian and does not ordinarily concern himself with theological issues; nonetheless, he offers phenomenological insights that help to display the manner in which Christian doctrine is an achieved "identity synthesis" known throughout and within the manifold of cultures and generations.[33] Further, through his use of "eidetic intuition," Sokolowski provides a conceptual framework for intelligibly distinguishing that which is essential to doctrine as opposed to that which is historically conditioned. Such reasoning could also be used to understand the kind of "nature" proper to humanity, a nature which itself warrants the achievement of an identity synthesis through time and culture.[34]

Sokolowski, with his emphasis on eidetic intuition, on grasping unity in difference, has little use for the originally (at least) Husserlian-inspired Derrida of philosophical deconstruction. He claims that Husserl and phenomenology handle the themes of difference and absence in a subtle way, without abandoning presence and identity. Consequently, he is forced to conclude that, when speaking of phenomenological genealogy, one only mentions deconstruction "with some embarrassment, the way a family might be forced to speak about an eccentric uncle."[35]

"Foundationalist" thinkers such as Rahner and Lonergan (and in his own way, Sokolowski) are certainly not interested in defending theological Cartesianism. On the contrary, they fought an Enlightenment concept of nature that gradually led to theological anthropologies fraught with extrinsicism. On the other hand, they do think that some kind of broadly metaphysical approach is necessary if one is to defend adequately fundamental positions regarding Christian teaching. These thinkers recognize that if the Christian faith holds for a notion of doctrine that, at least in essentials, is perduring and selfsame, universally valid and normative, despite profound changes in cultures and societies, then some metaphysical "foundation" is necessary or such doctrinal attributes could not possibly be logically/philosophically sustained.

If, on the other hand, one accepts postmodern and nonfoundationalist thought more fully, thereby abandoning some form of metaphysics, one's entire understanding of Christian teaching is deeply affected. Either the truth of the gospel, as mediated through doctrine, must simply be asserted, breaking its link with a philosophically elaborated infrastructure. Or, more likely, by opening a fissure between first philosophy and theology, one develops a quite different understanding of what the *depositum fidei* is, how it develops, and the type of continuity, universality, and selfsame identity proper to it. Also profoundly affected is the understanding of the type of truth mediated by it.

While the question of truth must wait for the next chapter, in the case of Lonergan and Rahner, the defense of some invariant transcendental structure and, in the case of Sokolowski, the grasping of essences in eidetic intuition, provides, ultimately, for some kind of philosophical "foundation" which, in turn, is able to offer a basis for unity amidst diversity, for identity within difference, for perduring continuity within the horizons legitimately illumined by much contemporary philosophy. It is to provide properly intelligible support for the way in which doctrine's meaning can remain intact despite cultural, linguistic, and sociological differences among men and women of every nation, custom, and epoch. Only a theological ontology of some sort can resist a fully historicized understanding of Christian doctrine.

While the theologies of Rahner and Lonergan are generally well-known, several others have also developed broadly metaphysical approaches in order to defend logically the claims of faith. Walter Kasper, for example, is very alert to the fact that Christian doctrine intends to say something universal and continuous, yet in conditions that are limited by all of the dimensions that concern contemporary thought. To this end, Kasper asserts, "What is considered the real cause of offense today is not so much the teaching about Christ [of Chalcedon], as the church and its dogma, which claims to be able to say something generally valid and timeless about God in terms that are historically conditioned."[36]

For Kasper, reconciling the universal and transcultural nature of the church's teachings with the requisite limitations of socio-cultural specificity constitutes the central crisis of truth besetting contemporary theology.[37] How does Kasper reconcile his claim that the church teaches truth universally with all of the issues raised by present-day philosophy? His first instinct is one of regret:

> The true and deepest crisis of present theology is that there is now no metaphysics. . . . One reason for this is to be found in philosophy, which in some quarters proclaims the end of metaphysics. Another reason is that the process of overcoming narrow and encrusted neo-scholastic metaphysics had led theology to divest itself radically of its Hellenized and metaphysical elements.[38]

But what does Kasper substitute here? He has, in the past, approvingly cited Lonergan's *Doctrinal Pluralism* as a useful attempt to underpin unity within diversity. Often enough, though, Kasper turns for help to Rahner's uniquely constituted transcendental subject, adding, however, that given the insights of contemporary philosophy, there must be a greater "interlacing of transcendentality and facticity." While supportive of some commodious notion of "metaphysics," and while hoping to incorporate current theoretical insights, Kasper himself has developed no independent philosophical position that would allow him to undergird logically the approach he clearly champions. This lacuna in his thought makes him less satisfying than other contemporary thinkers.

Wolfhart Pannenberg, too, has unambiguously recognized the importance of metaphysics for theology. He states, "In theology . . . the rejection of metaphysics cannot be successful over the long haul." Recognizing the central issue at stake, he asserts, "Theological discourse about God requires a relationship to metaphysical reflection if its claim to truth is to be valid. . . . A theological doctrine of God that lacks metaphysics as a discussion partner falls into either a kerygmatic subjectivism or a thoroughgoing demythologization—and frequently both at the same time!"[39] Pannenberg himself develops a philosophical approach that, while using Kant and Hegel, ultimately returns to a decided realism. As he says, "The critical interpretation . . . that I am suggesting makes contact with some of the views of transcendental Thomism in contemporary philosophy." For Rahner, an unthematized *Vorgriff* or foreconception is "the condition for grasping any finite essences at all. In making his case, Rahner appeals to some points of departure in Thomas Aquinas. . . . I agree with Rahner, as I do also regarding the impossibility of capturing this unthematized intuition through reflection."[40] As might be expected given Pannenberg's marked accent on the eschatological dimension of theology, wherein present givenness is anticipatory proleptic awaiting completion, he wants to intensify Rahner's notion of "unthematized anticipation," stressing the element of the "not yet" within the very reality toward which knowing is directed. Pannenberg further wishes to make clear, as the later Rahner did also, that inasmuch as we are "riveted to historicity, . . . the knowledge of Christian theology is always partial in comparison to the definitive revelation of God in the future of his kingdom."[41] Christian doctrine, then, while abidingly mediating revelation, can make no claims to exhaustiveness or ultimate adequacy which remain, essentially, eschatological ideals. The central issue here is not to examine how Pannenberg uniquely uses Hegel to make his realistic metaphysical points.[42] It is rather to recognize his understanding that if Christian claims are to be advanced as true, and this not simply by way of assertion, then some kind of first philosophy is needed to illuminate the logic of such statements.

John Milbank, profoundly under the influence of Henri de Lubac, also seeks to retrieve creatively some form of first philosophy, in this case Augustine's Christian neo-Platonism, in service to a theological overthrow of the secular pretensions of modernity. Human beings see all things in God's light, with grace being a further intensification of that original luminosity. Since all Christian thinking, and indeed all thinking, is oriented toward the beatific vision, then one's philosophical and theological anthropology must be commanded by that very fact.[43] Milbank's metaphysical approach, then, is of a natural order inscribed *ab ovo* within the supernatural order, always already intrinsically related to God. One cannot speak of human nature apart from the *unicus ordo supernaturalis*, as the Catholic neo-Scholastics tended to do, but neither can Milbank endorse Barth's antimetaphysical polemics, which he finds deleterious to theology's universal scope: "Therefore, while the Barthian claim is that post-Kantian philosophy liberates theology to be theological, the inner truth of his theology is that by allowing legitimacy to a methodologically atheist philosophy, he finishes by construing God on the model, ironically, of man without God."[44] For Milbank, Barth allows modern thought to dictate to theology, opening up a "secular" space without God, while Milbank himself, and all of Radical Orthodoxy, seeks to offer an alternative vision of modernity as oppressive and deracinated rather than theologically liberative.

Following Gilson's original analyses, Milbank traces the roots of much confusion in philosophical theology, as well as the rise of secularism (and here he moves past Gilson), to Scotus's univocal understanding of being. Scotism allowed for the development of an ontology prior to and unconstrained by theology and faith itself. Being was now an abstraction drawn from the twin notions of created and creating being. Once philosophy had imperialistically arrogated this knowledge of being to itself, theology was reduced to a "regional, ontic, positive science," concerned simply with one (religious) dimension of being.[45] Of course, much reflection on a "natural" order disconnected from faith and grace was mediated by Thomistic commentators themselves who often acted less as commentators on Aquinas than as coauthors. Gilson, for example, could say of Cajetan's celebrated commentary on the *Summa* that its proper description is not *commentarium Thomae sed corruptorium Thomae* so Scotus alone may not be considered the progenitor of secularism.[46] The crucial point here is simply that Milbank thinks that some theologically controlled understanding of metaphysics, in this case an Augustinian retrieval fused with Thomistic modifications, is essential for both deconstructing the "secular" logic of modernity and for properly explicating theological affirmations.

Finally, W. Norris Clarke, a Roman Catholic philosopher, offers a unique attempt to develop a renewed, contemporary metaphysics that may serve as a proper foundation for elucidating the universality and continuity of Christian doctrine. Clarke points out, as many have done, that Heidegger has misinterpreted the history of philosophy; Heidegger has continually lamented the 'forgetfulness of being' in modern thought, but Thomas Aquinas is the exception.[47] For Aquinas, Clarke observes, all beings are constituted as diverse participations in *esse*, the act of existence or *actus essendi*, which is the ultimate positive core of all real perfections. Insofar as *esse* concerns being as actual existence, it opens up for the inquirer a mystical vision of the universe of real being, of existing creation. This is so because the *actus essendi* introduces us to the mystery of being, allowing us to understand, admittedly slowly, the intensive and subsisting act of existence that is God himself.

In service to rethinking metaphysical anthropology, the kind of being proper to men and women, Clarke goes on to examine the notion of the person and his/her relationship to existence. Traditionally, concrete existing beings, such as persons, have generally been understood by way of substantiality, what Clarke calls an "in itself" dimension of being. One sees this in the classical Boethian definition of person as an individual and incommunicable substance of a rational nature. Clarke asks, however, if a rethinking of the tradition should not complement this accent on substantiality with that of relationality. He notes that there are several passages in Aquinas that indicate a sense of active being as communicative, so much so that Gilson can conclude, "To be is to act." Relationality then becomes for Clarke a primordial dimension of every real being "inseparable from its substantiality."[48] Consequently, he argues, "to be fully" is to be substance-in-relation: "The outgoing, self-expressive and self-communicating aspect must be an equally intrinsic and primordial aspect of every person as is its interiority and self-possession."[49]

Of course, the immediate question to pose itself theologically is the obvious one: If being is intrinsically communicative and relational, and such a notion is predicated of God, then how does this affect the doctrine of the absolute gratuity of creation? But that is not our primary interest here. The crucial point is that Clarke has developed an independent and creative metaphysical approach, a philosophical anthropology, but one now artfully rethought on the bases of hints in Aquinas himself, the influence of personalist philosophy, and dimensions drawn, as Clarke points out, from process philosophy and Balthasar. As such, Clarke provides theology with a unique notion of human nature and personhood, in the process developing a metaphysical foundation that is able to sustain and warrant philosophically, in and through socio-cultural specificity and historicity, the possibility of the continuity and material identity of Christian teaching.

With regard to providing a proper "foundation" for theology, one need not agree fully, or even at all, with any of the thinkers discussed. But two points are essential here. In the first place, all of these thinkers try, to a greater or lesser extent, to incorporate the exigent horizons of otherness, of historicity, of the tight web of sociocultural parameters, into their thought. At the same time, all believe there is a need for some kind of "foundation," for some philosophy with a metaphysical range, precisely to undergird and to illuminate the transcultural and transgenerational dimensions of Christian doctrine. As such, they resist a totally nonfoundationalist or postmodern understanding of reality that, with its abjuration of these kinds of "foundations" and with its subsequent turn to a thoroughly culturally and historically constituted subject, cannot easily give theoretical sustenance to the universal and continuous truth that essential Christian teaching mediates. Secondly, to the objection that some of these "foundational" approaches may be in conflict with each other, I would point out that what is sanctioned here is not a particular metaphysical system, but the recognition of the necessity of some such first philosophy in general. The encyclical *Fides et ratio* properly states that the church canonizes no particular system; neither does fundamental theology canonize one. Varying points of view may legitimately serve as "foundations" for the dogmatic claims of the Christian faith. Philosophers and theologians, of course, should seek that system most closely reflective of reality. Reflection on the theoretical exigencies of doctrine, however, need not endorse any particular philosophical approach.[50]

Jean-Luc Marion: Another Look

Finally, let us take another glance at the philosophy of Jean-Luc Marion, who, despite his seeming commitment to several postmodern and non-foundationalist themes, may offer a new way of thinking about Christian truth. Although he is primarily a philosopher, he has serious theological interests. Can his philosophy in any way support doctrine's claims and characteristics? For the Marion of *God without Being*, this seemed to be impossible. Metaphysics, in any sense at all, seemed to carry only the most pejorative connotations; it was the site of ontotheology, of the idolic rather than the iconic gaze.[51] Later, in his 1995 *Revue thomiste* article, Marion slightly modified his position, claiming that Thomas himself was not caught in the spider's web of ontotheology, that God was not reduced to *causa sui*, or to the "present-at-hand" status of *ens commune*. Despite this disclaimer, questions remain about Marion's thought. If it is true that many writers take postmodernism to mean "the overcoming of metaphysics" and the "end of onto-theology," then post-modern is surely a term characteristic of Marion's thought.[52] Does his unique brand of postmodernism allow for the theoretical buttressing of the claims of Christian doctrine?

Certainly, he poses some of his questions in ambiguous language. He writes, for example, "In short, can Christian theology as a theology evoked by Revelation remove itself in principle, if not in actual accomplishment, from the 'metaphysics of presence'—or is it, in the final analysis, reducible to metaphysics?"[53] The answer to both of Marion's questions appears to be a negative one. Theology can neither excise its metaphysical dimensions, nor can it be reduced to metaphysics. If metaphysics is, as Marion says, the philosophy of presence par excellence, then the presence mediated by metaphysics is far from exhaustive. Much of theology is about unknowing and absence. That God is essentially unknown is a commonplace of both the theological tradition and contemporary thought. Summary examples include Aquinas's claim, "We do not know what God is, only that he is and how he is related to us" (*SCG* I, 30), or Gregory Nazienzen's statement, written against Eunomius: "What God is in nature and essence no man ever yet has discovered or can discover" (*Orations* 28, 17). The chief doctrines of the church, while certainly affirming something true about Jesus of Nazareth and about his relationship to the Father and the Holy Spirit, leave most, by necessity, unsaid. Theology, by the very nature of its formal object, the triune God, is largely, though not entirely, an apophatic discipline, one that only cautiously intermingles presence and absence; the great theological tradition of Christianity has recognized this unreservedly. Marion, like Derrida, Caputo, and others, is interested in nonappearance, in the absence from which presence comes to light. From a theological point of view, one certainly cannot argue with this marked accent on unknowing or even nonappearance, for theology harbors intense elements of the apophatic, the apocalyptic, and the eschatological at the heart of its own self-understanding.

On the other hand, when one shows only disdain for metaphysics of any kind, even for theologically disciplined metaphysics, how then is presence, particularly the transcultural and transgenerational presence of perduring Christian truth, philosophically secured? One cannot but be haunted by Sokolowski's claim that while Husserl spoke about intending the absent, he also spoke subtly about identity and presence in a way that Derrida and others often forget.[54] The danger with Marion is that one suspects his condemnation of metaphysics and his concomitant interest in Dionysian thought, in agapic and mystical theology, leads to an assertion of Christian truth shorn of an intelligible structure. Theology is about "unknowing" and about "gift," but any attempt to secure this logically, even *a posteriori*, as an exercise in the *fides quaerens intellectum*, seems nothing more than an unwarranted rationalism that ultimately obscures and occludes the mystery of the given (divine) phenomena.

Even with this reservation in mind, there are elements in Marion's thought that offer hope for a reasonably grounded "foundation" for theology, even if this stands at some distance from more traditional metaphysical approaches and even from other phenomenological attempts. One such element is Marion's revaluation of Aquinas's theology/philosophy. Even though Marion's rethinking is done in a strongly Dionysian key, often following the intensely apophatic readings of Aquinas championed by the Dominican theologian A. D. Sertillanges, his attempt indicates at least some opening to a certain kind of first philosophy. Secondly, Marion asserts that "phenomenology need not have recourse, *at least in the first instance*, to the notion of being or Being."[55] This kind of thinking, reminiscent of John Paul II's assertion in *Fides et ratio* that thought must move from "phenomenon to foundation," seems to allow for some possible convergence between phenomenology and metaphysics. Is it possible, then, that Marion, although preferring the phenomenological image of "givenness" to "ground," may be thought of not simply as an inspired champion of "absence" but also as one providing a new approach to the traditional problem?

In his recent work, Marion continues to push beyond the metaphysics of presence, the "objectivity of objects" (characteristic of Descartes and Husserl) and even beyond the "Being of beings" of Heidegger.[56] As a phenomenologist, he wants to emphasize that no a priori horizon, neither the truncated transcendental subject of modernity nor even the Heideggerian ontological difference, may be philosophically adduced as an ultimate category because one must avoid all "prior constraints upon the self-giving of phenomena" and all initial determinations of what may "appear."[57] No preconceived horizon may serve to "block" or "obscure" "givenness" of any kind.[58] One must allow for the "impossible," for the unforeseeable, the unprogrammable, the *tout autre* that shatters the possible; it is the "impossible" which has, so to speak, ontological priority over "appearance."[59]

It is precisely at this juncture that Derrida and Marion register strong disagreement about the meaning of the "impossible." As Caputo has said, for Derrida, the impossible ultimately never comes; it never has an actual presence. The impossible always has to do with something that is not now and never can be given, that is always, in its essence, yet to be given, yet to come, and must not be confused with actual appearance. Derrida is here developing Husserl's notion that since human intentionality may be legitimately operative without actually being fulfilled by the intuition of phenomena, there may exist empty intentions, intentions that are never complemented by presence. This leads Derrida to examine the possibility that there is always a waiting, a structurally unfulfilled waiting, without givenness, in human intentionality.

For Marion, on the contrary, the impossible is not that which structurally can never come. It is, rather, excess and saturation; it is the gift par excellence, the gift which overflows every attempt to "comprehend" its givenness, to be fully understood. Marion also builds on Husserl's principles but takes them in a different direction. Husserl speaks of phenomenology as a discipline that is an encounter between human intuition and the given or donative phenomenon. As such, phenomenology is the a posteriori discipline par excellence. It simply allows the "given" to appear; it rids itself in the process of any a priori horizon that seeks to "limit" or to "determine" the uniquely donative phenomenon. One can expect, then, some of the invective Marion unleashes against the transcendentalism of modernity because phenomenology, unlike Kantianism, "no longer limits itself to sensible intuition but admits all intuition that is primarily donative."[60] So, Marion can say, the Husserlian *zu den Dingen selbst* has a corollary: "It is forbidden to forbid."[61]

Is it possible, Marion asks, that human intentionality cannot, at times, contain a given phenomenon, that it is *saturated* by the overflow of givenness, ultimately leaving human intentionality simply "to rub its eyes in wonder"?[62] Marion explores such examples of "saturated phenomena" as birth, death, love, and even the gift par excellence, the thought we cannot think, the *id quo maius cogitari nequit*—the God who is without being who is testified to in mystical theology.[63] For Marion, then, God saturates the human intention beyond understanding; certain donative phenomena are dazzling, even blinding in their brilliance, gifts beyond intentionality's expectation. So while Derrida's emphasis is on the structurally unfulfilled intention, Marion's is on a human intentionality that is saturated, overflowing with givenness, unable now to encompass the phenomenal appearing. One sees immediately the theological implications of such a point of view. Rather than thinking of the impossible as that which is structurally never to come, Marion is *philosophically* able to provide a kind of intelligible logic for revelation's claims. The "gift" given to us in revelation and the incarnation is impossible, yes, but impossible to comprehend fully, to envelop by human intentionality. The impossible is not that which will never come, but that which comes with such intensity that it is, in a certain way, itself ungraspable.

At the same time, one wonders what Marion's response would be if he were asked: what it is that allows Christian teaching on the incarnation, the person of Christ, and the Holy Trinity to be continuously and abidingly understood across generations and cultures—that is, what allows doctrines and their classical characteristics to escape complete historicization? I think it is certain that Marion would resist any kind of answer that bears similarity to the ideas of Rahner, Lonergan, or Pannenberg, with their emphases on invariant transcendental, metaphysical, or gnoseological structures that serve to warrant how meanings are permanent, how they are materially continuous from age to age and from culture to culture, even while recognizing—indeed, demanding—cultural and conceptual mutability.

It is more likely that Marion would say that such "impossible" teachings continue to "appear," to be "present" to men and women, to make their "identity" known, to be exemplars of the "donative." Surely this line of thought is promising for a theology well aware of the "impossibility" of revelation. But a thorny question remains: Is this enough, or must enduring and selfsame presence be pushed a bit further? That Marion seems assertive about faith is clear enough. John Caputo, for example, thinks his philosophy resounds of a kind of dogmatism: "Marion's heresy [in his departure from Husserl's ideas about intuition] falls in line with a very powerful dogma and dogmatics of a more authoritarian sort, which is a very odd form of heresy."[64] But is the dogmatic assertion that Caputo finds odd and others find appropriate itself sufficient? As Marion says, he resists the idea of a "ground" as inappropriate to phenomenology, which must concentrate only on appearance. But on what is this resistance based? He sometimes still writes as if *esse* is hardly what the tradition described as the "act of acts [*actus omnium actuum*] and perfection of perfections," but as the Heideggerian *Vorhandenheit* knowledge characteristic of objects.[65] And he still writes as if metaphysics pretends to be exhaustive about reality, even divine reality, when such is hardly the case.[66] In the last analysis, then, given the questions that cling to his work, one may harbor a certain ambivalence about Marion's project. Does Marion allow the truth of Christian doctrine, and the classical characteristics predicated of it, to be theoretically sustained? Is it enough to say that it "appears" to men and women of all ages and cultures without asking also about the very nature of human beings and their ability to grasp abiding meanings and enduring truth within cultural and conceptual change?[67] In this regard, one may wish that Marion followed Husserl more closely on the issue of "eidetic reduction," thereby allowing him to indicate how "humanity must be" in order for continual phenomenological disclosure to take place. And would not this lead Marion to at least something like metaphysics, at least in a convergent sense, without any pretense at exhausting either the mystery of the person and still less the mystery of divine truth? Similarly, is Marion relying too much on Dionysius, in a way that was not true of the later tradition? Can one place so much emphasis on the "givenness" exceeding all representation that the perdurance of the given (does one dare mention the conditions for the reception of the given?) remains unthought?

At the same time, Marion's examination of "saturated phenomena," as well as his thinking about the possibility of the impossible, has something very important to commend it. In speaking of phenomenology as "dona-tive intuition," Marion adopts a strongly realistic accent with a significant emphasis on the actual "givenness" of phenomena. Further, there is some-thing in his work that reminds one of Maurice Blondel, who avoided Thomistic metaphysics but who developed his own phenomenology of the will that ultimately opened up to what Blondel called the *unicum nec-essarium* and, from there, to revelation. As Robyn Horner properly points out, Marion's work, especially the later works of *Reduction and Givenness* and *Being Given* "open up onto a consideration of revelation as it might be said to enter the phenomenological sphere."[68]

Although Marion's attempt, in my judgment, needs further precision, with less fear of philosophy's metaphysical range, his thought offers sig-nificant and profound resources to theology that, ultimately, may be able to provide theoretical sustenance to the claims of Christian doctrine.

A Corollary: Purifying Philosophy

Since the theme of this chapter has been the theologically appropriate use of philosophical themes, it is worth making clear, even at this point, that the church never simply accepts a philosophy without molding and shap-ing it to the contours of revelation, to the gospel itself. Any metaphysics or first philosophy must be purified of alien elements before it can properly serve Christian truth. One could rightly object that the gospel would be sapped of its power if it were shown that Christian theologians merely placed the word of God within the preexisting Procrustean bed of ancient or medieval philosophy, unthinkingly adopting Hellenistic modes of thought. But is this, in fact, the case? As is well known, the historian and theologian Adolf von Harnack, largely disdainful of Christianity's dog-matic and conciliar tradition, described early Christian teaching as "in its conception and development a work of the Greek spirit on the soil of the gospel."[69] This is of a piece with his claim that "the victory of the Nicene Creed was a victory of the priests over the faith of the Christian people."[70] Such was the case, according to Harnack, because it was the philosophically (i.e., Hellenistically) educated clergy who had forced the "alien" definition.

Against such nineteenth- and early-twentieth-century Romantic longing for a "Christ without dogma," one may cite an entire catena of Christian thinkers who were acutely aware of the dangers of taking "spoils from Egypt." Origen is preeminent in this regard, but Augustine and the Cappadocians follow closely in his trail. Time and again Origen warned that a mishandling of Greek philosophy would lead not to the fashioning of instruments for proper worship, as the Israelites did with the silver and gold taken from Egypt, but rather to the building of the golden calf at Bethel. Aquinas, too, exercised great care in his appropriation of Aristotle, disagreeing with him at critical junctures where the philosopher's thought was irreconcilable with Christian truth.[71] Further, Aquinas adamantly opposed those radical Aristotelians, such as Siger of Brabant, who sought to reconcile the opposing claims of Christianity and Aristotelianism by arguing that a *veritas duplex* theory should be invoked: What was true theologically was not necessarily true philosophically and vice versa.

In a similar vein, one of Barth's complaints about Hegel was that he could not become the philosophical lodestar for Protestantism that Aquinas had been for Catholicism because, despite Hegel's kaleidoscopic brilliance, he had not properly understood the relationship between theology and philosophy.[72] Thinkers such as Joseph Maréchal and Pierre Rousselot sought to use, and concomitantly overcome, the phenomenalism and immanentism of Kant, hoping to mold his thought into a proper vehicle for the realism of the Christian faith. D. von Hildebrand, A. Reinach, M. Scheler, and E. Stein made great use of Husserl, without following him into the more idealistic dimensions of his transcendental reduction.[73] All of these thinkers considerably changed the philosophical ideas they used in accordance with their Christian faith. They were reflective of the position cited by Aquinas in *De Trinitate* 2, 3: "Those who use the works of philosophers at the service of faith in theology do not mix the water [of philosophy] with the wine [of theology] but rather change the water into wine."

As Henri de Lubac tirelessly argued, against the monistic hegemony of neo-Scholasticism in early twentieth-century Catholicism, theology is not limited to Thomism, but should fully employ every human thought, always shaping it, however, into the image of Christ.[74] And as W. Elert has observed, in some ways it is more accurate to speak of dogma as the "dehellenization" of the theology that had preceded it, that, in fact, "by its dogma the church threw up a wall against an alien metaphysic."[75] J. Pelikan adds that pure hellenization is found not in dogma but "in the speculations and heresies against which the dogma of the creeds and councils was directed."[76]

Is it possible that the church has at times relied a bit too much on philosophy, flying, Icarus-like, too close to the Hellenistic sun? Surely this is a debatable point. But what is certainly not debatable is the fact that the best Christian theologians were well aware of the difference between the philosophy that preceded them and their own Christian faith. It is also clear that the best of them made every effort to make philosophy malleable to the gospel rather than bend the church's faith to philosophical speculation.

A fuller account of the proper relationship between Athens and Jerusalem, and how this has been theologically understood, will need to await the considerations of chapter ten. Two points, however, need to be made here: (1) Taking "spoils from Egypt" is a continuous and perduring dimension of Christian theology; and (2) in its adoption of preexisting forms of thought, theology has generally been judicious, well aware of the risks it courts.

Conclusion

The contention of this chapter has been that theology requires certain theoretical exigencies in order to give its doctrinal claims architectonic structure and logical intelligibility. As such, I have argued that some kind of metaphysical horizon, some first philosophy, is essential if the characteristics attributed to Christian doctrine by both the universal church and a wide range of individual theologians—such as its universality, continuity, and material identity—are not simply to be asserted, without philosophical support or, conversely, understood in a way antithetical to the entire previous tradition.

The logical underpinnings proposed stem from the following questions: Do Christians today believe, in essentials, what Christians of the fourth century believed? Are the church's teachings materially identical and continuous through the centuries? If so, then what productive roles do the elements of historicity and of cultural particularity play in such understanding? How are the indefeasible dimensions of such horizons theologically incorporated? The answers to these questions have, of course, significant ramifications. If Christianity is to claim that the meanings of its doctrinal statements are transculturally and transgenerationally true, even, at times, irreversibly true, that they perdure in history largely identical and selfsame, then to sustain the logical intelligibility of these statements, some further claims appear equally needed. The stable nature of Christian doctrine, its ability to be grasped as fundamentally identical in and through history, surely implies something about human nature and reality itself that, while always existing within history, resists a total historicization.

On the other hand, given the insights of contemporary philosophy, with its movement toward nonfoundationalist and postmodern approaches, legitimate questions remain: Are the traditional approaches now simply wrong, that is, ontologically inappropriate given our newly presenced historical, cultural, social, and linguistic horizons? Does traditional ontology and metaphysics, even when theologically disciplined, simply paper over and thereby mask the ruptures and breaches within life and thought? Does it ignore the cross? If so, what meta-ontotheological or staurological discourse should be created as a replacement? What kind of language can show us that revelation is something utterly new? What kind of language is now suitable for "shattering the present horizons of possibility," for what Derrida calls *l'invention de l'autre*?

Some thinkers have turned to mysticism and doxology. This is the move that Marion makes, curiously approximating the nonreligious aesthetic and poetic mysticism of Adorno and the later Heidegger.[77] As Marion says, when speaking of the unique apophasis of mystical theology: Affirmation and denial alike belong to a constative or apophantic order, while the event of givenness belongs to an entirely different and *pragmatic* order of pure "reference" without meaning, of pure praise and prayer without apophansis.[78] But does this resolution into mysticism truly solve the persistent systematic issues? What is the truth-status of Christian doctrine here? Further, when one turns in this direction, how is the continuity and identity of the deposit of faith, of the perduring meaning of Christian confessions, intelligibly established?

The rejection of a philosophy with metaphysical dimensions leads, apparently, to two possibilities for understanding Christian doctrine: either a move toward significant mutability and flexibility in fundamental Christian teachings, or a fideistic assertion of the identity and truth of the gospel, prescinding from any attempt to establish such truth and identity philosophically as well, thereby opening a wide chasm between nature and grace.

Denying philosophical "foundations" of any kind, arguing that such positions are an unfortunate relic of a pre-Heideggerian, pre-Wittgensteinian way of thinking, inexorably leads to the conclusion that universal and per-during meanings and truth-claims are philosophically unsustainable. The indefeasible effects of temporality and culturally constituted life demand such an inference. Doctrine, then, becomes highly protean in content, with fundamental meanings subject to the changes wrought by historicity itself. Doctrinal claims are, by necessity, differently understood in disparate cultures and during various epochs. Of course, it is precisely in the hope of avoiding such conclusions that Rahner, Lonergan, and others have steadily labored to understand the ontologically productive effects of historicity and facticity in a way that is consonant with a universal, open, human nature. It is why Pannenberg says that theology needs metaphysics or it degenerates into demythologization. Only some account of substantial identity lends explicative force to the abiding claims of Christian doctrine.

On the other hand, one can simply assert the universality, identity, and continuity of Christian doctrine in the face of all evidence, but the danger here is the concession of logical intelligibility. Ultimately, this option begins with theology and ends with theology, failing to establish links with philosophical order and so, finally, privatizing faith and making the claims of Christian doctrine appear idiosyncratic.

There is no doubt, of course, that a program of renewed metaphysical thought must continue, and even more intensely, to take account of difference, historicity, and sociocultural particularity. From the critique of the nonfoundationalist and postmodern programs much can be learned: about the dangers of an unrelenting and lifeless sameness, about an ossified and deadening monism that ignores temporality, about a sterile univocity that excises the passion and love that is the heart of the Christian faith. To fail to affirm this critique would be to use first philosophy as a guise for what Rahner called "theological mummification"; it would be to degenerate into the kind of rationalism that missed Pascal's and Kierkegaard's God of Fire, using deductive philosophy as a way to avoid the bloody gaze of the crucified Christ.[79]

But many contemporary concerns can be incorporated without a collapse *tout court* of nature into culture, of essentials into convention. None of the thinkers outlined above—Rahner, Lonergan, Kasper, Pannenberg, or Sokolowski—defends a subjectless, contextless, ahistorical philosophy. The claim that "foundationalists" are interested in supporting ahistorical matrices, in endorsing perspectives that are "outside of history," is a red herring, lacking a *fundamentum in re*. The opposite is precisely the case with the thinkers identified, who take pains to show that unity is interlaced with plurality, that identity is intertwined with difference, that eidetic forms are only grasped in and through history. They argue that there is no pre-predicative grasping of objects, just as there is no noninterpretative observation or understanding. Even documents having some official ecclesiastical sanction, like the ITC statement of 1989, recognize that historicity is one of the main issues that must be appropriated by any intelligible contemporary theology. Every theologian will surely agree, then, with the comment of Levinas: If Husserl opened up phenomenological analysis, "it was Heidegger who first . . . showed that the phenomenological search for eternal truths and essences ultimately originates in *time*, in our temporal and historical existence."[80] And the reason they can agree is that the perduring question is not how history is to be circumvented, for such is neither possible nor desirable. It is, rather, how history is to be understood. Is it as a horizon that dissolves all grasping of lasting essences and forms, all totalities and finalities? Or is it, rather, a horizon within which such human grasping is possible? It is surely the latter that must be true if Christian doctrine is not to dissolve into an undifferentiated historical flux.

Christian revelation, a gift given in history, in the "fullness of time," has deeply historical dimensions, as witnessed in salvation history from the call of Abraham, through the history of Israel, through Christ and the church, to the consummation of the world. It is given in history and so necessarily imbued with historicity and its corollary effects. At the same time, the Christian church believes that revelation is in some central way completed and absolute in the incarnate person of Christ Jesus, whose teaching endures throughout history and tradition as what Scripture calls the "deposit of faith." It is precisely this intermingling of temporality and continuity, of historicity and finality, that is the basis for the theological interplay of presence and absence, of identity in the manifold, of unity within difference.

Christianity can no more now uncritically accept a new understanding of philosophy than it once did. The Christian faith accepted what it had received as the legitimate patrimony of reason, but hammered it into the cast of the gospel. Today the church *uses* philosophies that have been classified as metaphysical, and even, in some sense, "foundational" not because it is guilty of *Vergessenheit*, not because it is trapped in ontotheology, not because it is seduced by the intellectual wiles of a coquettish but perfidious Hellenism. The church employs these philosophies because it has been the judgment of theologians through the centuries that some "foundational"— that is, metaphysical or transcendental or realistically phenomenological— understanding is essential for logically preserving the material identity, continuity, and perpetuity of the salvific dialogue between God and his creatures. This is so because only some type of first philosophy logically supports identity, continuity, and universality in, through, and with history and culture.

No one, it must be repeated, endorses "more of the same" in the sense of a dreary apodicticism that borders on totalitarian rationalism, a thinking that can never begin to understand the gift given in revelation. On the other hand, nothing sounds so repetitive as Jesus Christ, the same yesterday, today and tomorrow, the alpha and the omega. Is this the result of monistic sterility, or confidence in the revelatory gift once given and never revoked? John Caputo has said that the "deconstruction of presence turns out to be not a denial of the presence of God but a critique of the idols of presence." But what are these idols? "It is idolatry to think that anything *present* can embody the *tout autre* or claim to be its visible form in history, the instantiation and actualization of *the* impossible."[81] Of course, no theology has ever claimed this for any teaching of the church, no matter how venerable its status as abiding dogma. However, is not something just like this said about the Word made flesh, *Verbum caro factum est et habitavit in nobis*, a Word not deferred but, as Marion says, given to excess?

Christianity can only defer presence, can only defer explaining continual "appearance" for so long before it no longer makes sense. At the same time, an appropriate use of any philosophy must itself be theologically authorized by the Christian faith. Certain theoretical positions can properly explicate and illuminate church teaching and the characteristics ancillarily associated with it; many others, while they have insights to contribute, cannot ultimately serve theology's purposes. For those who might protest that philosophy has its own autonomy apart from theological interests, these considerations must wait until later in the book. For now it is enough to say that while philosophy's autonomy is real, and capable of criticizing theology, this "autonomy" always exists within the wider horizon of revelation.

Having examined some contemporary challenges to any "metaphysics of presence," to the role of "first philosophy" in theology, we will now see that this dismissal of ontological "foundations," this very strong accent on the social, cultural, and historical construction of human nature and reality leads, logically, to the search for new forms of truth and rationality. Nonfoundationalist thought is not interested, of course, in demonizing reason, but calmly argues that, given our newly presenced situation, ontologically appropriate notions of how truth and rationality function must now be developed. To these attempts and their theological application we now turn.

Notes

1. Sally Haslanger, "Feminism in Metaphysics: Negotiating the Natural," in *The Cambridge Companion to Feminism in Philosophy* (ed. Miranda Fricker and Jennifer Hornsby; Cambridge: Cambridge University Press, 2000), 112. In what immediately follows, I use material first published in Thomas Guarino, "*Fides et ratio*: Theology and Contemporary Pluralism," *Theological Studies* 62 (December 2001).

2. Bruce Marshall, *Trinity and Truth* (Cambridge: Cambridge University Press, 2000), 50. For a similar definition, see Amos Yong, "What Evangelicals Can Learn from C. S. Peirce," *Christian Scholar's Review* 29 (2000): 563–88.

3. This was also the concern of Ronald Thiemann, *Revelation and Theology* (Notre Dame, Ind.: University of Notre Dame Press, 1985); and George Lindbeck, *The Nature of Doctrine* (Philadelphia: Westminster, 1984). Both authors wish to demonstrate that the word of God need not ultimately justify itself before other epistemic criteria. The books may appear somewhat "fideistic," however, in that they seem to rely on divine agency alone rather than on the search for proper philosophical warrants as well, in order to warrant logically the truth of Christian doctrine. Such explains the charge of Wainwright that Lindbeck succumbs to "ontological timidity." Geoffrey Wainwright, "Ecumenical Dimensions of Lindbeck's *Nature of Doctrine*," *Modern Theology* 4 (1988): 121–32.

4. Alvin Plantinga, *The Analytic Theist: An Alvin Plantinga Reader* (ed. James F. Sennett; Grand Rapids: Eerdmans, 1998), 333.

5. Ibid., 129.

6. Plantinga thinks that Aquinas is a classical foundationalist because his natural theology relies on the evidence of the senses as a condition for proper basicality. Consequently, Plantinga avers, Aquinas shares with nontheists such as A. Flew and B. Russell the position that belief in God is only basic when sufficiently justified and warranted. Joseph Greco argues against Plantinga that Aquinas was not a classical foundationalist in "Foundationalism and the Philosophy of Religion," in *Philosophy of Religion* (ed. Brian Davies; Washington, D.C.: Georgetown University Press, 1998), 34–41. For the argument that Aquinas was not a foundationalist of any kind, see Eleonore Stump, "Aquinas on the Foundations of Knowledge," *Canadian Journal of Philosophy*, supplementary vol. 17 (1991), 125–58. *Fides et ratio*, following Vatican I, affirms the natural knowability of God (nos. 8, 53). Whether this is necessarily reducible to the type of evidentialist foundationalism Plantinga decries is another question, especially given the various interpretations of both Aquinas's arguments and the statements of Vatican I itself.

7. Richard Rorty has defended this position in many works since the publication of *Philosophy and the Mirror of Nature* (Princeton, N.J.: Princeton University Press, 1979). Richard Bernstein has similarly done so, characterizing the tradition as saturated with "Cartesian anxiety" in his *Beyond Objectivism and Relativism* (Philadelphia: University of Pennsylvania Press, 1983); and, recently, in "Faith and Reason," *Books and Culture* (Philosophers Respond to *Fides et ratio*) 5 (July/August 1999): 30–32. John Caputo has condemned Western philosophy's search for fundamental *principia* and *archai* in many publications, including *Radical Hermeneutics* (Bloomington: University of Indiana Press, 1987); and *More Radical Hermeneutics* (Bloomington: University of Indiana Press, 2000). Gianni Vattimo, a well-known Italian exponent of *pensiero debole* (as opposed to the *pensiero forte* of metaphysics), seeks to move beyond the "violence" of traditional metaphysical thought in his *Belief* (trans. Luca D'Isanto and David Webb; Stanford, Calif.: Stanford University Press, 1999). See also Vattimo, *After Christianity* (New York: Columbia University Press, 2002).

8. A fine examination of the relationship of Christian doctrine to revelation, congruent, in my judgment, with my own position, is Avery Dulles, *Models of Revelation* (Garden City, N.Y.: Doubleday, 1983), 141–43.

9. I think that Bruce Marshall, despite his insights on many points, is mistaken when he argues that for *Fides et ratio*, "it's not just that accepting some other claims goes along with believing the gospel[;] . . . it's that the gospel itself fails to give you sufficient reason to hold these other claims true, and this epistemic deficit has to be made good from some other quarter." Marshall, "Reflections on Fides et ratio," unpublished paper written for Center of Theological Inquiry Project, May 2001; cited here with the kind permission of the author. I think the encyclical argues that, in fact, these other things must be true because of the gospel. At the same time, the encyclical also holds that one may come to many of these principles by the use of reason alone, even apart from explicit faith in revelation. It was precisely the insights of Plato and Aristotle that led the Schoolmen to believe that such reasoning was possible even on the basis of natural warrants. Colin Gunton is another astute thinker who, in his defense of the primacy of the theological order, may have too severely judged the encyclical, thereby taking the document's defense of philosophical self-sufficiency as equivalent to the claim of complete philosophical autonomy. See Gunton, "Varieties of Reason," in *Reason, Faith, and History: Essays in Honour of Paul Helm* (ed. Martin Stone; Aldershot: Ashgate, 2004).

10. This kind of "second moment," the *intellectus fidei* within the *auditus fidei*, was the response given to Barth by several of his Roman Catholic interlocutors on the question of analogy. While Barth was legitimately concerned that the *analogia entis* constituted an a priori *Grundprinzip* serving as a kind of predetermined horizon for revelation, Henri Bouillard and Hans Urs von Balthasar both argued that analogy was only used in an a posteriori manner, for the sake of providing intelligibility to the prior claims of the Christian faith. For Bouillard, see *Karl Barth* (2 vols.; Paris: Aubier, 1957). For Balthasar, see *The Theology of Karl Barth* (trans. Edward Oakes; San Francisco: Ignatius, 1992). Both Bouillard and Balthasar were under the influence of Gilson's famous Gifford lectures of 1931–1932, emphasizing that Aquinas's philosophy was always elaborated within a theological context. See Etienne Gilson, *The Spirit of Medieval Philosophy* (trans. A. H. C. Downes; Notre Dame, Ind.: University of Notre Dame Press, 1991). This theme is picked up today by Nicholas Wolterstorff, who argues against the philosophical attempt to impose evidentialist, post-Cartesian standards on Aquinas's thought. Wolterstorff, for example, takes the *quinque viae* as intellectual exercises within the *fides quarens intellectum*.

11. At this point the encyclical, in note 54, cites "*Humani generis*," *Acta apostolicae sedis* 42 (1950): 566, as a supporting document. But one is hard pressed to read anything quite like the sentence indicated here. The theme of that passage is that although the terminology used in the schools is capable of further perfection and refinement, it is clearly the case that such philosophy provides a sturdy foundation for church teaching. *Fides et ratio* is dated September 14, 1998. The official Latin text may be found in *Acta apostolicae sedis* 91 (1999): 5–88. An English translation may be found in *Origins* 28 (October 22, 1998): 317–47. Article numbers in the text refer to the document.

12. John Galvin, "*Fides et Ratio*," *Downside Review* no. 410 (January 2000): 1–16, has identified several others who, as John Paul II has at other times noted, have enriched the church with their thought.

13. Peter Henrici writes, "The two explicit references to Anselm of Canterbury (nos. 14, 42) and the allusions to the many Church Fathers who engaged in philosophy, as well as a series of more recent, and not altogether thomistic, Christian philosophers, can already generally be read as a certain relativising of the monopoly position of Thomism and

Scholasticism." Henrici, "The One Who Went Unnamed: Maurice Blondel in the Encyclical *Fides et Ratio*," *Communio* 26 (Fall 1999): 610.

14. Robert Jenson says, "It is a baneful instance . . . that theology, when it has acknowledged its own claim to universal scope has sometimes nevertheless thought it must achieve this by finding 'the right' metaphysics among those offered by officially designated philosophers." Jenson, *Systematic Theology*, vol. 1 (New York: Oxford University Press, 1997), 21. Although on the surface one may think that Jenson's comment serves as a proleptic criticism of *Fides et ratio*, I think his statement and the encyclical are largely convergent. *Fides et ratio* calls for philosophies of a universal scope and metaphysical range that logically support theology's claims. The document wishes to make clear that theologians should avoid certain philosophies, precisely because of their inability to provide warrants for the universal and transcultural claims to truth that Christian doctrine makes.

15. "[Classicism] . . . is not mistaken in its assumption that there is something substantial and common to human nature and human activity. Its oversight is its failure to grasp that that something substantial and common also is something quite open." Bernard Lonergan, *Doctrinal Pluralism* (Milwaukee: Marquette University Press, 1971), 8. Lonergan also seeks to balance nature and historicity in "Natural Right and Historical Mindedness," in Lonergan, *A Third Collection* (ed. Frederick Crowe; New York: Paulist Press, 1985), 169–83. Contrast his position with that of Rorty, who says, "There is no such thing as human nature in the deep sense in which Plato and Strauss use this term." See Richard Rorty, "Education, Socialization, and Individuation," *Liberal Education* 75 (1989): 5. In a similar manner, Clifford Geertz concedes biological similarity ("men can't fly and pigeons can't talk") but warns against "wiring your theories into something called the Structure of Reason" or the "Constitution of Man" and thereby insulating them from history and culture. Geertz, *Available Light* (Princeton, N.J.: Princeton University Press, 2000), 51–60.

16. Lonergan's position is outlined at length in Bernard Lonergan, *Insight* (New York: Philosopher's Library, 1958); and in *Method in Theology* (New York: Herder & Herder, 1972).

17. Lonergan, *Method in Theology*, 326.

18. Lonergan, *Doctrinal Pluralism*, 44, 53.

19. Lonergan, *Insight*, xxviii, 748.

20. Ibid., xviii.

21. For an account of Lonergan's "foundationalism," see P. B. Riley, "History and Doctrine: The Foundationalist Character of Lonergan's 'Christian Philosophy,'" *Religious Studies and Theology* 5 (1985): 79–96.

22. A convenient summary of these debates may be found in Carl Peter, "A Rahner-Küng Debate and Ecumenical Possibilities," in *Teaching Authority and Infallibility in the Church* (ed. P. Empie et al.; Lutheran-Catholic Dialogue 6; Minneapolis: Augsburg, 1978), 159–68.

23. Karl Rahner, "What Is a Dogmatic Statement?" in *Theological Investigations*, vol. 5 (trans. Karl-H. Kruger; Baltimore: Helicon Press, 1966), 55.

24. Karl Rahner, "Considerations on the Development of Doctrine," in *Theological Investigations*, vol. 4 (trans. Kevin Smyth; Baltimore: Helicon Press, 1966), 24.

25. Rahner's later position is evident, for example, in "Yesterday's History of Dogma and Theology for Tomorrow," in *Theological Investigations*, vol. 18 (trans. Edward Quinn; New York: Crossroad, 1983), 3–34.

26. See Karl Rahner, *Foundations of Christian Faith* (trans. William Dych; New York: Seabury, 1978); and "Experiences of a Catholic Theologian," *Theological Studies* 61 (2000): 3–15.

27. Henri de Lubac, *Surnaturel: études historiques* (Paris: Aubier, 1946).

28. Karen Kilby has recently given a nonfoundationalist interpretation to Rahner's thought. By this she means that Rahner is not elaborating an independent philosophy apart from Christian faith. It is Christian *belief*, then, that serves as Rahner's foundation, with his philosophical *Vorgriff auf esse* only elaborated a posteriori. So Kilby can say, "It is interesting to note that one can be a theological foundationalist in the sense just described [Christian belief as foundation] without in fact subscribing to philosophical foundationalism." See Kilby, *The "Vorgriff auf esse": A Study in the Relation of Philosophy to Theology in the Thought of Karl Rahner* (Ann Arbor: University Microfilms, 1994), 11 n. 10. As I have been using the term, Rahner is a "foundationalist" in that he continues to rely on a transcendental metaphysics that provides philosophical warrants for his marked emphasis on the universality and normativity of the church's doctrinal statements. My own formulation is not opposed to that of Kilby, although I am not certain that she, in distinction from my own position, would defend some kind of a posteriori "foundation" as essential for the logical intelligibility of Christian belief.

29. Karl Rahner, "Natural Science and Reasonable Faith," in *Theological Investigations*, vol. 21 (trans. Hugh Riley; New York: Crossroad, 1988), 21–22.

30. It is just here, perhaps, that Rahner's comments about Heidegger from a 1981 interview are appropriate: "Heidegger himself was, of course, convinced that after the pre-Socratics from Plato on up to and including German idealism a philosophy was being carried out that was based on an ultimate misunderstanding of being. I cannot share this opinion. I consider it false." Karl Rahner, *Karl Rahner in Dialogue* (translation ed. Harvey Egan; New York: Crossroad, 1986).

31. Robert Sokolowski, "Knowing Essentials," *Review of Metaphysics* 47 (1994): 697. He continues, "The task is phenomenological, to show how essentials manifest themselves, how they distinguish themselves from the accidental . . . We must also show how essence manifests itself, and it is our claim that this manifestation occurs when the essential distinguishes itself from the accidental" (706–7).

32. Robert Sokolowski, *Introduction to Phenomenology* (Cambridge: Cambridge University Press, 2000), 177.

33. Sokolowski does examine, using phenomenological themes, the type of divine disclosure intended by the Eucharist. See Sokolowski, *Eucharistic Presence* (Washington, D.C.: Catholic University of America Press, 1994).

34. Kenneth Schmitz has noted that many Christian phenomenologists, such as A. Reinach, E. Stein, and D. von Hildebrand, were influenced by the thought of Max Scheler, who himself refused to follow Husserl into transcendental subjectivity. Scheler's phenomenology was explicitly objectivist and realistic in character, providing for many philosophers an antidote to neo-Kantianism and ultimately influencing Karol Wojtyla's own philosophical and ethical theories. See Schmitz, *"Was heisst Philosophie?* One Hundred Years of German Catholic Thought," in *One Hundred Years of Philosophy* (ed. Brian J. Shanley; Washington, D.C.: Catholic University of America Press, 2001), 142. The influence of Scheler on Wojtyla is fully outlined in Rocco Buttiglione's comprehensive study, *Karol Wojtyla: The Thought of the Man Who Became John Paul II* (trans. Paolo Guietti and Francesca Murphy; Grand Rapids: Eerdmans, 1998).

Of course, as Karl Manheim noted, given the dependence of Husserl on Brentano, it is not surprising that certain themes in phenomenology lend themselves to a realistic philosophy. Manheim thought phenomenology had certain Catholic predispositions. Manheim, *Essays in the Sociology of Knowledge* (New York: Oxford University Press, 1952), 155; cited in Edward Farley, *Ecclesial Man* (Philadelphia: Fortress, 1975), 246 n. 17. Scheler was even accused of turning phenomenology into a "common whore" for the sake of apologetics, but Scheler himself thought that phenomenology had a deeper relationship with Christian thought than any philosophy since Descartes.

35. Robert Sokolowski, "Phenomenology in the Last Hundred Years," in Shanley, *One Hundred Years of Philosophy*, 213. He continues, "Husserl has a much more subtle treatment of absence and difference than Derrida gives him credit for, one that recognizes these phenomena but does not fall into the extremes of deconstruction."

36. Walter Kasper, *Theology and Church* (trans. Margaret Kohl; New York: Crossroad, 1992), 95–96.

37. "Diese Krise des Wahrheitsbegriffs und Wahrheitsverständnisses ist die Grundkrise gegenwärtiger Theologie." Walter Kasper, "Das Wahrheitsverständnis der Theologie," in *Wahrheit in Einheit und Vielheit* (ed. Emerich Coreth; Düsseldorf: Patmos, 1987). More recently, Kasper sounds the same theme: "Truth is now only understood in terms of the pluralism of truths. This understanding calls into question the . . . churches holding a general and universally valid claim on truth. . . . This seems to me to be the real challenge for the church." Kasper, *The Church and Contemporary Pluralism* (New York: Pastoral Life Center, 2002), 11.

38. Kasper, *Theology and Church*, 3. See also Kasper, "Postmodern Dogmatics," *Communio* 17 (1990): 181–91.

39. Wolfhart Pannenberg, *Metaphysics and the Idea of God* (Grand Rapids: Eerdmans, 1990), 5, 6. Pannenberg's either/or of "subjectivism" or "demythologization" is not too different from what is argued here, namely, that without metaphysics Christian doctrine is either asserted fideistically or becomes entirely historicized.

40. Ibid., 102–3.

41. Wolfhart Pannenberg, *Systematic Theology*, vol. 1 (trans. Geoffrey Bromiley; Grand Rapids: Eerdmans, 1988), 55.

42. For a good analysis of Pannenberg's attempt, see Francis Schüssler Fiorenza, "On Pannenberg's *Systematic Theology*, vol. 1," *Pro Ecclesia* 2 (Spring 1993), 231–38.

43. Milbank and Radical Orthodoxy lead Fergus Kerr to say that "the [Radical Orthodoxy] project is easy enough to locate, historically and textually, in terms of a controversy internal to Roman Catholic theology throughout most of the twentieth century." Kerr, "A Catholic Response to the Programme of Radical Orthodoxy," in *Radical Orthodoxy?—A Catholic Enquiry* (ed. Laurence Paul Hemming; Aldershot: Ashgate, 2000), 47. That controversy centered on the "natural" human desire for the beatific vision. Was this desire part of human nature, or did it already belong to the "supernatural order"? De Lubac, of course, (and after him Rahner) strongly defended the position that for the early Christian thinkers there was only the one, lived, graced, supernatural order. Any talk of the "natural" order could only be a philosophical abstraction. It is precisely a reprise of this position that Milbank defends, expanding its implications.

44. John Milbank, "The Theological Critique of Philosophy in Hamann and Jacobi," in *Radical Orthodoxy* (ed. John Milbank, Catherine Pickstock, and Graham Ward; London: Routledge, 1999), 22. Along the same lines, Milbank states, "Barth tends to embrace the post-Enlightenment notion of [a] fixed ascertainable limit to human reason, and also, at times, the idea of a valid secular autonomy within those limits." Milbank, "The Programme of Radical Orthodoxy," in Hemming, *Radical Orthodoxy?—A Catholic Enquiry*, 34. On the other hand, it may be argued that Barth was understandably concerned that a "separated" metaphysics presented itself as an a priori horizon delimiting the scope and nature of revelation. From this point of view, Kant's "destruction" of metaphysics was attractive insofar as it was emancipatory and liberative. Pannenberg argues that Barth certainly had a metaphysics, but one upon which he did not conceptually meditate. Pannenberg, *Metaphysics and the Idea of God*, 5–6.

45. One may see in Milbank's critique of Scotus a parallel with some of the criticisms leveled at Heidegger's notion of being. For Gilson's analysis of Scotus, see Etienne Gilson, *Being and Some Philosophers* (Toronto: Pontifical Institute of Mediaeval Studies, 1949), 84–95. The traditional criticism of Scotus accents his comments in *Ord. Prol.*, no. 168, where the medieval thinker holds that the theological knowledge possessed by humans does not have God in himself as object but God on the basis of the universal concept of being insofar as this concept transcends the difference between finite and infinite being. For a contemporary translation, see Scotus, *Prologue de l'Ordinatio* (trans. Gérard Sondag; Paris: Presses Universitaires de France, 1999), no. 168, 218ff. A good analysis of Gilson's critique of Heidegger's Scotism may be found in John Caputo, *Heidegger and Aquinas* (New York: Fordham University Press, 1982).

46. Etienne Gilson, *Lettres de monsieur Étienne Gilson au père de Lubac* (Paris: Cerf, 1986), 19, 74.

47. W. Norris Clarke, *The One and the Many* (Notre Dame, Ind.: University of Notre Dame Press, 2001), 9. John Caputo argues (against the claim of those like Clarke who state that Aquinas was exempt from Heidegger's condemnation of *Seinsvergessenheit*) that, from Heidegger's point of view, Aquinas was immersed in a particular notion, being as *actualitas*, not quite understanding the *Ereignis* from which being emerges and the "coming to pass" of being in time. Caputo, *Heidegger and Aquinas*, 2–7, 119–20.

48. W. Norris Clarke, *Person and Being* (Milwaukee: Marquette University Press, 1993), 12.

49. Ibid., 70.

50. In writing a systematic theology proper, a theologian is called upon, by necessity, to choose and develop a particular point of view most suitable for the intelligibility of Christian faith. This is not the case, however, for a work of fundamental theology.

51. A similar sentiment is echoed by L.-M. Chauvet, heavily influenced by Marion but now writing within the context of sacramental theology: "The god it [metaphysics] posits appears only in the perspective of a *causality* working as a foundation. The entire discussion is distorted by the passion to master the truth. Such an ambition inevitably degrades the truth into an unfailingly available foundation, a substantial permanence, an objective presence. This need for a reassuring plentitude is symptomatic of a visceral *anthropocentrism*: the need to begin with the certitude of the self . . . by which everything else in the world is ultimately to be measured." See Chauvet, *Symbol and Sacrament* (trans. P. Madigan and M. Beaumont; Collegeville, Minn.: Liturgical Press, 1995), 28. Chauvet seems to overlook the fact that many theologians seeking a theologically appropriate metaphysics begin not with an anthropological desire to master truth, but with the Christian faith as revealed.

52. See John Caputo and Michael Scanlon, introduction to *God, the Gift, and Postmodernism* (ed. John Caputo and Michael Scanlon; Bloomington: Indiana University Press, 1999), 16.

53. Jean-Luc Marion, "In the Name: How to Avoid Speaking of 'Negative Theology,'" in Caputo and Scanlon, *God, the Gift, and Postmodernism*, 23.

54. Sokolowski, *Introduction to Phenomenology*, 225.

55. Jean-Luc Marion, "Metaphysics and Phenomenology: A Summary for Theologians," in *The Postmodern God* (ed. Graham Ward; Oxford: Blackwell, 1997), 287 (emphasis added). This is an important claim because it allows some leeway for the position that one may move, at least secondarily, from appearance to foundation, that phenomenology and metaphysics need not necessarily be at antipodes.

56. See Caputo and Scanlon, introduction to *God, the Gift, and Postmodernism*, 6. Levinas saw in Heidegger's emphasis on being an ultimate norm against which all was to

be judged. But for Levinas, the Other cannot be prejudged on any terms, including that of being itself. The source of plentitude and gift is not being, but the Other that escapes being. Is it possible, however, to escape completely every designation of being? For the strong influence of Levinas's thought on Marion, see the insightful work of Robyn Horner, *Rethinking God as Gift* (New York: Fordham University Press, 2001).

57. See Marion, "Metaphysics and Phenomenology," 291. To some readers, Marion may sound like Barth in his early battle against the analogy of being. Barth was fearful that the *analogia entis* served as a predetermined horizon, a Procrustean bed that would illegitimately subvert the fullness of revelation and grace. Marion, too, in his attempt to out-*Differenz* Heidegger and even out-*différance* Derrida, is fearful that any such philosophical horizon "limits" the "appearance" of things (and, a fortiori, revelation) both on the predicamental and transcendental levels.

58. One can understand how a passage like this from Levinas might influence Marion's evaluation of Heidegger: "Heidegger's philosophy, the preeminence of Being over beings, of ontology over metaphysics—ends up affirming a tradition in which the same dominates the Other." Cited in Horner, *Rethinking God as Gift*, 56. Marion, wishing to understand God without Being, pushes in the same direction as Levinas, but Marion presses Pseudo-Dionysius into service as one who already saw this point.

59. On the priority of the "impossible," see John Caputo, "Richard Kearney's Enthusiasm: A Philosophical Reflection on 'The God Who May Be,'" *Modern Theology* 18 (2002): 90–91.

60. Marion, "Metaphysics and Phenomenology," 286. It should be remembered that many of Marion's attacks against metaphysics have a Cartesian and Kantian transcendentalism as the backdrop, especially their innate antipathy to phenomenology.

61. Ibid., 289. One may see in Marion's comments against predetermined horizons not only the aforementioned Barthian concerns but also some Balthasarian themes (also perhaps ultimately Barthian) regarding Rahner's transcendentalism. As noted, Balthasar argued that Rahner's use of philosophical idealism served, in the last analysis, to impose a human limit on God's grace, severely curtailing the totally unexpected and unforeseeable nature of the love shown in the paschal mystery. It is no surprise, then, that in his laudatory foreword to the English translation of Marion's *God without Being*, David Tracy says that Marion is more clearly a *Communio*-oriented Catholic rather than a *Concilium*-oriented one (Tracy, foreword to *God without Being*, by Jean-Luc Marion [trans. Thomas Carlson; Chicago: University of Chicago Press, 1991], xv). This means here that the former is less interested in "correlationist" theology than the latter. To a certain extent this is true; however, it should be remembered that Balthasar (the paradigmatic *Communio* Catholic) criticized Barth for failing to see that, in the last analysis, Catholicism's interest in philosophy (and particularly analogy) was for the sake of maintaining a rational infrastructure of revelation, developed only a posteriori. Consequently Balthasar, despite very clear sympathies with Barth's powerfully stated *church* dogmatics, resisted the kind of anticorrelationism that he found operative in Barth's theology. One wonders, along just these lines, if Balthasar would not also find Marion too "fideistic" and not sufficiently metaphysical in his thought.

62. Caputo and Scanlon, introduction to *God, the Gift, and Postmodernism*, 6. So, for example, Marion asks whether a phenomenon is possible "in which intuition would give *more, indeed unmeasurably more*, than intention even would have intended or foreseen." And again, "It is important to insist here particularly on this: this failure to produce the object [conceptually] does not result from a shortage of *donation* . . . but from an excess of intuition, and thus from an excess of *donation*." Jean-Luc Marion, "The Saturated Phenomenon," in *Phenomenology and the "Theological Turn*," by Dominique Janicaud et al. (New York: Fordham University Press, 2000), 195–96.

63. For a development of these arguments, see Marion, "Saturated Phenomenon." Also consult his trilogy on givenness and phenomena: *Reduction and Givenness* (trans. Thomas Carlson; Evanston, Ill.: Northwestern University Press, 1998; *In Excess: Studies of Saturated Phenomena* (trans. Robyn Horner and Vincent Berraud; New York: Fordham University Press, 2002); *Being Given: Toward a Phenomenology of Givenness* (trans. Jeffrey Kosky; Stanford, Calif.: Stanford University Press, 2002).

64. B. Keith Putt, "What Do I Love When I Love My God? An Interview with John Caputo," in *Religion with/out Religion*, ed. James Olthuis (London: Routledge, 2002), 175. The charge of dogmatism was also leveled at Marion by several French writers, who accused him of "chaining humanity to God and God to philosophy." See Horner, *Rethinking God as Gift*, 98.

65. So, for example, the theme of the essay "What Love Knows" is that knowing others by way of metaphysics necessarily reduces them to objectification/representation. Metaphysics here remains the site of the idolic imagination. So Marion can say, "In order to approach the question of charity, it is above all important not to suffer the influence of what metaphysics has thought about love." Jean-Luc Marion, "What Love Knows," in *Prolegomena to Charity* (trans. Stephen Lewis; New York: Fordham University Press, 2002), 168.

66. So Milbank correctly notes that while Marion agrees that Aquinas is not subject to ontotheology, it seems that for Marion "one must surpass metaphysics in a sense stronger than simply surpassing ontotheology." Ultimately, it seems, a general phenomenology must replace metaphysics. John Milbank, "The Soul of Reciprocity. Part II: Reciprocity Granted," *Modern Theology* 17 (October 2001): 488.

67. Horner hits just the right note when she says that the signification of an excess (saturating phenomenon) will always necessarily be left open. It therefore cannot be described as such. "It defies the capacity of the phenomenologist to go any further than signaling its 'presence.'" Horner, *Rethinking God as Gift*, 96.

68. Horner, *Rethinking God as Gift*, 81.

69. Adolf von Harnack, *History of Dogma* (trans. Neil Buchanan; New York: Russell & Russell, 1958), 1:20.

70. Ibid., 4:106.

71. See Fernand van Steenberghen, *Thomas Aquinas and Radical Aristotelianism* (Washington, D.C.: Catholic University of America Press, 1980). See also Pope Gregory IX's letter of July 7, 1228, "Ab Aegyptiis argentea," to the Parisian theologians on a proper use of philosophy in theology (DH 824). On the very point of "human nature," Scotus, in his prologue to the *Ordinatio*, says that philosophers regard nature as a finished whole, while theologians know it can receive a further perfection. See Scotus, *Prologue de l'Ordinatio*, 103.

72. Karl Barth, *Protestant Theology in the Nineteenth Century* (London: SCM Press, 2001), 384.

73. Robert Sokolowski, in his *Introduction to Phenomenology*, 212–13, has conveniently summarized the intentions of Husserl's Munich circle as opposed to that of his Göttingen followers. Sokolowski notes that the Munich group, with adherents such as Stein and von Hildebrand, was attracted to the realism that was inherent in phenomenology. In particular, Husserl's concept of intentionality seemed to overcome Descartes and the entire Cartesian problem of a "bridge" between objectivity and subjectivity. Sokolowski notes that this group distanced itself from Husserl's later transcendental reduction, thinking that such reduction veered too closely toward idealism.

74. Henri de Lubac, *Catholicism* (New York: Longmans, Green, 1950).

75. W. Elert, *Der Ausgang der altkirchlichen Christologie* (Berlin, 1957), 14; cited in J. Pelikan, *The Christian Tradition*, vol. 1, *The Emergence of the Catholic Tradition* (Chicago: University of Chicago Press, 1971), 55.

76. Pelikan, *Christian Tradition*, 1:55.

77. Others have moved in the direction of Gadamer and Habermas, as we will see later.

78. Caputo and Scanlon, introduction to *God, the Gift, and Postmodernism*, 9. As Marion says, "The de-nomination operated by prayer (and praise) . . . should not be surprising. In effect, it confirms the function of the third way, no longer predicative . . . but purely pragmatic." See Marion, "In the Name," 30. Caputo astutely notes, "Marion has very adroitly shifted the third way from a *modus predicandi*, an affirmative 'predication,' the affirmation of a finite and conceptually determinate predicate of God, into a *pragmatics*, a praise and a prayer." John Caputo, "Apostles of the Impossible," in Caputo and Scanlon, *God, the Gift, and Postmodernism*, 196–97.

79. For this reason, Ghislain Lafont, who defends the necessity of metaphysics in theology, also says that first philosophy must exhibit Pascal's *esprit de finesse* rather than the rationalistic *esprit de géométrie*. See Lafont, *Promenade en Théologie* (Paris: Lethielleux, 2003), 211.

80. E. Levinas, in Richard Kearney, *Dialogues with Contemporary Continental Thinkers* (Manchester: Manchester University Press, 1984), 51–52.

81. Caputo and Scanlon, introduction to *God, the Gift, and Postmodernism*, 5. Elsewhere Caputo, speaking in a Derridean key, notes that the "wholly other is always the one whose very appearance is constituted by nonappearance; if it ever appeared, then it would not be the wholly other. St. Augustine says the same thing about God; if you understand it, it is not God." If this is meant as Augustine meant it, having spent years thinking about the immanent relations of the Trinitarian *hypostases* (note well Augustine's comment about his *De trinitate*: I started it as a young man, finished it as an old one), fending off latent Sabellianism, full-blown Arianism, and other reductionist heresies in the process, it is easily understandable. But Caputo's citation may be disingenuous, because he wants it in service to a larger program, which, unlike Augustine's Christian neo-Platonism, has little use for metaphysics in service to Christian faith. See Caputo's comments in Putt, "What Do I Love When I Love My God?," 175.

CHAPTER 3

Christian Doctrine and Truth:
Contemporary Challenges

The Christian church has staked much on the affirmations that God is
triune, that Jesus Christ is both God and man, that the Lord and Giver
of Life sanctifies us, that the church is the body of Christ and the bride
of the Lamb. The church considers these beliefs, while necessarily held
with both the recognition of organic development and the exigencies of
theological nuance, as universally and abidingly true. Consequently, while
the last chapter asked if any particular notion of philosophy is implied by
the church's understanding of such enduring faith, this chapter asks a
related question: What notion of truth is implied by fundamental
Christian beliefs? The point of this chapter, then, is to determine the
kind of truth that Christian doctrine mediates, especially when the
claims of such teachings are placed in dialogue with the newer forms of
truth and rationality emanating from contemporary philosophy. Do
these newer understandings of truth serve as a suitable—that is, revelationally appropriate—vessel for the church's faith?

Selected Church Documents

It is not necessary to echo here the repeated ecclesial and theological
claims for doctrine's universality and objectivity that were displayed in
chapter one; nonetheless, a brief review of the historical material will be

useful. For example, the Roman Catholic Church, in a variety of documents, has defended the ability of Christian doctrine, as least in certain cases, to articulate enduring states of affairs. Such is illustrated most vividly, perhaps, during the time of the Catholic Modernist controversy, at the turn of the twentieth century, when some theological currents asserted a pragmatic and instrumental understanding of revelation that eviscerated dogmatic statements of any cognitive penetration into the mystery of God's own being and identity. The accent here was not on Christian doctrine's claim to truth but on a universal religious experience that issued forth in a variety of highly mutable statements.[1] The palpable fear was that the Modernist account of revelation and truth was nothing less than a forceful neo-Kantian intrusion into theology, simultaneously stressing intuited phenomenal experience and denying doctrine's capacity to mediate the noumenal world. Christian doctrine, apparently, was reducible to a changeable carapace, reflective not of the Godhead but of culturally constructed religious experience.

The fear of Kantian-influenced theological reasoning led to a flurry of magisterial documents. The decree *Lamentabili* (1907) and the encyclical *Pascendi* (1907), strongly reiterated the cognitive claims of revealed truth and endorsed, once again, the incontestable realism of Scholasticism and Thomism as sure philosophical bulwarks against philosophical idealism and various pragmatic positions. Of course, this was the Scholasticism that Leo XIII had already invoked in the encyclical *Aeterni Patris* (1879), against the Catholic neo-Kantianism of Georg Hermes and Louis Bautain.[2] The nineteenth-century document was intended to forestall the specters of immanentism and phenomenalism, of the claim that theological statements were largely symbolic and existentially illuminative rather than representational and ostensive. This magisterial fear of the theological tendency to attenuate the cognitive content of doctrine's universal claims continued well into the twentieth century.

One pertinent example is the encyclical of Pius XII, *Humani generis* (1950), which was a reaction to a French theological movement known by its opponents as the *nouvelle théologie*. There is no need to rehearse fully the issues involved in that debate.[3] It should be said, however, that the theologians of that time, who were themselves accused of Modernism, sought to defend not epistemological relativism, but the possibility of a legitimate conceptual pluralism born of changing sociocultural, linguistic, and historical horizons. Truth, including theological truth, never appeared "unalloyed," but was only displayed within particular socially and culturally constructed contexts. These indefeasible conditions of expression, however, were no denial of truth's universality or cognitive penetration. Pleading for the recognition of a plurality of such contexts, M.-D. Chenu, for example, wrote in 1937: "But it is the human condition that the spirit exists only in a body, that the immutable truth only expresses itself in time, where it is successively incarnated. Revelation itself is clothed by the human colors according to the age when it was manifested to us."[4] And Henri Bouillard, one of those involved in the thick of the movement, notoriously wrote in 1943:

> In order to maintain in new intellectual contexts the unity of an absolute affirmation, theologians have spontaneously expressed this affirmation in new notions. When the spirit evolves, an immutable truth is maintained thanks only to a simultaneous and correlative evolution of all the ideas, maintaining among themselves the same relations. A theology which was not current would be a false theology.[5]

The papal letter *Humani generis* saw in such statements, which really called only for a multiplicity of perspectives, the lingering shade of a cognitively attenuating Modernism (indicating how closely realism was tied, in the minds of many, with an Aristotelian-Thomistic system).[6] The encyclical made the mistake, under strong pressure from neo-Scholasticism, of confusing conceptual mutability and cultural-linguistic specificity, with the cognitive enervation of incommensurable judgments. Such confusion enfeebled the Catholic Church's ability to reconcile the doctrinal realism of the tradition with a plurality of legitimate theologies— and sapped its capacity to embrace the advances of the ecumenical movement. Such enfeeblement was even in evidence on the eve of Vatican II when the theological preparatory commission of the council issued a schema that was to serve as a kind of epistemological prolegomenon to the dogmatic constitution on revelation, *Dei Verbum*. Entitled *Schema constitutionis dogmaticae de deposito fidei pure custodiendo*, this proposed statement relied rather heavily on anti-Modernist documents.[7] The primary goal of this constitution was clearly to ward off theological relativism. Such a telos may be seen from the *Schema's* two major points: Truth is neither mutable nor subjective (citing *Lamentabili*), and the human intellect is capable of grasping necessary and immutable truth (citing *Humani generis*). But the *Schema* mistakenly links this legitimate concern for the truth-claims of Christian faith and doctrine to the notion that conceptual pluralism is philosophically detrimental to the life of the church (para.

22). It was precisely this philosophical shortsightedness that caused the *Schema* to be thoroughly scuttled before it reached the conciliar floor.

In contrast to the ill-fated prolegomenon, one of Vatican II's major achievements was its recognition of authentic theological and conceptual pluralism, a plurality trumpeted in several of the conciliar documents. And, while the council did not directly address the nature of theological truth, it did make several very clear statements, especially in *Dei Verbum*, regarding the finality and absoluteness of revelation manifested in Jesus Christ. The council also made clear that, in its judgment, the human intellect is connaturally structured to know reality and truth: "Intelligence . . . can with genuine certitude attain to reality itself as knowable, though in consequence of sin that certitude is partially obscured and weakened."[8]

As regards more recent ecclesial documents, one may point to an instruction entitled "On the Ecclesial Vocation of the Theologian" and to the papal encyclical *Fides et ratio*. The first statement contains significant sections on the nature of truth. It observes, for example, that "the object of theology is the Truth which is the living God and His plan for salvation revealed in Jesus Christ" (no. 8). The document further claims, "Despite the assertions of many philosophical currents . . . human reason's ability to attain truth must be recognized" (no. 10). *Fides et ratio* speaks not only of the "universal validity" of the contents of faith and of "certain and unchanging doctrine," but also asserts that "to every culture Christians bring the unchanging truth of God" and warns against the "negation of all objective truth" and the danger of historicism, "whereby the enduring validity of truth is denied" inasmuch as "what was true in one period . . . may not be true in another."[9]

This brief review of several documents of the Roman Catholic Church is usefully complemented by a final one, the important 1989 statement on the interpretation of dogmas issued by a body of theologians, the International Theological Commission.[10] The commission recognizes that in a philosophical climate dominated by legitimate concerns about historicity and culture, the truth question remains of essential importance: "Is there— not external to but within, the historical process of interpretation—a truth in itself? Are there statements which are to be affirmed or denied in all cultures and in all historical situations?"(A.I.1). The answer to these questions is proffered by the document itself:

> Truth, which is universal with respect to space and time and thus is universally valid, comes to be recognized as such in determined historical situations and exchanges, especially in the encounter between

different cultures. However, these contingent conditions ... must be distinguished from the unconditional claim to validity of the truth that is recognized therein. . . . The truth itself can only be one and therefore universal truth. What was once recognized as truth must therefore be acknowledged as true in an enduringly valid sense. . . . The one historically revealed Gospel . . . is nonetheless valid for all peoples and eras." (A.I.4)

A bit further along, the document declares, with regard to revelation and doctrine, "The truth of revelation . . . is universally valid and unchangeable in its substance" (A.II.1), and "this irreversibility and irreformability [of dogmas, *sensu stricto*] are implied in the church's infallibility under the guidance of the Holy Spirit" (B.II.1).

I have primarily examined teachings and hallmarks of the Roman Catholic Church. Because of a series of authoritative documents on this issue, drawing on such guideposts is relatively easy. Nonetheless, the statements about truth here adduced are hardly limited to Roman Catholicism; they belong to Christianity in general. While I will consider the work of several theologians later, in order that the ecumenical witness on this issue is clear even now I would like to cite the work of the American Lutheran theologian Robert Jenson. Jenson's position on doctrinal truth essentially echoes that of the documents cited above: "Theological proposals seem, however, never actually to appear as pure grammatical rules. Thus 'Christ is very God and very man in one hypostasis' seems to say something not just about language but also about an extralinguistic entity, the person Jesus Christ."[11] Because doctrinal statements have descriptive and representational force, because they state extralinguistic fact, Jenson takes to task George Lindbeck's *The Nature of Doctrine* for asserting that the correspondence between Christian language and the metaphysical structure of the Godhead is not doctrinally necessary for rule theory.[12] On the contrary, Jenson argues, this kind of "grammatical theory" is precisely what must be opposed inasmuch as it ignores the necessary correspondence between Christian language and existing reality that doctrine takes for granted. The logic of rule theory, then, needs to be supplemented by a concomitant interest in the reality actually displayed by Christian doctrine.[13] If theology is a grammar at all, Jenson holds, it is, in fact, a *prescriptive* grammar. Given theology's realistic claims, it is not surprising that logical positivism has derided it as "metaphysics," for theology knows dimensions of reality not available to the empirical sciences. This is why Jenson can say that theology "knows the one decisive fact about all things, so that theology must be either a universal and founding discipline or a delusion."[14]

What this catena of ecclesiastical documents and thinkers makes clear is that Christians hold not only that doctrine mediates truth that is universally valid but also that such teaching grasps and displays existing states of affairs, that it allows for certitude in some instances, and that it admits clear dimensions of finality and even of irreversibility. Of course, there is, unarguably, an apophatic and eschatological dimension to Christian doctrine that curtails the extent to which the *mysteria fidei* are known. Even with that said, however, it is a clear conviction of the Christian church that, here and now, it knows something universally, actually, and in some instances, irreversibly true about God's inner life.

This idea that Christian teaching, at least in certain instances, perdures with essentially the same meaning from age to age, is true across cultures and across generations, tells us something about God's inner life, and that, while open to further development, is conclusively true, implies certain characteristics clearly connected with first philosophy. For what is here necessarily affirmed, at least as a logical correlate, is the enduring actuality of a material unity, presence, and certitude that, according to significant swaths of contemporary thought, is inappropriate in light of the enveloping horizons of temporality, linguisticality, and sociocultural specificity. We now turn to the provocations such thought issues to the traditional understanding of the truth mediated by Christian doctrine. In the process of examining such challenges, we shall be asking if the newer forms of truth and rationality proposed are ultimately suitable and appropriate vessels for the claims of Christian doctrine.

Contemporary Understandings of Rationality and Truth

At the beginning of Boethius's *The Consolation of Philosophy*, Lady Philosophy visits the imprisoned Boethius to comfort him. Inscribed on the lower part of her robe is the Greek letter *pi*, standing for practical philosophy, while on the upper section is embroidered the letter *theta* for theoretical philosophy.[15] One suspects that in any nonfoundationalist version of Boethius's book, Lady Philosophy would be forced to undergo a serious fashion makeover.[16] This is so because certain philosophies hold that the deconstruction of metaphysics, of classical and modern ontologies, of substance and transcendental subject, means likewise the logical deconstruction of classical and modern notions of truth. The failure of traditional "foundationalist" systems to recognize the sociocultural embeddedness of rationality and the historical facticity of discourse has led, inevitably, to ontologically inappropriate ideas about what truth really is. Such non-foundationalist claims have occasioned one commentator to assert that the current battle against Enlightenment (and classical) thought is, at base, a rebellion against truth.[17] But surely this statement is, at best, only partially true. It *is* a rebellion against truth as traditionally understood; in this sense, it does amount to an abandonment of the theoretical notion of truth that was formerly philosophy's domain. But this abandonment is done consciously and in the interest of adjusting to further knowledge about finitude and contingency and, consequently, to the cognitive limitations of humanity.

Given our fully historicized and culturally determined life, thinkers such as Bernstein, Gadamer, Habermas, and Thomas Kuhn (under the influence of Heidegger and Wittgenstein, among others) are searching for new, apposite understandings of truth and rationality. What kind of truth is appropriate to our socially and culturally embedded life? These thinkers argue that a proper understanding of humanity and society must inexorably develop new notions of truth, notions that do not demonize reason, falling prey in the process to Nietzschean relativism, but notions that avoid the pitfalls of the now discredited foundationalism as well. These new understandings will recognize the enveloping horizons of historicity and finitude, of *lēthē* and *différe(a)nce*, and, in consequence, will be more supple and prudential than the universal and normative claims traditionally made for truth.

Richard Bernstein is one of the paladins of those seeking a via media between relativism and "foundationalism" or metaphysics. Bernstein's work continues to provide a useful taxonomy for the discussion since he neatly examines the dominant points of view. Further, many of the themes Bernstein explores have themselves become central to theological rethinking. Using categories similar to his, we shall briefly discuss traditional "foundationalism," then the seeming obviation of rationality and truth in some "deconstructive" philosophy, and finally and most completely, the middle path marked out by the *phronēsis* trajectory.

Foundationalism and Truth

As already noted, traditional "foundationalist" and metaphysical thought seeks some kind of substantial unity within history and culture; it tends toward certainties, finalities, and totalities. Since such metaphysical thinking is characterized by the search for a "ground" or "first principle," it encompasses the entire Platonic-Aristotelian-Thomistic-Cartesian-Husserlian axis. This search, as John Caputo has said, attempts to "stop the show" by means of assorted foundational principles such as *ousia, esse, eidos, res cogitans, Wille zur Macht, die Dinge selbst,* and so on. The "show" to which Caputo is referring, of course, is the historical flux, the encompassing dimensions of finitude and culture that have exposed metaphysical systems as ontologically inappropriate and therefore untenable.

The veridical counterpart to this notion of first philosophy often involves some type of empirical approach, correspondence theory, or a realistic phenomenological intuition. These theories generally hold that language mediates and displays states of affairs, that the "world," "noema," or some other designation is available to the "knower," "subject," or "human intentionality." Philosophical validity is thereby achieved when, to use only one possible language, the knower and the known become a unity, when the given or phenomenon is clearly manifested to human intuition. Theologically, this understanding of truth has been used in order to defend the position that Christian doctrine is able to mediate states of affairs as universally and normatively, even if not exhaustively so, correspondent to reality. It has been used to buttress the claim that God's "revealing" himself implies that this divine manifestation necessarily has a cognitive and referential dimension. It implies that the church can, in faith, grasp this revelation and make true statements (even with all of the proper qualifications perpetually true statements) about various states of affairs. It is precisely this abiding, referential, and conclusive understanding of revelation's cognitive claims that appears essential to Christian doctrine but has been called into question.[18]

Bernstein argues that the search for metaphysical grounds, and the notion of truth traditionally allied with it, has been philosophically exposed as inappropriate, as "Cartesian anxiety," by the theoretical uncovering of human finitude, of the socio-cultural construction of reality. Consequently, it is no longer possible to defend notions of truth or universal standards of rationality that are themselves based on discredited metaphysical principles. One must move beyond ahistorical matrices and Archimedean points, recognizing in the process that humanity, and so human rationality, is historically determined in its entirety.

Bernstein's insistence on the nature of our historicized life and thought is clearly evident in his essay on the encyclical *Fides et ratio*. He finds that document "dogmatic (in the pejorative sense)," because, while rightly praising the "journey" of philosophical inquiry, it insists that "the church already knows what this [philosophical] journey will discover."[19] Zeroing in on the heart of the truth question, Bernstein finds objectionable the encyclical's claim that "people seek an absolute[,] . . . something ultimate[,] . . . a final explanation, a supreme value[,] . . . a truth which confers certitude no longer open to doubt." In the first place, he points out, even if people do seek such an absolute, it hardly follows that such an absolute exists. Secondly, and more importantly, he states, "A variety of philosophers have questioned the very idea of such an absolute and final truth." He says that this is certainly not relativism but rather philosophical fallibilism. Fallibilism is "the conviction that knowledge claims are always open to further rational criticism and revision. Fallibilism does not challenge the claim that we can know the truth, but rather the belief that we can know that we have attained the final truth with absolute certainty." His accent, therefore, falls markedly on epistemological humility in the face of human finitude.[20] Bernstein turns, as many do today, to Peirce and James, who did, in fact, clearly defend objective truth (and from this point of view their thought is attractive) but, as Bernstein says, would have doubts about the "absolute and universal truth" that is championed by the encyclical.

For Bernstein, metaphysicians necessarily find solid Archimedean platforms and then build secure edifices of knowledge upon them by following strict rules and methods. Foundationalists seek intellectual self-purification, a retreat from history and culture, in order to construct epistemological fortresses. Bernstein's description, of course, echoes with the vibrant resonances of the projects conceived by Russell and the Wittgenstein of the *Tractatus*, that is, to create an ideal, atomistic language free from other influences. These epistemological projects were peerlessly satirized by Thomas Kuhn, who accused such thinkers of hoping the world would finally conform to their "retinal imprints."

On the other hand, simply because he has rejected metaphysics, Bernstein has no interest in demonizing reason, of moving from one "extreme," foundationalism, to its philosophical counterpart, relativism, thereby fleeing positivism for the sake of the Nietzschean "The truth is that there is no truth." In this regard, he has criticized Richard Rorty for falling prey to an untenable either/or—that is, one must be either a foundationalist or be reconciled simply to "useful kibbutzing," clearly implying that no truth of any kind is likely to be found. Bernstein, like several others seeking new dimensions of truth, avoids this disjunctive reasoning, either metaphysics or madness, either first philosophy or chaos. He is convinced a middle way may be discerned.[21] In fact, without such a via media, Bernstein fears what he calls the "realist reaction" or "anti-pragmatic backlash." By calling for the end of philosophy, Rorty himself has given the impression that any philosophical attempt to separate the better from the worse, the rational from the irrational, must lead back to metaphysics and ahistorical perspectives.[22] This lends urgency to finding middle paths that are neither "foundationalist" nor relativist in character. One must recognize that epistemological anarchism is not the only alternative to foundationalism.[23]

Truth as *Phronēsis*

Having rejected both first philosophy and anarchy as equally inappropriate, where does Bernstein now turn in order to establish an appropriate, nonfoundationalist understanding of rationality and truth? Primarily, he turns toward recent defenders of what may be called the "phronetic" trajectory, that is, those thinkers wishing to establish Aristotelian *phronēsis*, or practical reason, as the only truth proper to our fully historicized, culturally and linguistically determined thought and being. These defenders of *phronēsis*, it bears repeating, are not interested in a demonization of reason, a deconstructive postmodernism asserting that "truth" is simply another form of oppression and ideology. Rather, these thinkers usually develop some understanding of truth that is flexible and fallibilistic, one that eschews enduring, final, and irreversible claims in favor of notions that may support prudential and contingent affirmations. I will now discuss several of these contemporary "phronetic" thinkers.

Thomas Kuhn

In his famous 1962 manifesto, *The Structure of Scientific Revolutions*, Thomas Kuhn sought to challenge the foundationalism of positivist science, in the process arguing for a new understanding of both the scientific enterprise and the truth uncovered by it. Kuhn was legitimately reacting against an excessive Baconism that assumed that the scientific researcher qua knowing subject played a minimal role in observation and interpretation. Positivism argued that the rigorous following of specific scientific methodology led ineluctably to verifiable truth. Kuhn characterized this point of view as untenably rationalistic, forgetful of many of the constructive elements that saturate the interpretative endeavor. In particular, Kuhn launched an assault against the "worldless" observer, seeking to show that understanding—indeed, observation itself—is affected by many factors besides purely "objective" and "quantifiable" ones. Ultimately, Kuhn was contending that the natural sciences, no less than the *Geisteswissenschaften*, were deeply marked by historicity, finitude, and human subjectivity.

For Kuhn, then, the scientific researcher is never merely a passive receptor of "facts"; he or she is always an active and searching mediator and interpreter of that which is observed. Kuhn famously calls this "theory-laden interpretation," meaning, of course, that the scientist's observations are already deeply affected by a congeries of subjective elements. His point is simply that the historically embedded knower is always surrounded by certain horizons, constituting the *Vorverständnis* of the inquiring interpreter, which inexorably and profoundly affect the researcher's understanding of "observed facts." Consequently, Kuhn concluded there was no "basic vocabulary consisting entirely of words which are attached to nature in ways that are unproblematic and, to the extent necessary, independent of theory."[24] Insofar as the world is articulated in and through our own terminological and taxonomical schemas, one can hardly agree with the positivist claim that perceptual experiences are raw data, fixed occurrences not depending in any way upon prior judgment or interpretation.

Of course, Kuhn's heavy emphasis on theory-laden interpretation immediately brought to the fore the thorny question of how "facts" or the "world" serve as a norm or rule for various theories. And it is just here that Kuhn becomes more complicated. Is the theory-laden interpreter so dominated by his or her historical, cultural, and linguistic *Weltanschauung* that the "facts" themselves disappear? Some of Kuhn's critics, such as Karl Popper and Anthony O'Hear, are adamantine in their resistance, thinking that this is precisely what Kuhn is arguing. So, O'Hear insists, contra Kuhn, that despite cultural and social differences, "our common humanity and common world makes communication possible across theoretical and cultural divides."[25] Of course, O'Hear's claim is a rather straightforward assertion about a common human nature, leading us back to metaphysics. But it is precisely such assertions that Kuhn, in his desire to champion the socially and culturally determined subject, wishes to avoid. Karl Popper, similarly, was convinced that Kuhn's theory-laden subject and fact/theory commingling served to undermine the scientific enterprise altogether. To claim that the theory-laden subject was reasoning from a determinative matrix of sociocultural-ideological factors made it impossible to speak of intersubjective data, shared facts, or a common observational framework. Popper labeled this position "the Myth of the Framework," accusing Kuhn of being victimized by it. Popper does concede that "we are prisoners caught in the framework of our theories; our expectations; our past experiences; our language." He adds, however, "We are prisoners in a Pickwickian sense: if we try, we can break out of our framework at any time." He concludes that "the Myth of the Framework is, in our time, the central bulwark of irrationalism. My counter-thesis is that it simply exaggerates a difficulty into an impossibility."[26]

Adding to the fears of Popper and O'Hear are Kuhn's claims about incommensurability. While the precise meaning of incommensurability is still debated, one widely accepted understanding is that in varying construals of reality there exist profound differences in perception, standards of evaluation, and the meaning of key theoretical terms. Kuhn says, for example, that those with incompatible paradigms, such as Priestley and Lavoisier, Einstein and Newton, live "in different worlds." But it is just such language that worries his critics. Does living in different worlds mean the incomparability and mutual incomprehensibility of paradigms and theories? Does it, as Howard Sankey charges, render impossible mutual understanding and make all standards of appraisal internal to particular theories, paradigms, and lexicons?[27] One of Kuhn's sharpest interpreters, Paul Hoyningen-Huene, says that for Kuhn, theories are, in fact, incommensurable in certain ways. For example, the meaning of "planet" changed in the Ptolmaic and Copernican systems because in the latter, the sun and moon were no longer planets and the earth was now so classified. This hardly means, then, that theories cannot be compared or that there are no continuities between incommensurable systems.[28] But if incommensurability is taken in this apparently mild form, what does it mean to say, as Kuhn did in 1962, that after a scientific revolution "the world changes"? Surely this seems to indicate a totally different way of understanding reality. Kuhn himself admitted that he was unable to explain precisely the meaning of the assertion that after a revolution scientists practice their trade in different worlds, but he insists we must learn to make sense of these kinds of claims.[29]

Given that Kuhn has exposed the theory-laden subject, the commingling of fact and theory, and the incommensurability of paradigms, what notion of truth does he develop that is apposite for the historically, culturally, and linguistically embedded inquirer? For a start, debates about Kuhn's philosophical idealism have been taking place for many years. Virtually every commentator agrees that Kuhn is not a full-blown idealist, in the sense of denying the existence of, to use an unfortunate phrase, a "mind-independent" world. On the other hand, virtually all are similarly unanimous in the assertion that two "worlds" are operative in Kuhn's thought, one of which is independent of theory and another of which changes with theory—that is to say, between the world in itself and the phenomenal world, the one that is constituted by Kant's "totality of appearances." The two-world theory helps to explain Kuhn's assertion that though the world does not change with a change of paradigm, the scientist afterward works in a different world. This second world is the constructed one of the theory-laden scientist. Hoyningen-Huene finds strong affinities between Kant and Kuhn but notes that while the Kantian transcendental nature is stable, Kuhn has continually referred to himself as a "dynamic Kantian" since at least 1979.[30] Several thinkers have also called attention to Kuhn's reliance on Wittgenstein, claiming that there are deep affinities between their positions.[31]

I think it is relatively clear that Kuhn has profoundly idealistic tendencies. In overcoming positivistic empiricism, he has made clear that the subject is indefeasibly theory-laden and that our epistemological access to the world is circumscribed by our prejudices and prejudgments. While there is much in this statement that is true, Kuhn develops it through his own Kantian-influenced prism, claiming, in the process, that the theory-laden subject is limited to the phenomenal, constructed world of his own making. Unsurprisingly, then, he has little use for any kind of metaphysical realism, especially the kind espoused by correspondence theory. As he has said, "What is fundamentally at stake [in his work] is . . . the correspondence theory of truth. . . . It is that notion . . . that I'm persuaded must vanish together with foundationalism. What replaces it will still require a strong conception of truth, but not, except in the most trivial sense, correspondence truth." And again: "I earlier said that we must learn to get along together without anything like a correspondence theory of truth."[32]

Alexander Bird claims that Kuhn's rejection of both the correspondence theory of truth and of foundationalism in general is of a piece with his antirealism. Why does Kuhn reject them? His complaint is, "We could not *know* of the existence of such a match [between our theories and the world], because we could not have a theory-less access to reality." Kuhn's antirealism is not primarily a consequence of his rejection of the correspondence theory; it is instead caused by his "concern about our access to reality."[33] Hoyningen-Huene echoes this idea, arguing that for Kuhn, "it's essentially meaningless to talk of what there really is, beyond (or outside) of all theory. . . . It's impossible to see how talk of a 'match' between theories and absolute or theory-free, purely object-sided reality could have any discernible meaning."[34] Kuhn himself clearly supports such interpretations when he says, "There is, I think, no theory-independent way to reconstruct phrases like 'really there'; the notion of a match between the ontology of a theory and its 'real' counterpart in nature now seems to me illusive in principle."[35]

Such comments help to explain Kuhn's commitment to "two worlds," the world in itself and the phenomenal one available to us. At the same time, they point to a continuing concern that truth and falsity, for Kuhn, are simply relative to particular paradigms. It is not clear how the "world" serves as a norm and criterion for theoretical truth. If truth becomes purely intralexical, there are no independent standards of evaluation by which a theory may be judged. Of course, Kuhn rejects such universal standards, for as Bird says, there is no "Archimedean platform outside of history, outside of time and space."[36] Bird wonders, however, if this attack on realism is not tantamount to a deep metaphysical form of skepticism, or given Kuhn's lexicon-relative notion of truth, even of relativism. Kuhn himself comes quite close to relativism in his original work without, however, fully committing himself to it.[37]

Bird, for one, thinks that Kuhn's brush with relativism remains worrying. He argues that Kuhn is mistaken in claiming that because the subject is theory-laden he or she is ipso facto unable to know truth. He says, for example, "Knowledge of the truth of a theory can be had without some independent theory-less access to reality with which to compare the theory."[38] After all, in the last analysis, the very point of any theory is to provide us with access to truth and reality. Kuhn faces a similar problem (How is truth possible?) when discussing if and how there may be progress toward increasing verisimilitude. He writes, for example, in his 1969 postscript to *Structure*: "I do not doubt . . . that Newton's mechanics improves on Aristotle's and that Einstein's improves on Newton's as instruments for puzzle solving. But I can see in their succession no coherent direction of ontological development."[39] For Kuhn, theories help to solve puzzles in the phenomenal world, the world of appearances; they tell us virtually nothing about the world in itself. He would no doubt add that the world in itself is irrelevant because we have no theory-free access to it. One can understand, then, why Popper relentlessly opposed Kuhn, fearing that science was for him only an exercise in phenomenal puzzle-solving, not an instrument bringing us toward a fuller and more complete understanding of reality.[40]

In the last analysis, there is much to admire in Kuhn's work. He relentlessly exposed the inadequacies of positivist science, showing the epistemological importance of the theory-laden subject who was embedded within a socially, culturally, linguistically, and historically determined world. Having accomplished this, however, Kuhn seems not certain where to turn. He appears to be groping for a precise notion of truth by which he is able to steer between the Scylla and Charybdis of relativism and metaphysical realism. He stated earlier, in *The Road since Structure*, that we need a "strong conception" of truth, but he himself fails to develop one. The notion of truth he seems to champion is that in this phenomenal, constructed world, which is distinct from the world in itself, we are left with the ability only to solve empirically and contingently given phenomenal puzzles. Saying more than this violates the canons of theory-ladenness as Kuhn understands them. What is clearly evident in Kuhn is a move toward practical reason, toward a reason that is fully historicized, contingent, and socially constructed, but he fails to develop this in any extensive way.[41] The "strong conception" of truth he seeks seems still to elude him.

Perhaps Kuhn can be helped by other thinkers more philosophically and theologically influential who share his antipathy to positivism and metaphysics of any kind and who have sought, similarly, to sail between the rocky coasts of foundationalism and relativism, although perhaps with less explicit help from Kant's phenomenalism. Let us now turn to Hans-Georg Gadamer and Jürgen Habermas.

Hans-Georg Gadamer

Gadamer, like Kuhn, wants to overcome positivism, both the scientific variety and the kind arising from an Enlightenment modernity seeking a neutral subject shorn of the "world." Unlike Kuhn, however, the major theoretical influence on Gadamer is certainly not Kant, but Heidegger. It is Heidegger who is the machine in Gadamer's philosophical nonfoundationalism, his theory of interpretation, and his understanding of truth.

Heidegger is one of the chief proponents of nonfoundationalist thought and a significant progenitor of postmodernism. One significant dimension of Heidegger's groundbreaking project was a "presencing of the absent," an uncovering of the *lēthē* at the heart of *alētheia*. Heidegger was particularly intent on showing the extent to which historicity is the ultimately determinative horizon of thought. Historicity, thrownness, possibility, embeddedness, and immersion characterize the veiled but ontologically constitutive dimensions in which thinking is carried out. It is precisely the chief flaw of the metaphysical tradition since Plato—inclusive of the classical, medieval, and Enlightenment philosophical projects, with their dual emphasis on subjectivity and substantiality—that has "masked" the thinking of historicity and its correlative horizons, attempting, in the process, to find the ultimate foundation and ahistorical matrix for thought. In its continual quest to abstract "essences," "transcendental foundations," Archimedean platforms, and unshakeable first principles, Western philosophy has forgotten (*Seinsvergessenheit*) the nature of the "world" within which thinking is done, within which being comes to light. So, for example, Heidegger can say of Kant that, for all of his profundity, Kant failed to give a "preliminary ontological analytic of the subjectivity of the subject."[42] Kant, like his predecessors, stayed on the ontic level, examining elements of human subjectivity but not penetrating to the marrow of being's appearance in history. The same point is made by Heidegger's famous analysis of the "hammer." He wishes to show that a hammer's "ready-to-hand" utility escapes the theoretical gaze. When a hammer is examined theoretically, one misconstrues its essential function.[43] Heidegger's intention is to show that mere rationalism may conceal and obscure essential dimensions of existence. And this is in service to his thesis that *Dasein* has made the mistake of burying the "world," whose elements of historicity, facticity, and finitude constitute encircling horizons. Yet this forgetfulness, this inordinate fascination with subject and substance, has finally led to rationalism, to technocracy, to a thinking that is ontologically inappropriate for revealing intrinsic and constitutive dimensions of human life. It is precisely Heidegger's insights into the appearance of being that led him, increasingly in his later work, toward examining the more aesthetic and mystical dimensions of thought, elements more directly cognizant of the dyad of knowing and unknowing, of the absence at the heart of presence.[44]

For Gadamer, Heidegger's analysis of *Dasein* and his appraisal of Western philosophy since Plato is largely correct. Historicity and finitude are fully determinative of human life and thought; it is precisely this ontological point that has been philosophically and historically obscured. If, however, the Platonic-Aristotelian-Thomistic-Kantian-Husserlian axis of philosophy, with its dual emphasis on substance and subject, has now been deconstructed by Heidegger, if there is no "essence" or "transcendental foundation" or Archimedean matrix upon which to erect philosophy, then what notion of truth is now philosophically possible? What kind of knowing is ontologically appropriate given the horizons that Heidegger has unveiled? Past notions of truth and interpretation have assumed a certain first philosophy, one championing a stable human nature perduring from age to age, thereby mediating an actual and, in certain cases, an abiding notion of the intuited real.

For Gadamer, however, such notions of truth and interpretation are inextricably intertwined with an outdated and inapposite ontology. Any contemporary understanding of these issues must be reformulated in light of the Heideggerian rethinking of the tradition. Under this forceful influence, Gadamer argues that truth must now be mediated by the indefeasibly enveloping expanses of historical flux, societal norms, and cultural warrants. Any notion of truth must take account of an ever mutable humanity and society. To the extent that the terra firma of human nature (with its ontological constancy) has been abandoned—and there is no doubt that Gadamer thinks such a notion has been overcome by Heidegger—then in the same measure must our idea of truth be adjusted. An appropriate understanding of ontology has, necessarily, veridical effects. As Richard Campbell comments in just this regard, "If man's very humanity differs from age to age, from culture to culture [then] our own being varies relative to differing historical situations; in turn, that seems to imply that what is appropriated, the truths we claim to grasp, are likewise relative."[45]

Gadamer logically asserts that in our postmetaphysical, posttranscendental, post-Enlightenment age, any proper understanding of truth means a reversion to Aristotle's notion of practical reason as this is championed in book 6 of the *Nichomachean Ethics*. This is so because practical reason is "concerned with reason and with knowledge not detached from a being that is becoming, but determined by it and determinative of it."[46] Precisely what philosophy knows in the wake of Heidegger and Wittgenstein is that there is no form of rationality that is exercised apart from the contingent, finite, and delimiting horizons of the enveloping life-world.[47] Aristotle, of course, trapped as he is in the ontotheological tradition, mistakenly speaks of *epistēmē*, knowledge that deals with the eternal and the necessary (VI.1139b.20–22). He understands *phronēsis* as essential, but ultimately secondary to the pure and certain knowledge yielded by theoretical reason. Gadamer, on the other hand, argues that *phronēsis* is the prime analogue for *all* rationality in the postmetaphysical age. When Aristotle says, therefore, that practical reason is equivalent to "deliberating well" in contingent circumstances (VI.1140a.26–32), or when he says that practical reason issues in "some kind of correctness" (VI.1142b.8) properly understood as "hitting the best thing attainable by action" (VI.1141b.11), he is unwittingly describing the only exercise of reason truly available in our nonfoundationalist era.

As classically understood, practical reason is that dimension of human rationality that deals with mutable, changing circumstances; it was normally opposed to epistemic or theoretical reason, which grasped unchanging truth or essentials. Yves Simon is representative of this traditional distinction when he argues that practical reason is proper to contingent circumstances and does not have the universality proper to essences. Along the same lines, C. D. C. Reeve notes that *"phronēsis* is more concerned with particulars than with universals," for *"phronēsis* studies *endechomena*, things that admit of being otherwise."[48] For Gadamer, practical reason is the proper mode of all truth precisely because of finitude and historicity; these horizons have taught us that truth is necessarily contingent, is always reversible, is capable of being otherwise.

For Gadamer, the significance of historicity and the consequent overcoming of "foundationalism" is such that to speak of *epistēmē* is ontologically inappropriate. One cannot speak about necessary as opposed to contingent knowledge because all rationality is exercised in delimited circumstances. The knowledge yielded by deliberation in concrete situations, designated by Aristotle as practical reason, should, therefore, be taken as paradigmatic for knowing in general.[49]

Of course, while Gadamer has shown conclusively that reason is only exercised within history and tradition (something that appears undeniably accurate), and while he further argues that *phronēsis* is the only form of reason truly available to us, a claim more open to argument, in the final analysis, as Bernstein asserts, the concept of truth turns out to be one of the most elusive in Gadamer's work.[50] Bernstein observes that Gadamer rejects the traditional *adaequatio intellectus et rei* in favor of that truth emerging in dialogue with the tradition. But phenomenological hermeneutics must now offer some clue or criterion to distinguish that which is true and adequate in the tradition from that which is false and inadequate. If one is to forestall a random plurality, thereby emulating a mere relativism or a postmodern Nietzscheanism, it becomes necessary to offer some warrant for adjudicating exactly what is true in the tradition. It is here that Gadamer develops his notion of the "claim" as a clue to truthfulness. That which is true is that which continues to exercise a "claim" in and through tradition, prejudice, and effective-history. As Bernstein phrases it, for Gadamer, truth is what emerges from a "dialogical encounter with what makes a claim on us."[51]

The question that continues to haunt Gadamer is whether the notion of "claim" is a sufficient criterion for exorcising interpretive relativism. One recent commentator on Gadamer's thought, Ingrid Scheibler, is representative of many when she mentions "Gadamer's ambiguous and often unclear discussion of the 'claim to truth' of tradition."[52] Even Bernstein, a friendly critic, complains that Gadamer does not fully explain the "claim" to truth, does not offer any other warrants for distinguishing between varying elements of tradition, does not integrate anything positive about the Enlightenment, and, ultimately, is weak in clarifying the role of argumentative validation of truth-claims.[53] A somewhat less benign critic claims that the fundamental ambiguity in Gadamer's work is that "it becomes extremely difficult to distinguish between truth and nontruth, to say what is *not* true."[54] It is for these reasons that even philosophers sympathetic to Gadamer, who have sought to remain within the phronetic trajectory that he outlines, hope to supplement and strengthen his position with other points of view.

Of course, there is a great deal that is important and insightful in Gadamer's work, and his thought remains a valuable resource for contemporary theology.[55] However, does Gadamer's nonfoundationalist understanding of truth, despite its best attempts at avoiding relativism, at least in some sense fall prey to it and thereby limit its usefulness in theology? Does *phronēsis* rationality, with its marked emphasis on historicity and contingency, offer the necessary resources to explain a notion of Christian doctrine concerned with normative, perduring, and, at least in some instances, irreversible truth-claims? And is the notion of the continuing "claim" sturdy enough to handle Christian doctrine's pronounced stress on selfsame identity, presence, and continuity? Despite its weaknesses, Gadamer's thought has remained attractive to a wide range of theologians. Very appealing, in particular, is Gadamer's unmasking of the Enlightenment's claims to "traditionless" rationality, a claim now virtually without philosophical support. On the other hand, once metaphysics and its veridical correlates are left behind, as clearly occurs in Gadamer's philosophy, then the notions replacing it, such as *phronēsis* rationality, appear unable to sustain the substantive truth-claims made by Christian faith and doctrine.

We shall return to Gadamer's philosophy in the next chapter in order to examine his theory of interpretation. For the moment, our attention will turn to the thought of Jürgen Habermas. Habermas is adduced as one who, like Gadamer, accepts the Heideggerian stress on encompassing historicity and wants, therefore, to accent practical notions of rationality and truth. Unlike Gadamer, however, Habermas wants to redeem positive elements of the Enlightenment and seeks to supplement Gadamer's idea of the "claim" with stronger, more publicly available warrants for the validation of assertions.

Jürgen Habermas

Gadamer's rehabilitation of the *phronēsis* tradition, while applauded by many contemporary thinkers, is considered a bit too slippery when it

comes to the question of truth. The perduring issue is whether the phronetical "deliberating well" and "hitting the mark" provide adequate criteria
for determining, in any public way, coherence and intelligibility as
opposed to their opposites. Appealing to the epistemic authority of the
"claim" seems random and subjective, bordering on the idiosyncratic.

Because of this apparent weakness in Gadamer's thought, many
thinkers have turned to Habermas, seeking to supplement the tradition of
practical reason with his theory of communicative praxis.[56] Habermas, like
several other thinkers, resists foundationalist grounds—that is, metaphysical, epistemological, or transcendental first principles—as starting points
for philosophical inquiry. Despite his differences with Heidegger and
Gadamer, especially regarding the extent to which Enlightenment thinking may be positively redeemed, Habermas fully recognizes the thoroughly determinative and theoretically constitutive dimensions of
finitude, of the historically embedded and immersed subject.[57] Habermas
accepts much of Heidegger's critique of modernity as well as his censure
of the Western ontotheological tradition. Echoing Heidegger, Habermas
argues that the metaphysical imperative once consisted of digging out
persistent universals from fleeting particulars, the permanent from the
temporal, necessary and lawlike forms from accidental events.
Philosophers now recognize that one cannot simply ignore the contingent, the transitory, and the particular. Like Hegel, we realize that even
truth itself is drawn into the flux of time—"die Wahrheit fällt in die
Zeit."[58] Habermas further claims that Husserl's "thing itself" always slips
away in the cultural constructivism of speech-acts and truth-claims:
"Historicism and *Lebensphilosophie* have attributed an epistemological significance to the transmission of tradition, to aesthetic experience, and to
the bodily, social and historical existence of the individual; this significance had to explode the classical concept of the transcendental subject."[59]

Like Gadamer and Kuhn, Habermas has a deep and abiding respect
for the capacities of human rationality, but, like them, a rationality now
chastened by historicist, nonfoundationalist themes, which forbid and circumscribe the first principles established by classical and medieval
thought as well as by modernity itself. Despite these affinities, Habermas
is nonetheless fearful of the poetic mysticism of Heidegger and the ambiguity of the "claim" championed by Gadamer. If society is to avoid the
twin aporias of esotericism and privatism, it must have a public means to
adjudicate claims to truth within the contemporary *polis*. It is one thing
to stipulate that ontologically constitutive temporality and the assimilation of rationality to conventionally accepted language games demon-

strates the inappropriateness of metaphysics. It is quite another task, however, to provide democratic societies with political and philosophical guidance for the proper functioning of the marketplace of ideas in postfoundationalist society.

Here Habermas turns to his theory of communicative praxis, seeking to reclaim the positive heritage of the Enlightenment, with its concern to unmask the distortions of the tradition, to expose the power constellations that suppress rationality and to allow reason its properly liberative, transformative, and emancipatory role. In pursuit of these ends, Habermas speaks of the "ideal-speech situation," in which free and autonomous persons can exercise their critical faculties, seeking consensus in intersubjective communication and domination-free discussion. Habermas's goal, then, is to transform critical reason in light of the nonfoundationalist and postmodern horizons discussed earlier. Reason must not be understood as the instrument of foundationalist ontology, ruthlessly enforcing transcultural absolutes and relentlessly dominating through the mythology of universal truths. Rather, the rationality that sits deeply embedded in society, history, and language only solicits unforced and respectful conversation. Nonetheless, this critical reason may not retreat into mysticism or intralexical notions of truth; on the contrary, it must provide public redemption of warrants for the substantiation and validation of truth-claims. Without such publicly redeemable warrants, even if these are deeply embedded within the community, society cannot function. There is, then, certainly no denial of rationality, but there is a recognition that communicative reason is "a rocking hull—but it does not go under in the sea of contingencies, even if shuddering in the high seas is the only mode in which it 'copes' with these contingencies."[60] Habermas can claim, then, that while reason has lost its "metaphysical innocence," it cannot sanction those "anti-Platonic" attempts to "do away with any abstraction, idealization, or concept of truth, knowledge and reality that transcends the local *hic et nunc*," for to do so is to court performative contradictions.[61]

What type of truth is now characteristic of this "rocking hull" of communicative rationality? It is, of course, the truth of practical reason, now strengthened and fortified by means of a universal neopragmatics. Truth is reached by the community of inquirers through free, rational, and undistorted appeal, not by coercion or through the stipulation of first principles. It is true that reason is thoroughly historical and functions within highly delimited circumstances; nonetheless, historical, situated reason must offer public warrants for its assertions.[62] Only public redemption adequately allows the distinction between warranted claims and acts of ideological consciousness. This view does not provide us with the inappropriate security of metaphysics or transcendental thought, but neither does it lapse into anarchism or gnosticism.[63] The pragmatic understanding of truth, subtly structured as communicative praxis, has the further advantage of fundamental congruency with the aims of egalitarian liberal democracies increasingly heterogeneous in populations, views, customs, and mores. Defenders of neopragmatism appear to foster the creation of multivalent cultures of tolerance, while those expressing doubt about practical forms of truth seem to be a priori opposed to the inclusive ideals of liberal democracy itself.

The advance Habermas offers over Gadamer is that while both pursue the *phronēsis* tradition of rationality, the former, through the notions of communicative praxis and critical reason, has given concrete and public form to the task of "deliberating well" in contingent and finite circumstances. One speaks, therefore, not simply of "hitting the mark," but of publicly redeemable truth warrants for determining the *results* of proper deliberation.[64] What Habermas has developed is an ontologically appropriate rationality that gives determinate shape to how practical reason should proceed in a democratic society.[65]

What are the theological implications of this move toward pragmatic and praxis-oriented models of truth? Why have many theologians found the *phronēsis* trajectory, often supplemented by elements from Habermas's communicative theory, useful?[66] One reason for the attraction of Habermas's thought is that it may be marshaled to heal the split between the public and private domains. Religion, theologians argue, should not be excluded from the marketplace of ideas, the sphere of public interchange. Ghettoizing religion serves neither believers nor the societies in which they are citizens. But how can religion remain part of the public conversation without its demanding that it alone is true and all other "secular" philosophies must yield before it?[67] Can Habermas's communicative praxis give theology a significant role in wider society? Can it help provide a public validation of theology's assertions? Can it serve Christianity's claims to transgenerational, transcultural, and, at times, irreversible and conclusive truth? At first glance, Habermas seems an unlikely ally. Truth, in the ideal-speech situation, amounts to those validity claims that can be cognitively redeemed by public warrants. And there's the rub. To what extent can religion provide public warrants for its claims? Habermas says it cannot do so at all, ironically arguing that it might harm its very essence if it sought this goal.[68] The unavoidable consequence, however, is that religion must be excluded from communal discourse. Religion, with its a priori teleological view, cannot be allowed as a player in this discussion because—from the start and according to its very essence—it violates the rules of the game by limiting communicative freedom. This is why, for Habermas, the authority of consensus ethics must now replace the authority of the sacred: "The legitimizing function of religious views of the world is replaced by rationally motivated agreement."[69]

Despite this Habermasian refusal, some theologians seek to show that theology can become a viable player in the larger community of discourse according to neopragmatic rules. David Tracy and Helmut Peukert, for example, argue that the critical transformation of society may serve as a public warrant and criterion, validating and redeeming, to some extent, the truth-claims of Christianity. Habermas's theological conversation partners "argue that theology as a critical practical and public theology is self-confidently theology when it is not authoritarian[,] . . . when it is not sectarian but engaged in a discursive deliberation about its ethical content and when it advocates a method of critical correlation."[70] Religious and moral traditions are not simply warranted by authoritarian norms, but are validated by their continuing publicly illuminative value. Tracy most clearly represents this position when he argues for the public and imaginative character of theological truth, claiming, "The truth of religion is, like the truth of its nearest cousin, art, primordially the truth of manifestation."[71] Tracy and other theologians are seeking ontologically appropriate understandings of truth; they argue that theology cannot remain wedded to veridical notions intrinsically conjoined to discredited and untenable ontologies. Christianity, just as existence and thought itself, is radically historical; it simply excludes itself from democratic, public discourse when it insists on certain first principles that are posited rather than effectively argued for.

That Habermas is an influence in contemporary theology, then, is beyond question. That he has something to teach theology about the criteriological importance of consensus and publicly redeemable warrants (especially if these are used within a more comprehensive epistemology) is translucent. It remains to ask, however, if his phronetic, contingent notion of truth, despite its supplementation by other, critical warrants, can provide theology with a veridically appropriate point of view. This is not likely the case, at least ultimately, because as Habermas himself clearly recognizes, his neopragmatic consensus theory cannot allow for the kind of a priori, nonpublicly redeemable cognitive claims that are essential to religion in general and to Christian faith and doctrine in particular. While one may certainly agree with Tracy and Peukert that Christian faith and doctrine do have, to some extent, publicly illuminative value, the fact remains that Habermas's proscribing of any kind of metaphysics, and his consequent turn toward phronetic rationality, makes his philosophy useful to Christian thought only in a qualified way.

Summary

To this point, I have discussed thinkers seeking to develop new, ontologically appropriate notions of rationality and truth. It is essential to recognize that these new understandings are necessary because traditional notions of truth, with their emphasis on reference and correspondence, on certain dimensions of finality and conclusiveness, are necessarily tied to ontologically outdated, foundationalist systems. Such systems seek to "close down" effective history, to end historical consciousness. What is needed, instead, is a notion of truth that takes full cognizance of our historically, linguistically, and socioculturally embedded life and thought—a notion of truth that avoids the inappropriate "objectivism" of metaphysics but one that is equally chary of an anarchistic and unruly relativism.

Gadamer's *phronēsis*, Habermas's neopragmatic "rocking hull," and Kuhn's paradigm-based phenomenalism are attempts to provide nonfoundationalist notions of rationality and truth that are highly protean, able to continually change and adapt to the shifting dimensions of a culturally constructed society and humanity. They are properly called "phronetic" because they seek to obviate, as Habermas says, those philosophical dimensions associated with *theoria* and *epistēmē*, moving instead toward notions able to mediate the contingencies and particularities that are constitutive of life and being. Rorty, similarly, insists that notions of truth need to be developed that are not linked to an "unconditional, ahistorical, human nature. This attempt to put aside both Plato and Kant is the bond which links the post-Nietzschean tradition in European philosophy with the pragmatic tradition in American philosophy."[72] Many nonfoundationalist thinkers agree with Rorty when he says that the correspondence theory is "barely intelligible and of no particular importance—that it is not so much a theory as a slogan which we have been mindlessly chanting for centuries. We pragmatists think that we might stop chanting it without any harmful consequences."[73]

From a theological point of view, these newer notions of truth offer a pronounced challenge. Theology argues that Christian teaching is, at least often enough, normative, universal, enduring and, in certain instances, irreversible. Such attributes, for the sake of their theoretical intelligibility, require both some first philosophy, allowing for selfsame substantial identity, as well as some notion of truth that is able to sustain the kind of finality, referentiality, and perdurance intrinsic to Christian thought.

But from the point of view of the thinkers discussed above, these kinds of final, conclusive claims are largely untenable in light of our fully historicized life and culture. Theology's insistence on the absolute truth of its own doctrinal assertions is simply another instance of its unfortunate Platonic hangover. In making conclusive claims, theology ensures that the discipline must be excluded from the life of the *agora* since it knows the truth a priori, without publicly redeemable warrants and without a thoroughly fallibilistic accent.

There is, needless to add, something very important to be learned from the thinkers encountered here. Along with Heidegger, Wittgenstein, and others, they continue to mount challenges to a facile metaphysics and to an ahistorical transcendentalism. They properly point to the horizons of facticity and historicity that envelop life and thought, thereby overcoming a naïve positivism, a worldless subjectivity, an atomistic linguistic theory, and a wooden representationalism. In theology, such theoretical naïveté has at times led to a leaden dogmatism that failed to account for the paradigm-based, tradition-laden contextualization of knowing and, therefore, failed to account for the limited cognitive insight that epistemic activity, including that properly belonging to theology, can yield.

In the last analysis, however, theology can sanction only a qualified acceptance of these architects of *phronēsis*. In Kuhn's case, there is a loss of realism and referentialism, a reduction to the intralexical, Kantian-inspired, "constructed world" of the scientist or theologian, thereby emptying theology of its cognitive, "noumenal" content. In the case of Gadamer, the overarching flux of historicity has, despite his other strategies for continuity (themselves not without importance), ultimately undermined the possibility of a materially identical truth. The theoretical truth that someone like Aquinas spoke of is now ontologically inappropriate:

> For the true in the speculative intellect arises from the conformity of the intellect with the thing. . . . The true in the practical intellect arises from conformity with rectified appetite, a conformity which has no place in necessary things which do not come about because of the human will, but only in contingent things. . . . Therefore, only a virtue of practical intellect is concerned with contingent things.[74]

Only the latter notion, truth reached by practical reason, is now possible and appropriate, because it recognizes the contingent, historical, and contextual nature of reality. It is precisely such recognition that fuels Gadamer's universalization of phronetic rationality. But this understanding appears incapable of sustaining the kind of continuous and definitive truth that is characteristic of Christian teaching and doctrine.

Habermas, like Gadamer, endorses the truth of practical reason as the only ontologically acceptable form. But he seeks to strengthen this notion by emphasizing not only the consensus through which truth is reached but also the public redemption of warrants for the validation of truth-claims. His theory of communicative rationality comes quite close at points to the pragmatic philosophy earlier championed by Dewey. As Rorty says, "Dewey taught us to call 'truth' whatever beliefs result from a free and open encounter of opinions without asking whether this result agrees with something beyond the encountered." He adds that Dewey's "account of truth has been revived by Jürgen Habermas—and amounts to putting aside the notion that truth corresponds with reality."[75] The accent here is clearly on philosophical fallibilism, on a search for truth disengaged from substance and subject—from ironclad Archimedean points. There are no "unchallengeable" first principles that may claim to be "beyond" ideology, "beyond" the realm of politics or of particular interests. This is why Habermas thinks religious views are best sidelined, since society can only proceed by rationally motivated public agreement leading, at least asymptotically, to a universal consensus. In this kind of fallibilistic thinking, Rorty is justified in observing that there must be "cautionary use" of the truth predicate because while "p" may be well justified, it still may not be true.[76]

But if there continue to exist questions about the kind of truth proposed by these thinkers, then, on the affirmative side, which notion of truth is appropriate to theology? Which understanding of truth allows for the traditional claims of Christian doctrine, such as its universality, objectivity, and transgenerational perdurance? Which understanding of truth protects not only the above-named characteristics but is also cognizant of the legitimate themes uncovered by the nonfoundationalist, phronetic thinkers such as the embedded status of the knower and the consequent sociocultural conditioning of all noetic acts? We will examine attempts to develop just such theologically appropriate notions in the next chapter.

Notes

1. For a review of the cognitive intentions of Modernist thought, see E. Schillebeeckx, *Revelation and Theology*, vol. 2 (trans. N. D. Smith; London: Sheed &

Ward, 1968), 10–12; William Hill, *Knowing the Unknown God* (New York: Philosophical Library, 1971), 35–36; Yves Congar, *A History of Theology* (trans. Hunter Guthrie; Garden City, N.Y.: Doubleday, 1968), 190–92.

2. For more on the theologies of Bautain and Hermes, see Gerald McCool, *Catholic Theology in the Nineteenth Century* (New York: Seabury, 1977), 46–67.

3. For more on this issue, see Thomas Guarino, "Henri Bouillard and the Truth-Status of Dogmatic Statements," *Science et Esprit* 39 (1987): 341–43.

4. M.-D. Chenu, *Le Saulchoir: Une école de théologie* (Kain-Lez-Tournai: Le Saulchoir, 1937), 48. (A reprint of this work was issued in 1985 by Les éditions du Cerf, Paris.). Translations are the author's unless otherwise indicated. Chenu's work was placed on the Roman Catholic Church's Index of Prohibited Books in 1942. See *Acta apostolicae sedis* 34 (1942): 37.

5. Henri Bouillard, *Conversion et Grâce chez S. Thomas d'Aquin: Étude historique* (Paris: Aubier, 1944), 219.

6. For example, Bouillard's "Notions conciliaires et analogie de la vérité," *Recherches de Science Religieuse* 35 (1948): 251–71, is, in fact, a spirited defense of correspondence against the charges of R. Garrigou-Lagrange. The problem, as noted, was that any articulation of realism departing from the terminological lexicon of neo-Scholasticism was looked upon as suspect.

7. This schema was never discussed on the council floor. The complete text may be found in *Acta synodalia Concilii Oecumenici Vaticani II*, vol. I, part IV, 653.

8. *Gaudium et spes*, no. 15.

9. See *Fides et Ratio* nos. 84, 71, 90. "Fides et Ratio," *Acta apostolicae sedis* 91 (1999): 5–88. An English translation may be found in *Origins* 28 (October 22, 1998): 317–47. For a fuller analysis, see Thomas Guarino, "*Fides et Ratio*: Theology and Contemporary Pluralism," *Theological Studies* 62 (2001): 679 n. 6.

10. International Theological Commission, "On the Interpretation of Dogmas," *Origins* 20 (May 17, 1990): 1–14. Section numbers from this article are noted in the text.

11. Robert Jenson, *Systematic Theology*, vol. 1 (New York: Oxford University Press, 1997), 18. Jenson is not only concerned with confirming the referentiality of doctrinal statements but also with the irreversibility of certain such statements. See his comments on this matter on p. 17.

12. Ibid., 19 n. 45.

13. On Lindbeck's shortcomings with regard to truth and realism, a fine analysis may be found in Colman O'Neill, "The Rule Theory of Doctrine and Propositional Truth," *Thomist* 49 (1985). Alister McGrath has also argued that Lindbeck is palpably hesitant on the truth of doctrine. See *The Genesis of Doctrine* (Oxford: Blackwell, 1990), 26–32. McGrath has recently renewed this charge in *Scientific Theology*, vol. 2 (Grand Rapids: Eerdmans, 2002), 53. Also see Geoffrey Wainwright, *Is the Reformation Over?* (Milwaukee: Marquette University Press, 2000), 22–26. Here Wainwright expresses reservations about both Lindbeck's book and the work of Heinrich Fries and Karl Rahner, *Unity—An Actual Possibility?* for not being clear on the issue of incommensurability. The point of Wainwright's critique is: What exactly is held as true? Lindbeck's position will be discussed at greater length in chapter ten.

14. Jenson, *Systematic Theology*, 1:20. Jenson further asserts that this claim has been pressed most forcefully in contemporary thought by Pannenberg, whose own reflections on the matter are addressed later.

15. Boethius, *The Consolation of Philosophy* (trans. Richard Green; Indianapolis: Bobbs-Merrill, 1962), 4.

16. The understanding of "nonfoundationalism" and "foundationalism" used here is

explained in chapter 1, note 30.

17. Stanley Rosen, *Hermeneutics as Politics* (New York: Oxford University Press, 1987), 138. Rosen's text has now been reissued in a second edition by Yale University Press, 2003.

18. I am not contending here that revelation is collapsible to its cognitive and propositional content, thereby emptying it of personalist, existentialist, doxological, and symbolic dimensions. The point here is simply that revelation also includes a doctrinal dimension with its own attendant characteristics. Avery Dulles adeptly places doctrine in its proper relationship to the wider concept of revelation in *Models of Revelation* (Garden City, N.Y.: Doubleday, 1983), esp. 141–45 and 160–62.

19. Richard Bernstein, "Philosophers Respond to *Fides et ratio*," *Books and Culture* 5 (July/August 1999): 30–32.

20. Of course, there is much in Bernstein's comment that is reconcilable with Christian theology. This is the case because not only is Christian teaching always capable of further conceptual precision and wider contextualization, there is as well an eschatological dimension to such truth that will receive its complete realization only in the heavenly Jerusalem. Further, it is clearly the case that some Christian teachings have been and are, in fact, reversible. At the same time, it is clear that Bernstein would not sanction any assertion as a decisive, irreversible religious claim, since such would necessarily contradict fallibilistic methodology.

21. The encyclical *Fides et ratio* at times too quickly speaks of the pragmatic and prudential searches for truth as the wholesale abandonment of truth itself. But this is to misconstrue the chief challenge to the metaphysical realism that the encyclical itself champions—a fully historicized understanding of life and thought accenting contingency and cultural construction, but not proscribing the search for truth.

22. Richard Bernstein, "Philosophy in the Conversation of Mankind," *Review of Metaphysics* 33 (1979–1980): 768.

23. Bernstein would find unfortunate, then, Rorty's comment: "I should like to detach the notion of rationality from that of truth. . . . As I see it, the opposition between rationality and irrationality is simply the opposition between words and blows." Richard Rorty, "Emancipating Our Culture," in *Debating the State of Philosophy: Habermas, Rorty, and Kolakowski* (ed. Józef Niznik and John T. Sanders; Westport, Conn.: Praeger, 1996), 28. Of course, such comments lead some to conclude that nonfoundationalist thought is inextricably intertwined with the very relativism Bernstein hopes to avoid.

24. Thomas Kuhn, "Reflections on My Critics," in *Criticism and the Growth of Knowledge* (ed. I. Lakatos and A. Musgrave; Cambridge: Cambridge University Press, 1970), 266. In the following section on Kuhn, I rely on reflections I published as "Rosmini, Ratzinger, and Kuhn: Observations on a Recent Document of the Doctrinal Congregation," *Theological Studies* 64 (2003): 43–68.

25. Anthony O'Hear, *Introduction to the Philosophy of Science* (Oxford: Clarendon, 1989), 103.

26. Karl Popper, "Normal Science and Its Dangers," in I. Lakatos and A. Musgrave, *Criticism and the Growth of Knowledge*, 56–57. Popper's book on this theme, *The Myth of the Framework*, originally published in 1965, was reissued by Routledge in 1994.

27. Howard Sankey, *The Incommensurability Thesis* (Avebury, England: Aldershot, 1994).

28. Paul Hoyningen-Huene, "Kuhn's Conception of Incommensurability," *Studies in the History and Philosophy of Science* 21 (1990): 481–92.

29. Thomas Kuhn, *The Structure of Scientific Revolutions* (2nd ed.; Chicago: University of Chicago Press, 1970), 121. Kuhn's original work was published in 1962, but he preferred that the later edition be cited.

30. For Kuhn's close relationship to Kant, see Paul Hoyningen-Huene, *Reconstructing*

Scientific Revolutions (Chicago: University of Chicago Press, 1993), 31–42. On the same theme, consult the insightful work of Alexander Bird, *Thomas Kuhn* (Princeton, N.J.: Princeton University Press, 2000), 128–29.

31. For Kuhn's debt to Wittgenstein, see Kuhn, *Structure of Scientific Revolutions*, 44–45. Steve Fuller emphasizes Kuhn's proximity to Quine in *Thomas Kuhn: A Philosophical History for Our Times* (Chicago: University of Chicago Press, 2000), 391 n. 24. Grouping Kuhn with nonfoundationalist thinkers such as Wittgenstein, Quine, Sellars, and others seeking to overcome "Cartesian anxiety" is a theme that was fully explored by Bernstein in *Beyond Objectivism and Relativism* (Philadelphia: University of Pennsylvania Press, 1988). More recently, Trish Glazebrook's work, *Heidegger's Philosophy of Science* (New York: Fordham University Press, 2000) makes useful points comparing Kuhn and Heidegger, especially with regard to the relationship between thinking and technology.

32. Thomas Kuhn, *The Road since Structure* (Chicago: University of Chicago Press, 2000), 95, 99.

33. See Bird, *Thomas Kuhn*, 237. Bird further claims that Kuhn's arguments against correspondence have a distinct similarity to Otto Neurath's enduring image that science is like a boat that must constantly be rebuilt at sea: "There is no dry dock that allows rebuilding from the keel up" (234). This nautical image may remind some readers of Habermas's similar claim that reason is "a rocking hull—but it does not go under in the sea of contingencies, even if shuddering in the high seas is the only mode in which it 'copes' with these contingencies." Jürgen Habermas, *Postmetaphysical Thinking* (trans. William Mark Hohengarten; Cambridge, Mass.: MIT Press, 1992), 44.

34. Hoyningen-Huene, *Reconstructing Scientific Revolutions*, 263–64. This, of course, is very similar to Rorty's repeated claim that "Truth" must be left behind because there is no way of "breaking out of language to compare it with something else." Richard Rorty, "Pragmatism and Philosophy," in *After Philosophy: End or Transformation* (ed. Kenneth Baynes et al.; Cambridge, Mass.: MIT Press, 1988), 32–33.

35. Kuhn, *Structure of Scientific Revolutions*, 206.

36. Bird, *Thomas Kuhn*, 254.

37. Kuhn, *Structure of Scientific Revolutions*, 207.

38. Bird, *Thomas Kuhn*, 229. Bird argues, "Even if truth is a matter of a match between statement and reality, it does not follow that knowing a statement to be true requires a direct comparison of both together" (234). He offers inferential reasoning as another possibility. Lonergan and Rahner make similar arguments, such as that knowing the truth does not require an allegedly "higher viewpoint."

39. Kuhn, *Structure of Scientific Revolutions*, 206.

40. For a well-told journalistic account of Popper's disagreement with Wittgenstein over precisely the "yield" of philosophy, see David Edmonds and John Eidinow, *Wittgenstein's Poker* (London: Faber & Faber, 2001).

41. It is worth noting that Kuhn's understanding of truth was recently invoked by the philosopher Gianni Vattimo. Vattimo, echoing Heidegger, claims that philosophy necessarily thinks of Being as event and of truth, not as the reflection of reality's structure, but fundamentally as a historical message. This conception of truth, Vattimo claims, is upheld by a large part of the sciences, as Kuhn's famous work has clearly indicated. See Vattimo, *After Christianity* (New York: Columbia University Press, 2002), 6.

42. Martin Heidegger, *Being and Time* (trans. John Macquarrie and Edward Robinson; New York: Harper and Row, 1962), 45.

43. Ibid., 96–97.

44. It is not my intention to elaborate fully on Heidegger's project. I try here to capture what I believe to be his essential insight on the relationship between historicity and

the prior tradition of Western philosophy. Of the many books dealing with Heidegger and historicity, I recommend Christopher Fynsk, *Heidegger: Thought and Historicity* (Ithaca, N.Y.: Cornell University Press, 1993).

45. Richard Campbell, *Truth and Historicity* (Oxford: Clarendon, 1992), 402.

46. Hans-Georg Gadamer, *Truth and Method* (2nd rev. ed.; trans. Joel Weinsheimer and Donald G. Marshall; New York: Continuum, 2003), 312.

47. Wittgenstein's similarity to Heidegger is noted elsewhere by Gadamer: "But the really astounding thing is that Wittgenstein's self-critique [after the *Tractatus*] moves in a direction similar to the one we have seen in the evolution of phenomenology." (Gadamer is referring to Heidegger's abandonment of Husserl's transcendental idealism.) Hans-Georg Gadamer, *Philosophical Hermeneutics* (trans. and ed. David E. Linge; Berkeley: University of California Press, 1976), 174.

48. Yves Simon, *The Tradition of Natural Law* (New York: Fordham University Press, 1965), 23–27; Simon, *Practical Knowledge* (New York: Fordham University Press, 1991), 100–105; C. D. C. Reeve, *Practices of Reason: Aristotle's Nichomachean Ethics* (Oxford: Clarendon, 1992), 68, no. 2; 74.

49. "The distinction that Aristotle makes between moral knowledge (*phronēsis*) and theoretical knowledge (*epistēmē*) is a simple one. . . . A hermeneutics of the human sciences certainly has nothing to learn from mathematical as distinguished from moral knowledge. The human sciences stand closer to moral knowledge than to that kind of 'theoretical' knowledge. They are 'moral sciences.'" (Gadamer, *Truth and Method*, 314). At this point Gadamer still stressed the distinction between the human and natural sciences. Later, perhaps under the influence of Kuhn, he would extend the *phronēsis* trajectory: "Even in the domain of the natural sciences, the grounding of scientific knowledge cannot avoid the hermeneutical consequence of the fact that the so-called 'given' cannot be separated from interpretation." Hans-Georg Gadamer, "Text and Interpretation," in *Dialogue and Deconstruction: The Gadamer-Derrida Encounter* (ed. Diane P. Michelfelder and Richard E. Palmer; Albany, N.Y.: SUNY Press, 1989), 30.

50. Bernstein, *Beyond Objectivism and Relativism*, 151.

51. Ibid., 128.

52. Ingrid Scheibler, *Gadamer: Between Heidegger and Habermas* (Lanham, Md.: Rowman & Littlefield, 2000), 48.

53. Bernstein, *Beyond Objectivism and Relativism*, 168–69, 174. As Bernstein has elsewhere noted, "The precise meaning of truth for Gadamer still eludes us. What is even more problematic and revealing is that if we closely examine the way in which Gadamer appeals to 'truth' he is employing a concept of truth that he never fully makes explicit." Bernstein himself is arguing for a move toward Habermas, with his critical redemption of the Enlightenment. Richard Bernstein, "From Hermeneutics to Praxis," in *Review of Metaphysics* 35 (1982): 836.

54. Lawrence Hinman, "*Quid facti* or *Quid juris?* The Fundamental Ambiguity of Gadamer's Understanding of Hermeneutics," in *Philosophy and Phenomenological Research* 40 (1980): 513.

55. Some of Gadamer's contributions to theology, such as the overcoming of hermeneutical positivism, will be noted in chapter five.

56. In decidedly theological contexts, this is the move that has been made by David Tracy, *Plurality and Ambiguity: Hermeneutics, Religion, Hope* (San Francisco: Harper & Row, 1987); Thomas Ommen, "Theology and the Fusion of Horizons," *Philosophy and Theology* 3 (1988): 57–72; and Claude Geffré, *The Risk of Interpretation* (trans. David Smith; New York: Paulist Press, 1987). From the philosophical side, this move has long been championed by Richard Bernstein in, for example, *Beyond Objectivism and Relativism*, 180–200.

57. Some, like Fredric Jameson, properly see in Habermas's defense of the eighteenth century a reversion to the kinds of metanarrative condemned by postmodernity. See Jameson, *Postmodernism* (Durham, NC: Duke University Press, 1991), 61. However, while it is true that Habermas, contra Heidegger and Gadamer, has argued that the Enlightenment cannot simply be eradicated from the humanist tradition, his defense of that universalism is clearly nonfoundationalist in kind and so, ultimately, quite different from the Enlightenment itself. See Habermas, *Philosophical-Political Profiles* (trans. Frederick Lawrence; Cambridge, Mass.: MIT Press, 1983), 197.

58. Jürgen Habermas, "Coping with Contingencies," in Niznik and Sanders, *Debating the State of Philosophy*, 7.

59. Jürgen Habermas, *Postmetaphysical Thinking* (trans. William Mark Hohengarten; Cambridge, Mass.: MIT Press, 1992), 40. Similarly, "The growing awareness that the contingencies of history had gained philosophical relevance increasingly undermined the extramundane status of an ahistorical and disembodied transcendental subject." Habermas, "Coping with Contingencies," 13.

60. Habermas, *Postmetaphysical Thinking*, 144.

61. Habermas, "Coping with Contingencies," 4.

62. So Habermas can say that he agrees with Rorty's criticism of "truth as correspondence" as well as "accept(ing) the Deweyan proposal to explain 'truth as warranted assertability.'" Habermas, "Coping with Contingencies," 20.

63. Of course, this is not to say that Habermas himself has not been accused of seeking an inappropriate security. For example, Lyotard says, "Is legitimacy to be found in consensus obtained through discussion as Jürgen Habermas thinks? Such consensus always does violence to the heterogeneity of language games. And invention is always born of dissention." See Jean-François Lyotard, *The Postmodern Condition: A Report on Knowledge* (trans. Geoff Bennington and Brian Massumi; Minneapolis: University of Minnesota Press, 1984), xxv. For Lyotard's spirited discussion of Habermas, see 60–65.

64. Richard Rorty, for example, says the principal difference between Habermas and himself is the notion of universal validity. But since Habermas is searching for undistorted communication and not attempting "to get from appearance to reality, this difference may not be so very important." Rorty, "Emancipating Our Culture," 28.

65. The alleged inability of Heidegger and Gadamer to develop a truly *intersubjective* theory of practical reason is the ultimate basis for Habermas's reservations about their thought. So against Heidegger, thereby linking him with Husserl, Habermas says, "But the priority of the lifeworld's intersubjectivity over the mineness of *Dasein* escapes any conceptual framework still tinged with the solipsism of Husserlian phenomenology." Habermas, *The Philosophical Discourse of Modernity* (trans. Fredrick Lawrence; Cambridge, Mass.: MIT Press, 1987), 149.

66. Relatively recent works illustrating the influence of the *phronēsis* model, with elements often drawn from both Gadamer and Habermas, include David Tracy, "Beyond Foundationalism and Relativism," in *On Naming the Present* (Maryknoll, N.Y.: Orbis, 1994), 131–39; and Paul Lakeland, *Theology and Critical Theory: The Discourse of the Church* (Nashville: Abingdon, 1990). Lakeland says, for example, that the only two choices for theology are Habermas or Derrida/Foucault. Otherwise, he claims, theology will "degenerate into senescence by a fearful retention of a precritical outlook" (99). Other theologians deeply influenced by Habermas may be found in *Habermas, Modernity, and Public Theology* (ed. Don S. Browning and Francis Schüssler Fiorenza; New York: Crossroad, 1992); and in *Habermas et la théologie* (ed. E. Arens; trans. D. Trierweiler; Paris: Cerf, 1993).

Tracy, in his most recent work discussed in chapter one, has moved away from Habermas toward Marion with his stress on "non-reductive saturated phenomena" and the "impossible." In this regard, Tracy has been concerned to recover "fragments" of religious insights—how they undermine reified, rationalist totality systems, thereby shedding light on modernity's "concealment" of religious experience.

67. This issue concerns both David Tracy and Richard John Neuhaus. Each seeks to mend the rift between the "sacred" and "secular" realms. Tracy does so by adopting, in large measure, *phronēsis* rationality and mutually critical correlation. Only such mutuality, and the abandonment of a priori truth claims, allows religion to be taken seriously by the democratic publics of the academy and society. Neuhaus, on the contrary, thinks that religious citizens of the American republic must insist on a public voice and are under no necessity to relinquish their unique truth-claims. Such relinquishment would continue the relegation of religion outside of the "public square" begun in the Enlightenment. Both Tracy and Neuhaus are close to the classical Catholic position of validating at least some of Christianity's truth-claims on the basis of public warrants. For Neuhaus, this involves a turn to the natural law tradition; for Tracy, a turn to discourse theory.

68. "In the Federal Republic of Germany . . . it was primarily a group of Catholic theologians who, having always maintained a less troubled relation to the *lumen naturale*, were able to draw upon this tradition [of conversation with the humanities and social sciences]. Yet, the more that theology opens itself in general to the discourse of the human sciences, the greater is the danger that its own status will be lost in the network of alternating takeover attempts." See Habermas, "Transcendence from Within, Transcendence in the World," in Browning and Fiorenza, *Habermas, Modernity, and Public Theology*, 231. It remains surprising to see Habermas take a position perhaps most closely associated with a kind of Barthianism, or at least one interpretation of Barth, that the church can easily become contaminated by its association with the "world."

69. Francis Schüssler Fiorenza, "The Church as a Community of Interpretation," in Browning and Fiorenza, *Habermas, Modernity, and Public Theology*, 70. This point has also been made by William Meyer, who concludes that while Habermas has made some concessions to the existential usefulness of religion, he continues to deny that religion has any cognitive dimension. See Meyer, "Private Faith or Public Religion? An Assessment of Habermas's Changing View of Religion," *Journal of Religion* 75 (1995): 371–91.

70. Francis Schüssler Fiorenza, "Introduction: A Critical Reception for Practical Public Theology," in Browning and Fiorenza, *Habermas, Modernity, and Public Theology*, 15.

71. David Tracy, *Dialogue with the Other* (Grand Rapids: Eerdmans, 1990), 43. Stanley Rosen disapprovingly notes (in a nontheological context) that "there can be no doubt that the thesis that art is worth more than the truth is the dominant principle of our time." Rosen, *Hermeneutics as Politics* (New York: Oxford University Press, 1987), 138. But this, I think, misses the central point. What is being argued is precisely that the truth of art illuminates and reveals an *appropriate* understanding of what truth is. Of course, the enduring theological issue is the potential reduction of truth to its imaginative, creative, and symbolic dimensions. Adorno sought to redeem the modern pathologies of positivism and dominative reason by turning toward art. But is aesthetic redemption appropriate for theology? Is there necessarily in theology a representative and referential dimension that is not intrinsic to art? And must all nonartistic notions of truth lead to instrumental and reificatory thinking?

72. Richard Rorty, "The Challenge of Relativism," in Niznik and Sanders, *Debating the State of Philosophy*, 31.

73. Ibid., 32.

74. *ST* I-II, q. 57, a. 5, ad 3; cited in Ralph McInerny, *Aquinas on Human Action* (Washington, D.C.: Catholic University of America Press, 1992), 155.

75. Richard Rorty, "Education, Socialization, and Individuation," *Liberal Education* 75

(1989): 5. As Rorty says elsewhere, the issue is "to choose between truth as 'what is good for us to believe' and truth as 'contact with reality'" (Rorty, *Philosophy and the Mirror of Nature* [Princeton, N.J.: Princeton University Press, 1979], 176). In his later work, *The Consequences of Pragmatism* (Minneapolis: University of Minnesota Press, 1982), Rorty avers, "For the pragmatist, true sentences are not true because they correspond to reality, and so there is no need to worry what sort of reality, if any, a given sentence corresponds to—no need to worry about what 'makes' it true" (xvi). There are clear differences between Rorty's and Habermas's notions of truth, with the latter being more concerned about ensuring as great a consensus as possible, that is, universal validity as asymptotic ideal. On the kind of truth pursued, however, that of practical reason, there is a significant convergence between them.

    76. Rorty, as cited in Habermas, "Coping with Contingencies," 20.

CHAPTER 4

Christian Doctrine and Truth: Renewals

Renewed Notions of Theological Truth

If, as Vatican II says, God's revelation abides perpetually in its full integrity for all generations (*DV*, art. 7), if God has communicated himself and the eternal decisions of his will (*DV*, art. 6), if, indeed, revelation, linguistically articulated as doctrine, makes certain normative claims, as all Christians assert, then revelation and doctrine need some notion of truth that can support such conclusive and abiding assertions, that can logically sustain the affirmations of Christian belief. It comes as no surprise, then, that a papal encyclical on the relationship between faith and reason, *Fides et ratio*, finds the notion of truth proper to the Christian understanding of revelation and doctrine a central and neuralgic issue. The document asserts, "To every culture Christians bring the unchanging truth of God [*immutabilem Dei veritatem*]" (no. 71). It criticizes historicism whereby "the enduring validity of truth is denied. What was true in one period . . . may not be true in another" (no. 87). The encyclical also inveighs against the nihilistic "negation of all objective truth" and asserts that "the neglect of being inevitably leads to losing touch with objective truth and therefore with the very ground of human dignity" (no. 90).

In the passages cited, one may see clearly an emphasis on universal, and enduring, truth. Such characteristics are defended, of course, because

the encyclical recognizes that contemporary philosophy, which tends to underscore the local, contextual, and heteromorphous nature of knowing, is often enough at odds with the kind of truth essential for theoretically sustaining Christian teaching. Any notion of truth that is to fulfill what the document calls the *officium congruum*, or "suitable office," of philosophy must be able to buttress fundamental Christian teaching; it must be capable of adequately mediating the truth of revelation; in short, it must be a notion of truth that is revelationally and doctrinally appropriate. The universal and enduring claims of Christian belief, then, must be able to be logically and philosophically supported.

Having argued that any revelationally appropriate thought must be able to "know the truth" and to "reach objective truth" (no. 82), *Fides et ratio* further claims that this should be done by means of the *adaequatio rei et intellectus* "to which the Scholastic Doctors referred" (no. 82). Indeed, the encyclical is correct in defending some kind of metaphysical realism as philosophically and theologically essential to revelation, for realism alone allows the church to defend Christian doctrine as not only symbolic, disclosive, and existentially illuminative but also as ontologically true.[1] Inasmuch as Christianity is concerned with mediating states of affairs, human and divine, some form of philosophical realism, profoundly stamped by the subjective and constructive dimensions intrinsic to knowing and productive of it, and equally stamped by the apophatic nature of all theological speech, must be adduced. Just as theological language has analogical, apophatic, and doxological dimensions, it must have ostensive and "representational" ones as well.[2] The breakdown of realism leads, it appears, to unfettered constructivism (and so to idealism), to conceptual pragmatism, or to a narrative unsure of its precise ontological status. This is why the encyclical rightly insists that theological language and interpretation can never simply "defer" in the Derridean sense, but must ultimately offer us a "statement which is simply true; otherwise there would be no Revelation of God, but only the expression of human notions about God" (no. 84).[3]

While the encyclical properly defends realism, one must ask if realism needs to be as tightly bound to the *adaequatio* as this document presumably requires. While there is nothing wrong with the *adaequatio* in itself, is this the only possible way to defend the theological and philosophical realism that Christian doctrine demands? In response to *Fides et ratio* one may ask: Was Newman a representative of a bare *adaequatio*? Was Lossky, mentioned favorably by *Fides et ratio* yet who nevertheless harbored such deep reservations about Aristotelianism and Western theological "rationalism"?

Was Edith Stein, also cited in the encyclical, with her Husserlian and phenomenologically inspired approach? In defending realism, should the Christian theologian and philosopher be bound to a thirteenth-century conceptual apparatus? This seems hardly in the spirit, countenanced by the encyclical, of developing philosophies that proceed through the Fathers and Scholastics while simultaneously taking account of modern and contemporary thought (no. 85).[4]

Related to the issue of realism and objectivity is the matter of human subjectivity in noetic acts. For the most part, the encyclical ignores important dimensions of knowing that, of themselves, do not frustrate the realism that *Fides et ratio* wishes to defend. One sees very little, for example, about the turn to the subject, horizon analysis, theory-laden interpretation, the constructive dimensions of knowledge, or the tacit and intuitive elements of epistemology. Failing to acknowledge the subjective elements constitutive of knowing counts as a significant omission in a document discussing human rationality and its relationship to faith. The encyclical, it is true, avoids some of the blind alleys in the epistemology of modernity. One wonders, however, if by ignoring the anthropological dimensions of knowing prominent in modern thought, the encyclical does not ignore modernity itself, thereby militating against its own goal of establishing a new synthesis that takes account of the entire philosophical tradition.[5]

Although the encyclical limits itself to classically accepted thinkers, there are, in fact, many sophisticated theological defenders of metaphysical realism. They advance this theoretical point of view precisely because they are convinced that such an epistemological position is able to logically explicate Christian truth and teaching. These thinkers are also well aware of the "scandal" given by theological claims. As Walter Kasper has bluntly stated, "The real cause of offence today is . . . the church and its dogma, which claims to be able to say something valid and timeless about God in terms that are historically conditioned."[6] In fact, he writes elsewhere, "This crisis of the concept of truth and the understanding of truth is the *Grundkrise* of contemporary theology."[7] The scandal lies in the fact that the Christian church claims to teach, at least in certain instances, that which is actually and even irrevocably true, even though such truth is always grasped in historically contingent situations and in a limited way. Kasper observes that the contemporary problem has roots extending deep into the Enlightenment. Lessing's ring parable, for example, had already made transparently clear that, for some, the true ring, or true religion, is beyond knowing. This religious nescience "led to tolerance and the relativization of all claims to a universal and absolute truth, as well as to the requirement to subject all validity claims to the rules of reason common to all human beings. . . . The Christian religion was to renounce its universal claim in the sphere of public life and to yield to reason."[8] Kasper then notes, as he did in his earlier work, that both contemporary philosophy and the common Zeitgeist "call into question the . . . churches holding a general and universally valid claim on truth." The inescapable conclusion is that all claims, including those of Christianity, "have a provisional character."[9]

Since the truth-question is vital to both contemporary philosophy and theology, it is worth examining several theological defenders of metaphysical realism who seek to take account of the legitimate questions brought to the fore by nonfoundationalist thought.

Bernard Lonergan

Bernard Lonergan has a famous essay on truth, now over thirty years old, that illustrates some of the major themes discussed here. The context of his essay was a book written by Leslie Dewart that called for the "dehellenization of dogma." The argument, now familiar, was in many ways reminiscent of Harnack's claims about early Christianity: The problem with the Christian faith is that it has been seduced by an incompatible and insidious Hellenism from which it needs to shake itself free. John Caputo has recently exhumed Dewart's book and hails it as an early forerunner of postmodern philosophy, of a Christian thought proleptically seeking to incorporate certain postmodern themes.[10]

Lonergan begins by outlining one of Dewart's main philosophical *bêtes noires*, namely, truth as the *adaequatio intellectus et rei*. Tracing this opposition to the light Dewart has received from phenomenology as well as to his misinterpretations of Scholasticism, Lonergan argues that Dewart misconstrues precisely what the correspondence theory of truth, in fact, entails.[11] Dewart, like many, assumes that this theory necessarily presupposes that we could witness from a "higher" viewpoint the union of a subject and an object. This would assume that the knower could rise to a "God's-eye" view, thereby properly adjudicating the success or failure of the alleged correspondence. But such thinking, asserts Lonergan, "is involved in a grave confusion" (73). This confusion results from thinking that there is some kind of "higher viewpoint," which Lonergan famously ascribes to naïve realism, holding for the "super-look," which encompasses both the looking and the looked at.[12] On the contrary, Lonergan argues, "the union of object and subject is a metaphysical deduction from the fact of knowledge, and its premise is the possibility of consciousness objectifying not only itself but also its world" (73).

To Dewart's evisceration of both the correspondence notion of truth and the dogmatic theology that depends on it, Lonergan opposes the claim that dogmas have a mediating role in God's revelation to humanity. To assent to dogmas is to assent to what the dogma means: *Verum est medium in quo ens cognoscitur*. Any attempt to separate dogmatic claims from truth—or to interpret truth, including religious truth, in some other way than a judgment that something "is"—remains for Lonergan simply an inability to distinguish the great strengths of Hellenism from its clear limitations (80). This statement, of course, is of a piece with Lonergan's other claims about dogmas, such as that dogmas harbor meanings that are continuous and permanent because these meanings "convey the doctrine of faith revealed by God." Further, "the meaning of dogmas is permanent because that meaning is not a datum but a truth and that truth is not human but divine."[13] For Lonergan, Christian doctrine aims at "a clear and distinct affirmation of religious realities: its principal concern is the truth of such an affirmation." In fact, "doctrines are concerned to state clearly and distinctly the religious community's confession of the mysteries so hidden in God that man could not know them if they had not been revealed by God."[14] With regard to the believer's assent, Lonergan states, "assent to such doctrines is the assent of faith, and that assent is regarded by religious people [he is no doubt thinking of Aquinas's comments here] as firmer than any other."[15] Dewart's proposal, by attacking the correspondence notion of truth, constituted for Lonergan an illegitimate attack on Christian doctrine, on the truth manifested by God that is knowable in faith. At the same time, Lonergan, seeking an epistemological via media, resisted what he saw as a Roman Catholic overemphasis on objectivity and realism (to the detriment of subjectivity), with a consequent devaluation of historicity (and conceptual mutability).

In order to oppose just these latter tendencies, Lonergan spent a good part of his career trying to move Catholic theology away from an exaggerated anti-Kantianism that blinded theologians to the central noetic role played by historicity and subjectivity. It is no surprise, then, in his classic 1968 essay on "The Subject," that Lonergan tries to balance the objectivity of truth with the enveloping and indefeasible dimensions of finitude constitutive of knowing in general. Of truth's objectivity, Lonergan has no doubt. He says, for example, "A subject may be needed to arrive at truth, but, once truth is attained, one is beyond the subject and one has reached a realm that is non-spatial, atemporal, impersonal."[16] He immediately adds, however, that one should not be fascinated by truth's objectivity, for if it is intentionally independent of the subject, "ontologically it resides only in the subject: *veritas formaliter est in solo judicio*" (70). Truth resides in the subject because the subject is capable of self-transcendence, that is, of going beyond what he or she imagines, thinks, and feels to what, in fact, is so. But the subject himself or herself is situated and contextualized because the laborious process of coming to know the truth requires a gestation and parturition that is "not independent of the subject, of times and places, of psychological, social, historical conditions. The fruit of truth must grow and mature on the tree of the subject, before it can be plucked and placed in its absolute realm" (71). Similarly, he says that "one can be fascinated by the objectivity of truth[,] . . . one can so emphasize objective truth as to disregard or undermine the very conditions of its emergence and existence" (71). He points out that the failure to take account of these subjective elements has led, at times, to an alienation from the dogmas of Christian faith. This alienation "is not unconnected with a previous one-sidedness that so insisted on the objectivity of truth as to leave subjects and their needs out of account" (71). To this end, Lonergan notes that the problem with Baroque Catholic Thomists, such as Suarez and de Lugo, was that they "thought of truth as so objective as to get along without minds" (71–72). Lonergan's judgment on those who fail to attend to the embedded and historical subject is transparent:

> The neglected subject, then, leads to the truncated subject, to the subject that does not know himself and so unduly impoverishes his account of human knowledge. He condemns himself to an antihistorical immobilism, to an excessively jejune conjunction between abstract concepts and sensible presentations, and to ignorance of the proleptic and utterly concrete character of the notion of being. (75)

There is no question, then, that Lonergan thinks that sociocultural, linguistic, and historical elements are essential to any theory of truth. At the same time, even with all of his concern for the mediating subject and its determinative role in epistemology, Lonergan has little time for a historicist construction of truth. The context of discovery does not delimit the truth of the "absolute realm" at which the subject arrives. Further, Lonergan continues to rely on the theory of invariant cognitional structure first elaborated in *Insight* and briefly discussed in chapter 2. Human beings have an intentional self-transcendence, which allows them to make true judgments, but this intentionality is a compound of many immanent operations, including inquiry, investigation, experience, understanding, and judgment. Only in judgment does one sharply distinguish between what one imagines and thinks and, finally, "what is so."

In the last analysis, Lonergan, like Rahner and Pannenberg, remains a "metaphysical" or "foundational" thinker, seeking to develop a notion of truth sensitive to constructive and historical horizons, but ultimately remaining a defender of metaphysical realism, of truth as a correspondence mediating being and reality.[17] Although Lonergan develops this notion philosophically, it is in service to the theological claim that Christian doctrine mediates truth and, as he says, a permanent truth that is not human but divine.

Karl Rahner

Karl Rahner has written on the truth question in many contexts, both philosophical, especially during his early years, and with explicit theological intent, especially during the post-Vatican II period when he reflected more intensely on changeable and unchangeable elements in the Roman Catholic Church. In this section, I will examine Rahner's understanding of the kind of truth displayed by Christian doctrine and his philosophical attempt to explicate this position.

In his explicitly theological writings, it is unsurprising that Rahner begins with revelation and the church's claims to teach revealed truth. There is, in fact, never any question in Rahner's work, from beginning to end, about the kind of truth mediated by Christian doctrine. While it is certainly true that, as time passed, Rahner placed increasing emphasis on both the mystery and the pluriformity of human experience, on the socially and culturally constructed dimensions of religious formulations, his positions on the truth displayed by Christian affirmations remain virtually unchanged.

Even early on, Rahner accented the importance of historicity and the inseparability of doctrinal statements from their sociocultural specificity. He observes, for example, that "propositions . . . even though they express an *abiding truth* are nevertheless subject to history."[18] Although the dogmas of the Council of Trent, for example, remain in force, one must draw a distinction between the "essential point in its abiding validity" and a "conceptual model used at that time."[19] But conceptual mutability does not call into question the validity of doctrine's claims to truth. Indeed, in certain propositions, "the believer . . . is enabled in the concrete to grasp that *absolute and irrevocable* self-utterance of God to which he assents with hope."[20] Further, the church holds certain "true and indestructible propositions" that are constitutive of faith; such teachings of Christian doctrine are always, in fact, "ultimately binding and valid."[21] Finally, "if the believer failed to understand the content of his faith as enduring *finally and definitively* in this world[,] . . . he could not recognize Jesus as the final and definitive Word of God's self-utterance to the world."[22]

These kinds of Rahnerian claims could, in fact, be endlessly duplicated. They indicate, clearly, that Rahner regards the fundamental judgments of Christian doctrine as enduringly, universally, and, at times, irrevocably true. Of course, he recognizes that such terms are applicable only to certain essential and definitive teachings of the Christian faith. There are other teachings, less authoritative, that are, of course, open to fundamental revision and even complete reversal. But this acknowledgment exists side-by-side with a referential realism that recognizes the truth reached by essential Christian teaching as definitive and perduring.

At the same time, Rahner wants to make clear that the claims of Christian doctrine do not exist in an ahistorical bubble, apart from the effects of historicity, ideology, and culture. In the context of his hermeneutical theory, for example, Rahner observes again and again that theological affirmations are inextricably intertwined with highly delimited concepts. One never "has" the truth apart from the conceptual and cultural conventions of a given age and of a specifically constituted linguistic community. He says, for example, that the Christian must be aware that dogma is never "chemically pure"; there must be an awareness of the "relativity" of the truth proclaimed by the church, relativity in "the conceptual models by means of which something is expressed."[23] Even though some Christian doctrines are binding and valid, they "are always expressed in terms which are conditioned by history, from the standpoint of ideas which are historically conditioned and subject to change." He continues, "Dogma, even in its most ultimate and binding form, is open to the future."[24] Rahner seeks to balance, then, his accent on the abiding and universal validity of certain doctrines with a similar stress on the irrefragable importance of historically and culturally constituted conditions in which such claims are formulated.

While Rahner's hermeneutics of doctrine will be discussed later, it is worth returning for the moment to one of his early writings in order to examine more fully his understanding of the truth question. There is no need to rehearse here, once again, Rahner's perception of humanity's implicit preapprehension of Absolute Being, a notion that grounds his entire oeuvre. This idea, developed in dialogue with Aquinas, Kant,

Hegel, and Heidegger, and elaborated in his two early works, *Spirit in the World* and *Hearers of the Word*, has been amply explicated.[25] It is enough to say, with Jack Bonsor, that in these early works "the reference of Christianity's truth-claim is the God manifested in humanity's constitutive noetic, free transcendence."[26] Our attention will focus instead on an essay dating from the same period as the two larger works, but which has the notion of truth as its specific concern.

In this exposition, dating from 1938, Rahner begins with an examination of Aquinas's understanding of truth as the *adaequatio rei et intellectus*.[27] The phrase, he points out, appears easy to understand on the face of it (reminding one of Rorty's "mindlessly chanted slogan"), but discerning the actual meaning takes a bit more work. Echoing the consensus that was becoming prominent among many Thomistic commentators of his time, Rahner states that a key element in this formulation is that truth is not located in the process of conceptualization or abstraction, but rather in the further intellective act of the judgment of affirmation or negation. He then sets about formulating his argument.

Rahner first asks about the basis for the "universality and validity of metaphysical propositions, namely the first principles" (24). He locates this basis, using traditional terminology, in the light of the agent intellect, which is itself a formal, a priori principle that is "ontologically speaking, nothing else than the dynamic movement of the intellect as such outwards towards the absolute totality of all possible objects of the human intellect" (24). Rahner holds that Aquinas recognizes, as Hegel did after him, that this spontaneous, dynamic movement of the intellect is in some ways a "hunger." The individual object or sensible singular is recognized by the intellect as that which is finite and as failing to measure up, because of its limitations, to the depth and power of the intellect's own dynamism. In a classic statement of this message, Rahner can say, "Once the absolute epistemological ideal is applied to it as a standard, it is shown to be *a* being as compared with being itself, and so as a 'this,' a finite *individuum*" (24). In distinguishing the finite sensible singular as an *individuum*, one also recognizes the universal; in distinguishing the concrete, finite "this," one recognizes being in the absolute, as the ultimate horizon of thought. Aquinas here departs from Kant because the Kantian a priori principle does not extend beyond the basis provided by sensory perception, while for Aquinas, "the intellect's transcending power avowedly bears upon being in the absolute" (25). For Aquinas, the intellect's agency extends beyond the sphere of the senses, "thereby opening up a knowledge of being as such, and providing the basis on which metaphysics . . . becomes possible" (25).

To accept the range of transcendence opened by the intellect is to accept "the transcendental conditions enabling an intellect endowed with self-knowledge to make objective judgments upon, and so to know, the objects of sense perception" (25). Consequently, Rahner continues, "while it is true that knowledge of the world based on judgment . . . does not afford any direct view of the metaphysical dimension, still it does implicitly involve what is the enabling condition of this, namely the acceptance of transcendental being and of its ultimate structures" (25–26). The validity of the transcendental principles he has outlined "makes knowledge possible in the material world" (26).

Concluding in a manner very similar to Lonergan, Rahner states, "Thomist epistemology cannot be accused of basing its theory of the adequateness of truth upon the naïve assumption that it is possible to compare the reality in itself with the reality as known and so to establish an agreement between the two" (27). While Lonergan calls this fallacy the "super-look" of naïve realism, which fails to understand the metaphysical deduction involved in the *adaequatio*, Rahner claims this misconstrual is based on a failure to understand that the actuality of finite knowledge is based on the a priori *Vorgriff* of the intellect. The opposition to the *adaequatio*, then, is ultimately based, not on the inability to establish a "higher viewpoint" (which is impossible) but on the failure to reflect on the nature of what is involved in the act of understanding itself: "This truth, this *proportio ad rem* of the act of judgment, is realized not, as we would expect, by a reflecting upon, or looking at, the reality itself, but by the understanding reflecting upon itself" (27). In other words, Rahner is saying, only by understanding what is involved in one's own intentional self-transcendence (the transcendental principle of the *Vorgriff auf esse*) will one understand properly the nature of the *adaequatio*.

One sees that Rahner is very close here to Lonergan's point that the *adaequatio* is a metaphysical deduction based on the possibility of consciousness objectifying itself and the world, in the process achieving intentional self-transcendence. For both theologians, truth consists in a judgment upon the "thing in itself" that is ultimately based upon metaphysical (transcendental) first principles, opening out to Absolute Being; these first principles constitute the foundational basis for individual judgments. Rahner's conclusion verifies his claim that the validity of the truth reached in individual judgments is based on those transcendental conditions allowing one to constitute objects of knowledge as such: "Our chief point . . . is that man, by the very fact of accepting the validity of his own transcendental a priori, and thereby the first principles of being as such, in every judgment he makes, accepts also that it is in principle possible to know a being as such" (29).

Of course, one need hardly accept Rahner's philosophical attempt to establish the objective validity of judgments, or to interpret the traditional *adaequatio* on the basis of a transcendental analysis of intellective action. Needless to add, his approach has had many opponents over the years, both from a traditionally Thomist point of view (such as Gilson, who saw this as an illegitimate Kantian reading of Aquinas) and from a Wittgensteinian-influenced one (such as Fergus Kerr's claim of markedly Cartesian elements in Rahner's thought).[28] The point here, however, is clear enough—namely, that Rahner holds, from his earlier to later writings, for an understanding of truth that is meditative, abiding, universal, and ultimately in service to Christian doctrine. While he places pronounced accents on the sociocultural constitution and limitations of doctrinal formulas (with their mutable conceptual frameworks), while he certainly admits that many Christian teachings are revisable and even reversible, and while he stresses that doctrine has an eschatological dimension belonging to its essence, Rahner decidedly resists full-blown fallibilistic and phronetic understandings of truth that, with their accent on the primacy of contingency, are ultimately unable to sustain the normative and perduring truth of essential Christian teachings.

Wolfhart Pannenberg

Wolfhart Pannenberg is another theologian who, like Rahner and Lonergan, is a strong, although unique, defender of realism and a referential view of truth. In his well-known *Systematic Theology*, Pannenberg examines this notion at some length. He begins, for example, by affirming that "in the concept of theology, the truth of theological discourse as discourse about God that God himself has authorized is always presupposed. Talk about God that is grounded in humanity, in human needs and interests, or as an expression of human ideas about divine reality, would not be theology."[29] In just this regard, he observes approvingly that Vatican I spoke of *fidei dogmata* (Denzinger-Schönmetzer 3017), which are true and to be believed as revealed by God (DS 3001; *tamquam divinitus revelata credenda proponuntur*).[30] He further states, "Theology deals with the universality of the truth of revelation and therefore with the truth of revelation and of God himself" (51). Pannenberg, then, like Lonergan and Rahner, begins with the truth of revelation and with its formulation as Christian doctrine. After all, dogmatics is concerned with "the divinely grounded universality of its content, which embraces the reality of the world from its creation to its eschatological consummation" (48–49). It is, then, from a starting point deeply rooted in Christian faith that he develops his understanding of the kind of truth proper to theology.

Pannenberg argues that "by its very nature truth precedes subjective insight, for seekers after knowledge may either hit upon the truth or miss it. Here is the element of 'correspondence' to the object, the actual truth which is foundational to the epistemological aspect of the concept of truth." Of course, in many cases, judgments are reformable and are open to better formulations. This, however, "does not alter the fact . . . that *presupposed* truth can be grasped only in the medium of knowing it *as* truth" (24). Pannenberg also explains why theology needs a veridical approach differing from many of the phronetic positions outlined earlier: "The absolute priority of truth . . . is especially important in the case of theology and its self-understanding. Involved here is the absolute priority of God and God's revelation over all human opinions and judgments" (24). Judgments are subjectively conditioned and thereby open to error. Truth, however, in its "binding universality" precedes our idiosyncratic judgments. "We presuppose it [truth] and seek to correspond to it. . . . This insight was the decisive step in Augustine's argument for the divinity of truth" (52).

Pannenberg accents the importance of metaphysics in theology and expresses concern about a contemporary dégringolade into kerygmatic subjectivism or an epiphanic notion of revelation unable to sustain logically the perduring claims of Christian truth. Similarly, he thinks some kind of correspondence notion is theologically essential, finding the contemporary emphasis on consensus understandings to be ultimately without great value for the discipline. As he says, "The consensus theory of the truth of dogma shares the weakness of a mere consensus theory of truth in general. Consensus can express and denote the universality of truth but it can also express mere conventionality among the members of a group, society, or culture" (12). So, Pannenberg argues, the earth's place at the center of the universe was accepted as unimpeachably true for centuries until this was unmasked as a mere convention.[31] He concludes that "even where there is widespread or, indeed, universal consensus, this consensus alone is not a sufficient criterion of truth" (13).[32]

Pannenberg appears more willing to accept the coherence account of truth as theologically appropriate. Coherence in things allows for proportion and logical unity. Apparently unconcerned about the charge of ontotheology, he continues: "This [emphasis on coherence] gives new force . . . to the idea of truth in Parmenides and Augustine which relates the idea of truth to that of being and also to the thought of God as absolute and all-embracing. God alone can be the ontological locus of the unity of truth in the sense of coherence as the unity of all that is true" (53).

For those familiar with Pannenberg's thought, there is, unsurprisingly, together with his emphasis on the truth mediated by dogmatics, a very strong accent on the incompleteness of knowledge, on dogmatic asser- tions as proleptic claims only to be completely revealed and compre- hended eschatologically. He says, for example, that dogmatics "cannot give concrete reality to the truth of God as such. It cannot present it in packaged formulas. Sincerely as it strives to grasp and present the truth, its possible correspondence to the truth of God is linked to an awareness that theology is a matter of human knowledge and is riveted as such to the conditions of finitude" (54). Here one sees several themes central to Pannenberg's own theology, as well as his attempt to present a concept of truth properly disciplined by the elements of finitude, historicity, cultural constructivism, and all of the dimensions appropriately championed by *phronēsis*-oriented thinkers. The accent here is on the realization that theological truth is always eschatologically constituted, that revelation itself will come to fullness and final fruition only at the end of time. The Heideggerian element of Pannenberg's thought is also thrown into strict relief here, especially his claim that humanity is "riveted . . . to the condi- tions of finitude." As Pannenberg says, "The historicity of human experi- ence and reflection forms the most important limit of our human knowledge of God. Solely on account of its historicity all human talk about God unavoidably falls short of full and final knowledge of the truth of God" (55). Pannenberg recognizes, of course, that Christian truth is concerned with the perduring, with the lasting, with that which is not perpetually mutable. So he can flatly state, "The biblical understanding of truth, like the Greek, equates the true with the lasting and reliable. This is what is identical with itself" (54). He rightly adds, however, that this identity is not grasped *apart* from history, "behind the flux of time." On the contrary, this identity is grasped in and through our condition as limited beings, enmeshed in history. Pannenberg is very clear that although we exist as finite beings in historical times and places, "relativity does not have to mean that there is nothing absolute and that there is thus no truth, which as such is always absolute." However, this "absoluteness of truth" is only accessible to us "in the relativity of our own experience and reflection" (54).

Ultimately, it appears, even while remaining acutely aware of finitude and facticity, of the limitations of human formulations (part of "theological sobriety"), Pannenberg, like Lonergan and Rahner, although clearly in a different way, thinks that some kind of correspondence notion of truth (embedded in a coherence account), and some kind of metaphysical realism, is essential for theology. This is the case given the very nature of doctrinal assertions, their claim to perduring, conclusive, and universal truth. It remains equally true, of course, that Pannenberg fully agrees with the Rahnerian claim, "Dogma, even its most ultimate and binding form, is open to the future," and he thinks that human finitude compels us to say that "our talk about God becomes doxology in which the speakers rise above the limits of their finitude to the thought of the infinite God" (55). But he adds that "in the process, the conceptual contours do not have to lose their sharpness." Doxology here functions for Pannenberg not as a way to eviscerate the cognitive content of doctrinal formulas, to collapse realism into mysticism, but as a way of explaining how human concepts are properly predicated of God—enabling him to circumvent some of the aporias he thinks are attached to the traditional notion of the *analogia entis*.[33] This doxological emphasis, legitimate in that it preserves an apophaticism at the heart of linguistic attribution, should not, however, be taken as meaning that Pannenberg ultimately calls into question the importance of adducing some notion of truth that can appropriately mediate the perduring and universal claims of Christian faith and doctrine. On the contrary, his entire theological oeuvre testifies to his attempts at defending the absoluteness of those claims, while concomitantly acknowledging the productive dimensions of human finitude.

Robert Sokolowski

Another thinker who strongly supports realism is the philosopher Robert Sokolowski, who does so largely in nontheological contexts and with Husserlian themes, rather than with more traditional Augustinian and Thomistic approaches. Leslek Kolakowski has recently stated that it is the kind of truth proposed by Husserl that pragmatism and contemporary constructivism are seeking to overturn; consequently, Sokolowski's reliance on Husserl should alert us to the nature of his project.[34] In a significant compendium of phenomenology, Sokolowski distinguishes two kinds of truth: the truth of correctness and the truth of disclosure.[35] Both have their place. In the former, it is simply a matter of verifying whether a claim is true. For example, we may confirm the statement that the roof leaks when it rains by verifying whether or not this is, in fact, the case. "If the results confirm the assertion, we can say that the statement is true because it does express the way things are" (158). The latter kind of truth, the truth of disclosure, is more basic and elementary. It is simply the display of a state of affairs to us. For example, we walk to our car and see that the tire is flat. The truth is simply displayed to us. We have not been thinking about it or anticipating it; neither are we trying to confirm or verify some claim that has been made to us. "It is the simple presencing to us of an intelligible object, the manifestation of what is real or actual" (158).[36] The truth of correctness ultimately depends on disclosive truth, since it is the latter that displays what is in fact the case.

Building on this distinction, Sokolowski argues that a true proposition "matches" that which is disclosed. A statement or presentation of the world that was previously tentative and unsure, that was simply a display of the world as proposed by someone else to us, is now confirmed by the disclosure of a direct display of the world presenting itself to us. "It is these propositions, these states of affairs as proposed, that become candidates for the truth of correctness and they acquire such truth when they are seen to blend with what is given, once again, in the truth of disclosure"(159). Comments such as these indicate the forcefully realistic aspects of phenomenology, of the world as disclosed, displayed, and intuited, as truly "given" to us as intentional knowers.[37]

The reaction against Kant's transcendental philosophy, which preceded and often surrounded Husserl's own work, is here clearly evident; categorical objects are displayed to us, intentional consciousness constitutes— that is, makes present—the world, and human beings are the receptive "datives of display."[38] Sokolowski adduces these profoundly realistic themes, rooted clearly in Husserl himself, without hesitancy. He then applies these principles to the correspondence understanding of truth. Sokolowski notes that, at least traditionally, "the issue of truth seems to require some sort of meaning, concept or judgment between us and the thing"(98). After all, when we say we hold a particular truth, do we not imply that the meanings we have "correspond to what is out there"? Are not meanings and judgments, then, some kind of mental entities serving as bridges between us and the world we intend? Or are meanings and judgments, when thought of as mental entities, more likely to lead to philosophical aporias?

Sokolowski argues that one of phenomenology's strengths is that it treats judgments and meanings neither as mental entities nor as intermediaries between the mind and things; judgments, rather, are dimensions of presentation that arise out of our focusing on particular states of affairs. Even in judgments, we are simply referring to the world as proposed to us, intended by us, given to us, not developing a mental entity as a kind of *tertium quid* or "bridge." The emphasis here falls markedly on human intentionality in knowing, on, as Sokolowski says, the "world directedness of all intentionality." This understanding allows Sokolowski to offer a phenomenological clarification of the correspondence theory of truth. As we have already seen, the major problem with such a theory (addressed by Rahner and Lonergan) is explaining the "match" or bridge between propositions and existing states of affairs. For phenomenology, however, no such problem of explaining this bridge exists. Propositions are only states of affairs "in the world" now linguistically articulated. They are the "world" as projected or proposed by the speaker. But when a state of affairs is proposed or intended, how does one know its truth? Sokolowski responds that one first adopts a propositional attitude, that is, an attitude of reflection, turning toward judgment. The judgment is not a thing in this case, a mental entity; it is a change in the world's presentation when we change our focus, a change in how the world is now "grasped" by intentionality. To finally confirm or disconfirm a particular proposition, Sokolowski responds, one, in essence, simply returns to examine the state of affairs existing in the world. One inquires and inspects regarding the issue or "given" at hand. The outcome of this inquiry will determine if a particular proposal "does correspond to the way things are" (101). A particular state of affairs is no longer simply proposed. It is confirmed or disconfirmed on the basis of inquiry and reflection.

One need agree neither with Sokolowski's use of phenomenology nor with his understanding of Husserlian themes such as presentation, judgment, intentionality, registration, and disclosure. What is incontrovertible, however, is that he offers a clear defense of philosophical realism along with a profound stress on the objectivity of truth. One sees in his formulations the Husserlian, at least the early Husserlian, objections to both Kantianism and the subjectivism of modernity at large.[39] As Sokolowski says, "Husserl shows that when we articulate things, when we judge or relate or compose or structure things, we do not merely arrange our own internal concepts or ideas or impressions; rather, we articulate things in the world."[40] This is why, for Husserl and subsequent phenomenology, one does not try to "prove realism"; rather, "one displays it."[41]

When theologically adopted, Sokolowski's understanding provides a very useful theory for explaining the nature of doctrinal claims. Such claims mediate states of affairs that are constituted, that is, made present, by human intentionality. Of course, there is no possibility in theology of examining "presentation" as one would categorical objects. But theology has its own criteria of presentation, primarily Scripture and the mediation of Scripture through certain central moments of ecclesial tradition; these constitute the primary loci through which reflective judgment grasps truth in its disclosive and correspondent aspects. As such, Sokolowski's development of Husserlian themes provides new and largely unexplored avenues for developing a notion of theological truth that would be largely preservative of the normative and objective claims of Christian teaching.

Radical Orthodoxy

A final realist understanding of truth to be examined will be the one advanced by John Milbank and Catherine Pickstock in their work *Truth in Aquinas*.[42] They argue that not only is a realist, correspondence understanding of truth essential to theology, but such theory is, in fact, theological in its very essence. The first essay in the collection, entitled "Truth and Correspondence" and written by Pickstock, constitutes an extended commentary on a few questions from Aquinas's *De veritate*. The thrust of the essay, expected now from those associated with the movement called Radical Orthodoxy, is that any proposed theory of truth must ultimately be rooted in God's own life. Trying to develop a notion of truth, or any other philosophical idea, apart from a divine source, as does modernity and as does a certain philosophically inspired theology, is to betray, in this particular case, the inner logic of Aquinas's own intentions and arguments.[43]

Pickstock begins by asserting that opponents of the correspondence theory of truth consistently argue that since we have access to the world only via our own determinate knowledge, it is impossible to verify the accuracy of such knowledge, that is, its "match" with the world, by means of a higher viewpoint. This is the position (the need for a "God's-eye view") that Lonergan derided as the naïve "super-look" encompassing both the looker and looked-at, failing to see that correspondence is, in actuality, a metaphysical deduction. Rahner, similarly, claimed that this primary objection to correspondence is largely derived from those failing to reflect on the nature of understanding itself, especially the dynamism of the intellect, which, in its constitution of the concrete sensible singular, the finite *individuum*, reveals its wider *Vorgriff* to absolute being. Pickstock, taking a different tack, claims that the major objection adduced against the correspondence theory is important and, indeed, "perhaps unanswerable."

Nonetheless, she staunchly picks up the gauntlet—not, however, on purely philosophical grounds (Pickstock, of course, would deny that such grounds are possible). Rather, she seeks to show that "things appear to us," that "states of affairs appear to be the case," on the basis of an interpretation of correspondence that is, unlike many modern formulations, highly theological. As she says, "Whereas for modern correspondence theory and some other theories . . . one first has a theory of truth and then might or might not apply it to theology, for Aquinas, truth is theological without remainder" (6). Thus, one discovers in Aquinas's thought "a defence of a realist theory of truth of a very extreme kind (for here one's mind corresponds to the ways things are at the very deepest level), against claims that truth reduces to whatever is the case according to convention or pragmatic motivation or phenomenal appearances" (6).

What is this correspondence theory that goes to the "very deepest level"? For Pickstock, there is continuity between the way things are in the material world and in the mind; however, this continuity is not simply a matter of our thoughts or judgments being "true to the facts." There is, rather, a dynamic aspect to truth so that, given the *ratio* or parallel that exists between the way things are in material substances and how they are in our minds, "our thought occasions a teleological realization of the formality of things and, in so doing, is itself brought to fruition" (8). This bringing to fruition occurs because, as she says, invoking Aquinas, truth is less properly in things than in the mind, in the judgment. This she interprets to mean that knowing concrete sensible singulars actually and dynamically brings them, and the knower, to their proper telos.

By way of example, Pickstock pictures a willow tree overhanging the river Cherwell: "Our knowing of it would be just as much an event in the life of the form 'tree' as the tree in its willowness and its growing. An idea of a tree, therefore, is not in any way a mere representation" (9). Here she tries to answer the primary objection to correspondence: "Its truth is not, as modern realism assumes, ever tested by a speculative comparison with the thing itself. Indeed, the very notion of a 'thing itself' is radically otherwise, for it is only 'itself' in its being conformed to the intellect of the knower. . . . Truth is not 'tested' in any way, but sounds itself or shines outwards in beauty" (9). The truth of correspondence, then, is never proven, since that would be impossible; it is, rather, simply displayed by means of an object's givenness to human intentionality.

Even though it is in the knowing that both the knower and the known are brought to fruition, Pickstock claims a thing is true when it fulfills its proper end, when "it is *copying God in its own manner*" (9). So, for example, a tree copies God when it is true to its treeness, rain when it is true to its rainness, and so on. A thing is truest when it is directed toward its proper telos because, in that instance, it is copying God and tending toward existence in the divine Mind. For Aquinas, Pickstock avers, "truth is primarily in the mind of God and only secondarily in things as copying

the Mind of God" (10). Consequently, Aquinas's realism and correspondence theory "is qualified by this subordination of all things to the divine
intellect" (10).

Of course, this interpretation is in accord with Radical Orthodoxy's
project of continuing what Milbank calls the "de Lubac revolution," that
is, of healing the grace/nature duality, a split between the natural and
supernatural orders, a rupture seminally located by the movement in the
work of Duns Scotus.[44] The "natural" order, employing "reason" alone,
apart from God, is a myth, and Pickstock argues that Aquinas knew it.
On the contrary, a proper Thomism, and a proper Thomistic theory of
truth, is an inherently theological matter. So she can say that truth in
Aquinas is such that he "seems to suggest that when one knows a thing,
one does not know that thing as it is by itself, but only insofar as one
meaningfully grasps it as imitating God" (10).[45] Thus, Pickstock wishes to
make clear that the Thomist theory of the *adaequatio* differs significantly
from other theories, especially contemporary ones, elaborated independently of God's intrinsic involvement in the cognitive process.

The marked emphasis in Pickstock's thought is on Aquinas's participationist ontology and its convertibility with a correspondence theory of
truth. This accent on the neoplatonic, and so Augustinian, dimensions of
Aquinas's philosophy was first brought to the fore by C. Fabro and L.
Geiger in the early 1940s (in relative opposition to the highly Aristotelian
interpretations of Gilson and Maritain) and is now, in Pickstock, creatively
applied to Aquinas's notion of truth. Her reasoning might be reconstructed as follows: All beings participate in *esse*, while God may be designated as *Ipsum Esse Subsistens*. Participating in *esse* is, in some sense, an
ontological imitation of an attribute possessed fully by God. Since being
and truth are convertible as transcendentals, one may say that "truth is also
a *property of all finite modes of being* insofar as they participate in God"
(11). When one knows truth, therefore, one always necessarily knows it as
imitating God. By way of example, a proper correspondence notion of
truth cannot simply say, "It is the case that this is a stone"; on the contrary,
one should say that this is a stone teleologically directed and so copying
God after its own manner. Or as Pickstock says, a tree "only exists at all—
as imitating the divine, what we receive in truth is a participation in the
divine" (12).[46] The knower should recognize that he or she knows the tree
and its analogical relationship to God "according to the mind's divine
inner light of divine illumination" (11). One may not, therefore, attribute
to Aquinas a notion of truth that is not always already in the one and only
"supernatural" order; one may not speak of a knower not already in this

same *unicus ordo supernaturalis*. Rather, the Augustinian note is here sounded loudly: To reason truly one must be already illumined by God, while revelation itself is but a higher measure of such illumination.

Of course, as with all of the earlier thinkers discussed, one need not agree with the unusual claims for the correspondence theory advanced by Pickstock and Milbank. In fact, many Thomists would disagree with the statement that the mind is divinely illuminated for Aquinas, or that Aquinas holds that the concrete sensible singular comes to ontological fruition in the very act of knowing.[47] Such criticism, however, is not the central point here. The point, rather, is that Radical Orthodoxy represents another significant theological movement defending realism and a correspondence notion of truth, uniquely interpreted, which has, at least as one aim, the logical undergirding of Christian doctrine.

Summary

We have examined several notions of truth seeking to defend the claim that there are continuously true propositions reflective of actual states of affairs and accessible to knowing subjects. Often enough, such ideas are placed at the service of theology's doctrinal claims. Rahner, for example, speaks of "true and indestructible" and "irrevocable" propositions. Lonergan invokes the "absolute realm" of truth. Avery Dulles says, "Historically and . . . providentially, Catholic faith has been linked with the metaphysical realism of classical thought, and has refined that realism in the light of revelation."[48] John Milbank and Catherine Pickstock state, "For while, certainly, human access to truth can only be time-bound, if truth has no connotations of the eternal and abiding, then it is hard to see why it is called truth at all."[49] These thinkers, then, appear to be at odds with those who take historicity as the ultimately determinative horizon of thought and who, therefore, defend practical, contingent notions of truth as alone ontologically appropriate. Of course, those defending realism and an abiding notion of truth agree with the assertion that truth is necessarily mediated in and through an intricate web of societal norms and historical-cultural flux. They insist equally, however, that any notion of truth that can adequately serve Christian doctrine, providing what the encyclical *Fides et ratio* called the *officium congruum*, cannot, at least ultimately, be phronetic or fallibilistic in kind, limiting itself to historical contingencies. Pragmatic, phronetic, and fallibilistic understandings of truth, at least seemingly, are born from nonfoundationalist constructions of human life and being that cannot sustain the kind of universal, materially identical, transgenerational, and enduringly referential truth proper to fundamental Christian doctrine.[50] Even from a purely philosophical point of view, L. Kolakowski claims:

> [Husserl's] unflagging pleas for Truth—spelled with upper case—in the face of the relativist corruption of European civilization went largely unheeded and this was not so because his arguments were necessarily faulty but rather because the prevailing cultural trends were going in another direction and eradicated . . . the belief in perennially valid standards of intellectual work, in the regulative ideal of *epistēmē* and finally in the very usefulness of the concept of truth.[51]

Kolakowski asserts that this trend, begun in the Enlightenment, has now reached its apogee in our times. Of course, it is not that truth today is considered useless; it is that determinate ideas of truth, especially those marked by realism or by insistence on perduring and universal dimensions, are often considered ontologically inappropriate and therefore candidates for replacement by truly apposite pragmatic and fallibilistic forms. Even if these notions are not always identical with Rorty's own claims, as indeed they surely are not, they merge closer to those of Rorty's heroes, such as Thomas Kuhn, who thinks that science "should not be thought of as moving toward an accurate representation of the way the world is in itself," or such as William James, who believes that the "true" is simply the "expedient in the way of believing."[52] These are the thinkers, Rorty says, who reject the Greek distinction "between the way things are in themselves and the relations which they have . . . to human needs and interests" (31). But such highly constructivist forms of truth appear themselves inappropriate for mediating Christian revelation and doctrine.

The defenses of metaphysical realism offered above are not, of course, unaware of absence at the heart of presence. While the thinkers discussed defend some form of realism and correspondence—and this, often enough, in service to enduring Christian doctrine—they are equally aware that doctrinal assertions offer no exhaustive claim to truth. To argue, therefore, that Christian teaching has a decided and definitive cognitive content capable of being known as enduringly true, must immediately be balanced by eschatological and apophatic dimensions that circumscribe the knowledge proper to revelation. A fuller exposition of this issue must wait until chapters seven and eight which discuss the nature of theological language. It should be noted even here, however, that such recognition is a theological commonplace. The International Theological Commission of the Roman Catholic Church has said, for example, "To be sure, we now recognize the truth only as in a mirror and in vague contours; only eschatologically will we see God face to face, as God is. Thus, our knowledge of truth exists in tension between the 'already' and the 'not yet'" (B I.1). As Gerhard Sauter states, "No dogma is formulated for all time or for eternity. If it could be, it would be a definite, i.e., final statement of truth, but that would anticipate the conclusive judgment of God."[53] Similarly, Pannenberg says, "The knowledge of Christian theology is always partial in comparison to the definitive revelation of God in the future of his kingdom (I Cor. 13.12). . . . Christians should not need to be taught this by modern reflection on the finitude of knowledge that goes with the historicity of experience."[54] Of course, it is hardly contemporary philosophical reflection that teaches this lesson to theology. At the height of nineteenth-century rationalism, Vatican I's dogmatic constitution on revelation, *Dei Filius*, thought it necessary to make this forceful and unambiguous statement: "The divine mysteries so exceed created human nature that even when these mysteries are given in revelation and received by faith they remain covered with the veil of faith itself and shrouded in darkness as long as in this mortal life 'we journey to the Lord, for we walk by faith and not by sight' (2 Cor. 5.6, ff)."[55] So when E. Levinas, in his critique of Husserl, claims that theoretical consciousness does not and cannot envelop the given, this is certainly true, at least theologically speaking, when applied to God and revelation. This is surely how Karl Barth should be understood when he says, "The dogma after which dogmatics inquires is not the truth of revelation, but it is on the way to the truth of revelation. . . . [Dogmas] are propositions which grasp and reproduce the truth of revelation only as far as they strive towards it."[56]

The point here is simply that the Christian tradition is well aware that one should not confuse the truth mediated by doctrine, its actual cognitive content, its mediation of states of affairs, with a search for a complete and exhaustive apodicticity, with an Enlightenment positivism, or even with an inability to recognize that only in the heavenly Jerusalem will the ultimate truth of revelation become entirely clear to us.

Conclusion

For many contemporary thinkers, realism and the correspondence theory of truth, with their emphasis on *die Sache selbst* and *Ansichsein*, on enduring and stable presence, cannot be maintained in light of human finitude, sociocultural specificity, linguistic conventionality, and contextualized and embedded rationality. Heidegger and Wittgenstein exposed these philosophical horizons, and they have been intensified and expanded by postmodern reflection. In light of these newly presenced dimensions, the contemporary task is to develop notions of rationality and truth consistent with our socially constructed and historical natures, with our finitude and contingency. From this starting point, nonfoundationalist thinkers, while eschewing relativism, have explored the pragmatic and phronetic understandings of truth emerging from Peirce's community of inquirers, James's coherent, ethical pragmatism, Gadamer's universalization of *phronēsis*, and the ideal-speech situation of Habermas's communicative praxis. Only these notions of truth and rationality are now "ontologically appropriate," that is, consistent with the philosophically constitutive horizons exposed by the seminal thinkers of historicity and culture.

The problem with these understandings, in my judgment, is that Christian doctrine makes cognitive claims that are intended to be universally and, in a certain sense, conclusively true.[57] Insofar as doctrine is the linguistic articulation of revelation, of God's determinate self-manifestation to us, it is a reflection of the *locutio Dei* that is in some substantive manner continuous, identical, and universal. This perpetuity, of course, must be clearly and unambiguously nuanced by a variety of theological qualifications, but it unmistakably contains an element of stability and unchangeability—and is classically denominated as the *depositum fidei*. Christian doctrine, therefore, needs a notion of truth that can support some measure of realism and referentialism, as well as one that can support normative and even perpetual claims. This is what is ultimately behind the theological use of "adequation" and "correspondence." Phronetic notions of truth, on the contrary, do not appear able to provide logical support for such assertions without betraying their own understanding of ontological and veridical appropriateness.[58]

In order to illustrate the issue at hand, let us take, by way of example, the Nicene claim that Jesus is the incarnate Son of God, *homoousion* with the Father. For the historic and orthodox Christian faith, this assertion is universally and enduringly true, mediating an actual state of affairs. Emphasis here is placed on the substantial and material continuity of God's revelatory Word. The truth stated is not warranted simply by consensus nor by its continuing "claim" in history; neither is it open to fallibilistic reversibility.[59] The ability of such a statement to mediate the "world," whatever one may add about its ultimately eschatological incompleteness, is not called into question. But how would such a statement, definitively taught by Nicea, be understood by phronetic thought? For those championing *phronēsis*, the truth mediated by revelation and doctrine would not be, as in the example given, one that perdures substantially through generations and cultures. It would, rather, be more epiphanically conceived, resonant with the dialectic of absence and presence, of veiling and unveiling. The truth emerging from revelation is not, then, enduringly descriptive and "representational." It may offer insight, yes, but that insight always appears in the moment of the historical flux; it cannot stake a permanent claim to normativity. The truth of Christian doctrine may perdure, but the perdurance is more formal than material in kind. Jesus of Nazareth may indeed still make a claim on men and women, and humanity may continue to receive flashes of insight and glimmers of presence regarding his truth. One would be entirely mistaken, however, to insist on the continuing identity and perduring truth of one particular way of understanding who Christ is. The truth about Jesus is "given" in one way to the ancient world and another way today. Different understandings reveal themselves successively over time. This is required by the very nature of historical contingency. In Heideggerian terms, it is part of the givenness of Being, the series of messages, *Seinsgeschicke*, which, in the West at least, began with Anaximander. The different understandings that emerge are not simply the result of fresh approaches, new perspectives, or complementary points of view. Rather, these new understandings are occasioned by honestly accepting the deeply lethic and apophatic dimensions of historicity, finitude, and sociocultural specificity. This is what it means to say that truth is an Event wherein Being manifests itself by both revealing and concealing. So traditional Christian doctrine about Jesus cannot be taken as normative in the sense that it, in some final and conclusive way, mediates the truth about Christ, and so about God. It is true that these doctrines may still make an enduring claim on us, may even still garner a consensus. But the truth of the doctrine is not irreversible, nor does it preclude other possible construals, even contradictory ones.

Nonfoundationalist thinkers, once again, do not intend to construct a tower of Babel, an unintelligible polyglotism. But they do think that only notions of rationality and truth that fully respect the enveloping tide of contingency, finitude, and cultural immersion can honestly avoid inappropriate and now unmasked foundationalist ontologies. A phronetic construal of truth requires contingent and fallibilistic models because such truth, by its very nature, deals with what Aristotle called *endechomena*, matters admitting of being otherwise.

One theological representative of this position, Mark Cladis, calls for a "mild-mannered pragmatism" that "rejects metaphysical foundationalism . . . but . . . aims for truthfulness."[60] For Cladis, theology needs to embrace finitude and to avoid foundations and methods, while concomitantly prizing rationality itself (20). Of course, the rationality so prized is that of practical, fully historicized reason. In his most revelatory sentence, the author asserts, "In sum the sectarian knows from the start the outcome of Augustine's *faith seeking understanding*. Faith will be vindicated. The mild-mannered theological pragmatist, in contrast, must wait and see" (32). The problem with Cladis's position is that it accepts a particular notion of finitude, excises metaphysics of any kind, limits itself necessarily to a phronetic understanding of truth and then—revealingly but logically—cannot assert that the claims of Christian revelation and doctrine will be vindicated. The tides of historicity and contingency need first be served.[61] At a particular moment, faith may illuminate one's existential and historical situation, but faith cannot make universal and abiding cognitive claims; to do so is to be "sectarian." Traditional themes, such as a subsisting *depositum fidei*, must necessarily disappear from this point of view. Of course, it is precisely the pragmatic notion of truth here advanced that appears finally unacceptable, for it cannot sustain logically the Christian understanding of revelation and doctrine as that which remains, substantially the same, throughout generations and cultures.

This is not to say, of course, that theology can learn nothing from a nonfoundationalist construal of truth and rationality. The contrary is, in fact, undeniably the case. Gadamer's emphasis on the importance of tradition as well as his unmasking of Enlightenment claims of a "neutral" subject is entirely welcome. Kuhn can be thanked, once again, for his accent on the culturally constituted paradigms that are operative in all human thought. Habermas has shown the dangers of ideology and the continuing significance of a warranted and validated consensus. All of these positions have something to contribute to a notion of truth capable of sustaining Christian doctrine. They have helped to undermine a worldless Cartesianism and an Enlightenment apodicticism; they have assisted in the development of a postpositivist understanding of theology, philosophy, and science. In their accent on the constructive and contextual dimensions of knowing, they have helped theology overcome a naïve realism and a wooden conceptualism. And in their championing of historicity's effects, they have aided theology in its understanding of conceptual mutability and its consequent sanctioning of a complementary pluralism. In turn, this welcoming of a wide variety of formulations and perspectives has become an essential cornerstone of contemporary ecumenical agreement.

On the other hand, any notion of rationality that ultimately deconstructs the idea of truth as some kind of realistic, disclosive correspondence, or that fails to sustain the idea of perduring, continuous, and transcultural truth cannot, it seems, serve as a suitable vessel for Christian doctrine. This is the case because Christianity holds that certain teachings constitute irreversible cognitive claims, normative states of affairs with selfsame meanings that are at antipodes with the kind of philosophical contingency supported by the phronetic trajectory. The truth mediated by Christian doctrine is not simply the reversible truth of time and history. To so conceive of it is to understand doctrinal claims as highly constructivist in kind, leading ultimately to an understanding of revelation and doctrine that is doxological but nonreferential or fallibilistic and so contingent—which, of course, is to conceive of it very differently from the tradition heretofore. As Lonergan said in his defense of realism against Dewart, "It seems of the essence of Dewart's prolegomenon to exclude the correspondence view of truth. Such an exclusion is as destructive of the dogmas as it is of Dewart's own statements. To deny the correspondence view of truth is to deny that, when the meaning is true, the meant is what is so. Either denial is destructive of dogmas."[62] This is why theologians such as Lonergan, Rahner, and Pannenberg continue to defend some form of correspondence. It is why thinkers such as Sokolowski, Pickstock, and Milbank are not seeking fundamentally new forms of rationality but hope, rather, to creatively rethink realistic and abidingly referential notions of truth.

Christian faith and foundational doctrine serve, ultimately, as an Archimedean point, a decisive matrix for theology. And Christian theologians have defended realism and correspondence, along with some notion of perduring truth, not because faith was unconsciously imprisoned by Aristotelianism or because it was a victim of *Dasein's Vergessenheit*. Theologians have enlisted a certain type of realism precisely because they believe it essential for defending Christianity's understanding of revelation and doctrine as having a definitive content and as exhibiting determinate characteristics. Of course, these same thinkers have sought to shade and nuance this defense so that a leaden objectivism is surpassed. One thinks of Newman's emphasis on notional and inferential knowledge, of Marcel's attempt to incorporate existentialism and phenomenology, of the Kantian dialogues of Rousselot and Maréchal. This trend continues with theologians such as Pannenberg, Rahner, and

Lonergan, with their qualified interest in Kant, Hegel, and Heidegger—and with Milbank and Pickstock's marriage of traditional realism with postmodern concerns. In the last analysis, Christian theologians have judged through the centuries that some notion of metaphysical realism is essential for preserving the idea that God has manifested himself to his people and that the church has some enduring and abiding knowledge of the salvific acts of the triune God.

It is precisely because revelation and doctrine need a notion of truth that perdures across generations and cultures, that mediates something of God's inner life, that is able to sustain, at least in certain instances, a conclusive finality, that a particular notion of truth is required.[63] Nonfoundationalist construals of truth are only partially suitable as philosophical warrants for Christian faith because they are, at least ultimately, unable to maintain this understanding. There may exist, then, only two options for Christian theologians on the truth question: (1) to adopt the new notions of truth and phronetic rationality that have emerged, thereby supporting a largely historicized understanding of fundamental Christian doctrine, or (2) to say that essential Christian claims are, in fact, mediative (of course not exhaustively so) of states of affairs, normatively, enduringly, and conclusively displaying something of God's own life and being.

The theme of the first and second chapters was that the Christian notion of revelation and doctrine requires some type of first philosophy to properly sustain and explicate the notion of perduring and continual presence purported by its claims. The theme of the last two chapters has been that this same notion of revelation and doctrine requires a certain understanding of truth that, once again, may sustain the abiding and universal affirmations of Christian faith. The next chapter will be concerned with the kind of hermeneutical theory proper to Christian claims. I will argue that only a particular range of hermeneutical theories, those which allow for material continuity with the intended meanings of the prior tradition, is ultimately suitable for sustaining Christian faith and doctrine.

Notes

1. At the same time, one does well to take account of John Haldane's assertion regarding the encyclical's endorsement of realism: "Quite generally, much more work needs to be done on the issue of the range of tolerable 'realisms' and none of us can afford to be triumphant about the 'tradition' or dismissive of other's ways of going on." Haldane, "The Diversity of Philosophy and the Unity of Its Vocation: Some Philosophical Reflections on *Fides et ratio*," in *Fides et Ratio: The Notre Dame Symposium 1999* (ed. Timothy Smith; Notre Dame, Ind.: St. Augustine's Press, 2001).

2. Needless to add, the representationalism proper to knowledge of created realities is essentially different from that proper to theology, which is never, in Heideggerian terms, *Vorhandenheit* in nature. The apophatic and analogical nature of theological language, which will be treated in chapter eight, is built upon just this premise.

3. At the same time, Aquinas's important statement should be clearly invoked: We cannot grasp what God is, but only what he is not and how other things are related to him (*SCG*, I, 30). Even if this classic text, omitted from the encyclical, refers to our inability to know God quidditatively, it reminds us of Aquinas's own profound apophaticism and the danger of naïve representationalism.

4. One wonders, for example, whether the encyclical would not have been strengthened had it observed, as Louis Dupré does, that while correspondence should certainly not be rejected, speaking about truth as "disclosure" serves to protect the truly religious nature of truth while standing at some distance from the subjectivism of modernity. See Dupré, *Religious Mystery and Rational Reflection* (Grand Rapids: Eerdmans, 1998), 19–40. At one point, the encyclical does try to place the truth question in a wider context (see nos. 28–34), but its observations remain mostly at the level of adumbration.

5. M. Blondel and J. Maréchal, two thinkers who knew the tradition well and yet sought to incorporate the "fundamental achievements of modern and contemporary thought" (no. 85), were not mentioned in the encyclical. One reason for this may well be the document's relative disinterest in the subjective dimensions of noetic acts. *Fides et ratio* speaks pejoratively of an "immanentist habit of mind" (no. 15), but the immanentism (no. 91) and phenomenalism characteristic of Kant can hardly be predicated of either Blondel or Maréchal. Henrici's claim that the encyclical does not wish to bind thinkers strictly to Blondel (or to anyone else) as *Aeterni Patris* had bound them to Aquinas appears entirely too benign an interpretation. Henrici, "The One Who Went Unnamed: Maurice Blondel in the Encyclical *Fides et ratio,*" *Communio* 26 (Fall 1999): 620–21. While Blondel is implicitly endorsed when the document applauds those who produced philosophies "starting with an analysis of immanence" (no. 59), one nonetheless wonders if Garrigou-Lagrange's charge that Blondel understood truth as nothing more than an *adaequatio vitae et mentis* rather than a true correspondence finds a certain resonance in the encyclical. As for Maréchal, one may well take note of Balthasar's claim in 1946: "The methodology carried out by Joseph Maréchal can be adduced as the most perfect example of such a clarifying transposition [spoils from Egypt] in the present age. . . . Kant has never been understood more deeply and thoroughly by a Catholic philosophy—understood and at the same time applied and overcome." "On the Tasks of Catholic Philosophy in Our Time," *Communio* 20 (Spring 1993): 161.

6. Walter Kasper, *Theology and Church* (trans. Margaret Kohn; New York: Crossroad, 1989), 95–96.

7. Walter Kasper, "Das Wahrheitverständnis der Theologie," in *Wahrheit in Einheit und Vielheit* (ed. E. Coreth; Düsseldorf: Patmos Verlag, 1987), 175.

8. Walter Kasper, *The Church and Contemporary Pluralism* (New York: National Pastoral Life Center, 2002), 9.

9. Ibid., 11, 13. Later in this essay Kasper goes on to claim, rightly, that the Christian claim to universal truth is intrinsically linked to the belief that all men and women are free, that no one is obliged to believe: "Christianity's claim of absoluteness—rightly understood—is then not totalitarian, but on the contrary it is radically anti-totalitarian" (18).

10. See John D. Caputo, "Metanoetics: Elements of a Postmodern Christian Philosophy," in *The Question of Christian Philosophy Today* (ed. Francis J. Ambrosio; New York: Fordham University Press, 1999), 192 n. 5. It is certainly true that Dewart's book was

one of the first Catholic attempts to argue for "God without Being." See Leslie Dewart, *The Future of Belief* (New York: Herder & Herder, 1966).

11. Bernard Lonergan, "The Dehellenization of Dogma," in *The Future of Belief Debate* (ed. Gregory Baum; New York: Herder & Herder, 1967), 72. Citations in the text are from this essay. The same article may be found in Bernard Lonergan, *A Second Collection* (ed. William F. Ryan and Bernard J. Tyrrell; Philadelphia: Westminster, 1974), 11–32.

12. Lonergan outlines here the rather frequent misconstrual of what the correspondence theory holds. This need for a "super-look" is precisely how Kuhn understands correspondence and is the central reason he opposes it.

13. Bernard Lonergan, *Doctrinal Pluralism* (Milwaukee: Marquette University Press, 1971), 44, 53. He repeats much the same claim the following year when he says that dogmas are permanent because they have been revealed; consequently, our understanding of them is to be *"eodem sensu eademque sententia"* with previous understandings. Bernard Lonergan, *Method in Theology* (New York: Herder & Herder, 1972), 352.

14. Lonergan, *Method in Theology*, 349.

15. Ibid., 349. For Aquinas on this point, see *ST* I, a. 8, ad 2.

16. Bernard Lonergan, "The Subject," in Ryan and Tyrrell, eds., *Second Collection*, 70. Further citations in the text will refer to this essay. The essay may also be found in Lonergan, *The Subject* (Milwaukee: Marquette University Press, 1968).

17. For an excellent study of Lonergan's "foundationalist" inclinations and their relationship to his understanding of truth, see Ulf Jonsson, *Foundations for Knowing God* (Frankfurt: Peter Lang, 1999).

18. Karl Rahner, "Basic Observations on the Subject of Changeable and Unchangeable Factors in the Church," in *Theological Investigations*, vol. 14 (trans. David Bourke; New York: Seabury, 1976), 11 (emphasis added).

19. Ibid., 13. Some of these examples also help explain Rahner's hermeneutical theory, which will be more fully examined in chapter six.

20. Karl Rahner, "Does the Church Offer Any Ultimate Certainties?" in *Theological Investigations*, vol. 14 (trans. David Bourke; New York: Seabury, 1976), 53 (emphasis added).

21. Ibid., 57, 62–63.

22. Ibid., 55 (emphasis added).

23. Karl Rahner, "The Faith of the Christian and the Doctrine of the Church," in *Theological Investigations* 14:40–41.

24. Rahner, "Does the Church Offer Any Ultimate Certainties?" 63–64.

25. For a recent insightful exposition of the meaning of these works, see Brian Shanley, *The Thomist Tradition* (Dordrecht: Kluwer Academic Publishers, 2002), 166–78. See also Gerald McCool, *From Unity to Pluralism* (New York: Fordham University Press, 1989).

26. Jack Bonsor, *Rahner, Heidegger, and Truth* (Lanham, Md.: University Press of America, 1987), 49. Bonsor's fine work treats of Rahner's notion of truth *in toto*, but with particular attention to Heidegger's influence.

27. Karl Rahner, "Thomas Aquinas on Truth," in *Theological Investigations*, vol. 13 (trans. David Bourke; New York: Crossroad, 1983), 13–31. Further citations in the text will refer to this essay.

28. For Gilson's 1939 manifesto against "critical Thomism," see Etienne Gilson, *Thomist Realism and the Critique of Knowledge* (trans. Mark Wauck; San Francisco: Ignatius, 1986). For Fergus Kerr on Rahner, see Kerr, *Theology after Wittgenstein* (Oxford: Blackwell, 1986), 14.

29. Wolfhart Pannenberg, *Systematic Theology*, vol. 1 (trans. Geoffrey Bromiley; Grand Rapids: Eerdmans, 1991), 7. Further citations in the text will refer to this work.

30. Pannenberg also expresses the hope that "reception" by the whole body of Christian believers as a necessary indication of doctrinal consensus is not ruled out by the well-known claim of Vatican I that certain teachings made by the papal magisterium are valid and inalterable *ex sese non autem ex consensu Ecclesiae* (Denzinger-Hünermann 3074). At the same time, he notes that "consensus" alone cannot serve "on its own as an adequate criterion of the truth of doctrine." The reason for this, Pannenberg notes, is that "the consensus theory of the truth of dogma shares the weakness of a consensus theory of truth in general" (Pannenberg, *Systematic Theology*, 12). His objections to consensus will be noted later.

31. Pannenberg agrees here with A. Beckermann, who notes that Habermas "still has to have recourse to the idea of 'competent' judgment to be able to distinguish an objective from a purely conventional consensus" (12, note 19).

32. Of course, the ultimate problem with Habermas, not pointed out fully by Pannenberg, is not that he fails to recognize that even a universal consensus may be simple conventionality. This requires only a fallibilistic approach, which Habermas surely countenances. The problem is that he explicitly rejects any realist understanding of the correspondence view of truth and cannot, therefore, with the use of the nonfoundationalist, Deweyan "warranted assertibility" he accepts, sustain central elements of Christian faith and belief.

33. See Wolfhart Pannenberg, *Basic Questions in Theology*, vol. 1, trans. George Kehn (Philadelphia: Fortress Press, 1970), 182–210. For more on Pannenberg and analogy, see chapter eight.

34. Leslek Kolakowski, "A Remark on Our Relative Relativism," in Niznik and Sanders, *Debating the State of Philosophy*, 73.

35. Robert Sokolowski, *Introduction to Phenomenology* (Cambridge: Cambridge University Press, 2000). Citations in the text are from this work.

36. Of course, truth as disclosure is normally connected with Heidegger and his discussion of "disclosive" as opposed to "correspondence" truth in *Being and Time*, no. 44, and in his essay "On the Essence of Truth," in *Basic Writings* (ed. David Farrell Krell; San Francisco: HarperSanFrancisco, 1993), 115–38. Heidegger argues that truth needs to be understood as disclosive; it is the fundamental relationship between human beings and the world in which they live. This open comportment to the disclosiveness of beings is, of course, a fundamental insight of phenomenology, especially when viewed against the neo-Kantian horizon of a priori transcendental categories. Sokolowski uses disclosure in the sense spoken of by Heidegger, but without the polemic against a correspondence view of truth that is found in Heidegger's work.

37. As Robyn Horner appositely observes, "For Husserl, as for Brentano before him, 'intentionality' refers to the relationship between consciousness and object. Consciousness is always consciousness of something." Horner, *Rethinking God as Gift* (New York: Fordham University Press, 2001), 46.

38. Sokolowski's comments on such themes may be found, for example, in Robert Sokolowski, *Husserlian Meditations* (Evanston, Ill.: Northwestern University Press, 1974).

39. I have already noted in chapter two that many of Husserl's early disciples, such as Scheler, Stein, and Reinach, found Husserl's later transcendental interests to be at odds with the clear realism of his earlier work. On this score see Robert Sokolowski, "Phenomenology in the Last Hundred Years," in *One Hundred Years of Philosophy* (ed. Brian Shanley; Washington, D.C.: Catholic University of America Press, 2001), 202–15, esp. 204.

40. Robert Sokolowski, *Introduction to Phenomenology* (Cambridge: Cambridge University Press, 2000), 216. Very similarly, Sokolowski had earlier written about philosophy's problems: "The central confusion philosophy must handle is the rejection, in principle, of the truthfulness of ordinary perceptions and common sense. The claim is made

that the manifest world must give way to the idealized or constructed world of science in matters of truth and being." Husserl's intention was to oppose this kind of "double-world." Sokolowski, *Husserlian Meditations*, 268.

41. Sokolowski, "Phenomenology in the Last Hundred Years," 207. In an essay written in 1940, Karl Rahner wrote that in *Being and Time* Heidegger, under the continuing influence of Husserl, understood that "the question of laying a foundation for the existence of an external reality always comes too late and, in short, constitutes a philosophical pseudo-problem. Man is not first a 'closed' subject who . . . would somehow have to force his way clear . . . and thus gain access to an 'external world.'" Rahner, "The Concept of Existential Philosophy in Heidegger," *Philosophy Today* 13 (1969): 132.

42. John Milbank and Catherine Pickstock, *Truth in Aquinas* (London: Routledge, 2001). Page numbers cited in the text will refer to this work.

43. As Milbank says, Radical Orthodoxy "allows for no entirely autonomous realms of secular discourse (even where these do not directly concern God or redemption)." John Milbank, "The Programme of Radical Orthodoxy," in *Radical Orthodoxy?—A Catholic Enquiry* (ed. Laurence Paul Hemming; Aldershot: Ashgate, 2000), 34.

44. For de Lubac, see John Milbank, "Truth and Vision," in Milbank and Pickstock, *Truth in Aquinas*, 38. For the claim that Scotus is the *fons et origo* of the reason/revelation, nature/grace split, see, inter alia, John Milbank, "The Theological Critique of Philosophy in Hamann and Jacobi," in *Radical Orthodoxy* (ed. John Milbank, Catherine Pickstock, and Graham Ward; London: Routledge, 1999).

45. Pickstock is arguing here that when one cognitively grasps an object, one grasps it simultaneously (on the basis of participation) as imitating God. While this is certainly at a remove from Rahner's transcendental theology, one may surely see resonances here with Rahner's claim that one can only grasp the concrete sensible singular insofar as one athematically and concomitantly affirms the Infinite horizon of Being. Of course, Pickstock (and Milbank) have little use for Rahner's transcendental starting point. So, for example, in this same volume, *Truth in Aquinas*, while Milbank cheers the work of Blondel and de Lubac, he regards Rahner's project as "very flawed" (123 n. 75). But Rahner, like Maréchal, used transcendental terminology to overcome the rationalism of modernity (using Heidegger's *existenzialen* to the same purpose). Further, Rahner's influence in overcoming theological rationalism—and in the process the dualities of Enlightenment modernity—was unparalleled in modern Roman Catholic theology. It should also not be forgotten that de Lubac, despite differences in language, saw his own project as tacking close to that of Rahner. See Henri de Lubac, *A Brief Catechesis on Nature and Grace* (trans. Br. Richard Arnandez; San Francisco: Ignatius, 1984), 25 n. 31.

Perhaps a better Thomistic predecessor for Radical Orthodoxy's attempt at emphasizing cognitive dynamism, that in knowing things one also grasps something of God, is Dominick De Petter, the Dutch Thomist who, like Maréchal, was dissatisfied with interpretations of Aquinas that were overly conceptual and representational and who argued, instead, for a nonconceptual dynamism toward the Absolute. He spoke not of transcendental subjectivity but of an implicit intuition of the Infinite found in the knowledge of the real. This more phenomenologically based dynamic intuition of the Infinite affirmed concomitantly in the knowledge of things is not exactly what Pickstock is arguing for here, but there are similarities nonetheless. For a good summary of De Petter, see Shanley, *Thomist Tradition*, 15–16; and Hill, *Knowing the Unknown God*, 89.

46. Along the same lines, Pickstock concludes, "This means that rather than correspondence being guaranteed in its measuring of the given . . . it is guaranteed by its conformation to the divine source of the given." C. Pickstock, "Truth and Consequences," in *Truth in Aquinas*, 18.

47. For a review that points out some of the classical Thomistic difficulties with Pickstock's thesis, see Adrian Pabst, *Revue thomiste* 101 (2001): 475–79.

48. Avery Dulles, *The Craft of Theology* (New York: Crossroad, 1992), 133.

49. Milbank and Pickstock, *Truth in Aquinas*, xii.

50. Precisely because of these characteristics, Adolf von Harnack stated that infallibility is essential to dogma: "A dogma without infallibility means nothing. This was already settled by Luther's position at the Leipzig Disputation, although Luther himself never fully realized the implications of his assertions. . . . This is why already in the first edition of my *History of Dogma* I set the fall of dogma in the sixteenth century." "Erik Peterson's Correspondence with Adolf von Harnack," trans. Michael J. Hollerich, *Pro Ecclesia* 2 (1993): 337. Harnack clearly recognizes here that without the church's ability to know truth infallibly, dogma always consists of practical reason's *endechomena*, "reversible matters." Harnack's criticism of Luther, however, is largely misplaced. Luther moved the locus of infallibility from pope and councils to the Scriptures themselves (and those councils clearly reflective of Scripture). He hardly denied that the truth of revelation could be known infallibly. The precise locus of knowing infallibly, however, is not the issue here. The issue is that for virtually all Christians, truth can be decisively, even infallibly, known.

51. Kolakowski, "Remark on Our Relative Relativism," 69.

52. Rorty, "Challenge of Relativism," 31. As Rorty says a bit later, the word "relativist" or even "social constructionist" should not be permitted since it allows the terms of the "Platonists," or metaphysicians, to set the debate (33–34).

53. See ITC, "On the Interpretation of Dogmas," 5; and Gerhard Sauter, *Gateways to Dogmatics* (trans. G. Bromiley; Grand Rapids: Eerdmans, 2002), 41.

54. Pannenberg, *Systematic Theology*, 1:55.

55. DH 3016. It is worth reading J. Franzelin's theological *votum* (an opinion written for the council) where he resurrects Eunomius, the opponent of Gregory of Nazienzen, as the predecessor of modern rationalism. For a summary of Franzelin's essay, see Thomas Guarino, "Vincent of Lerins and the Hermeneutical Question," *Gregorianum* 75 (1994): 491–523.

56. Karl Barth, *Church Dogmatics* I/1, *The Doctrine of the Word of God* (trans. G. T. Thomson; Edinburgh: T&T Clark, 1949), 307. For this reason, Barth was fond of Aquinas's definition of the *articulus fidei* as "*perceptio divinae veritatis tendens in ipsam*" (*ST* II-II, q. 1, a. 6). It is precisely, of course, the "*tendens*" that appeals to Barth because of its eschatological nature.

57. As W. Norris Clarke says, Christian revelation "presupposes the truth, the same truth, is universally accessible to all human beings, across all boundaries of culture and time and that this same universal truth can be faithfully expressed, with sufficient effort, in many different languages." Clarke, "John Paul II: The Complementarity of Faith and Philosophy in the Search for Truth," *Communio* 26 (1999): 557–70. Roger Haight notes, to the contrary, "The very claim for the existence of a universal truth has become associated with a narrow, sectarian outlook." Haight, *Jesus, Symbol of God* (Maryknoll, N.Y.: Orbis, 2000), 188.

58. I wish to be clear that *phronēsis* does have an important role in theology, especially with regard to the making of particular moral judgments and the complexus of contingent elements involved in coming to the act of faith. John Henry Newman, for one, clearly exploited phronetical thinking in his elaboration of the illative sense, especially as this is found in his *Grammar of Assent* (London: Longmans, 1985). But the scriptural and ecclesial judgments represented by certain doctrines attain a dimension of finality and irreversibility that, at least in some aspects, surpass the historical contingency necessarily attaching to phronetical notions of truth.

59. Fallibilistic "reversibility" is not possible here because the denial of Jesus Christ as the incarnate Word of God is not admissible. On the other hand, a qualified fallibilism is always endorsable if one means by this that every statement requires further thought and elucidation, that every assertion is open to reconceptualization and reformulation, and that no statement comprehensively exhausts truth, much less divine truth.

60. Mark Cladis, "Mild-Mannered Pragmatism and Religious Truth," *Journal of the American Academy of Religion* 60 (Spring 1992): 19–33. Page numbers cited refer to this article.

61. I point out later in this book that Aquinas himself holds that faith cannot be repugnant to reason—and John Paul II, in the encyclical *Fides et ratio*, strongly defends the legitimate autonomy of philosophy. In this case, however, the author appears to be first committed to the results of reason's investigations rather than to the affirmations of Scripture and tradition. The proper correlation between faith and reason will become clearer in chapter ten.

62. Lonergan, "Dehellenization of Dogma," 74. S.-T. Bonino makes the same point when he says that the theological implications of the debate on the nature of truth are immediate: "yes or no—the act of faith, by and through dogmatic statements, does it attain the Real?" See "Avant-propos," *Revue thomiste* 104 (2004): 6.

63. It is not surprising, then, to find Avery Dulles stating that "for the sake of progress, the Church needs a relatively stable philosophical tradition," approvingly noting the claim of the encyclical *Humani generis* (1950) that Christianity needs a philosophy that safeguards "the mind's ability to attain certain and unchangeable truth." Dulles, "Is Neo-Thomism Obsolete?—Vatican II and Scholasticism," *New Oxford Review* 57 (May 1990): 8.

CHAPTER 5

Interpretation and the Nature of Christian Doctrine

Hermeneutics and Christian Faith

Chapters three and four argued that Christian doctrine required a particular notion of truth, one that allowed for both ostensive and representational dimensions and that could logically sustain the continuous and abiding content of certain affirmations of faith. Consequently, only a qualified use of the nonfoundationalist notions of truth and rationality, as developed in some quarters of contemporary philosophy, is possible. This chapter, concerned chiefly with the hermeneutics of doctrine, will argue that Christian claims, held as universally, normatively, and transculturally true, require not only a particular notion of truth but also a determinate understanding of interpretation, a specific hermeneutical theory. This thesis will be largely discussed in dialogue with the philosophically and theologically influential approach outlined by Hans-Georg Gadamer.

Selected Church Documents

As with earlier chapters, it is important to recall, once again, the understanding of revelation and doctrine that has been traditionally advanced. *Dei Verbum*, Vatican II's Dogmatic Constitution on Revelation, states clearly, "Through divine revelation, God chose to show forth and communicate himself and the eternal decisions of his will" and "God has seen to it that what he had revealed for the salvation of all nations would abide perpetually in its full integrity and be handed on to all generations" (art. 7). The council's marked emphasis on the enduring truth and normativity of revelation has been echoed repeatedly by many other official ecclesial documents. For example, the recent declaration on the salvific universality of Jesus Christ, *Dominus Iesus*, issued by the Roman Catholic Church's Congregation for the Doctrine of the Faith, is replete with affirmations concerning the universality and conclusive nature of revealed truth.[1] Another such statement is John Paul II's encyclical *Fides et ratio*, wherein the pope speaks of the "universal validity" of the contents of faith, of "certain and unchanging doctrine," and of the "unchanging truth of God." The document also warns against the danger of historicism, whereby "the enduring validity of truth is denied. What was true in one period . . . may not be true in another." This last reference, of course, is directed against the position that what the church has taught as essentially true in the past has now fundamentally changed or may be understood in a quite different manner.[2] This is the point of the encyclical's explicit assertion about interpretative theory that while current developments in hermeneutics are often helpful, some theorists "tend to stop short at the question of how reality is understood and expressed, without going further to see whether reason can discover its essence" (no. 84). It worries that such positions "tend to obscure the contents of faith or to deny their universal validity" and in so doing "disqualify themselves" as possible helps for illuminating Christian truth.

Of course, *Fides et ratio* certainly presents us with neither a clear examination of hermeneutical theories, nor with the philosophical positions underlying them. However, it does recognize that several current interpretative approaches have difficulty sustaining the universal and normative contents characteristic of Christian faith and doctrine. This is why the same encyclical states that "dogmatic statements, while reflecting at times the culture of the period in which they were defined, formulate an unchanging and ultimate truth." Since the claims of historicism are unable to express the "absoluteness and the universality of truth," what is needed is a "hermeneutic open to the appeal of metaphysics" (no. 95). Two points need to be made here: (1) the encyclical recognizes that one must ultimately reconcile the sociocultural limitations of particular formulations with the universality of truth, and (2) an appropriate hermeneutical theory must be able to employ metaphysics, at least in some broad and commodious sense. Both of these crucial issues will be addressed later. For the moment, it is enough to say that the encyclical clearly thinks that certain affirmations central to the belief of the Christian church endure as universally normative.

A final useful statement to peruse is, once again, that issued in 1989 by the International Theological Commission of the Roman Catholic Church entitled "On the Interpretation of Dogmas." The very title indicates that hermeneutics will be a central concern of the document. In fact, the declaration turns out to be carefully attuned to central contemporary issues, hoping to avoid in the interpretative process both anarchic relativism and woodenheaded dogmatism. Like *Fides et ratio* and innumerable other ecclesial pronouncements, this statement affirms the traditional emphasis on the perduring and normative truth of Christian doctrine. For example: "Theology proceeds from the conviction of faith according to which (a) . . . dogmas that are transmitted therein validly express the truth revealed by God in the old and new covenant and (b) the truth of revelation transmitted in the *paradosis* of the church is universally valid and unchangeable in substance (A.II.1)."[3] Further: "The one historically revealed Gospel . . . is valid for all peoples and eras" (A.I.4). In a statement replete with implications for hermeneutical theory, the commission observes that while development of dogma certainly takes place, "the development occurs within the same sense and meaning (*eodem sensu eademque sententia*). Thus, the council [Vatican I] taught that in the case of dogmas, the meaning must be continually adhered to which was once set forth by the church" (B.II.1).[4] At the same time, the commission is well aware that its accent on doctrinal objectivity and universality must necessarily be balanced with the fact that all truth comes to language only within history. The declaration, therefore, identifies the proper relationship between history and truth as one of the principal issues facing contemporary theological thought. Prior to addressing the commission's attempt to come to terms with that issue, however, it is worth examining some earlier theological ventures that hoped to reconcile the universality of truth with the limitations imposed by human finitude, by the cultural-linguistic webs within which all thinking is necessarily accomplished.

Background

The Christian church first came up against the question of history and truth in a significant way during the Enlightenment. The Reformation had issued a vigorous protest against a lifeless and often bastardized Scholasticism that had occupied the late medieval and early modern role of "Christian philosophy." But the Reformation was not, at least in any self-conscious way, concerned with the epistemological impact of historicity and culture. Its concern, rather, was the restoration of a more pristine, scripturally based notion of Christian life and truth than was widely available in the sixteenth century. This restoration was accomplished on the basis of the dogmatic assertion of Scripture alone and faith alone as the unique rule of Christian belief. Certainly there was a recognition that history could lead to corruption, that tradition could be profoundly defective. But this assertion did not inspire any significant reflections on the fundamental correlation between historicity and truth. The logical conclusion of the Reformation was that tradition, if taken apart from the inspired scriptural text, was often nothing more than the theological innovation of sinful men. Tradition could and did distort the inspired word of God and needed, therefore, to be firmly held to a normative scriptural standard.

It is only with the Enlightenment, with Lessing's positing of the "broad, ugly ditch" between history and reason, and with his like-minded ring parable—with its subtext that history and culture relativizes religion's cognitive, if not humanitarian, claims—that theology was confronted with the unalloyed acids of historicity head on. Later, Ernst Troeltsch became the most significant purveyor of the claim that history necessarily attenuated the absolutist claims of the Christian faith—that the truth-claims of religious belief are necessarily limited to the cultural matrix in which they arose.[5]

In many ways, contemporary Christian theology is an attempt to respond to the challenges first issued by Lessing and Troeltsch. It seeks to reconcile continuing doctrinal claims for truth with the irrefragable demands of cultural and historical fluidity. Of course, at its heart, this is the central issue of hermeneutical and interpretive theory. For if certain Christian assertions are championed as normatively, perduringly, and transculturally true, then theology needs some notion of hermeneutics that can sustain precisely these characteristics while concomitantly respecting the legitimate demands of history and change, of the encompassing sociocultural horizons that indefeasibly stamp all truth, including revelational and doctrinal claims.

The question then remains: How can the universality and continuity of doctrine's claims be philosophically sustained and logically explicated given historicity's ontologically freighted impact? In the following section, I shall limit myself to examining various attempts to answer this question in Roman Catholic thought. All Christian churches, however, have been faced with the same challenge, and the answers, though varied, are similar across theological traditions.

Vatican II and the Emergence of the Form/Content Hermeneutical Approach

A significant philosophical crisis in the Roman Catholic Church's life was caused by the Modernist crisis at the turn of the twentieth century. Under the legitimate pressures of historical-critical biblical studies, of history of religions research, and of Troeltsch's cultural analyses, several "Modernists" came to the conclusion that an entirely new approach to Christian dogmatics was required. To their credit, the Modernists recognized that all doctrinal statements bore the identifying marks of their social and cultural birthplace. But they also seemed to hold that Christian doctrines were little more than linguistic carapaces, achieving no other cognitive penetration than that allowed by the amorphous religious experience that underlay them. The danger, of course, to use one metaphor, was that doctrinal statements were understood as a kind of removable "husk" that could be entirely jettisoned in favor of the valuable and genuine experiential "stalk." The "content" of Christian doctrine was not, in itself, important. What remained of significant interest was the authentic religious experience that issued forth in particular doctrinal crystallizations.[6] The reaction of the Roman Catholic magisterium to Modernism was swift and understandable, although in many cases unreasonable.[7] What the magisterium feared, clearly enough, was a pragmatic enervation of the cognitive status of Christian doctrine, a neo-Kantian evisceration of the truth mediated by revelation so that religious knowledge, ultimately, was limited to sensible and experiential intuition. To counteract the Modernist critical assault, the magisterium once again called for a philosophical adherence to Thomism, an approach that had already been sanctioned in 1879 by Leo XIII's encyclical *Aeterni Patris*, itself a reaction to alleged Kantian and rationalistic trends in theology. Unfortunately overlooked by this furious official reaction were the legitimate questions the Modernists had raised in light of biblical criticism and Troeltsch's relentless historicism. To what extent were dogmatic formulations limited by the cultural-linguistic matrices in which they came to expression? What was the relationship between revelation's claims and the sociohistorical contexts that attend every human formulation? The unyielding magisterial reaffirmation of Thomistic philosophy simply denied that significant questions existed, preferring instead to view Thomism as a universally applicable philosophy not itself subject to historicity. But this "solution" was to provide only temporary theoretical balm.

All of the issues that were denied at the turn of the century were given new life again in the 1940s in the Roman Catholic theological movement known by its opponents as the *nouvelle théologie*. The allegedly pejorative (no longer *ancienne*) designation, of course, makes clear the project's intentions. The theologians involved in this movement argued that precisely what theology must learn from Troeltsch, from Newman, from biblical criticism, from history of religions research, and even from the Modernists themselves is that theology cannot be limited to the language, thought, and conceptual framework of the thirteenth century any more than it could once be limited to the thought patterns of the fourth or fifth century. Their intention was not to follow the Modernists into a pragmatic evisceration of dogma's cognitive content; rather, the *nouveaux théologiens* argued that the Modernists rightly understood that Christianity could neither meet the intellectual challenges of the day, nor speak with authority to the contemporary age, by using the language and concepts characteristic of and limited to the Scholastic philosophy of the Middle Ages. M.-D. Chenu argued for the mutability of conceptual patterns of thought and so for a certain amount of theological pluralism: "But it is the human condition that the spirit exists only in a body, that the immutable truth only expresses itself in time, where it is successively incarnated. Revelation itself is clothed by the human colors according to the age when it was manifested to us."[8]

It was not Chenu's work, however, but a volume published by Henri Bouillard in 1943 that set the simmering discussion ablaze. This work was largely concerned with grace and conversion in Aquinas's thought, and how Aquinas adjusted his theological formulations after discovering the condemnations of semi-Pelagianism by the fifth-century Council of Orange. In the last pages of the book, however, Bouillard turned his attention to theological epistemology, and it is these pages that remained at the center of the controversy. There Bouillard argues that doctrinal and theological formulations are always products of their time, deeply conditioned by the historical and linguistic communities from which they emerge. In the case of Aquinas, for example, several Aristotelian terms and concepts were borrowed for the sake of explaining Christian revelation, just as earlier Christian writers had often used Platonic notions. So, Bouillard claims, "It may be seen that the notions utilized by S. Thomas are simply some Aristotelian ideas applied to theology. In this regard, they differ notably from the theological ideas utilized by the Fathers of the Church or even by moderns."[9] For Bouillard, a careful comparison between Augustine and Aquinas clearly displays that which is contingent in their conceptual frameworks as well as that which is constant and unchanging. There is always, Bouillard avers, a similarity of fundamental affirmations within a variety of conceptual representations. For example, the fundamental idea that grace is a free gift of God by which human beings are justified and empowered to do the good is a theme found in Scripture, Augustine, Aquinas, Trent, and post-Tridentine theologians.[10] Each used different paradigms and concepts in order to protect and to express the same central affirmation.

The Eucharist serves as another example. Before the twelfth century, Bouillard says, the word "transubstantiation" was unknown in the Christian world. Yet Augustine and other early Christians firmly believed in the actual presence of Christ in the Eucharist. The use of "substance" and "accident" is one way of expressing this mystery, one that was particularly useful in the Middle Ages. It is not, however, essential for expressing the Christian faith. As history teaches, other formulations have been used in the past, and new ones may be coined in the future. Even the Council of Trent recognized this when it said that one speaks of "transubstantiation" *aptissime* and *convenienter et proprie* (DH 1642; 1652).

These examples illustrate Bouillard's fundamental epistemological and hermeneutical point: "Ideas, methods, systems change with the times, but the affirmations which they contain remain, although expressed in other categories."[11] For Bouillard, the temporality of the theological inquirer precluded the possibility of Christian truth subsisting in abstract purity. Such truth is always embedded in the contingent schemas that constitute its rational structure. Of course, precisely at this point the critical question arises: Does the contingency of conceptual systems, that is, the historical and limited nature of paradigmatic schemas, enervate the cognitive status of dogmatic statements thereby leading inexorably to theological relativism? Bouillard argued that the relativity of theological schemas does not inevitably vitiate Christian doctrine, for an absolute exists at the heart of evolving representations.

Through the agency of this affirmation/representation distinction, a unique hermeneutical approach, Bouillard hoped to encourage theological pluralism, to show that pluralism is, in fact, demanded by historicity, linguisticality, finitude, and a host of other factors, while at the same time maintaining an identity within plurality that would forestall relativizing dogmatic statements. Different theologians had indeed developed varying "grammars," but an invariant affirmation could be discovered at the heart of representational contingency. So while the Council of Trent surely speaks about justification using the Aristotelian language of formal causality, it certainly did not intend to canonize a particular philosophy— only to say that justification involves an interior renewal and not only a forensic imputation of Christ's merits.[12]

Bouillard was convinced that the great conceptual systems of the thirteenth century no longer served the purpose of exhaustively illuminating and transmitting the mysteries of faith. If theology was to take seriously not only the perduring cognitive content of doctrinal statements but also the historical horizon within which these come to language, then dogmatic statements were not only patient of, but in fact often required, reconceptualization.[13] As Bouillard said, "Theology is linked to its times, linked to history—at the same time exposed to their risks and so capable of progress."[14] With a hermeneutical approach allowing for a fundamental content expressed in a variety of schemas, forms, or representations, Bouillard could argue for a healthy theological pluralism, open the door for greater ecumenical agreement, and concomitantly defend the normative, universal, and objective meanings found in Christian doctrine. Bouillard thought he had offered an interpretative trajectory that at the same time reconciled the universality of the church's faith with the necessarily delimiting (although also epistemologically productive) factors of historicity and sociocultural constitution.

The reaction to this Bouillardian affirmation/representation, content/context hermeneutical schema was both quick and fervent. Bouillard had issued a major challenge to the conceptual monism of neo-Scholasticism, and its proponents responded by charging him with relativism and an ill-advised return to Modernism. There is no need to rehearse that battle here.[15] The point here is simply to spotlight Bouillard's attempt to develop a hermeneutical theory that would reconcile the universality and normativity of doctrine with its historically and culturally limited context of formulation.[16] Despite the neo-Scholastic opposition to Bouillard, his subsequent removal from his teaching position at Lyon-Fourvière, and the issuance of Pius XII's encyclical of 1950, *Humani generis* (which expressed doubts about the reconceptualization of dogmatic statements), Bouillard saw something like his interpretative theory confirmed when John XXIII, in his opening speech at Vatican II (October 11, 1962) entitled *Gaudet mater ecclesia*, famously stated that "the substance of the ancient doctrine of the *depositum fidei* is one thing; the way in which it is formulated is another."[17] Soon after the council's conclusion, Yves Congar pointed out that the entire conciliar corpus gave testimony to these few words.[18] After the council, the curial Congregation for the Doctrine of the Faith issued a declaration entitled *Mysterium ecclesiae* (1973), further reinforcing the context/content hermeneutical approach.[19] One of the reasons Congar, Alberigo, and others have supported the context/content approach is because it allows for a variety of conceptual systems and frameworks, thereby encouraging a modicum of theological pluralism and allowing for much greater chance of ecumenical convergence.[20] The neo-Scholasticism that had been dominant from the issuance of the encyclical *Aeterni Patris* until just before Vatican II could now be complemented, and at times surpassed, by other methodologies.

Ultimately, the advantage of the context/content trajectory was that it protected the universality and material identity of Christian truth while clearly recognizing that this truth could be expressed in a variety of different ways (with new elements thereby unveiled)—and so incorporating many of the horizons attendant on historically and linguistically constituted existence. Over time, theologians of many stripes made significant use of the context/content distinction. However, this distinction has not escaped significant criticism.

Theological Reservations about the Context/Content Approach

The context/content interpretive trajectory continued to be endorsed by the Roman Catholic Church—and, insofar as it is a theoretical cornerstone of ecumenical agreements, by other Christian churches as well—as a legitimate and viable hermeneutical strategy.[21] But with the aforementioned document of the International Theological Commission (ITC), "On the Interpretation of Dogmas," one begins to find some reservations expressed.[22] The ITC document is in many ways intended to acknowledge the importance of historicity while at the same time avoiding the aporias of liberal Protestantism where, as Brian Gerrish has said, "dogma was an early casualty in the invasion of historical thinking."[23] The statement affirms the unity, historical identity, and normativity of revelation. And in its cogent attempt to incorporate the productive dimensions of historicity, it asserts that there can be no view of truth separate from its finite mediation. In the process of affirming these two dimensions, the universality of truth and its historical expression, the statement comes close to confirming the context/content hermeneutical trajectory. So, for example, the ITC statement avers that "these contingent conditions for the knowledge in question and the context of its discovery must be distinguished from the unconditional claim to validity of the truth that is recognized therein" (A.I.4). Further, one should attend "to the distinction between the immutable deposit of faith (or truths of faith) and the way in which they are expressed. This means that the teaching of the church . . . must be transmitted to people in a manner that is alive and appropriate to the exigencies of the day" (B.II.2). Finally, "Without doubt, the permanent and valid content of the dogmas is to be distinguished from the way in which they are formulated" (C.III.3). These sentences make clear that the ITC, at least in a qualified way, continues to endorse the form/content trajectory.[24] At the same time, the ITC wants to make clear that the context/content distinction cannot be made with surgical or mathematical precision. So, for example, in qualified opposition to the comments above, the document states that "no clear-cut separation can be made between the content and form of the statement. The symbolic system of language is not mere external apparel, but to a certain extent the incarnation of a truth" (C.III.3). Also, "the images and concepts (employed in the proclamation) are not *arbitrarily* [emphasis added] interchangeable" (C.III.3). Finally, "the truth of revelation nevertheless remains always the same 'not only in its real substance (content) but also in its decisive linguistic formulations'" (C.III.3).

These statements express decided reservations about the context/content distinction. Given the context of the entire document, two observations are called for: (1) the statements above testify to the difficulty of speaking of a form/content distinction as if in each case the "essential" reality is easily distinguishable from the "accidental" form (a point made consistently by Rahner, as we shall see); and (2) the document defends the point of view taken by Paul VI's encyclical *Mysterium fidei* (1965), as well as that of the declaration *Mysterium ecclesiae* (1973), that the truths of revelation are truly mediated by the terms in which they are defined *if one continues to use that particular conceptual system*. It is not here a question of the exhaustiveness of a particular formulation but of its continued adequacy.[25] In recognizing an undeniable coinherence between form and content, the magisterium is not trying to establish a "backdoor" conceptual monism, but is recognizing, in fact, that no facile distinction between context and content is possible.[26] Of course, if this legitimate caution hardens into a denial of the possibility of the form/content distinction, then it becomes very difficult to maintain its original telos—namely, the reconciliation of Christian doctrine's universal, transcultural, and normative claims with the indefeasible horizons of historicity and linguisticality attaching to all formulations. The other options become (1) a conceptual monism that denies, *de facto* if not *de jure*, the effect of historicity, or (2) a stress on historicity to the point that the original cognitive claim of doctrine is now quite different (and not simply complementary to) that which was originally intended.

A recent papal document very cautious about the context/content distinction—and in the process moving, at least potentially, toward conceptual monism—is the encyclical *Fides et ratio*.[27] This statement, unsurprisingly, invokes the importance of "certain and unchangeable doctrine" (no. 92) and rejects the historicist claim that "what was true in one period . . . may not be true in another" (no. 87). However, this expected emphasis on the identity and perpetuity of doctrine's truth is not balanced with earlier ecclesial accents on the possible variety of conceptual formulations. The crucial passages regarding pluralism found at Vatican II, such as those in *Gaudet mater ecclesia, Gaudium et spes,* and *Unitatis redintegratio,* are not cited by the encyclical.[28] Furthermore, the encyclical's sole reference to *Mysterium ecclesiae* cites that part of the declaration defending the claim that the meaning of dogmatic statements remains constant (no. 96, note 113), while ignoring the significant passage pertaining to the possible plurality of conceptual expression cited above.[29]

How should these omissions be understood? Is there an intentional brake placed on theological reconceptualization and the legitimate plurality of expression? Has the encyclical given up on the very desire that gave birth to the context/content distinction, the desire to wed the universality and normativity of doctrine's claims with varying social and cultural dimensions imposed by history itself? This does not seem to be the case inasmuch as the entire document is calling for pluralism, at least within certain limits. Perhaps the failure to cite the relevant conciliar and post-conciliar passages is provoked by the encyclical's clear desire to preserve the ancient terminology, a language it is at pains to protect. So *Fides et ratio* rejects "disdain for the classical philosophy from which terms of both the understanding of faith and the actual formulations of dogma have been drawn" (no. 55, citing *Humani generis*). And one may surmise that the encyclical also has in mind the sensible warning of *Humani generis* that the church cannot tie itself to philosophical systems that have flourished for only a short period of time. Nonetheless, the encyclical's failure to cite the germane texts endorsing some type of context/content distinction is a significant omission (especially in a document that eagerly adduces elements from the entire Roman Catholic tradition) and is likely the result of excessive caution.[30] The statement would have better preserved the theological insights of recent times if it had stated that the context/content distinction is indeed sanctioned by the church and had encouraged theologians to seek an intelligible language and appropriate methodology for their times, while concomitantly asserting that the tradition provides a theological terminology and conceptual framework of great sophistication not easily surpassed and, at least in several cases, worthy of preservation. As it stands, the encyclical seems to backslide, at least on occasion, into the conceptual monism that existed prior to the council. It also causes one to wonder what kind of hermeneutics of doctrine the encyclical can now sanction. Is it one that is capable of reconciling the universal truth and material identity of Christianity's cognitive claims with the delimiting (although also ontologically productive) factors of sociolinguistic embeddedness and historical conditioning?

As we shall see, the ITC's and encyclical's reservations about the form/content hermeneutical trajectory are not limited to those seeking to maintain and uphold traditional terminology. Such an interpretative theory is also opposed, although for very different philosophical reasons, by those maintaining that any attempt at a context/content distinction is based on ontologically inappropriate grounds.

Wider Implications of the Context/Content Trajectory

The form/content or context/content hermeneutical approach rests on certain presuppositions that should at least be mentioned before investigating the contemporary critique. The most important of these elements is that, for the very distinction to be made, ultimately a reconstructive or objective notion of interpretation is necessary. This means that texts have a stable and determinate meaning that may be reconstructed and recovered (given, of course, proper philological and sociocultural analysis) as well as re-presented and re-expressed by an interpreter centuries or even millennia later. By way of example, one may state that the definitions authorized by the Councils of Nicea and Chalcedon may be recovered and reconstructed, that is, the central ideas intended by and embedded in the original texts may be appositely understood by a much later interpreter. This same meaning may also be re-expressed and reformulated in other terms, with the recognition, of course, that a new terminology, a new lexical-semantic taxonomy, will necessarily uncover new shades of perspective and nuance while still protecting the essential and determinate meaning of the text.[31] This is the basis for the theological claim that Christianity still follows the path of the early councils (inasmuch as they represent the faith of Scripture) while allowing for further organic and architectonic development of the conciliar definitions. Reconstructive or objective hermeneutics, therefore, is completely in agreement with the claim that every interpretation is necessarily productive and creative. The indefeasible horizons of historicity and subjectivity demand such hermeneutical effects. It adds, however, that these interpretations are also legitimately mediative of an original textual meaning.

Of course, an argument on behalf of reconstructive hermeneutics as uniquely congruent with the Christian faith carries with it a certain philosophical freight. One such element, even if it is not always clearly explicated, is the underlying notion of the fundamental unity of human nature perduring through history. An eidetically discernible common nature, however understood, whether classically or transcendentally, ultimately grounds and warrants the recoverability of a textual meaning now centuries or millennia old.

Even a document with some reservations about the context/content distinction, the ITC statement of 1989, says without hesitation, "The unity, mutual understanding and peaceful coexistence of humanity as well as the mutual recognition of an identical human dignity presuppose that there is a human element (*humanum*) common to all people despite far-reaching differences between cultures and thus that there is a truth common to all" (A.I.4).[32] *Fides et ratio*, harboring its own concerns about the form/content distinction, unself-consciously speaks of the universality of "human nature" at many points, taking for granted its conceptual transparency. But it is precisely the denial of "human nature" and the metaphysics that necessarily accompanies it that is under unremitting attack today by both nonfoundationalist and postmodern thought, giving rise, in the process, to much more fluid and protean understandings of the hermeneutical task. Of course, these newer approaches are themselves rife with theological implications.

Nonfoundationalist Construals of Hermeneutical Theory

Just as the nonfoundationalist notions of existence and thought have unmasked allegedly inappropriate theories of truth, developing newer approaches to rationality in the process, so this same unmasking is applicable to hermeneutical theory.[33] Heidegger's unveiling of an ontologically constitutive temporality and Wittgenstein's presencing of linguistically and culturally constituted communities has deconstructed truncated interpretive theories and the misguided philosophical foundations on which they rest. What Wittgenstein and Heidegger have shown is that shared essences or natures, common transcendental constitutions or invariant structures of knowing now represent historically outmoded and properly deconstructed patterns of thought. Such attempts typify the consistently Platonic thrust of Western philosophy, the "escape" from time and chance, thereby theoretically obscuring and veiling the ontologically productive effects of finitude, facticity, and historicity.[34]

Heidegger's fundamental project was intended as a "presencing of the absent," an uncovering of the *lēthē* encompassing *alethēia*. To that end,

Heidegger relentlessly revealed those unannounced but constitutive and determinative structures of thought and being: historicity, thrownness, otherness, and sociocultural immersion. Both classical and Enlightenment thinkers, blindly concentrating on a worldless substance and subject, on the ontical and the existentiell, have left unthought precisely that which is ontologically decisive: the enveloping life-world of historicity. Kant and Descartes, the philosophical progenitors of modernity, simply appropriated medieval ontology, transferring its original metaphysical concerns to transcendental subjectivity. But modern as well as ancient and medieval thinkers are guilty of the same solipsistic forgetfulness of slipping into the *Vergessenheit* that overlooks the constitutive horizons encircling *Dasein*.

For Heidegger, on the other hand—and this is the central point that much contemporary thought has appropriated—the truly important philosophical quest does not revolve around isolating the worldless, ahistorical entities of substance and subjectivity. It revolves, rather, around an examination of why *Dasein* tends to bury and to conceal the "world" in its theoretical search for ahistorical matrices and rigorous foundations. The absence at the heart of presence, the world that constantly "slips away" and veils itself from view constitutes, for Heidegger, the truly interesting philosophical issue.

Inasmuch as Heidegger has brought to light the ontologically inappropriate search for substance and subject, thereby attacking the metaphysical jugular that is the theoretical basis for reconstructive hermeneutics, Hans-Georg Gadamer can now claim that a new, *ontologically appropriate* understanding of hermeneutics is philosophically necessary. The reconstructive theoretical basis has been effectively dismantled. This allows Gadamer to claim that any attempt at a context/content distinction is fallacious, needing to be replaced with an interpretative theory that rigorously takes account of a fully temporized human life and thought.

Gadamer's Hermeneutics

Hans-Georg Gadamer's groundbreaking study, *Truth and Method*, presupposes and in some ways intensifies the deconstruction of philosophy advanced by Heidegger, bringing it, in the process, to hermeneutical fruition. The metaphysical anchorage of Western thought has now been unmoored by Heidegger's uncovering of the historicity and facticity of the *Lebenswelt*; the primordial basis of existence is temporality, and full ontological weight must now be accorded to finitude and historical immersion.[35] But this metaphysical unmooring now has determinate and irrefragable hermeneutical effects. Gadamer rejects the context/content and understanding/application distinctions of traditional hermeneutical theory because these are necessarily rooted in some type of metaphysics or so-called foundationalist ontology.[36] To speak, as traditional hermeneutical theory does, of a stable and determinate textual meaning, or of the difference between a text's meaning and its significance, is rooted in a naïveté born of a failure to appreciate fully the deconstructive power of Heidegger's fundamental ontology.[37] It is to woefully underestimate the deeply lethic consequences of historicity. Heidegger had already revealed the extent to which *Dasein* is always already constituted by preunderstanding, historical immersion, thrownness, and finitude. Gadamer has extended the Heideggerian project to interpretive theory, showing how the "worldhood of the world" and the encompassing horizons of temporality are now essentially constitutive of all textual readings. This is the basis of Gadamer's vigorous remarks against Dilthey and Husserl, both of whom seek to preserve some notion of "first principles" that Gadamer deems untenable. Dilthey, for example, asserts that *Verstehen* presupposes an ultimate substratum of common human nature that serves as the matrix for reconstructive understanding.[38] Husserl, of course, finally posited the transcendental ego of subjectivity as the Archimedean point and ground from which to establish a rigorous science. For Gadamer, however, Husserl's later, transcendental philosophy is simply an eleventh hour attempt to rescue hypostasized consciousness from historical contingency.[39] It is now precisely the Platonic-Kantian-Husserlian foundationalist axis that Gadamer rejects as ontologically and, a fortiori, hermeneutically, inappropriate. Gadamer's rejection of Dilthey, Husserl, and others follows a highly coherent logic: Metaphysics and "foundationalism" holds for some consistent notion of "human nature" serving as a substratum of *Dasein*. In turn, this Archimedean point warrants and buttresses the notion of reconstructive hermeneutics, whereby one may "recover" the perduring meaning embedded in a text, even centuries or millennia later. This in turn leads to hermeneutical distinctions such as the difference between content and context and between understanding and application. In both cases, there is a determinate textual meaning that can be recovered. In the former, this meaning can now be re-expressed and reconceptualized in a new linguistic and categorical formulation even while preserving the central "recovered" content; in the latter, this stable, enduring meaning can now be "applied"—such as in preaching—to various circumstances and cultures. It is precisely this logic, both ontological and hermeneutical, that Heidegger has dismantled.

Having rejected the notion of an "essence," a selfsame matrix in *Dasein*, and with it any warrant for a reconstructive hermeneutics accenting the recovery of textual meaning, Gadamer must now constructively establish the kind of ontologically appropriate hermeneutics that may legitimately flourish in light of Heidegger's philosophical deconstruction of the prior tradition.[40] How does Heidegger's overcoming of metaphysics positively affect hermeneutical theory? For Gadamer, an ontologically *apposite* theory of interpretation necessarily excises the notion of a stable meaning "recoverable" over time (there is now no warrant for it), and it excises as well the form/content and understanding/application distinctions (which themselves rest on the discredited notion of "recoverability"). If the horizons of temporality and finitude, as well as the forestructure of understanding, are accorded their proper philosophical weight, then reconstructive hermeneutics necessarily yields to an interpretive theory that allows for a plurality of new and even essentially different interpretations of a text's meaning. Such plurality is demanded by the historicity of understanding, by the newly presenced dimensions of the life-world itself.[41]

Of course, Gadamer is not a hermeneutical relativist, and he would strongly repudiate such a description. But how does he avoid hermeneutical anarchism once he rejects the "recoverability" of meaning warranted by the unity of substance and subject? Having rejected any traditional "foundation" for interpretative unity and validity, Gadamer must now seek some other form of continuity, one that successfully avoids interpretative relativism. A different continuity from the type established by reconstructive or so-called Romantic hermeneutics must now be found.[42] Gadamer argues, instead, that there is a fundamental unity within history itself, so that, in the very act of interpretation, there is always a "fusion" or "melding of horizons" (*Horizontverschmelzung*) from which a new meaning or interpretation emerges. The unity of history itself provides a formal continuity (rather than a material continuity of perduring meanings) that allows Gadamer to defend, simultaneously, the importance of tradition (since all interpretations take place, necessarily, in dialogue with historical "tradition") as well as a plurality of textual readings (since a determinate and recoverable meaning is theoretically forbidden).[43]

In consequence, although Gadamer's hermeneutics proscribes reconstructive understanding, his accent on historical tradition allows him to hold that interpretation is always related to the past. This must not, of course, be understood in the sense that one "recovers," by means of philological, historical, and sociocultural analysis, the stable meaning of a text. Such is to lapse into an inappropriate interpretive theory, misunderstanding the impact of historicity.[44] Rather, given the unity of history and the "fusion of horizons" between text and interpreter, a new "interpretation" of a text must emerge, one that may be essentially different (not just newly appropriated from a different perspective) from prior interpretations. This is the basis for Gadamer's conjunction of the traditionally distinct moments of understanding and application. Every understanding is, by strict ontological necessity, always already, and in Gadamer's unique sense, an application.[45] A nonfoundationalist construal of rationality and hermeneutics, one honest about the constitutive dimensions of historicity, demands such a conclusion.

Because of Gadamer's rehabilitation of elements overlooked and suppressed by the Enlightenment—such as the forestructure of understanding, the constitutive role of tradition, and the ontological productivity of history—his hermeneutical theory has had an impressive and, in many instances, a positive effect on contemporary philosophy and theology. His triumph has been so convincing and thorough that one finds hermeneutics frequently spoken of as a replacement for metaphysics and epistemology.[46] As Jean Grondin says, hermeneutics is a successful postmetaphysical philosophy, "a *prima philosophia* without metaphysics."[47] Given this overwhelming success, one may ask how his hermeneutical theory now affects theological interpretation.

If taken to their logical conclusion, certain theological consequences of Gadamer's hermeneutical construals are pronounced. One may no longer claim that the meaning of conciliar, dogmatic, or doctrinal statements is recoverable and applicable as an adjudicatory norm for a later period. All textual statements, including the essential statements of Christian doctrine, are now subjected to historical understanding alone rather than historical understanding in relationship to a common *humanum* or *physis*, thereby allowing for new interpretations, possibly quite different from those that preceded it.[48] Significant interpretative plurality appears to be the inevitable result.[49] Of course, Gadamer is no friend of hermeneutical anarchism, and he adduces the unity of history as one way of avoiding the disparate interpretations of random pluralism. Nonetheless, with his decided emphasis on interpretative plurality rather than on recoverable textual meaning, he is compelled to offer some standard for adjudication between varying approaches. It is here that Gadamer develops the notion of the "claim" as a clue to the truth and validity of an interpretation. That which is true is certainly not that which is commensurable with a stable and recoverable textual meaning. Such an understanding would constitute an unwarranted return to ontologically truncated reconstructive theories.

Rather, that which is true is that which continues to exercise a "claim" in and through tradition and effective-history. As Richard Bernstein phrases it, truth is that which emerges from "dialogical encounter with what makes a claim on us."[50]

Of course, the question haunting Gadamer is whether the notion of the "claim" is a sufficient criterion for wholly exorcising interpretive relativism. Does it provide an adequate standard for establishing validity in interpretation? Or does Gadamer's hermeneutics, despite its significant contributions in certain areas, fall short in establishing criteria for stability in interpretation? And does such failure not qualify its theological use in explaining revelation and the central characteristics of Christian doctrine—its normativity, universality, and perduring truthfulness—that have been invoked earlier? Does Gadamer's thought allow one to affirm, simultaneously, the continuity and selfsame identity of Christian truth while also taking account of historical contingency, finitude, and all the other horizons associated with a hermeneutics of facticity?

While many theologians have been strongly influenced by Gadamer, I will limit myself here to discussing the thought of David Tracy.[51] When discussing hermeneutical theory, Tracy repeats many distinctive Gadamerian themes, which may also be used by those contending for a renewed reconstructive approach. For example, Tracy says that "we need to interpret in order to understand";[52] that to understand texts is to understand differently (16); that there is no ahistorical nonlinguistic correspondence of subject and object (122 n. 5); that we have no unalloyed reality (47); that we understand in and through language (48); and that the route to reality passes through the plurality and ambiguity of language and history (82). None of these texts is particularly troublesome for those seeking to defend reconstructive hermeneutics and to maintain something like the context/content distinction. The neuralgic issue is *not* the claim that reality is only grasped in and through language, history, and culture. Such an assertion is undeniable. The foundational *punctum saliens* is this: Is historicity entirely determinative of *Dasein*, or may we also speak of a common *humanum* or nature?

Tracy's accent on the plurality and ambiguity of language and history is of a piece with his acceptance of Heidegger's emphasis on human finitude and his rejection of the Platonic-Aristotelian-Thomistic classical metaphysical approach as well as the Cartesian-Kantian-Husserlian transcendental axis.[53] He clearly opposes the search for the stable and recoverable textual meaning, the context/content distinction, and the metaphysical grounds upon which this distinction, with its goal of uniting universal truth and historical contingency, rests.[54]

At the same time, Tracy, like Gadamer, does not want the excision of reconstructive hermeneutics to collapse into an inappropriate relativism. He asks if epistemological anarchism is not inevitable if one accepts the deeply lethic consequences of historicity and finitude, the deconstruction of a selfsame matrix in *Dasein* and, in Derridean terms, the decentering of the subject. Tracy, however, rejects random pluralism, pointing out that to say all interpretations are equal is to deny the possibility of knowledge (61). The day comes when even the pluralist must utter his "Here I stand" (92). Of course, the lingering question remains: Having proscribed reconstructive interpretation, on precisely what grounds does one take this "stand"? Ultimately, Tracy appropriates Gadamer's notion of the claim but, recognizing its elusive character as a sufficient warrant for validity in interpretation, seeks to buttress its ability to adjudicate conflicting interpretative views with help from Habermas's understanding of emancipatory praxis. Tracy realizes that there are no mechanisms in Gadamer to guard against the systemic distortions that the tradition offers and that the notion of "claim" offers only a "soft" criterion for interpretive adequacy. With the dual warrants of both Gadamer's "claim" and Habermas's "liberative and transformative praxis," Tracy believes he can establish the "relative adequacy" of varying interpretations.[55] Like several others, Tracy wants to avoid relativism and skepticism but has rejected the metaphysical warrants that underlay reconstructive and objectivist hermeneutical theory. The logical question, then, is this: Can the newer warrants introduced, the "claim" and "emancipatory praxis"—both advanced now as ontologically *appropriate* in light of the horizons presenced by contemporary philosophy—preserve the perduring material identity of Christian faith and doctrine?

In my judgment, it is difficult for Tracy's hermeneutical approach to protect adequately the abiding identity and universal truth of doctrinal statements.[56] His accent on historicity, on the delimiting horizons of societal, cultural, and linguistic determination, *in nuce* on human embeddedness, is undoubtedly legitimate. However, lacking any kind of first philosophy as a "foundation," Tracy is seemingly left only with the adjudicatory criteria of the "claim" and of "emancipatory and liberative praxis" as authentic warrants for doctrine's truth. These may indeed be legitimate auxiliary criteria for establishing hermeneutical adequacy, but they cannot, ultimately, establish the perduring truth and identity of doctrine because these criteria—developed as an alternative to that which best establishes hermeneutical adequacy, namely, reconstructive interpretation—cannot, and certainly recognize that they cannot, hope to recover and reproduce the determinate meaning embedded in the original texts.

Tracy's work, then, appears subject to the same criticism as that directed toward Gadamer's, even though Tracy has buttressed his point of view with Habermasian insights. Once one has abandoned metaphysics of any kind, it appears difficult, if not impossible, to intelligibly establish, as opposed to fideistically assert, the material identity and perduring truth of central Christian affirmations. Instead, these affirmations themselves become entirely subject to interpretative history, as Gadamer has argued. There will be a *formal* continuity of various statements, the continuity provided by history and tradition itself (since doctrinal affirmations will always be interpreted in dialogue with the prior tradition), but this cannot be confused with the claim that there is a *material* identity such that the same, equivalent meaning (not, of course, the same language or formula) is affirmed from age to age.[57] What is affirmed is a continuity of *symbols and texts* which, in their polyvalent and historical character, open themselves to speculative reflection and interpretation; an identity of (recovered) meaning through history, however, is, in the last analysis, ontologically and hermeneutically naïve. There is simply no legitimate philosophical warrant for such "recoverability." Supplementing Gadamer's understanding with that of Habermas may better help to uncover systemic distortions within the tradition, but inasmuch as Habermas fundamentally accepts Heidegger's critique of the philosophical canons of substance and subject, he is subject, ultimately, to the same criticisms. I do not see, then, how a profoundly Gadamerian-influenced approach clearly maintains the fundamental continuity and abiding character of Christian doctrine. Such perdurance, in my judgment, is better preserved by reconstructive or objectivist hermeneutics, to which we now turn.

Notes

1. "Dominus Iesus," *Acta apostolicae sedis* 96 (2000): 742–65. An English translation may be found in *Origins* 30 (2000): 6–8. I have previously observed that this document received a good deal of unfounded criticism. It is certainly true, however, that its failure to speak of the significant advances in ecumenical and interreligious dialogue since Vatican II diminished its effectiveness.

2. Of course, this is hardly to state that there have not been reversals in the history of church teaching. The contrary is clearly the case, as has been shown many times. One may cite, by way of example, Walter Principe's "When 'Authentic' Teachings Change," *Ecumenist* 25 (1987): 70–73. The salient point here is that certain fundamental affirmations of Christian doctrine, such as those about Christ and the Trinity, make irreversible and normative claims.

3. International Theological Commission, "On the Interpretation of Dogmas," *Origins* 20 (May 17, 1990): 3–14.

4. The reference here is to the statement of Vatican I: "That meaning of the sacred dogmas is to be perpetually retained which Holy Mother Church has once declared and there must never be a deviation from that meaning on the specious ground and title of a more profound understanding" (DH 3020). Of course, development was not here excluded since the document immediately cites the claim of Vincent of Lerins to the effect that there must always be growth and progress in understanding *in eodem sensu eademque sententia.*

5. See, for example, Ernst Troeltsch, *The Absoluteness of Christianity and the History of Religions* (Richmond, Va.: John Knox, 1971).

6. For this point of view, see George Tyrrell, *Through Scylla and Charbdis* (London: Longmans, Green, 1907). For evaluations, see E. Schillebeeckx, *Revelation and Theology*, vol. 2 (trans. N. D. Smith; London: Sheed & Ward, 1968), 10–12; Yves Congar, *A History of Theology* (trans. Hunter Guthrie; Garden City, N.Y.: Doubleday, 1968), 190–92; Aidan Nichols, "G. Tyrrell and the Development of Doctrine," *New Blackfriars* 67 (1986): 515–30; William Hill, *Knowing the Unknown God* (New York: Philosophical Library, 1971), 35–36; David Schultenover, *View from Rome: On the Eve of the Modernist Crisis* (New York: Fordham University Press, 1993). Tyrrell himself recognized that he might have fallen into Auguste Sabatier's pragmatic view of revelation and doctrine. See his comments to Wilfred Ward as recounted in Nicholas Sagovsky, *"On God's Side": A Life of George Tyrrell* (Oxford: Clarendon, 1990), 146–47, 187–88.

7. See Etienne Gilson, *Lettres de monsieur Étienne Gilson au pére Henri de Lubac* (Paris: Cerf, 1986), 76: "Modernism was wrong, but its suppression was conducted by unreasonable men whose pseudo-theology made a modernist reaction inevitable."

8. M.-D. Chenu, *Le Saulchoir: Une école de théologie* (Kain-Lez-Tournai: Le Saulchoir, 1937), 48. (A reprint of the work was issued in 1985 by Les éditions du Cerf, Paris). The work was placed on the Roman Catholic Church's Index of prohibited books in 1942. See *Acta apostolicae sedis* 34 (1942): 37.

9. Henri Bouillard, *Conversion et Grâce chez S. Thomas d'Aquin: Étude Historique* (Paris: Aubier, 1944), 213.

10. Bouillard, like many Catholics writing in the 1940s, did not take much account of the work of Reformation-based thinkers. He would go on in the next decade, however, to write elegantly and at great length about Barth's (and Bultmann's) theological achievements.

11. Bouillard, *Conversion et Grâce*, 220.

12. Ibid., 222.

13. Ibid., 224.

14. Ibid., 223.

15. For more on Bouillard and the theological reaction to him, see Thomas Guarino, "Henri Bouillard and the Truth-Status of Dogmatic Statements," *Science et Esprit* 39 (1987): 331–43.

16. Aidan Nichols correctly concludes that the neo-Scholastics of the 1940s were "wrong in allowing so little *droit de cité* to the *nouvelle théologie*. It is not the case that, grudgingly, the other theologies [or philosophies] are permitted to exist until Thomism has absorbed their better insights (whereupon, like the Marxist State, they can wither away)." Nichols, "Thomism and the *Nouvelle Théologie*," *Thomist* 64 (2000): 19.

17. *Acta apostolicae sedis* 54 (1962): 792. An exhaustive study of the opening speech may be found in Giuseppe Alberigo et al., *Fede Tradizione Profezia: Studi su Giovanni XXIII e sul Vatican II* (Brescia: Paideia Editrice, 1984). For Vatican II formulations similar to that found in *Gaudet mater ecclesia*, see *Gaudium et spes*, no. 62 and *Unitatis redintegratio*, nos. 4, 6, 17. It is worth noting that Karol Wojtyla, speaking about "Schema 13," which later became *Gaudium et spes*, claimed that his criticisms were not directed at doctrine,

but at the proposed mode of expression: "non de corpore doctrinae, sed de modo loquendi." See Kenneth Schmitz, "Faith and Reason: Then and Now," *Communio* 26 (Fall 1999): 595–608.

18. Congar, *History of Theology*, 18–19. More recently, Giuseppe Alberigo has called this distinction one of the decisive motifs of the council. See Alberigo, "Facteurs de 'Laïcité' au Concile Vatican II," *Revue des sciences religieuses* 74 (2000): 211–25.

19. "The truths which the Church intends to teach through her dogmatic formulations are distinct from the changeable conceptions of a given age and can be expressed without them." *Acta apostolicae sedis* 65 (1973): 403. Other comments about dogmatic statements, equally pointed, may be found in section five of the declaration.

20. *Ut unum sint*, the encyclical of John Paul II that strongly endorses the necessity of ecumenism, unhesitatingly makes the context/content distinction, citing Vatican II's *Gaudium et spes*, no. 62. See *Ut unum sint*, no. 81.

21. It is precisely this hermeneutical position—that a fundamental and enduring content may be expressed in a variety of schemas and concepts—that undergirds, for example, the Joint Declaration on Justification between Lutherans and Roman Catholics, as well as countless other such agreements.

22. Of course, very soon after Vatican II ended, Oscar Cullmann already called into question the form/context distinction, claiming that it is useless to make such a distinction if one cannot say clearly what is the form and what is the content. Cullman, "Sind unsere Erwartungen erfüllt?" in *Sind die Erwartungen erfüllt?* (ed. K. Rahner, O. Cullmann, and H. Fries; Munich: Max Hueber, 1966), 41. But Cullmann may be too positivistic here. It is not a matter of surgically separating the two elements, which coincide here in any case. It is a matter of the distinction becoming clear only gradually, ultimately with the guidance of the Holy Spirit.

23. Brian Gerrish, "From 'Dogmatik' to 'Glaubenslehre': A Paradigm Change in Modern Theology?" in *Paradigm Change in Theology* (ed. Hans Küng and David Tracy; trans. Margaret Kohl; New York: Crossroad, 1989), 162.

24. John Thiel has stated that the ITC document can be read as an extended statement of dissatisfaction with the context/content trajectory. I think the statements just adduced indicate that such a claim must itself be placed within a wider context, as I argue in *Revelation and Truth* (Scranton, Pa.: University of Scranton Press, 1993), 34–37. Thiel is correct in saying that the ITC document indicates legitimate reservations, but, as Thiel himself recognizes, these are lodged while simultaneously affirming several elements central to the distinction. For Thiel's comments, see Thiel, *Senses of Tradition* (Oxford: Oxford University Press, 2000), 227 n. 72.

25. So, for example, the 1973 declaration says, "It must be stated that dogmatic *formulas* of the Church's magisterium have suitably communicated revealed truth from the very beginning and that, remaining the same, these formulas will continue to communicate this truth forever to those who interpret them correctly" (citing *Mysterium fidei*). *Acta apostolicae sedis* 65 (1973): 403.

26. Not long ago Christopher Hill complained that the magisterium at times seems to be insisting on adherence to certain sixteenth-century formulas, showing, perhaps, that "there is still not a sufficient appreciation of the truth that there is indeed a distinction between a doctrinal formulation and the deposit of faith it is designed to express." Hill, "The Decree on Ecumenism: An Anglican View," *One in Christ* 26 (1990): 25. In light of the recent Joint Statement on Justification, an agreement concluded between Lutherans and Catholics, it is difficult to express that sentiment baldly today, although certain statements in the encyclical *Fides et ratio* may give substance to Hill's plaints, as we shall see.

27. The official Latin text may be found in *Acta apostolicae sedis* 91 (1998): 5–88. An English translation is available in *Origins* 28 (October 22, 1998): 317–47. Paragraph numbers from this text are cited in parentheses.

28. With regard to John XXIII's opening allocution at Vatican II, for example, the extract cited by *Fides et ratio* (no. 92) is found just before the overlooked but hermeneutically critical passage: "Est enim aliud ipsum depositum Fidei, seu veritates, quae veneranda doctrina nostra continentur, aliud modus, quo eaedem enuntiantur, eodem tamen sensu eademque sententia" (The deposit of faith itself, or the truths which our venerated doctrine contains is one thing, the manner in which these are expressed is another, always according to the same meaning and judgment).

29. See note 19 above for *Mysterium ecclesiae.* The encyclical does briefly state (no. 95) that a question must be raised concerning the universality of truth and the historical and cultural conditioning of formulas. But instead of then invoking the conciliar distinction between the *depositum fidei* and the conceptual mode of expression, the encyclical immediately turns to the claim of *Humani generis* that it is wrong to depart from traditional terms and notions (no. 96, note 112).

30. This is especially the case given that the Roman Catholic Church's theological and ecumenical praxis is clearly based on some kind of context/content distinction. Another such example, besides that of ecumenism, may be drawn from Christian anthropology. For example, Joseph Ratzinger observes, with dismay, that in the post–Vatican II revision of the Roman Missal, under the influence of studies by Paul Althaus and Oscar Cullmann, the term *anima*, or "soul," was excised from the liturgy for the dead and the ritual for burial. It is fair to say that the point of such suppression was likely fueled by the search for new ways of speaking about the unity of the human person as well as the avoidance of terms connected, in popular imagination if not in theological explication, with an untenable dualism. The intention, of course, was to maintain the meaning that "soul" intended to convey while seeking a terminology appropriate to the times. It is no surprise then that the Congregation for the Doctrine of the Faith itself, in its 1979 Letter on Eschatology, says that the church affirms the subsistence and continuation of a spiritual element after death, an "*ego humanum*," that the church has traditionally designated as "soul." One notices that the letter hardly makes "soul" language the only terminology possible, but seeks to maintain the fundamental meaning that such a word has traditionally conveyed. For Ratzinger's comments, see Joseph Ratzinger, *Eschatology* (trans. Michael Waldstein; Washington, D.C.: Catholic University of America Press, 1988), 105–6. For the Letter on Eschatology, see DH 4650ff., which bears a mistaken heading.

31. Throughout this chapter, I will refer to the "meaning of the text," the "intention of the text" and "textual intention." I use these phrases in order to avoid what I regard as the inappropriate language of *mens auctoris*. Every text, of course, is the result of a communicative act by a communicative agent. However, one determines the meaning or intention of the text not by peering into the "mind of the author," as if this were possible, but by examining the actual text-in-the-world (while taking account, of course, of the issues that interest the author, his or her sociocultural world, the concepts used, etc.). One is not concerned, then, at least not primarily, with what an author *thinks* he or she said, or what an author *claims* he or she said, but what the text itself is able to sustain from an examination of it. This latter constitutes the proper standard for hermeneutical validity. For this reason, the language of "textual intention" or "textual meaning" is at a remove from a bald *mens auctoris*. This will be explained more completely below.

32. The ITC is not referring here to mere biological similarity, which even Clifford Geertz concedes: "Men can't fly and pigeons can't talk." At the same time, Geertz has little use for any metaphysical understanding of human nature such as "wiring your theories

into something called the 'Structure of Reason' or the 'Constitution of Man' thereby insulating them from history and culture." Geertz, *Available Light* (Princeton, N.J.: Princeton
University Press, 2000), 51–60.

33. See note 30 in chapter one for the precise meaning I am giving to the terms "foundationalism" and "nonfoundationalism."

34. Gadamer can rightly say of Heidegger's work: "What being is was to be determined from within the horizon of time. Thus, the structure of temporality appeared as
ontologically definitive of subjectivity. But it was more than that. Heidegger's thesis was
that being itself is time. This burst asunder the whole subjectivism of modern philosophy—and, in fact, as was soon to appear, the whole horizon of questions asked by metaphysics, which tended to define being as what is present." Gadamer, *Truth and Method*
(2nd rev. ed.; trans. Joel Weinsheimer and Donald G. Marshall; New York: Continuum,
2003), 257.

35. Of course, in accepting these Heideggerian convictions, Gadamer recognizes that
he must avoid a performative contradiction: "It is no objection [refutation] to affirming
that we are thus fundamentally conditioned to say that this affirmation is intended to be
absolutely and unconditionally true, and therefore cannot be applied to itself without contradiction. The consciousness of being conditioned does not supersede our conditionedness." Gadamer, *Truth and Method*, 448. One author, who defends a kind of
Enlightenment rationalism, nonetheless properly identifies the heart of Gadamer's
thought: "Thus, according to historicity, and in contrast to Aristotle, the only essence of
human beings is that there is no essence. The nature of human beings is ontologically
determined by the historical situation in which we exist." James Harris, *Against Relativism:
A Philosophical Defense of Method* (Lasalle, Ill.: Open Court, 1992), 109.

36. I say "so-called" in order to alert the reader, once again, to the particular way in
which I use the term "foundationalism," that is, as an employment of metaphysics that is
theologically controlled. Foundationalism is an inappropriate word here if one means by it
some philosophical intuition or epistemological standard more basic than revelation. I use
this term because I am convinced that in much contemporary discourse, any invocation of
first philosophy, even for the express purpose of theological explication guided by revelation, is regarded as foundationalist in nature and, therefore, illegitimate. An example of
this is Richard Bernstein, "Faith and Reason," *Books and Culture* (Philosophers Respond
to *Fides et ratio*) 5 (July/August 1999): 30–32.

37. It is worth noting that despite Heidegger's own use of the words "fundamental
ontology" (*Being and Time* [trans. John Macquarrie and Edward Robinson; New York:
Harper and Row, 1962], 34), Gadamer questions the appropriateness of the term because
it appears to provide still *another* foundation for *Dasein*, to lapse again into ontotheological thinking and to inadequately capture the radicalness of Heidegger's thought. Hans-
Georg Gadamer, *Philosophical Hermeneutics* (trans. David Linge; Berkeley: University of
California Press, 1976), 171. By rejecting this term, Gadamer wishes to make clear precisely what is at stake given *die Geschichtlichkeit des Verstehens*.

38. Although he ultimately disagrees with Gadamer, Habermas defends him against
Dilthey, observing, "As Gadamer has explained, the interpreter would not understand any-
thing if he were not located within a process in which both the interpreter and his object
are embedded from the start. Since there is no way out of this context for the interpreter,
his interpretation is no less a manifestation of historical life than the interpretandum is."
Jürgen Habermas, "Coping with Contingencies," in *Debating the State of Philosophy:
Habermas, Rorty, and Kolakowski* (ed. Józef Niznik and John T. Sanders; Westport, Conn.:
Praeger, 1996), 11. Of course, as will be clear below, no one is denying that interpreters
are embedded in the historical process. Nor is anyone denying that all interpretations are
necessarily perspectival and therefore contextual and that precisely this "conditionedness"

is itself hermeneutically productive. The metaphysical questions are not directly addressed by Habermas here since he has elsewhere simply accepted the Heideggerian critique of the earlier tradition. See, for example, *Postmetaphysical Thinking* (trans. William Mark Hohengarten; Cambridge, Mass.: MIT Press, 1992), 40.

39. Gadamer severely evaluated Husserl's Cartesian tendencies, saying, "Unlike Marburg Neokantianism and Husserl's Neokantian reshaping of phenomenology, Heidegger himself refused to remain with a tradition of modifying and perpetuating the heritage of metaphysics." Hans-Georg Gadamer, "Destruktion and Deconstruction," in *Dialogue and Deconstruction: The Gadamer-Derrida Encounter* (ed. Diane P. Michelfelder and Richard E. Palmer; Albany, N.Y.: SUNY Press, 1989), 110. Of course, Heidegger himself was convinced that Husserl's thought remained tinged with Kantian transcendental subjectivity and so had not finally broken through to an unalloyed phenomenology. Husserl's reduction was, for Heidegger, simply another attempt at establishing a "worldless transcendental ego." See *The Encyclopedia of Phenomenology* (Dordrecht: Kluwer Academic Publishers, 1997), 333–39.

40. Joseph Dunne correctly identifies the fundamental basis of Gadamer's criticism of reconstructive hermeneutics: "But this critical assumption [the recovery of meaning] was usually buttressed by another more affirmative one which provided an escape from the flux of history onto the *terra firma* of a kind of metaphysical psychology. This psychological element in nineteenth-century hermeneutics postulated 'human nature as the unhistorical substratum of its theory of understanding.'" Dunne, *Back to the Rough Ground: "Phronesis" and "Techne" in Modern Philosophy and in Aristotle* (Notre Dame, Ind.: University of Notre Dame Press, 1993), 108, citing Gadamer, *Truth and Method*, 290 (see note 42 below). Reducing the notion of a common human nature to its "psychological element" may be true of some nineteenth-century thinkers, especially those under the influence of Romanticism, but it is really metaphysics itself, in both its classical and transcendental forms, that is severely questioned by Gadamer.

41. So, Gadamer says, "The discovery of the true meaning of a text or a work of art is never finished; it is in fact an infinite process." Gadamer, *Truth and Method*, 298. Of course, in one sense Gadamer's comment is wholly true since any text is newly appropriated in each age, from a new perspective. But Gadamer does not want merely a new appropriation of a stable meaning; this would be to revert to a "discredited" understanding/application distinction. For suggestive comments on Heidegger's hermeneutics, also applicable to Gadamer, see Robert Detweiler, *Breaking the Fall* (Louisville: Westminster John Knox Press, 1989), 34–36.

42. Gadamer says, "Romantic hermeneutics had taken homogeneous human nature as the unhistorical substratum of its theory of understanding and hence had freed the congenial interpreter from all historical conditions." Gadamer, *Truth and Method* (2nd rev. ed.; trans. Joel Weinsheimer and Donald G. Marshall; New York: Continuum, 2003), 290. Gadamer, and now others in his wake, repeatedly use the term "Romantic" in order to identify certain nineteenth-century theories accenting psychological empathy with the author. But "Romantic" is a misleading term and unnecessarily limits the scope of the tradition that Gadamer seeks to overturn, a tradition as wide as Heidegger's condemnation of the philosophy that preceded him. The wider reality Gadamer intends to scuttle is better named "reconstructive" or "objectivist." William Hill rightly notes that some contemporary thinkers seek to dismiss concerns with "truth" and "objectivity" simply by equating this with Romanticism. See Hill, *The Three-Personed God* (Washington, D.C.: Catholic University of America Press, 1983), 246.

43. John Caputo charges that Gadamer's reversion to a Hegelian ontologization of history, for the sake of some kind of unity, ultimately domesticates Heidegger's most radical insights about the flux of historicity. See Caputo, "Gadamer's Closet Essentialism," in

Michelfelder and Palmer, *Dialogue and Deconstruction*, 258–64. Gadamer, of course, rightly recognizes that without the unity now attributed, Hegel-like, to history, interpretative claims would be indistinguishably chaotic.

44. In a telling passage, Gadamer says, "Reconstructing the original circumstances, like all restoration, is a futile undertaking in view of the historicity of our being. What is reconstructed, a life brought back from the lost past, is not the original. In its continuance in an estranged state it acquires only a derivative, cultural existence." Gadamer, *Truth and Method*, 167.

45. Gadamer can calmly reason, "We too [like Aristotle but now globally] determined that application is neither a subsequent nor a merely occasional part of the phenomenon of understanding, but codetermines it as a whole from the beginning." Gadamer, *Truth and Method*, 324.

46. As Kevin Vanhoozer states, "The rise of hermeneutics parallels the fall of epistemology." Vanhoozer, *Is There a Meaning in This Text?* (Grand Rapids: Zondervan, 1998), 19. But as Robert Jenson rightly observes, "But when hermeneutics becomes universal, they just so become metaphysics." Jenson, *Systematic Theology*, vol. 1 (New York: Oxford University Press, 1997), 20. What Gadamer is proposing is, in fact, a kind of metaphysics—or, perhaps better, a meta-metaphysics—one now properly chastened by Heidegger and so appropriately adjusted to previously unthought dimensions.

47. Jean Grondin, "Hermeneutics and Relativism," in *Festivals of Interpretation: Essays on Hans-Georg Gadamer's Work* (ed. Kathleen Wright; Albany, N.Y.: SUNY Press, 1990), 47. See also Grondin's essay, "Gadamer's Basic Understanding of Understanding," in *The Cambridge Companion to Gadamer* (ed. Robert J. Dostal; Cambridge: Cambridge University Press, 2002), 36–51.

48. Of continuing interest on this point is the dialogue conducted between Leo Strauss and Gadamer after the publication of *Wahrheit und Methode*. Strauss protested to Gadamer that the book overthrows the stability of textual meaning. Gadamer responded, "What I believe to have understood through Heidegger (and what I can testify to from my Protestant background) is, above all, that philosophy must learn to do without the idea of an infinite intellect. I have attempted to draw up a corresponding hermeneutics." Hans-Georg Gadamer, "Correspondence concerning *Wahrheit und Methode*," *Independent Journal of Philosophy* 2 (1978): 10. For Gadamer, it appears, both the Reformation and Heidegger teach humanity about finitude, about epistemological limitations. This is not the place for an exposition of Heidegger's use of Luther, but Gadamer tends to think, like Heidegger, that religion is not about perduring cognitive affirmations but about reflection on "faith-filled *Dasein*" (a Heideggerian tendency, it should be noted, strongly opposed by Karl Barth). This tendency is perhaps ratified by this comment of Gadamer: "All of his [Heidegger's] efforts to sort things out with himself and with his questions were motivated by a desire to free himself from the dominating theology in which he had been raised—so that he could be a Christian." Hans-Georg Gadamer, *Heidegger's Ways* (Albany, N.Y.: SUNY Press, 1994), 170. It would be worth investigating precisely how Gadamer's understanding of Protestantism (including the thought of Bultmann) influenced his hermeneutical theory.

49. Of course, as one of Gadamer's well-known axioms goes, "It is enough to say that we understand in a *different* way *if we understand at all.*" Gadamer, *Truth and Method*, 297. This sentence may be properly understood, of course, as simply emphasizing the undeniably unique perspective of any interpreter. In Gadamer, however, with his marked reliance on the ontological effects of temporality and his rejection of first philosophy, such a claim indicates the possibility of a wide interpretative plurality. The same is true of Gadamer's claim, "Understanding is not merely reproductive but always a productive activity as well." *Truth and Method*, 296.

50. Richard Bernstein, *Beyond Objectivism and Relativism* (Philadelphia: University of Pennsylvania Press, 1983), 128.

51. More recently, Gadamer plays a decisive hermeneutical role in Roger Haight, *Jesus, Symbol of God* (Maryknoll, N.Y.: Orbis, 2000).

52. David Tracy, *Plurality and Ambiguity: Hermeneutics, Religion, Hope* (San Francisco: Harper & Row, 1987), 9. Pages are noted in parentheses in the text.

53. Tracy's dyslogistic regard for metaphysics appears invariable in his work, especially in *The Analogical Imagination* (New York: Crossroad, 1981), esp. 319ff. and 372ff., and may be found more recently in his essay "Fragments," in *God, the Gift, and Postmodernism* (ed. John D. Caputo and Michael J. Scanlon; Bloomington: Indiana University Press, 1999), 170–81. One may wonder, however, given Tracy's notion of disclosure (a disclosure encompassing dimensions of analogy, participation, and creation), why genuinely metaphysical elements have so little role in his thought. For Tracy on participation and analogy, see David Tracy, "A Theological View of Philosophy: Revelation and Reason," in *The Question of Christian Philosophy Today* (ed. Francis J. Ambrosio; New York: Fordham University Press, 1999), 142–62.

As is well known, Tracy's distinction between the analogical and dialectical imaginations (later expanded to the prophetic-mystical imagination) has provided a typology that is very useful for many theologians. Nonetheless, it should be acknowledged that Tracy's understanding of "analogy" is, because of his rejection of metaphysics, quite different from the use of analogy in the theological tradition. In fact, from the traditionally analogical point of view, Tracy's theology may seem dialectical and interruptive, rather than analogical in kind.

54. For Tracy's rejection of the form/content distinction, see his "Evil, Suffering, Hope: The Search for New Forms of Contemporary Theodicy," *Proceedings of the CTSA* 50 (1995): 26, where he firmly opposes such an approach. Edward Farley also criticizes the context/content distinction at great length in his book *Ecclesial Reflection* (Philadelphia: Fortress, 1982). He observes that for many Catholic theologians "the search is on to locate that *about* dogma, that element *in* dogma, beneath the relativity and errancy of the time-bound and human formulations, which is inerrant" (96 n. 19). Farley, on the other hand, accepts as valid what he calls the epistemological presupposition of contemporary philosophy: "Every entity occurs in an ever-changing situation and is itself . . . an ever-changing situation" (138). From this principle, Farley infers that the recognitive identity assumed by the context/content distinction is unattainable. One may not conclude that an equivalent meaning perdures in a new conceptual framework, since to do so massively ignores the historicity of understanding.

55. Tracy, *Plurality and Ambiguity*, 118 n. 28, 129 n. 2. The use of Habermas's notion of communicative rationality and critical praxis as validity-warrants supplementing Gadamer's emphasis on the "claim" has been explored by several thinkers who are supporters of the Gadamerian trajectory, such as Richard Bernstein, *Beyond Objectivism and Relativism*, and, in a theological context, Claude Geffré, *The Risk of Interpretation* (trans. David Smith; New York: Paulist Press, 1987). These thinkers, however, do not tackle Gadamer's consistent challenge to Habermas: Once one allows for a "higher viewpoint" (the Enlightenment) vis-à-vis the tradition, one veers quite close to a "foundationalist" ontology. See Gadamer, *Philosophical Hermeneutics*, 18–43.

56. It is perhaps not surprising, then, that in his own work on hermeneutics, Claude Geffré speaks of dogmatics and hermeneutics as antitheses. See Geffré, *Risk of Interpretation*, 46–64.

57. It is perhaps useful at this point to note once again that what is at stake here is not a mere repetition of concepts or formulae, which are mutable, but of enduring meanings, restated from new perspectives. This, of course, was the entire intention behind the original context/content hermeneutical approach.

CHAPTER 6

Renewing the Hermeneutics of Christian Doctrine

Rethinking the Hermeneutics of Doctrinal Statements

The widespread triumph of Gadamerian hermeneutics has been criticized by those, such as John Caputo, who argue that it represents an abandonment of Heidegger's most radical instincts.[1] Gadamer, the alleged defender of Heidegger's accent on temporality, is, no less than Husserl, a "false friend" of historicity. Why is this the case? Because despite Gadamer's criticisms of metaphysics in general and of Husserl in particular, he is, in fact, ultimately dependent on Hegel and Hegel's ontologization of history. In one stroke Gadamer rejects a selfsame matrix in *Dasein*, homogenizes history, and elides difference.[2] The radical *Abbau* of traditional metaphysics that Heidegger had unleashed in *Being and Time* is, according to Caputo, "constrained and domesticated" by Gadamer. The notion of the *Horizontverschmelzung* is simply a transcendental residue, an eleventh-hour attempt to find some ultimate unity in history; it is a last-gasp effort to ward off the death rattle of metaphysics (113). In the end, avers Caputo, Gadamer introduces as much change as possible into the philosophy of unchanging true and immobile verity; he seeks, by means of a Hegelian residue, to temper the radicality of the flux (111).[3]

A similar attempt to unmask Gadamer's hermeneutics as nothing more than thinly veiled logocentric metaphysics is that of Jacques Derrida. For Derrida, meaning is hardly stable, centering on presence; it is, instead, always differing and deferring. This Derridean indeterminacy of meaning, with its corollary of "undecideability," was brought to a head in the Parisian dialogue between Gadamer and Derrida in 1981. Gadamer opened with a straightforward statement on textual interpretation, while Derrida offered only an obscure, barely intelligible response. To this rhetorical ploy, Gadamer responded:

> Is he [Derrida] really disappointed that we cannot understand each other? Indeed not, for in his view this would be a relapse into metaphysics. He will, in fact, be pleased, because he takes this private experience of disillusionment to confirm his own metaphysics. But I cannot see here how he can be right only with respect to himself, be in agreement only with himself.[4]

For Derrida, Gadamer is furtively, and untenably, clinging to a last shred of metaphysics, presence, and logos-centered thought.[5] But regardless of the criticisms of Gadamer launched by Caputo and Derrida, it is not these that primarily concern us here.[6] It is neither Caputo's nor Derrida's but rather Gadamer's hermeneutics that have had the most significant influence in contemporary theology.

The concern caused by the success of Gadamerian interpretative theory is linked to certain theological consequences. In particular, as regards the nature of doctrine, it is very difficult to claim that the formal dogmatic statements of the church, such as the creeds of Nicea, Constantinople, and Chalcedon, statements recognized by virtually all Christians as reflective of biblical truth, are able to exist, identical and selfsame, as perduringly true through various generations and decidedly different cultures. It is difficult to see as well, of course, how these dogmatic statements may serve as criteria for the adjudication of other, necessarily different, constructive theological proposals. This is so, of course, because Gadamer holds that reconstructive understanding is ontologically flawed.[7] One must substitute instead an interpretative trajectory excising the stable determinacy of textual meaning in favor of the *Horizontverschmelzung*, issuing forth in a new understanding linked to the prior one, not by the material continuity of meaning but only the formal continuity of history and tradition itself.

Of course, there is a great deal in Gadamer's hermeneutics that is valuable and legitimately attractive. He rebels against the Enlightenment annihilation of the interpreting subject, he conclusively shows that all interpretation is not simply repetition but is also, necessarily, creation and mediation, and he rehabilitates the forestructure of understanding, thereby accenting the necessity of perspectivism, that is, of how historicity, finitude, and human embeddedness positively affect interpretation. These insights must be welcomed in any creative hermeneutical retrieval.[8]

Both theologically and philosophically, however, Christian thought needs a hermeneutical theory that, while incorporating certain Gadamerian insights, can safeguard the church's ability to recover, restate, and reformulate those doctrinal and dogmatic texts in which central aspects of Christian faith are displayed and that can serve as an adjudicatory norm for further theological proposals. Christian theology needs a hermeneutics that can account for textual stability and enduring meanings. It needs a hermeneutics that can intelligibly explain the normative and universal truth of Christian doctrine as mediated in and through a variety of languages, cultures, and socially constituted communities. In other words, it needs a hermeneutics that can support the possibility of reconstructive and reproductive understanding, one that allows for the advances of reconceptualization, that explicates the legitimacy of contemporary ecumenical discussions, and that provides useful clues for the development of doctrine.

The hermeneutical approach able to fulfill these goals is, in fact, the reconstructive hermeneutics noted earlier. Incorporating many Gadamerian themes, but within a context that is much more favorable to theological concerns about the continuity of Christian teaching, is the work of Emilio Betti. In fact, much of what Gadamer, Betti's chief interlocutor, claims about finitude, the forestructure of understanding, and the productive role of the interpreter, is also acknowledged by Betti himself. What separates Gadamer and Betti—and, a fortiori, the Gadamerian from the objectivist construal of hermeneutics—is that reconstructive theory requires some kind of (broadly conceived) metaphysical approach.

Emilio Betti

Emilio Betti's fundamental hermeneutical theory may be found in several works. His magnum opus, however, is *Teoria generale dell'interpretazione* (*TGI*; 1955), an exhaustive, two-volume study that traces virtually the entire history of hermeneutics.[9]

Emilio Betti came to hermeneutical issues not by way of philosophy or theology but by way of his study of legal decisions and their applicability in various circumstances over the course of time. This interest gradually drew him to the theological and philosophical debates over interpretive theory that had already been underway for decades.[10] In particular, Betti spent a great deal of time countering certain aspects of Gadamer's hermeneutical theory, aspects which, Betti argued, tended toward an unacceptable subjectivism. Despite his prominence in the hermeneutical debate and the utter seriousness with which Gadamer himself has taken his criticisms, Betti remains relatively unknown in the English-speaking theological world. Where he is known, his thought is often conflated with that of E. D. Hirsch, another defender of reconstructive hermeneutics whose work is more accessible. But Betti and Hirsch, although certainly thinking in a similar direction—that of realistic, reconstructive hermeneutical theory—are hardly coincident in their thought.[11] Both clearly hold that the role of the interpreter is to discover the meaning embodied in the text (which is also called by Betti the "Form" or "Representative Form"). Both are also dependent, at least to some extent, on Husserl and phenomenology, allowing for a move away from a "psychologizing" notion of authorial intention.[12] Nonetheless, in my judgment, Betti's hermeneutical theory is far more comprehensive than Hirsch's, since Betti's thought encircles virtually the entire history of interpretation, especially as this developed in Germany from Schleiermacher onward. Betti also has more completely developed his thinking on crucial issues, such as the actuality or topicality of interpretative acts.

I argue in the following section that Betti's hermeneutical theory incorporates much of what is best in Gadamer's thought, especially Gadamer's emphasis on the actuality of interpretation, while at the same time hewing more closely to the recovery of a stable textual meaning. I will move in three steps: (1) Betti's hermeneutical theory, (2) an evaluation of his thought, and (3) some of the crucial differences between Betti's and Gadamer's notions of interpretation.

Betti's Hermeneutics

In his major two-volume work, Betti presents an exhaustive phenomenology of the hermeneutical situation.[13] The cornerstone on which his work rests is the determinate and invariant structure of the interpretive act. This movement is triadic in structure. It involves, first, the interpreter who is called to understand the meaning of texts, symbols, musical scores, monuments, and so on. Betti calls these "products" of the creative spirit, "Representative Forms," or, less frequently, Objectifications of the human spirit. It involves, second, the "other" spirituality who calls and speaks to the interpreter though the Representative Form, and, third, the Form itself. Betti offers a detailed analysis of each of these constitutive elements.

In all noetic situations, the interpreter finds himself or herself before a Representative Form. This Form or Objectification may be defined as perceptible material (whether text, musical notation, or work of art), mediating an endowment (message) that is embodied within it. The Form now serves as the inaugurator of a colloquy between the interpreter and the spiritual endowment living within the Objectification. The correlation between the Form's message and the interpreter to whom it speaks marks the beginning of an actual historical dialogue. What interests hermeneutical theory, Betti says, is precisely the process of understanding, whereby one person responds to the message of another communicating by means of the Form.

Where Betti differs from several contemporary hermeneutical theorists, such as Gadamer, is in his analysis of the message embodied in the Representative Form. Betti emphasizes both the determinate meaning affixed within the Form and the possibility of its recovery and re-cognition by the historical interpreter. The Form embodies a meaning and message that has been objectified by the creative act of an "Other." The process of re-cognition involves the reconstruction and re-expression of precisely the message now mediated through the specific Objectification.

The recognitive act of the interpreter seeks to be as faithful as possible to the meaning embodied in the Representative Form. Insofar as the interpretative act succeeds the creative act, a proper hermeneutics demands some type of controllable subordination of the interpreter to the Form itself. Only this kind of interpretative fidelity to the text or Objectification protects both the unique individuality of the Form itself as well as the classical hermeneutical criterion: *Sensus non est inferendus sed efferendus.*[14]

It is precisely this subordination of the interpreter to the Representative Form that emphasizes the "Other" before whom the interpreter stands. This otherness, the voice of a *different* human spirit, engenders the hermeneutical project itself. However, the very otherness affixed in the Form must be protected from attempts to level its message to the horizon and self-understanding of the interpreter. If the interpreter's subordination and fidelity to the Form is ignored, the "otherness" of the spiritual endowment (message) is forgotten and there intrudes a temptation to validate understanding by means of a framework that is imposed subjectively and a priori.

For Betti, the "otherness," the "alien" nature of the Form, does not stand as a barrier to the re-cognition (recovery) of its affixed endowment. Because of the common humanity that the interpreter shares with the Other who speaks, the interpreter is able to reconstruct the Form's meaning. It is here that metaphysical questions begin to loom. For the moment, however, it is enough to say that for Betti, two demands always accompany the

hermeneutical task: (1) objectivity, that is, re-cognition and re-presentation must be faithful to the "otherness" of the meaning embedded in the Representative Form, and (2) mediation, that is, such objectivity is possible only insofar as the interpreter perceives the Form from his or her unique visual angle. Each interpreter, therefore, necessarily interprets from a unique historical, factical standpoint. Betti insists, however, that it is a misunderstanding to conclude that historical context so governs content that any search for the determinate meaning of the Representative Form is illusory. This is to confuse the essentially reconstructive and mediative tasks of *interpretation* with the creative and productive tasks characteristic of the original *creation*.[15] It is to misunderstand, therefore, the bipolar nature of the hermeneutical task.

Betti is not opposed to "productive" and "creative" readings, which he generally labels "speculative" interpretation.[16] He simply claims that such a procedure must be distinguished from a hermeneutical approach which, although recognizing that understanding is necessarily conditioned by the interpreter's unique visual angle, and which, therefore, contains creative and productive elements, nonetheless seeks, as an interpretative goal, to protect the meaning embedded in the Representative Form itself. This latter approach is primarily concerned with safeguarding the "otherness" and "autonomy" of the message affixed in the independent Form.

The triadic structure of the hermeneutical process noted above—the interpreter, the person "speaking" to the interpreter through the Form, and the Representative Form itself—gives rise to four canons governing the hermeneutical process.

Autonomy of the Text, or Form. This canon is intended to preserve the "otherness" affixed in the Representative Form, the objectification of the human spirit. The Form must not be interpreted by way of any heteronomous or extrinsic standard. All tendencies to reduce or relativize the text to one's own horizon or a priori prejudices must be suppressed in favor of the text's own internal and immanent coherence and rationality.[17] The text must be taken in its uniqueness as an objectification of the human spirit, with its own autonomous meaning. One cannot allow attitudes that contravene the "otherness" of the Representative Form to intrude upon the hermeneutical task.

Reciprocal Illumination. This canon calls attention to the correspondence existing between the whole and the parts of the Representative Form. The interpreter, respecting the Form's autonomy, must excavate from individual elements the meaning of the whole, while understanding the individual elements themselves in function of the whole. According to Betti, this is simply another way of calling attention to the Form's autonomy. By stressing the critical norms of totality and internal coherence, Betti hopes to avoid the deficiencies of what he sees as hermeneutical "extrinsicism."

The Actuality (Topicality) of Interpretation. The emphasis in this third canon is markedly on the side of the interpreter's contribution to the hermeneutical moment. The interpreter necessarily approaches the "otherness" of Representative Forms with his or her own interests, concerns, and horizons. The Form constitutes an embodied spiritual endowment that the interpreter must reconstruct and reproduce in accordance with his or her own sensibilities and place in history, what Betti frequently refers to as the interpreter's "conditioned perspective" (100–102). Interpretation, then, is never the mechanical reproduction of the Representative Form; on the contrary, one must necessarily interpret from the "unique visual angle" of one's perspective. It would be absurd to aspire to strip oneself of one's own subjectivity, as if one could have unalloyed contact with the "world," a noncontextual access to reality.[18] In fact, Betti avers, it is precisely the contextual subjectivity of the interpreter that is the indispensable condition for the possibility of hermeneutical reconstruction.[19] However, the importance of subjectivity, of the historical perspective of the interpreter, must not be confused with those theories concluding from the interpreter's historicity to an excision of a stable meaning embedded in the Form. Interpretation is, for Betti, always mediation. At the same time, he insists that the act of interpretation both succeeds and is subordinate to the prior creative act of giving birth to the text or musical score itself (231).

Hermeneutical Consonance. In this fourth canon, Betti posits a certain "congeniality" that must exist between the interpreter and the Representative Form, a "fraternal disposition" between the interpreter and the objectified spiritual endowment. It represents a sense of *pietas* before true *humanitas*. This attitude of empathy is meant to underscore the necessary excision of prejudices, amounting to a certain self-abnegation, in the interpreter's meeting with the "alien" Form. It serves to accent the fact that, if spirit is to speak to spirit, then a true unity, a harmony, must ensue. This must not be confused with a rigid identity, which, in any case, is impossible. It must be understood, Betti says, as a dialectical unity. The interpreter, always from his or her unique visual angle, must seek to understand the "Other" through the Form in which he or she has communicated a message. There is an accent, certainly, on the essential importance of the horizon of the interpreter, while always maintaining the autonomy of the "alien" textual intention.

The Goal of Interpretation

Given these four hermeneutical canons, offered as aids to the interpretive task, one may achieve, according to Betti, a determinate goal. The primary end of interpretation is always the re-cognition (recovery) of the spiritual endowment affixed in the Representative Form. However, as Betti also makes clear, this re-cognition is never simply imitation, endless mimetic and iterative repetition, but is also, in some sense, a creation. This is necessarily the case since the *new* Representative Form achieved by the interpreter reflects a distinct visual angle, a conditioned perspective.[20] Further, this new Form is meant for a new circle of hearers; its very purpose is to re-express an original meaning in a diverse manner, accessible to a new "audience."

Interpretation, then, never results in simple identity. This would be impossible given the two horizons confronting each other in the hermeneutical situation. However, Betti observes, some theorists confuse identity and correspondence. The former, outside of mathematics, is epistemologically impossible. It assumes that the consonance between two spiritual totalities could result in a rigid identity. The latter, however, is the achievable telos of interpretation. Betti describes correspondence as the *equivalency of meanings* in various Representative Forms (324). This consonance may not be understood as an antidialectical identity that ignores the two horizons; rather, it represents the highest goal of interpretation, namely, a dialectical unification. Precisely because the process of re-cognition and reconstruction can only be in accord with the historicity and subjectivity of the interpreter—that is, with his or her social, cultural, and educational categories—the new understanding achieved will be *equivalent* to the original Representative Form, not identical to it. As Betti states, "It is a gnoseological error to believe that the subject is able to 'contact' the object directly without need of his own categories" (326). On the other hand, Betti cannot countenance hermeneutical theories that discount the possibility of equivalent re-cognition.[21] What is always at stake in interpretation is the tension between the dual criteria of the autonomy of the Form and the actuality and historicity of the interpreter. For Betti, the hermeneutical ideal demands allowing the Form to speak, even as one understands it within one's own perspective.[22]

The hermeneutical task, properly fulfilled, results in the issuance of an equivalent Representative Form that expresses the original meaning in a different manner or perspective. At this point, Betti makes a distinction between understanding as pure re-cognition and as reproduction. Even re-cognition is, in a certain sense, reproduction (i.e., suffused with a productive, creative element) because of the unique visual angle and conditioned perspective of the interpreter. However, while recognitive interpretation stresses correspondence with the Representative Form—such as in reading a text—reproductive interpretation consciously emphasizes the uniqueness of the representative dimension. This is to say that while even reproductive understanding is always essentially recognitive (concerned with the recovery of meaning), it more forcefully assumes the office of substituting a different, although equivalent, Representative Form. As such, reproductive understanding does not simply seek to understand, but to make something *newly understood* (*TGI*, 1:347–48; *TGI*, 2:636). Unlike recognitive interpretation, reproductive interpretation is never exhausted *in interiore hominis*; it always seeks a dimension of transposition.

As transitive and social, reproductive understanding presents a new Representative Form, sometimes quite different from (although ultimately equivalent to) the original one. Especially here, given the new Objectification, the critical demands of fidelity and subordination to the original Representative Form must be rigorously invoked. The original remains the standard by which the fidelity of the reproduction is judged. But precisely because of the inevitable lacunae that exist in any Representative Form, the reproduction will draw out new perspectives lying fallow in the original (*TGI*, 2:641). Of course, only by following the hermeneutical canons will reproductive interpretation achieve its fundamental goal, namely, the communication of a corresponding, equivalent message to a circle of listeners different from the one to which the Original Form was first addressed.[23]

Betti's hermeneutical theory, like Gadamer's, seeks to integrate the insight that the horizons of temporality and finitude are ontologically constitutive of understanding and interpretation. The actuality or topicality of interpretation means that each interpretation necessarily takes place from what Betti calls a unique visual angle, a "conditioned perspective." However, Betti's admission of the productivity of history is not equivalent to a denial of recognitive and reproductive hermeneutics. For Betti, the rejection of the recovery of meaning, in favor of a Gadamerian-influenced fusion of horizons, is a reprise of a historicism as misguided as the naïve autonomy espoused by the Enlightenment.

Of course, it is undeniable that Betti himself allows for a certain type of *Horizontverschmelzung*. The horizon of the interpreter is always confronted with the spiritual endowment affixed in the Representative Form. Further, the interpreter approaches the Form with all of the philosophical, cultural, sociological, and psychological categories that constitute his or her individual subjectivity. A *Horizontverschmelzung* must take place, but it is a fusion that gives rise to a "correspondence," not to a rigid identity or to an understanding rejecting the material continuity of meaning. There is, then, no denial of the historical dimensions suffusing noetic acts, but there is, simultaneously, an affirmation of the recognitive and reproductive powers of the interpreter in and through history. Betti, of course, wants to defend the coherence of recoverable meaning affixed in the historically given Form. He sees in Gadamer's position (i.e., that reconstructive understanding is ontologically naïve) an idealistic overlay extraneous to realistic interpretative theory. Gadamer's work constitutes a turn to a "speculative" kind of interpretation that, for Betti, may only be called hermeneutics in an analogous sense (102).[24]

As a corollary to the fusion of horizons, one must emphasize Betti's positive valuation of tradition. It is precisely the "prejudice" of tradition that endows the interpreter with his or her unique visual angle. Any denial of the subject's presupposed *Lebenswelt*—saturated as it is with "conditions" of every kind, the *Vorhabe* and *Vorverständnis* highlighted by both Heidegger and Gadamer—results merely in Enlightenment mythology. Betti, however, seeks to conjoin the indefeasible forestructure of understanding with the critical rationality of the interpreter. While it is true that all thought and understanding come to light within a particular linguistic and historical tradition, and while the worldless ideal of certain eighteenth-century thinkers has been exposed as untenable, Betti argues that the achievement of critical rationality lies precisely in the interpreter's awareness of the preunderstanding "attending" all reading, the "world" penetrating all of his or her formulations, ultimately allowing the interpreter to perceive the differences between himself/herself and the endowment embodied in the Form.[25] Far from obviating the possibility of recognitive interpretation, Betti holds that the elements constituting the historicity and facticity of the interpreter both allow it and, especially in reproductive interpretation, enrich it.[26]

Therefore, with regard to the two axioms epigrammatically characterizing Gadamerian hermeneutical theory, Betti stands in qualified agreement: (1) Understanding is always interpretation, and (2) understanding is an event over which the interpreting subject does not ultimately preside.[27] Both axioms seek to emphasize the nameless but ever-present "world" that saturates the hermeneutical moment. With the presence of this "world," Betti is in complete concordance. With the inference that the "world" inexorably vitiates the possibility of recognitive and reproductive interpretation, he firmly disagrees.

One may hardly accuse Betti, then, of defending a mechanical notion of interpretation, one arguing for mere wooden replication. This is simply inaccurate. Further, while it is true that Betti thinks certain "canons of interpretation" are essential to the proper understanding of the hermeneutical project, he hardly proposes these be followed leadenly, with the intention of establishing an exact, positivistic methodology. The charge of "methodism," therefore, would be here misplaced.[28]

The Metaphysical Question: The Difference between Gadamer and Betti

Despite the exhaustive exposition of hermeneutical theory that Betti offers, and despite his outlining certain differences with Gadamer's thought, Betti never quite explicates or defends the ontological assumptions on which his interpretive theory rests. He does make some references to the solidarity of human nature as the basis for reconstructive understanding, invoking along the way the works of Husserl and especially Nicolai Hartmann.[29] For the most part, however, these remarks are quite brief and philosophically undeveloped even though they represent, in fact, the crux of the difference between realistic, reconstructive hermeneutics and the Gadamerian variety.

For example, Betti criticizes Heidegger, since for Heidegger "understanding ceases to be a universal human fact, accessible in virtue of a common mental structure to whoever has reached the necessary level of spiritual maturity" (*TGI*, 248–49). In the same section, Betti condemns Heidegger's "existential limitation on understanding, with its failure to recognize the spiritual basis of this in a common humanity, leading to the inhuman and barbaric result of raising insuperable barriers among circles of men reciprocally excluding them and attributing an absolute value to particularism" (249).[30] Similarly, in a discussion of Bultmann, Betti notices the exegete distancing himself from Dilthey's claim that the possibility of recognitive interpretation rests on the "spiritual communion given by common human nature" (251). This distancing leads inexorably, Betti concludes, to a Bultmannian hermeneutics more concerned with inferring meaning rather than extracting it from texts. Finally, Betti asserts that, in hermeneutics, "knowing is re-cognitive . . . so that through the objectified forms, one speaks to the thinking spirit, feeling close to him in one's *common humanity*" (260–61).[31] In the fundamental thrust of his work, then, Betti would agree with Stanley Rosen: "If there is no human nature that remains constant within historical change . . . then reading is impossible." Rosen further claims that the rise of hermeneutics is partially caused by "an intensifying conviction that nature, and so human nature, is an historical myth."[32] Rosen here is simply recognizing, along with Leo Strauss, that, lacking some notion of a common human nature, there cannot be transcultural readings that protect both the stable determinacy of textual meaning and the ministerial office of the interpreter.[33]

Without doubt, then, it is on the basis of this largely unexplicated metaphysical/transcendental anthropology, the ontology warranting reconstructive hermeneutics, that Betti rejects the radically historical approach he finds characteristic of Heidegger, Gadamer, and Bultmann. It is certainly true that Betti does not understand himself to be tied to a particular notion of metaphysics even if, at times, his language approaches that of phenomenology, with its emphasis on intentionality.[34] Perhaps precisely to avoid quarrels he thinks extraneous to the hermeneutical task, Betti leaves this area of his thought undeveloped. It remains true, nonetheless, that he is working within parameters and presuppositions that thinkers such as Gadamer find virtually indistinguishable from traditional metaphysics of any kind.[35]

Of course, it is just this "metaphysical" jugular advanced by Betti, this undeveloped "foundation," that Gadamer attacks. As Joseph Dunne has remarked, it is precisely the idea of a "common human nature" that Heideggerian hermeneutics thinks untenable and philosophically inappropriate.[36] Knowingly or not, Gadamer argues, Betti's hermeneutical stance is based on an illegitimate metaphysics.[37] Betti is positing some selfsame matrix of human nature in order to undergird the very possibility of reconstructive interpretation. But it is precisely the inappropriateness of Betti's *ontological* grounds that has led him to erroneous *hermeneutical* conclusions. To speak, as Betti does, of a recoverable meaning affixed within the text indicates a hermeneutical naïveté borne of a failure to understand the depth of Heidegger's critique of the prior metaphysical tradition. Heidegger has unmasked precisely the constitutive horizons of historicity and finitude that *Dasein* has ceaselessly buried. The entire weight of contemporary nonfoundationalist thought, with its accents on temporality and facticity, is thus brought to bear on Betti's hermeneutical project. Betti fails to recognize, in Gadamer's judgment, that the interpreter is fully enmeshed and embedded in history, and so he remains trapped within the parameters of traditional metaphysics and its allied interpretative theory.

Excursus: Kevin Vanhoozer's Realistic Hermeneutics

Although he is, like many of those writing in English, largely unaware of Betti's thought, Kevin Vanhoozer, in a recent work, offers a contemporary rendition of many of the central themes of reconstructive hermeneutics. Vanhoozer has the further advantage of writing in a theological key so that his ideas have immediate relevance to some of the issues under discussion.

Vanhoozer's stated goal is to show, in the shadow of Derrida, Stanley Fish, and postmodernity generally that, indeed, "there is a meaning in the text, that it can be known and that readers should strive to do so."[38] In this, as in several other matters, Vanhoozer's hermeneutical approach is similar to that of Betti. In the following sections I will, firstly, outline the similarities and differences between Betti and Vanhoozer; secondly, I will discuss reconstructive hermeneutics in relationship to the nature and development of doctrine; finally, I will return to a consideration of the content/context distinction.

On several crucial points, especially regarding the goal of interpretation, Betti and Vanhoozer are quite close. For example, of primary importance to both of them is the claim that some kind of recognitive interpretation is possible. Vanhoozer points out that he is a hermeneutical realist, who holds that there is "something prior to interpretation, something 'there' in the text, which can be known and to which the interpreter is accountable" (26).[39] He asserts that the text represents the "communicative act of a communicative agent" (225); consequently, textual meaning enjoys an integrity of its own thanks to this intended communicative action (234).[40] Vanhoozer further holds that "the goal of interpretation is to recover the original meaning of the text" (46); the interpreter is fundamentally accountable to the text, wherein there exists a determinate textual meaning (47). Interpretation, then, is primarily about recovering the message and meaning embedded in the text. With this pronounced accent on the recoverability of textual intention, Betti would certainly agree.

Vanhoozer also defends, again in common with Betti although with assuredly different accents, the meaning/significance distinction that Gadamer, on his own theoretical principles, forcefully denies as ontologically truncated. Vanhoozer argues that such a distinction relies on one's ability to recover textual meaning; the significance of this recovered meaning, however, may be adjudged differently at different times and by different interpreters.[41] Consequently, he concludes, "with regard to interpretation, the meaning/significance distinction continues to be meaningful and highly significant" (260).

Vanhoozer's central claim is that when examining a text, a score, or a work of art, the interpreter is seeking to understand the communicative act of a particular agent. Meaning, therefore, exists where there is a "meant," a "communicative action of a genuine 'other'" (234).[42] For both

Betti and Vanhoozer, then, there is clearly a sense in which interpretation is truly recovery and re-cognition and not simply new creation. Although they have different emphases, both thinkers are seeking some hermeneutical via media between wooden repetition and interpretative relativism, between mechanistic identity and interpretative indeterminacy, or, as Vanhoozer has it, between absolute and anarchic interpretation (136).[43]

On the other hand, there are clearly differences between Betti's and Vanhoozer's construals of the hermeneutical task. In the first place, Vanhoozer is entirely wedded to the language of authorial intention. The author, for Vanhoozer, is the one who "commands and controls meaning" (46); the author is the "ground of the 'being' of meaning" (47). Indeed, the central problem of postmodern interpretation is that "the author cannot fulfill the role of stabilizing signs that the metaphysics of meaning would seem to require" (66). It must immediately be added that Vanhoozer has reservations about speaking of hermeneutics as "recover[ing] the author's consciousness" (25). There is no doubt, however, that his emphasis is on authorial intention as the hermeneutical key for ascertaining meaning; it is the primary guide for validity in interpretation (43–44). Betti, on the other hand, uses sparingly the language of authorial intention, preferring to stress the text or the Form, in which the author's meaning is embedded. It is certainly true that the textual meaning Betti is trying to understand ultimately stems from the communicative act of an intentional agent. In this sense, then, authorial intention surely plays an important role. But Betti's accent is on understanding the Representative Form, thereby placing his emphasis squarely on the public availability of the text in-the-world rather than on the hidden, inaccessible consciousness of the author or, still less, on strict authorial interpretative control.[44]

Is there a legitimate difference between Betti and Vanhoozer? Vanhoozer is careful to note that insofar as a text is the "communicative act of a communicative agent," the ground for meaning is found "in the communicative activity not the subjectivity of the author" (225).[45] He states further that one's communicative action, unlike one's consciousness, is "publicly accessible" (225). However, throughout his work, Vanhoozer frames his argument within the language of authorial intention, which tends to mislead the reader. Betti's language, of the message embedded in the "Representative Form," better preserves, in my judgment, the public notion of available meaning, moving away from any psychologizing consciousness irreducibly associated with the language of authorial intentionality.[46] The influence of Husserl here, who himself sought to break with what he thought was an illegitimate neo-Kantian accent on transcendental consciousness, clearly finds useful resonances in Betti's hermeneutics.

A second difference between the two authors, perhaps the central one, is that Betti, although not always explicitly, recognizes that there is an important metaphysical difference between himself and Gadamer, meaning by this that Betti's entire hermeneutical project assumes an eidetically discernible "human nature" common to all men and women. He makes several references to such a metaphysical idea and says that the failure to recognize such commonality raises insuperable barriers among men and women.

Vanhoozer, for his part, is certainly aware of some of the metaphysical issues at stake. He refers, for example, to the Derridean claim that metaphysics is the attempt to detextualize reality, the endeavor to escape from the freeplay and instability of signs (63–64). He further points out that the contemporary postmodern hermeneutical challenge is primarily to the realistic "metaphysics of meaning," that is, to the claim that the meaning of a text clearly gives us access to the "world" (99). And he avers that "Gadamer and Ricoeur have tried to explain how interpretation is still possible after the metaphysical shift away from the author and the epistemological shift away from Newtonian objectivity" (106).[47]

Vanhoozer, however, although explicitly abjuring Cartesian anthropology (231), scarcely mentions Heidegger, whom Betti rightly recognizes as the philosophical machine ultimately powering significant swaths of contemporary hermeneutical theory. And he fails to recognize clearly that it is the large-scale adoption of Heidegger's "fundamental ontology" that guides Gadamer's own interpretative approach. On this point, it seems, Betti has more clearly and carefully identified, without developing, the central issue—namely, that the overthrow of classical and transcendental metaphysics is the primordial basis for contemporary philosophical opposition to the entire trajectory of realistic hermeneutics. Of course, it may be noted that Vanhoozer is much more interested in Derrida and Fish than he is in Heidegger and Gadamer. But it remains the case that the latter duo has had much more theological influence than the former and that the latter group is the ultimate foundation on which the former thinkers have built.[48]

The Hermeneutics of Doctrine: Theological Development

Betti, Vanhoozer, and E. D. Hirsch represent thinkers with similar interests, especially regarding the possibility of realistic, recognitive, and reproductive hermeneutical theories. I have discussed some of their differences earlier,

especially those regarding the language and meaning of "authorial intention." Vanhoozer's stress on authorial intention is often meant to serve a
particular purpose, namely, protecting the traditional notion of *sola scriptura* as the sole criterion by which the truth of ecclesial assertions may be
judged. This essential criterion will only have force, Vanhoozer argues, if
it is possible to have access to the literal meaning intended by the author.
This goal has prompted Roger Lundin to assert that the reconstructive
work of Hirsch is "enormously influential in evangelical biblical studies."
Hirsch is attractive to "conservative Christians seeking to ground their
faith without deference to tradition or recourse to a developed doctrine of
the church."[49]

I would contend, however, that it is not simply evangelical thinkers
who find Hirsch's thought attractive. An adherence to the possibility of
recognitive and reproductive interpretation, to use Betti's terms, and a
defense of the stable determinacy of textual meaning are important not
only to those seeking to defend a particular notion of *sola scriptura* but also
to those wishing to develop a hermeneutics of doctrine capable of supporting the identity and continuity of doctrinal statements as reflective of
scriptural affirmations.[50] So one need not, as Lundin suggests, simply concern oneself with reconstructive hermeneutics for the sake of *avoiding* tradition and a "developed doctrine of the church." On the contrary, one may
seek a determinate meaning of Scripture while concomitantly defending
the necessity of doctrinal development and the amplification of biblical
meaning that must always be an organic and architectonic maturation of
it. This is precisely what Vincent of Lerins meant in the fifth century
when he argued that there is indeed development within the tradition but
that it must always be a *profectus*, never a *permutatio*; it must always be *in
eodem sensu*, not *in sensu alieno* with the deposit of faith.[51] This understanding recognizes the productivity of history and tradition, as Gadamer
has argued, but without the concomitant loss of recognitive and reproductive hermeneutics. The actual fact of the matter is that Catholicism,
Orthodoxy, and many Protestant representatives of historic Christian
orthodoxy see the biblical intention embodied in the apostolic and doctrinal tradition of the church, thereby allowing for organic development
without strictly identifying Scripture and the church. Timothy George,
for example, has said that evangelical Protestants recognize the need to
take account of developing the "inexorable implications" of Scripture.[52]
Roman Catholics and others will fully agree with this, while adding that
these determinate, inexorable elements are made clearer and fuller by
ecclesial dimensions such as the liturgy, the councils, the doctors of the

church, the lives of the saints—in other words, by all of those elements grouped around a proper understanding of tradition. It is anachronistic, therefore, to argue that historic Christian orthodoxy is uninterested in the literal and determinate meaning of Scripture. Such orthodoxy is, however, surely uninterested in saying that every implication of Scripture is thereby exhausted by the literal sense.[53]

Reconstructive hermeneutics are also particularly helpful in explaining how one may simultaneously affirm the identity of Christian doctrine along with the importance of its architectonic development. Just here, one recalls that Betti makes a distinction between recognitive and reproductive interpretation. Both interpretative strategies seek to understand the meaning embedded in the text. But while the former type seeks simply to understand, the latter seeks both to understand and to make the message of the Form/text newly understood. As such, reproductive interpretation issues forth in a new Form/text, often somewhat creative in its own right, even if essentially faithful to the original Form.

Theologically speaking, one may use Betti's principles to affirm the unity and identity of doctrine through the ages without thereby becoming victim to doctrinal immobility. For example, the doctrinal definitions issuing from the Councils of Nicea, Constantinople, and Chalcedon are ecclesially constitutive statements. Most Christians believe these doctrinal affirmations to be abidingly, universally, and normatively true. On the basis of recognitive interpretation, one may claim that the meanings of these conciliar affirmations may be recovered by later generations. Betti, for example, would say that the Nicene Creed has a particular meaning, which is the fruit of a communicative act by the bishops gathered in council. The meaning of the text is recoverable, not by thinking we can peer into the minds of the fourth-century authors, but by examining the text in its proper context (e.g., its sociohistorical location, the controversies arising at the time, the concepts in use). The standard here for validity in interpretation is the recovery of meaning sustainable by the text (in its original context). The definitions proposed by the Council of Nicea (and the other councils), the recovered meaning of these conciliar texts, are now able to serve as contemporary christological standards.

Does this then mean that realistic and reconstructive hermeneutics countenances only an immobile and positivistic theory, disallowing any development of doctrine or any contemporary reconceptualization; that Chalcedon, for example, à la Rahner's famous essay, is now only an end and not also a beginning? Such is hardly the case, for two reasons: In the first place, even recognitive interpretation, an interpretation seeking strict fidelity to the original "Other," is necessarily grasped from the unique visual angle and historical situation of the interpreter. There will be a "productive" moment, therefore, in any interpretation, given that even the most faithful rendering (remember that Betti has abjured any mathematical notion of "identity" that is inseparable from mechanical repetition) will have a chiaroscuro effect, accenting some elements while letting others remain more obscure. Secondly, as Betti says, reproductive understanding seeks to go a step beyond recognitive interpretation, trying not only to understand a text/Form but also to make the text *newly understood*. The accent here, clearly, is on contemporary actualization and topicality. Once again, Betti rightly insists that the recognitive moment must be protected. It is not a question of primarily speculative thought, of abandoning faithfulness to the meaning of the original Form; it is a matter of allowing the textual meaning, in its legitimate autonomy and "otherness," to speak again, to speak newly.[54] It is a matter of reconceptualization, of trying to say what was originally said in a way that uses language, images, and concepts in a new and different way, even while protecting the original meaning. In this process of reproductive thought, new ideas, points of view, and, of course, new formulations emerge. A determinate meaning—let us say, that of Nicea or Chalcedon—is recast in new images, reconceptualized according to the patterns, language, and concepts of the day, and thereby made intelligible to a new generation, without betraying the original textual intention. This accent, clearly on the actualization of interpretation, is in full accord with Gadamer's claims that to understand is to understand differently, that history and tradition are ontologically productive, that there is a fusion of horizons between text and interpreter, but without accepting his philosophical suspicions about recognitive thought. History is not here simply a chasm that is to be overcome. On the contrary, historicity, social location, and cultural-linguistic specificity are all necessarily productive of the interpretative act. A *Horizontverschmelzung* truly occurs because the meaning of the text/Form is now reconceptualized, rethought, and re-expressed even while preserving the autonomy of the original insight.

Examples of just such a procedure may be adduced from the tradition. Aquinas certainly recognized that he departed from Augustine (as well as from Dionysius and Damascene) in many of his central concepts and in several of his unifying principles. Nonetheless, it is virtually certain that he saw himself as "repeating" the great tradition, as making newly understood, in a new language, patient of new insights, the perduringly true and selfsame faith that Augustine, and the others, had believed. The same is surely the case, at least in essentials, with the great thinkers of the Reformation. And the phenomenon repeats itself during the attempts of various theologians to enter into dialogue with modernity, with the thought of Descartes, Kant, and Hegel now expressing the faith in terms drawn from modern philosophy. The intention, once again, was to maintain the substance of the great dogmatic tradition while making this intelligible in contemporary terms and, in the process, uncovering new insights. In the twentieth century, theological attempts to incorporate existentialist and phenomenological categories were elaborated with the same goal in mind.

Surely most contemporary ecumenical agreements are also an exercise in both recognitive and reproductive understanding. In the first place, a council's thought—let us say, by way of example, Trent on justification— is recovered by an examination of the documents, the conciliar acts, and so forth. Secondly, the meaning of the council is reproduced not simply by repeating the scholastic lexicon utilized in the sixteenth century, but by seeking new ways of expressing, conceptualizing, and formulating the conciliar intention on the nature of humanity's renewal through Christ's salvific actions. Precisely such reproductive interpretation has yielded, from the Roman Catholic side, the affirmations found in the Joint Declaration on Justification.[55]

It is not the case, of course, that all theological attempts at reproductive interpretation, of making the truth of the deposit of faith newly understood, are equally successful.[56] However, the fundamental point should be clear: It is the constant state of the church that theologians seek to reconceptualize the Christian faith, to understand it and make it newly understood, from the perspective, standpoint, and sociocultural-linguistic horizons of their own age. The newly wrought interpretation is mediative because it seeks to present an equivalent meaning in a more intelligible framework; it is productive and creative because the new conceptual system necessarily reflects a unique visual angle and historical moment. The newly proffered reproductive understanding will also be able to develop some ideas hidden and obscured that have lain fallow in the original Form. This reproductive attempt, accenting equally the ontological productivity and the hermeneutical fidelity of the interpretative act, serves as one significant means of the development of doctrine.[57]

Development of doctrine occurs, then, when the church tries to understand the "inexorable implications" of Scripture; to make its faith, as articulated in Christian doctrine, newly understood; and to make the truth that has been handed on, that constitutes the deposit of faith, intelligible to a new age, an age that thinks, lives, and speaks in a new intellectual universe. It is what Bouillard and Chenu refer to as the "law of the incarnation." It is the meaning of Bouillard's controversial but penetrating comment, "Une théologie qui ne serait pas actuelle serait une théologie fausse" (a theology which was not contemporary would be a false theology). And it is what Newman meant in his oft-cited remark that "to be perfect is to have changed often."[58] In all cases, it is a matter of maintaining the fundamental content of the doctrine of the church, of recognizing its normativity and perduring truthfulness while speaking it in new contexts, with unique accents, different perspectives, new appropriations, and a renewed lexicon.

The Hermeneutics of Doctrine: A Return to Context/Content

Having examined the reconstructive thought of Betti and Vanhoozer and having discussed the role that reconstructive hermeneutics plays in the interpretation of doctrine, it is now appropriate to return to the context/content distinction adduced at the beginning of chapter five. This distinction has been useful from several perspectives. Its citation by John XXIII at the opening of Vatican II helped Catholicism to overcome the theological strictures of neo-Scholasticism, thereby allowing a true theological pluralism to flourish. Christian doctrine had been and could once again be expressed in a variety of forms, incommensurable with each other (Augustinian and Thomist paradigms, for example), but ultimately commensurable with the *depositum fidei*. The encyclical *Fides et ratio* offers a vigorous endorsement of just such theological pluralism, with the proviso, of course, that such plurality remains commensurate with the essential teachings of the Christian faith. This notion, that the church can express its enduring faith within a variety of conceptual systems, is behind the encyclical's claim that although Christianity first encountered Greek philosophy, "this does not mean at all that other approaches are precluded" (no. 72). Even more strongly, the document asserts that "the church has no philosophy of her own nor does she canonize any one particular philosophy in preference to others" (no. 49). Still again, "I have no wish to direct theologians to particular methods, since that is not the competence of the magisterium" (no. 64). In all of these instances, one sees the assertion that the content of the Christian faith may be expressed in a variety of contexts or forms. It is precisely this idea that is behind the letter's eulogistic citation of a variety of thinkers using very different methodologies, both classical, such as Augustine, the Cappadocians, and Aquinas, and modern, such as Newman, Soloviev, and Stein.[59]

The context/content distinction has also been a major engine in virtually all ecumenical discussions. The very premise of such bilateral agreements is that each church is working from a particular point of view, *Denkstil*, or unique visual angle that, in its own conceptually determined and lexicon-specific vocabulary, preserves the essential teaching of the *depositum fidei*. The Joint Declaration on Justification between Lutherans and Catholics serves a prime exemplar ratifying this approach. While for Roman Catholics the Tridentine decree on justification is couched in the Aristotelian-Thomistic language of causality, the Lutheran approach avoids entirely this classical/scholastic framework in favor of a Pauline/existential model. Yet each church in its own way affirmed the statement that justification is a free gift of God resulting in the renewal of the human person.[60]

Each of the reconstructive thinkers discussed earlier can support the context/content hermeneutical distinction because each concludes that the meaning of a text, in its essential intentionality, may be recovered and then subsequently re-expressed. For each, a sameness of content may be preserved even when re-expressed within a different context or form (and not only re-expressed, of course, but productively revisioned). One need not agree with Derrida, then, that the "iterability" of signs is necessarily destructive of a stable and determinate meaning. On the contrary, non-identical repetition does not mean the loss of meaning, since re-expression from a new point is essential to understanding, without, of course, abandoning recognitive interpretation in the process.[61] The claim that we are not lost in textual instability and indeterminacy, in a Derridean iterability that destabilizes textual meaning, in a Gadamerian collapse of the meaning/significance distinction, is essential for Betti. For the "reconstructive" position, it is a matter of respecting the autonomy of the text, of respecting its genuine "otherness" while, at the same time, acknowledging the productive element that is an essential part of the interpreter's "unique visual angle."

Of course, even while endorsing the distinction between context and content, it must be immediately added that this distinction can only be made gingerly and with caution. If too mechanistically and positivistically understood, the form/content distinction represents an immobile theory disallowing true development and ignoring the necessary coinherence between the two elements, a coinherence clearly illustrated by the worlds of literature, art, and music.[62] One may not speak as if the content may be surgically removed from the form by means of algorithmic processes, as if the form were merely a convenient and discardable shell. On the contrary, the form is often an important indicator of the meaning intended, since literary genre is a significant clue to textual intentionality. Pierre Hadot, for example, has successfully argued that if one does not see that the form of ancient philosophy was essentially "therapeutic"—much like Wittgenstein's later thought—one will miss the primary intention of its message.[63] But neither immobility nor hermeneutical naïveté constitutes the intention of the context/content approach. Precisely the opposite is the case, that is, such an approach encourages an organic and architectonic development that necessarily incorporates new perspectives and points of view. Theologically, the church continues its task of expressing the Christian faith, the faith enshrined primarily in Scripture, and then in the conciliar definitions of the early church, to every culture and generation. A deeper understanding of this task is what John XXIII, Vatican II, and the 1973 declaration *Mysterium ecclesiae* were aiming at when they made a distinction between the fundamental teachings of the church and manner in which these are expressed. This distinction opened the door to conceptual plurality, to the ongoing task of reproductive interpretation and reconceptualization, of making the Christian faith, always within its perduringly true identity, newly understood. It is what Henri de Lubac meant when he said that the church is a perpetual construction site, although built on the foundation of the apostles.[64]

The advantages of the form/content hermeneutical approach are several. Does not the very idea of historicity and of sociocultural plurality demand new formulations that will, at the same time, protect the fundamental teachings of the church? Is this not especially necessary as the church in various parts of the world theologically matures? Does not the context/content distinction also protect the proper creativity of the theologian who, while always conserving the deposit of faith, must contribute to its proper development as well? Does not this distinction allow the theologian to reap the fruits of his or her dialogue with contemporary philosophy, anthropology, and the physical and social sciences? Does not this distinction recognize the ontological productivity of tradition and history as well as a proper understanding of the fusion of horizons? Does it not help solve the question of unity within multiplicity, of identity within difference? Further, given the many ecumenical agreements that have been reached, has not this distinction borne significant fruit for the noble cause of Christian unity?

Some Theologians
A great number of theologians have supported the distinction between context and content without always reflecting on the hermeneutical

theory and theoretical presuppositions that underlie and warrant it. Since I have treated some of these supportive thinkers in the past, I will offer only a very brief review of their thought here.[65] Walter Kasper bluntly asserts that the main "offense" caused by the Christian church today "is not so much the teaching about Christ [of Chalcedon], as the church and its dogma, which claims to be able to say something generally valid and timeless about God in terms that are historically conditioned."[66] He observes that both contemporary philosophy and the common Zeitgeist "call into question . . . the churches holding a general and universally valid claim on truth." The inescapable conclusion is that all claims, including those of Christianity, "have a provisional character."[67]

Arguing that we must hold these two elements together, namely, perduring validity and historical context, Kasper notes approvingly that both Pope Paul VI and John Paul II ratified declarations with non-Chalcedonian churches, intending to preserve the fundamental *content* of the Chalcedon definition without using the specific *terms or forms* of the conciliar decree. He points out that, from an ecumenical point of view, one may often achieve a unity in faith by means of complementary perspectives.[68] Kasper nods in the direction of the metaphysical issues that undergird the context/content hermeneutical perspective, even if he fails to develop this aspect of his thought fully: "The true and deepest crisis of present theology is that there is now no metaphysics . . . . One reason for this is to be found in philosophy, which in some quarters proclaims the end of metaphysics. Another reason is that the process of overcoming narrow and encrusted neo-scholastic metaphysics had led theology to divest itself radically of its Hellenized and metaphysical elements."[69] One sees in Kasper an affirmation of the importance of the context/content hermeneutical trajectory, even if he leaves unsaid some of its presuppositions.

Bernard Lonergan makes his adherence to the context/content distinction clear at several points. One example is his statement, "The permanence of dogmas, then, results from the fact that they express revealed mysteries. Their historicity . . . results from the fact that 1) statements have meanings only in their context and 2) contexts are ongoing and ongoing contexts are multiple." He concludes that while dogmas are permanent, the classical culture in which they were first expressed is not.[70] For Lonergan, changing historical and sociocultural contexts inexorably lead to the mutability of concepts, even while an enduring truth of judgment is maintained. It is the doctrinal judgment that abides, even when specifically delimited contexts and concepts are subject to fluidity. At the same time, Lonergan says, contexts may be reconstructed, original meanings may be ascertained, and these meanings may be reformulated in new and different contexts.[71] Of course, Lonergan grounds the possibility for context/content distinction on his metaphysical claims. He argues, for example, that classical culture was right in assuming there was a universal human nature, but misunderstood the extent to which this essential nature was open.[72] In conjunction with this premise, Lonergan develops a transcendental philosophy outlining the invariant structures of human consciousness while tirelessly defending, against neo-Scholasticism, the necessary flexibility of conceptual constructs. It is just Lonergan's metaphysical principles, ultimately, that warrant his endorsement of reconstructive hermeneutics and that allow, therefore, for a fundamental, material unity in and through historical and conceptual change.

Karl Rahner has been one of the most sophisticated thinkers on the nature of the form/content distinction. Rahner claims that "the Church can distinguish, within the mixed-up mass of what is human and what is divine in Tradition, between that which really represents a handing on properly-so-called of the original tradition and the rest which cannot make any such claim. One will absolutely have to concede this instinct to her because of the assistance of the Holy Spirit promised to her."[73] While endorsing the context/content distinction, Rahner has also claimed that one cannot speak of this distinction facilely, as if the church always knows precisely how to distinguish context and content. On the contrary, dogmatically binding truths are often couched in modes of understanding and conceptual models (Rahner calls these "amalgams") that later turn out to be entirely without normative power.[74] The force of historicity and sociocultural location inexorably changes our models, paradigms, and forms. Rahner is insistent, however, that even within such change there is an underlying identity: One "must of course make simultaneously clear that the sameness of dogma in the old sense is assured and the effort to do this must not be regarded in principle as dubious, as a feeble and cowardly compromise."[75] Rahner further asserts that when a formula evolves, there is naturally some friction precisely because it is difficult to see, at least initially, if the substance of faith is being changed or if, rather, it is merely the mutable "formula" handed down with it. Pannenberg makes this same point when speaking of Vincent of Lerins: "Vincent saw clearly that the formulation can evolve, and when this happens conflict inevitably rises over whether the new formulation preserves the identity of the faith content."[76]

Rahner's context/content hermeneutical theory is grounded and buttressed by the theological ontology he had elaborated in his early works *Spirit in the World* and *Hearers of the Word*, with their consistent attempts to defend some universal notion of humanity (with its *Vorgriff* toward Absolute Being), while simultaneously seeking to overcome an Enlightenment naturalism that saw human nature as a self-enclosed entity wholly unrelated to God.

The crucial point here is that, even as he increasingly defended otherness, historicity, absence, and mystery in theological knowing, Rahner continued to maintain his invariant transcendental ground, which served as a foundation for understanding humanity's intrinsic relationship to God and as a warrant for explaining the possibility of reconstructive understanding and so the enduring, material identity of "content" within varying contexts. Even toward the end of his life, Rahner noted that the question of a "metaphysical theology" occurs when the "knowing subject . . . asks itself, in a total return to itself, about the conditions of the possibility of the subject and of a knowledge and a freedom which have a reflexive knowledge of themselves. . . . In this transcendental reflection on oneself there is contained a metaphysical anthropology."[77] As with Lonergan, it is not a matter of deciding on the adequacy of Rahner's philosophical theology; it is matter of recognizing that he saw clearly that only such a philosophical foundation (what is really a theological ontology) would allow for the permanency, universality, and material continuity of the church's doctrine to be intelligibly and logically defended.[78]

Other supporters of the context/content trajectory include William Hill, who, while endorsing the traditional hermeneutical distinction, calls for caution: "Truth and its form (vêtement) and expression can never be separated—as if one could peel away and discover a transcultural truth at its core. But the impossibility of a real separation is no denial of grounds for a *distinction*.[79] Theology is never mere repetition; there will always be changes in style and conceptual expression. It is a failure, however, to allow theology "to collapse into historicism and relativism."[80] Avery Dulles, too, tries to balance the mutability of historically stamped expressions with an enduring (even if also historically influenced) doctrinal truth. He argues that "the abiding truth of the Gospel never comes to human beings except in provisional, historically conditioned forms."[81] Pronouncements made in particular historical and cultural situations may require reinterpretation or modification with the passage of time. Consequently, Dulles asserts that "the core teaching is constant, but the forms in which it is conceptualized and verbalized are fluid."[82]

The point of this brief review of significant theologians has been to indicate that the context/content hermeneutical distinction continues to be important both ecumenically and doctrinally in the life of the church.

It has offered a significant interpretative model for conjoining the universal and materially identical affirmations of faith with the historical, social, and cultural particularity endemic to finite existence.

Conclusion

The thrust of chapters five and six is clear enough: The Christian faith holds that certain beliefs, linguistically articulated as doctrinal statements, are universally, normatively, and continuously true, through varying generations and cultures. It claims that, in essentials, these beliefs are stable and selfsame, with a fundamentally perduring dimension throughout history. At the same time, these fundamental beliefs undergo change on two levels: (1) There are often changes in conceptual construct, that is, in the formulation or *Denkstil* in which a particular belief or judgment is rendered and conceptualized; and (2) there is also, often enough, the change of organic development, continuing the fundamental thrust of the original doctrine or idea but now extending and amplifying it in consonance with the original meaning.[83]

In consequence of such claims, Christian theology needs a hermeneutical theory that is able to sustain these conjunctive elements—on the one hand perduring identity, on the other, a decided modicum of change and development. What is needed, then, is a hermeneutical theory able not only to take account of the enveloping horizons of historical embeddedness, of sociocultural delimitation, but one also able to explicate and display the material continuity and identity of the Christian faith throughout that history. What is needed is an interpretative theory corresponding to the insight of Pascal: A pluralism that cannot be integrated into unity is chaos; unity unrelated to plurality is tyranny.[84]

One argument of these chapters has been that the hermeneutical via media proposed by Gadamer, which seeks to navigate between the Scylla of wooden repetition and the Charybdis of interpretative anarchism, can only be appropriated by Christian theology in a qualified manner. Of course, about certain elements in Gadamer's work theology should be entirely enthusiastic. With Heidegger, he has unmasked the "worldless subject," thereby centralizing Heidegger's attempt to exhume the *Lebenswelt* from the obsequies pronounced by a bloodless transcendental philosophy; he has convincingly argued that hermeneutical positivism, with its exaltation of subjective annihilation, is entirely untenable; he has shown that "the standpoint beyond any standpoint . . . is pure illusion"[85]; he has overcome a naïve objectivism by indicating that any understanding must always already be interpretation, that is, a true *Horizontverschmelzung* takes place between interpreter and the interpreted; he has maintained the axial importance of tradition while superseding a stolid traditionalism forestalling growth and development; and he has shown that any "listening" is always already "appropriative listening," and that any seeing is already a "seeing as."

Nonetheless, the appropriation of Gadamer's thought by Christian theology must be qualified, in my judgment, because his approach is ultimately unable to provide theoretical support for the claim that revelation and doctrine represent a true *locutio Dei*, that is, a manifestation that is materially continuous and abidingly true from culture to culture, from generation to generation. At stake here is the need to defend revelation and doctrine as encompassing elements of *material*, and not simply formal and historical, continuity. The definitions of Nicea, Constantinople, and Chalcedon, with their fundamental meanings intact, must be able to norm Christian belief today as clearly as in the early church. But in order to maintain the material continuity of the salvific, revelatory narrative, its normative identity in history, the integral transmission of Christian doctrine requires, for the sake of its logical explication, the possibility of reconstructive understanding. Gadamer's theory, relying ultimately on Heidegger's "fundamental ontology," has rejected realistic hermeneutics out of hand, holding that this approach is both ontologically and hermeneutically truncated.

Theologically, then, if one takes an unqualified Gadamerian hermeneutics as one's philosophical koiné, with historicity and finitude as first principles, one is left defending interpretations that may differ widely from age to age, from culture to culture, from epoch to epoch. Of course, Gadamer tries to stem the tide against interpretative relativism with what Caputo has called his "Hegelian ontologization of history" as well as with his notion of the enduring "claim." It is difficult to see, however, how the formal unity of history, absent the material unity of content, allows this hermeneutical approach to sustain the self-understanding of historic Christian faith.[86] In my judgment, the hermeneutical work of Emilio Betti provides an alternative interpretative theory which, like that of Gadamer, seeks to establish a via media between leaden repetition and interpretative anarchy, but does so in a way that is able to preserve recognitive and reproductive interpretation and, in so doing, is better able to explicate theoretically the material continuity of Christian faith and doctrine.

Betti, like Gadamer, wishes to take account of the ontological productivity of history and of the indisputable centrality of temporality and social location, but in such a way that recognitive interpretation is not thereby excised. Betti's thought allows for, indeed demands, reconceptualization while at the same time protecting the autonomy of the original text/Form. Consequently, his thought is able to support a subtle understanding of the context/content hermeneutical trajectory, whereby the teachings of the church may be differently and creatively re-expressed while maintaining a stable identity throughout history and culture. This approach allows Christian theologians to argue for unity within historicity, for identity within cultural difference. It allows for change and development because it calls for the importance, indeed necessity, of reconceptualization while concomitantly maintaining the fundamental stability of the dialogical narrative between God and humanity called revelation. It endorses and encourages continuing ecumenical dialogue because it recognizes that differing perspectives and formulations of Christian faith need not preclude a more fundamental unity. It strikes the proper balance between historicity and identity without "dehistoricizing" hermeneutics (as would those seeking to maintain only conceptual monism) and without entirely "historicizing" them (as would those arguing that any "stable" content is philosophically untenable). In both cases, the context/content distinction is opposed, but for very different reasons. One option has difficulty explaining historicity, the other with explaining identity.

One can understand the concerns of the conceptual monists. A certain terminology has been used for centuries, and it is very easy to think that a lexicon purified in the fire of controversy and honed by centuries of theological thought is irreplaceable. But historicity requires an idea to be presented anew, in a different conceptual and lexical/semantic context, if it is to be once again intelligible.

One can also understand the plaints of the Gadamerian-influenced theoreticians. They wish to emphasize, properly, all of the sociocultural and linguistic horizons within which "presence" comes to light. They wish to show, appropriately, that all understanding is already, in some sense, interpretation. Further, we can say that the "overcoming of metaphysics" that Gadamer adopts from Heidegger is entirely correct if by this we mean a baroque, encrusted ontotheology that reduces the God of mystery to what Heidegger calls calcified, *Vorhandenheit* thinking, the *causa sui* before whom one cannot dance or sing, or to what Jean-Luc Marion condemns as the reifying, conceptually idolatrous imagination. This overcoming of metaphysics is also entirely correct if metaphysics is here understood as an imperialistic discipline placing revelation and theology in an illegitimate Procrustean bed, failing to recognize the absolute epistemic primacy of the revelatory narrative for a Christian understanding of both being and God.

These aberrations, however, are not the performative, theologically disciplined metaphysics that is the best of the Christian tradition. And it is just this disciplined metaphysics that resists a profoundly historicized construal of thought and being ultimately issuing in a fluidity of textual meaning, despite the other strategies Gadamer has proposed, and so a fluidity in doctrinal statements that, in my judgment, strays beyond the acceptable development and organic growth characteristic of the tradition.

Revelation is about the *Deus Revelatus*, the God who has entered into a dialogue with his creatures and manifested to us something of his inner Trinitarian life. This "unveiling" persists, continuously and normatively, in the Christian church. It is for this reason that some construal of reality explaining this continuous presence, this perduring revelation, has led theology to use some kind of metaphysics (understood in a commodious sense), and thereby some particular kind of hermeneutics, to aid in theological explications of faith. This metaphysics exists, it must always be emphasized, not as theology's lord but as theology's servant, as its *ancilla*, given the epistemic primacy of God's revealing love. One should not think that metaphysics endures simply because Christianity quickly took root in a Hellenistic culture; it is surely only an illegitimate Harnackian bias that sustains this claim. On the contrary, a certain kind of rationality and first philosophy has endured because it has helped to illuminate the continuous and perduring, if inexhaustible, presence characteristic of Christian faith and thought.

Robert Jenson is correct when he says that when hermeneutics becomes universal, it thereby becomes metaphysics.[87] The point here is that Christian faith and doctrine needs the kind of hermeneutics, and so the kind of metaphysics, that can support abiding presence, that can support the normative and universal truth characteristic of certain Christian beliefs and affirmations. Such a claim does not constitute resistance to history, which would be a futile and worthless undertaking in any case. It does constitute, rather, a clear recognition that truth, in its abiding nature, may be grasped within history—and that such grasping says something about the very nature of humanity. In my judgment, Betti's hermeneutical position, while not without its own imperfections, provides, more clearly than does Gadamer's, the theoretical support that Christian affirmations need.

The theme of chapters three and four was that Christian theology needs a certain notion of truth that can logically explicate and sustain its perduring and normative claims. I have argued in chapters five and six that a hermeneutical theory sustaining such claims is similarly needed. In chapters seven and eight, I shall examine the kind of language needed to explicate properly and appositely Christian faith and doctrine.

Notes

1. However much Caputo may diverge with Gadamer on their respective interpretations of Heidegger, they are at least in agreement on this formulation: "But there is no place for Archimedean centers and onto-theo-logical levers once one has started down the hermeneutic path. Hermeneutics spells the end of metaphysics." John Caputo, "Radical Hermeneutics and Religious Truth," in *Phenomenology of the Truth Proper to Religion* (ed. Daniel Guerrière; Albany, N.Y.: SUNY Press, 1990), 149.

2. John Caputo, *Radical Hermeneutics: Repetiton, Deconstruction, and the Hermeneutic Project* (Bloomington: University of Indiana Press, 1987), 96. Page numbers cited refer to this text. In a later work, Caputo says that Gadamer's thought "is decisively marked by Hegel and the metaphysical tradition generally." Caputo, *More Radical Hermeneutics* (Bloomington: Indiana University Press, 2000), 43.

3. In place of Gadamer's phenomenological thought, Caputo substitutes what he calls a "meta-onto-hermeneutics," which is, for the most part, simply a retrieval of Heidegger's own deconstructionist and metaontological tendencies, absent now the Hegelian elements introduced by Gadamer. Gadamer's mistake was in repeating the error embedded in the entire history of philosophy, namely, thinking he had finally found the "winning" name for Being. This was, in the last analysis, to fall into the trap of ontohermeneutics. Caputo, however, gives little thought to the question of conflicting interpretations, an issue with which Gadamer surely struggles, even if, in my judgment, unsuccessfully. As Caputo says, the search for criteria or warrants for the adjudication of interpretations results simply from the foundationalist compulsion, from "Cartesian anxiety" (*Radical Hermeneutics*, 261). Ultimately, Caputo opts for a free society in which public debate serves as a forum for competing viewpoints.

In his later work, Caputo has turned away from Heidegger as insufficiently postmodern, as ultimately remaining within the horizon of being, and has moved instead toward Derrida's "undecideability" as a philosophically appropriate flight from the violence of cognitive determination. For Caputo's disenchantment with Heidegger, see *Demythologizing Heidegger* (Bloomington: Indiana University Press, 1993). For his appreciation of Derrida, see *The Prayers and Tears of Jacques Derrida: Religion without Religion* (Bloomington: Indiana University Press, 1997). From the viewpoint of revelation and Christian doctrine, concerned as it is with identity, continuity, and perduring presence, Caputo's hermeneutics offers, seemingly, very little help.

4. Hans-Georg Gadamer, "Reply to Jacques Derrida," in *Dialogue and Deconstruction: The Gadamer-Derrida Encounter* (ed. Diane P. Michelfelder and Richard E. Palmer; Albany, N.Y.: SUNY Press, 1989), 56.

5. See Jacques Derrida, "Three Questions to Hans-Georg Gadamer," in Michelfelder and Palmer, *Dialogue and Deconstruction*, 52–54.

6. The hermeneutics of postmodernity, and Derrida in particular, are examined at great length in Kevin Vanhoozer, *Is There a Meaning in This Text?* (Grand Rapids: Zondervan, 1998), esp. 38–193.

7. The rejection of reconstructive understanding has proceeded so far that Francis Noël can say: "The notion that we read a text to understand its meaning is now regarded

in most elite circles of academic study of literature as something fit for a glass case in the Concept Museum. It is, if anything, even quainter to speak of an *author's* meaning." Noël, *The Writer Writing: Philosophic Acts in Literature* (Princeton, N.J.: Princeton University Press, 1992), 133.

8. Although I think that Gadamer's hermeneutics may be theologically accepted only in a qualified sense, I do not intend to underestimate his significant strengths. In particular, I think that Gadamer's notion of effective-history, or *Wirkungsgeschichte*, is unobjectionable when he uses it to say, for example, "We should learn to understand ourselves better and recognize that in all understanding, whether we are expressly aware of it or not, the efficacy of history is at work." Gadamer, *Truth and Method* (2nd rev. ed.; trans. Joel Weinsheimer and Donald G. Marshall; New York: Continuum, 2003), 301. Gadamer rightly points out that we stand within history and tradition and so our reasoning, and reading, is always accompanied by its effects. Such insights may be very helpful in developing, for example, an understanding of how tradition develops over the course of time. They may also be useful in understanding the "anamnetic" character of Christian doctrine, that is, how ancient creeds, for example, may be effectively and historically present. I do think, however, that because of the polemic against metaphysics that animates Gadamer's discussions (and, of course, it must be recognized that, in the first place, he is arguing against "positivism" and "methodism" as a path to truth), he fails to recognize that, along with the unity of history there is a unity of an eidetically discernible human nature that allows for reconstructive understanding and for standards warranting validity in interpretation, standards about which Gadamer, in my judgment, remains unclear. I am not arguing, therefore, that my objections to Gadamer entirely vitiate his theological employment, only that such employment needs to be carefully discriminating.

9. Emilio Betti, *Teoria generale dell'interpretazione* (Milan: Dott. A. Giuffrè, 1955). Citations in the text are from this work. For the sake of wider circulation, he translated the work into German as *Allgemeine Auslegungslehre als Methodik der Geisteswissenschaften* (Tübingen: J. C. B. Mohr, 1967). This text of Betti's constitutes the fundamental basis for my summary. Also important, however, is a 1962 work Betti originally wrote in German, entitled *Die Hermeneutik als allgemeine Methodik der Geisteswissenschaften* (Tübingen: J. C. B. Mohr, 1962). More recently, this was translated into Italian as *L'ermeneutica come methodica generale delle scienze dello spirito* (Roma: Città Nuova, 1990). The primary purpose of this later book was to offer a direct response to Gadamer's *Wahrheit und Methode*, itself published in 1960. Of course, Betti was intimately familiar with Gadamer's interpretive theory even in his earlier work, so the later book simply intensifies the critique originally offered in his *TGI* of 1955.

10. Also defending the reconstructive position deftly, although much less comprehensively than Betti, and primarily from the standpoint of literary criticism, is E. D. Hirsch, *Validity in Interpretation* (New Haven, Conn.: Yale University Press, 1967); and *The Aims of Interpretation* (Chicago: University of Chicago Press, 1976). Also see E. D. Hirsch, "Meaning and Significance Reinterpreted," *Critical Inquiry* 11 (1984): 202–25.

11. The influence of Betti upon Hirsch is evident throughout *Validity in Interpretation*. Such influence is acknowledged in E. D. Hirsch, *Teoria dell'interpretazione e critica letteraria* (Bologna: Il Mulino, 1973), 8ff., and mentioned in Gaspare Mura, "Saggio Introduttivo," in *L'ermeneutica come methodica generale delle scienze dello spirito*, by Emilio Betti (Roma: Città Nuova, 1990), 37.

12. For the meaning of the terms "textual intention" and "textual meaning," see chapter five, note 31. For Hirsch on Husserl, see *Validity in Interpretation*, 58. Vanhoozer examines the influence of Husserl on Hirsch in *Is There a Meaning in This Text?* 75–78, and cautions that one should not misunderstand Hirsch's accent on "authorial intentionality" in a psychological manner. For Hirsch, the author's intention means the object (message)

of which the author was conscious. What is important is the meaning, the message, someone wills to convey by a particular sequence of signs.

13. Still very useful in his examination of Betti's principles is Richard Palmer, *Hermeneutics* (Evanston, Ill.: Northwestern University Press, 1969), 54–60; and Josef Bleicher, *Contemporary Hermeneutics* (London: Routledge & Kegan Paul, 1980), 27–50. I have examined Betti's interpretative theory with regard to specifically theological issues in my article, "Emilio Betti and the Hermeneutics of Dogma," *Thomist* 53 (1989): 635–54. Parts of that article are included below. Also helpful, from a point of view concerned with semiotic theory, is a work by Betti's English translator: Susan Noakes, *Timely Reading: Between Exegesis and Interpretation* (Ithaca, N.Y.: Cornell University Press, 1988).

14. This phrase "meaning is not imposed but is drawn out" is repeated by Betti throughout his work and serves as an epigrammatic clue to his entire hermeneutical project. Of course, in his own way, Gadamer agrees with this axiom, but while for Betti interpretative coherency is to be found primarily in the recovery of the Form's message, for Gadamer, concern with such "recovery" overlooks other dimensions of the hermeneutical process (such as the "world" saturating the interpreter's perspective). Of course, the deeper ontological questions here intrude. Betti sees Gadamer as tending toward subjectivism, while Gadamer thinks Betti is mired in a notion of human nature characteristic of nineteenth-century Romanticism. See Gadamer's remark on human nature in note 42 in chapter 5.

15. Betti argues that those who accent interpretation as "new" creation are necessarily locked into a constraining particularism. He states, with clear metaphysical import, "The existential limitation of understanding, which ignores the spiritual basis of interpretation within common humanity, leads to the inhuman and barbaric result of raising insuperable barriers among circles of men reciprocally excluding them and attributing an absolute basis to particularism" (249). This passage is likely excessively harsh, but Betti is convinced that a pronounced accent on historicity (absent some notion of a common "nature") necessarily leads to tribalism.

16. Betti asserts, for example, that this kind of "speculative" interpretation is characteristic of Heidegger's readings of Kant and Nietzsche as well as Gadamer's retrieval of Plato (102). Betti thinks these kinds of readings are legitimate on their own terms (i.e., if recognized for their primarily speculative character), since they are generally governed by a priori theoretical considerations and are primarily inventive rather than mediative in character (231).

17. Of course, all are familiar with Gadamer's claim that "the fundamental prejudice of the Enlightenment is the prejudice against prejudice itself, which denies tradition its power." Gadamer, *Truth and Method*, 270. Betti should not be seen as fundamentally disagreeing with this, if it is taken to mean that tradition and history have an important, unexcisable role to play in the hermeneutical process. On the other hand, Betti would argue that "prejudice" cannot so overwhelm the interpreter that the autonomy of the text, and the "alien" message embedded within it, is reduced to the subjective horizon of the interpreter. Of course, the different valuations of "prejudice" here are themselves rooted in ontological issues, which will be discussed later.

18. Betti is not, therefore, subject to Frank Lentricchia's assertion (in an evaluation of E. D. Hirsch) that this reconstructive hermeneutics is ultimately Cartesian since it requires a "massive act of dispossessing" oneself. Any study of Betti will recognize that he hardly countenances "dispossessing" oneself since not only would this be metaphysically impossible, but it would also lose the essential and productive perspective of the interpreter. See Lentricchia, *After the New Criticism* (Chicago: University of Chicago Press, 1980), 263;

cited in Roger Lundin, "Interpreting Orphans: Hermeneutics in the Cartesian Tradition," in *The Promise of Hermeneutics* (ed. R. Lundin, C. Walhout, and A. Thistleton; Grand Rapids: Eerdmans, 1999), 37 n. 79.

19. Betti points out, "While it is true that the office of interpreter is that of research-ing and understanding the meaning of the 'other,' this can hardly be understood so that the interpreter is an inert recipient with a passive and mechanical operation" (315–16).

20. One can see how far Betti is from Richard Bernstein's bald claim that the state-ment "all understanding involves interpretation" is "scandalous to those who hold for objective interpretation." This excessive overstatement does not strengthen Bernstein's legitimate case against philosophical and scientific positivism. Bernstein, *Beyond Objectivism and Relativism* (Philadelphia: University of Pennsylvania Press, 1983), 138.

21. Betti would be largely, although not entirely, in agreement with Leo Strauss: "The task of the historian of thought is to understand the thinkers of the past exactly as they understood themselves, or to revitalize their thought according to their own interpreta-tion. If we abandon this goal, we abandon the only practicable criterion of 'objectivity' in the history of thought." Strauss, *What Is Political Philosophy?* (Westport, Conn.: Greenwood Press, 1959), 67. Betti's differences with Strauss would be similar to those he has with Schleiermacher's well-known axiom (see the following note).

22. Betti is appreciative of the hermeneutical axiom characteristic of Schleiermacher, Boechk, Dilthey, and Wach: The goal of the interpreter is to understand the author better than he understood himself. At the same time, Betti explains that the formula is some-what equivocal inasmuch as one must take account of the qualitative difference between the author and the interpreter. The author never presupposes a true "other"—and has the further difficulty of placing himself or herself at a remove from the Form or text. The interpreter, properly disposed, has a more profound knowledge of the reflexive conscious-ness of the author by means of the hermeneutical perspectives embodied in the canons (338–39). Betti's point here is that the author is, only with great difficulty, a proper inter-preter of his or her own work.

23. For the sake of clarity it should be remembered that although Betti has here made a distinction between recognitive and reproductive interpretation, his most significant contrast is ultimately between reproductive interpretation (which is essentially recognitive) and what he calls "speculative" interpretation, which dismisses on philosophical grounds the possibility of recognitive interpretation. For Betti, the work of Heidegger, Gadamer, and Bultmann is more analogous to, rather than representative of, the actual hermeneuti-cal task because their work is more "creative" than "mediative."

24. Ultimately, Betti, while at complete antipodes with John Caputo's hermeneutics, would agree with Caputo's charge that Gadamer tries to "save appearances" by means of an eleventh-hour ontologization of history. Of course, Caputo, from his Derridean posi-tion, sees this as an illegitimate turn to a certain kind of "metaphysics," while Betti sees it as a rejection of proper interpretative theory.

25. Of course, Gadamer's response to this was cited earlier: "The consciousness of being conditioned does not supersede our conditionedness." Gadamer, *Truth and Method*, 448.

26. In a recent volume, Anthony Thiselton argues that hermeneutical theory must steer between the Scylla of "mechanical replication" and the Charybdis of "unrestrained pluralism." One can, of course, argue that Betti's hermeneutics provide just this kind of via media. The authors in this volume have only a slight familiarity with Betti's thought and so are fundamentally unaware of his attempt to achieve their own stated goal but with different presuppositions. They do speak of E. D. Hirsch, one thinker clearly representative

of realistic hermeneutics, although his thought is not entirely congruent with Betti's. Thiselton, "Communicative Action and Promise in Interdisciplinary, Biblical, and Theological Hermeneutics," in Lundin, Walhout, and Thiselton, *Promise of Hermeneutics*.

27. Betti's agreement with this first axiom should be obvious; his agreement with the second is based on the fact that the interpreter is necessarily subordinate to the Representative Form and so is not, therefore, preeminent in the actual practice of interpretation.

28. Gadamer implicitly charges Betti with "methodism" when he writes, perhaps a bit disingenuously, "Fundamentally, I am *not proposing a method*; I am describing *what is the case*." Gadamer, *Truth and Method*, 512. Betti, of course, could make exactly the same claim.

29. Throughout *TGI*, Betti cites Hartmann at some length as the philosophical thinker most supportive of his work. Hartmann, like many thinkers at the turn of the twentieth century, had reacted against a strict Kantianism and moved toward a more realistic point of view. It is likely this realism, and especially Hartmann's criticism of Heidegger, is what attracted Betti to him. For more on Hartmann's rejection of neo-Kantianism and his move toward a Husserlian phenomenology of intentionality, see James Collins, "The Neo-Scholastic Critique of Nicolai Hartmann," *Philosophy and Phenomenological Research* 6 (1945–1946): 109–22. Pannenberg's astute comment on Hartmann should also help to explain why he is attractive to Betti: Hartmann, precisely because of his unabashed pursuit of metaphysics, remained an "outsider" in German thought after Ritschl. Wolfhart Pannenberg, *Metaphysics and the Idea of God* (Grand Rapids: Eerdmans, 1990), 4–5.

30. Betti's concern to overcome particularism is partially echoed in a recent essay by Alisdair MacIntyre who, while fully acknowledging Gadamer's proper emphasis on our historical embeddedness, also says we may "appeal to standards of rationality and truth that do in some measure transcend the limitations of historically bounded contexts." MacIntyre, "On Not Having the Last Word: Thoughts on Our Debts to Gadamer," in *Gadamer's Century* (ed. Jeff Malpas et al.; Cambridge, Mass.: MIT Press, 2002), 158.

31. Betti adds that "common humanity as the presupposition of understanding" may be found in Humboldt, Wach, Ast, Dilthey, and others. In addition, a symbolic prefiguring of this common humanity, notwithstanding the diversity of tongues, may be found in the "glossolalia" of Pentecost (*TGI*, 261 n. 12). Of course, for the Christian theologian, this common "human nature" may never be the properly rejected *natura pura* that de Lubac unmasked as a neo-Scholastic error and that Karl Rahner, in his own way, has done so much to overcome. More recently, of course, John Milbank has claimed the mantle of the "de Lubac revolution."

32. Stanley Rosen, *Hermeneutics as Politics* (2nd rev. ed.; New Haven, Conn.: Yale University Press, 2003), 146–47. A summary of Rosen's arguments and a response to them from a Gadamerian perspective may be found in Joseph Margolis, *Interpretation Radical but Not Unruly* (Berkeley: University of California Press, 1995), 56–64.

33. For Strauss, see note 21 above. Gertrude Himmelfarb lodges a similar concern with regard to contemporary historiography. See Himmelfarb, *On Looking into the Abyss* (New York: Alfred A. Knopf, 1994), 131–61.

34. At other times, Betti's language does obviously display the spirit of Romanticism, perhaps an overlay from his interest in nineteenth-century theorists. This aspect of his theory, with its language of "empathy" and "spirit," would need to be rethought in a full-blown updating of his approach.

35. As Richard Palmer correctly observes, Betti advances as axiomatic precisely those presuppositions that Heidegger has called into question. See Palmer, *Hermeneutics*, 163.

36. See note 40 in chapter 5.

37. Gadamer has commented on Betti at some length, regarding him as the foremost contemporary representative of the reconstructive position. For Gadamer's evaluations of Betti, see *Truth and Method*, 324–25, 510–12.

38. See Kevin Vanhoozer, *Is There a Meaning in This Text?* (Grand Rapids: Zondervan, 1998), 24. Page numbers in this section will refer to this text.

39. Vanhoozer points out that while meaning is embedded in the text, "it is inaccessible apart from human constructions. This more moderate realism claims neither that interpretations are absolutely true, nor that interpretations are only useful fictions" (90–91 n. 23).

40. As Vanhoozer says, from his own evangelical perspective but with legitimate implications for all reconstructive hermeneutical theory, "Ultimately, Luther stands for the possibility that the text and its meaning remain independent of the process of interpretation and hence have the ability to transform the reader." I do not think that the word "independent" is the *mot juste* here for two reasons: (1) The text never remains "independent" of the interpreter, so as to exclude all subjectivity and historicity. The salient point is that its stable meaning may be grasped in and through particular, historical perspectives. (2) Vanhoozer's formulation fails to clarify how a tradition of interpretation may actually be *productive* of understanding drawing out previously unseen dimensions. However, Vanhoozer's central point—that the text has a determinate meaning that can serve as a norm for interpretative validity—is well taken (467). Further, and here I believe Vanhoozer is locked into an untenable confessionalism, the central difference between Catholics and Protestants is not necessarily the Reformation principle *Scriptura sui interpres.* The issue is that Roman Catholics (and other Christians) see the patristic and conciliar tradition, in its most important affirmations, as the place where the meaning of the scriptural text, its inexorable inner logic, receives its proper organic and architectonic development and amplification. This point, not the literal meaning of Scripture *in se*, is the root of the difference. I have discussed this at greater length in "Catholic Reflections on Discerning the Truth of Sacred Scripture" *Your word Is Truth* (ed. C. Colson and R. Neuhaus; Grand Rapids: Eerdmans, 2002), 79–101.

41. Vanhoozer says that when a text has a clear perlocutionary goal and intent, such as trying to persuade someone of something, even if it should fail in its goal, the meaning of the text is still embedded and recoverable. For Hirsch on the meaning/significance distinction, see *Validity in Interpretation*, 63.

42. Vanhoozer ultimately develops his own theory of reconstructive hermeneutics. Borrowing primarily from Austin and Searle, but also judiciously from Habermas, Vanhoozer proposes a notion of meaning as communicative action with three elements: prepositional content, illocutionary force, and perlocutionary effect. To inquire into what a text means is to ask, therefore, "what the author has done in, with and through the text." Vanhoozer, *Is There a Meaning in This Text?*, 260.

43. One may argue, of course, that this is the goal of virtually all hermeneutical theorists. See, for example, Thiselton's stated interpretative intent in note 26 above. The differences are rooted in the ontological presuppositions accompanying the task.

44. For comments about the language of *mens auctoris*, see note 31 in chapter 5. Betti also has serious reservations about the claim that an author is the best interpreter of his or her work. Like Vanhoozer, Hirsch also speaks of authorial intention. However, when one reads Hirsch's works *Validity in Interpretation* and *The Aims of Interpretation*, he explains that he is not speaking of authorial consciousness per se but of the meaning embedded within the text. See Hirsch, *Validity in Interpretation*, 58. In my judgment, the language of "authorial intention" smacks of investigating the hidden consciousness of the author. Betti's emphasis on the textual message or Form, with its accent on public availability, provides a welcome alternative.

45. As he later says, "Rationality in interpretation is not a matter of having absolute evidential foundations, either of the history of the text's composition or of the author's strategic intentions" (301).

46. Such language would also more clearly reflect Vanhoozer's own reservations about the Schleiermachian dictum that the interpreter should seek to know the author better than the author knows himself. While Betti thinks the dictum is equivocal, not clearly recognizing the qualitative differences between author and interpreter, Vanhoozer thinks that it is at best "quixotic" and at worst "Cartesian" in that it assumes access to the "consciousness" of the author (231).

47. Vanhoozer is surely right in saying that Gadamer and Ricoeur seek to provide legitimate hermeneutical theories after the demise of "Newtonian objectivity." But he appears to overlook the fact that there are several "post-Newtonian" theories available, separated, however, by quite different presuppositions.

48. Perhaps Vanhoozer's reticence with regard to metaphysical questions stems from the influence of Hirsch, who claims, "A precocious ascent into the realm of ontology is just what needs to be avoided in the descriptive, analytical side of hermeneutical theory." Hirsch, *Aims of Interpretation*, 81. But Hirsch goes on to observe, correctly, that the avoidance of such an ascent is warranted because realistic hermeneutics may be explicated by several metaphysical theories. In this, he is in full agreement with Betti. One wonders if Vanhoozer's own theory of communicative action, essentially a *linguistic* theory, can carry the freight that metaphysics traditionally carried in reconstructive interpretative theory. Can the "linguistic turn" entirely replace metaphysics? Vanhoozer does not address that question, but it is one that must ultimately be addressed if realistic hermeneutics is to be fully defended.

49. Lundin, "Interpreting Orphans," 36–37.

50. This is not simply a Catholic theme. Several evangelical thinkers—for example, J. Daryl Charles—claim that a better formulation than a naked *sola scriptura* is instead *prima scriptura*, which recognizes Scripture's normative place while simultaneously taking account of the interpretative community of the church. See Thomas Guarino, "Catholic Reflections on Discerning the Truth of Sacred Scripture," in *Your Word Is Truth* (ed. Charles Colson and Richard John Neuhaus; Grand Rapids: Eerdmans, 2002), 96.

51. Pannenberg has noted that Vincent of Lerins has always appealed to Catholics because Vincent "saw clearly that the issue was the identity of the matter, not the formulation." I think Vincent should appeal to all Christians concerned with the heritage of the great tradition because Vincent is concerned with continuity amid difference, with development amid change. I have treated Vincent as a model of doctrinal hermeneutics in "Vincent of Lerins and the Hermeneutical Question," *Gregorianum* 75 (1994): 491–523. Vincent was not cited by Vatican II because, according to J. Ratzinger's commentary on *Dei Verbum*, his emphasis on the *semper, ubique et ab omnibus* seemed misplaced given the council's new thrust. Of course, it is Vincent's "second rule"—that development must be *in eodem sensu*, always a proper *profectus*—which sheds light on the issue of continuity within change. For Pannenberg, see *Systematic Theology*, vol. 1 (trans. Geoffrey Bromiley; Grand Rapids: Eerdmans, 1991), 11. J. E. Kuhn presciently called Vincent's *Commonitorium* a *goldenes Büchlein* precisely because it began to meet the challenges of historicity.

52. Timothy George, "An Evangelical Reflection on Scripture and Tradition," in Colson and Neuhaus, *Your Word Is Truth*, 9–34.

53. Although I have briefly mentioned biblical hermeneutics here, the accent in this chapter is primarily on the hermeneutics of doctrine. Obviously, Scripture, given its unique status as the inspired word of God, carries with it its own set of interpretative issues. A

fuller discussion of these would require investigations into the works of, inter alia, de Lubac, Balthasar, and Raymond Brown. For biblical interpretation at Vatican II, see Ignace de la Potterie, "Interpretation of Holy Scripture in the Spirit in Which It Was Written (*Dei Verbum*, 12c)," in *Vatican II: Assessment and Perspectives*, vol. 1 (ed. René Latourelle; New York: Paulist Press, 1988), 220–66. Also important in this regard is the 1993 statement of the Pontifical Biblical Commission clearly endorsing the "literal sense," without thereby claiming that this sense exhausts the possibilities of interpretative method. See "The Interpretation of the Bible in the Church," *Origins*, January 6, 1994. One may also usefully consult the commentary by Peter Williamson, *Catholic Principles for Interpreting Scripture: A Study of "The Interpretation of the Bible in the Church"* (Chicago: Loyola University Press, 2002).

54. I am reminded here of another of Vincent of Lerins's dicta, virtually coincident with what Betti would say about reproductive understanding: *noviter non nova* (newly, not new things). It is not without interest that Pannenberg is fully supportive of Betti's central hermeneutical point against Gadamer, even while finding him underdeveloped in other areas: "For all the inadequacy of his arguments, Betti's insistence on the requirement of 'objectivity' in historical interpretation is nonetheless justified." Wolfhart Pannenberg, *Theology and the Philosophy of Science* (trans. Francis McDonagh; London: Darton, Longman & Todd, 1976), 167.

55. Examples from ecumenical dialogues could be ceaselessly duplicated. A fine analysis of how conciliar statements may be reconstructed while preserving their original intention may be found in Avery Dulles, *The Survival of Dogma* (Garden City, N.Y.: Doubleday, 1971), 171–84.

56. Betti had said that insofar as reproductive interpretation attempts to go beyond mere recognitive interpretation, to make an original meaning newly understood, it always courts the danger of infidelity to the original Representative Form or text.

57. Needless to add, I am hardly offering here an entire theory of doctrinal development, for such a theory, besides dealing with aspects of reconstructive hermeneutics, would also need to show how there is organic, architectonic development and productive appropriation *beyond but in hermeneutical consonance with* the originally intended and recoverable doctrinal meaning—that is, how there exists what Vincent called development *in eodem sensu* not *in alieno sensu* with the previous tradition. This would require showing how a dynamic, developmental sense of tradition, as endorsed for Catholicism by *Dei Verbum*, is essential in the life of the church. Such would also demand an accounting of how various loci (e.g., *sensus fidelium, schola theologorum*, the liturgy, the lives of the saints, and the magisterium) are interwoven in an authentic theological criteriology. The more circumscribed but crucial goal here is to show that a hermeneutics that allows for recognitive and reproductive interpretation is the necessary platform from which any such theory of development must properly begin.

58. For Newman, see the illuminating article by Ian Ker, "Newman, the Councils, and Vatican II," *Communio* 28 (Winter 2001).

59. I have mentioned both John XXIII's opening speech at Vatican II and the encyclical *Fides et ratio*. But it should also be again noted that Vatican II itself clearly sanctioned this kind of context/content, commensurable pluralism distinction. Clear conciliar texts supporting such an approach may be found in *Unitatis redintegratio*, nos. 4, 6, and 17; and *Gaudium et spes*, no. 62.

60. Avery Dulles observes, similarly, that the Council of Florence, when discussing the *Filioque*, acknowledged "that conceptually diverse formulations may co-exist in different sections of the Church." Dulles observes further that "dogmatic formulas must be kept under constant review" since, as our perspectives change and our knowledge deepens,

formulations reflecting the "style" of another age may be "outmoded" and inadequate. Dulles, *Survival of Dogma*, 163–65.

61. For Derrida, "iterabililty" means nonidentical repetition, understood, however, so that context is entirely determinative of content. There is, he argues, no determinate textual meaning, simply various contexts in which the signs are embedded. See Jacques Derrida, "Signature, Event, Context," in *Margins of Philosophy* (trans. Alan Bass; Chicago: University of Chicago Press, 1982), 307–30.

62. John Thiel has recently argued that the context/content distinction "no longer explains the workings of tradition well." The reason behind such doubts appears to be the fact that there is, as he rightly says, no "hypostatized 'content'" of tradition that transcends its historical expression. Thiel further asserts that "tradition's truth cannot stand apart abstractly from the conditions of historicity." Two distinct issues are at stake here. The first is the question: Is reconstructive interpretation possible? That is, is it possible to recover the meaning of past doctrinal texts? If so, as I have argued here, then continuity in and through history has to do, in the first place, with the re-cognition of abiding meanings of conciliar and dogmatic statements. Of course, reconstructive hermeneutical theory hardly ignores the "conditions of historicity," but it does, ultimately, involve a commitment to certain commodious metaphysical principles, something that Thiel appears to avoid. See, for example, Thiel, "Pluralism in Theological Truth," in *Why Theology?* (*Concilium*; ed. Claude Geffré and Werner Jeanrond; London: SCM Press, 1994), 57–69. A second issue is this question, raised by Thiel: How is continuity established if one abandons simple repetition? His claim is that those defending the context/content distinction seek to isolate "content" from history and tradition in a way that is "indefensible." In response, it should be said that the context/content approach hinges primarily on the recoverability of textual meaning. The further step, which distinguishes between context and content over the course of time, cannot be understood positivistically or algorithmically, as if the essential "content" is easily and quickly discernible across various periods. Such "content" or material continuity may only become clear over the course of time and, in many cases, with some friction, as Rahner has indicated. Such continuity must also be open, as the history of theology clearly witnesses, to consonant developments that are in accord with original, universally sanctioned claims (the *idem sensus* of Vincent of Lerins). At the same time, it must also be clearly stated that some measure of "continuity" is surely determinable even by an impartial observer investigating the meanings of various texts. For example, any historian would be able to see the continuities and discontinuities between the Tridentine decree on justification (1546) and the Joint Declaration on Justification (1999). The more recent document does not use the language of causality to explain how we are justified, but both documents make clear that justification is achieved through the gratuitous action of God in Christ and its result is a real, graced, ontological renewal of human beings. Such is determined by the Catholic Church to be the essential "content" of the Christian faith, even if the Aristotelian-Scholastic language of final, formal, efficient, and material causality (characteristic of the sixteenth-century document) is now deemed as the inessential (although not incorrect, it is important to add) "context." When Thiel says, then, that with the demise of the context/content distinction, "what remains is theological interpretation judged to be true by the present community because it is deemed continuous with, while at the same time it renews, past theological interpretations," he is surely correct in pointing to the essential role of the interpreting subject/community. Insofar as the community stands in a unique historical/cultural place, it will always interpret the tradition from its own perspective. However, it is equally important to affirm, in a way that Thiel does not, that the interpreting community itself must always be guided by the previous, recoverable, doctrinal meanings. This is simply to say that the interpreting community's

judgments must always be rooted in a *fundamentum in re,* namely, prior determinate textual meaning. For Thiel's comments, see his *Senses of Tradition* (Oxford: Oxford University Press, 2000), 88–89.

63. Among his many writings with this theme, see Pierre Hadot, *Philosophy as a Way of Life* (trans. Michael Chase; Oxford: Blackwell, 1995).

64. Henri de Lubac, *Catholicism* (trans. Lancelot C. Sheppard; London: Longmans, Green, 1950).

65. For a fuller exposition of these theologians on the hermeneutics of doctrine, see Thomas Guarino, *Revelation and Truth* (Scranton, Pa.: University of Scranton Press, 1993), 38–56.

66. Walter Kasper, *Theology and Church* (trans. Margaret Kohl; New York: Crossroad, 1989), 95–96.

67. Walter Kasper, *The Church and Contemporary Pluralism* (New York: National Pastoral Life Center, 2002), 11, 13.

68. Kasper, *Theology and Church,* 144–45. See also Kasper's later article, which makes many of the same points, "Unité ecclésiale et communion ecclésiale dans une perspective catholique," *Revue des sciences religieuses* 75 (2001): 6–22. On the recent agreements with non-Chalcedonian churches, see Antonio Olmi, *Il Consenso Christologico tra le Chiese Calcedonesi e non Chalcedonesi (1964–1996)* (Rome: Editrice Università Gregoriana, 2003).

69. Kasper, *Theology and Church,* 3. See also Kasper, "Postmodern Dogmatics," *Communio* 17 (1990): 181–91. In the *Communio* article Kasper says, "The regaining of the metaphysical dimension appears to me, therefore, one of the most important tasks of contemporary theology" (189).

70. Bernard Lonergan, *Method in Theology* (New York: Herder & Herder, 1972), 326. See also Lonergan's claims in *Doctrinal Pluralism* (Milwaukee: Marquette University Press, 1971), 10–11 and 44–45. An excellent work on Lonergan's interpretative interests is *Lonergan's Hermeneutics* (ed. Sean McEvenue and Ben F. Meyer; Washington, D.C.: Catholic University of America Press, 1989).

71. Lonergan, *Doctrinal Pluralism* 10–11.

72. "[Classicism] . . . is not mistaken in its assumption that there is something substantial and common to human nature and human activity. Its oversight is its failure to grasp that that something substantial and common also is something quite open." Lonergan, *Doctrinal Pluralism,* 8. Lonergan's comment is similar to the one preferred by W. Norris Clarke in his discussion of the unity of substance that characterizes the human person. Substance is the "principle of continuity and self-identity throughout the whole spectrum of accidental change. . . ." But substance does not mean "something static, inert, totally unchanging and immutable. . . . *Self-identical* is not the same concept as *unchanging* or immutable." See *The One and the Many* (Notre Dame: University of Notre Dame Press, 2001), 128–29. Lonergan also seeks to balance nature and historicity in "Natural Right and Historical Mindedness," in *A Third Collection* (ed. Frederick Crowe; New York: Paulist Press, 1985), 169–83. Contrast his position with that of Richard Rorty: "There is no such thing as human nature in the deep sense in which Plato and Strauss use this term." Rorty, "Education, Socialization, and Individuation," *Liberal Education* 75 (1989): 5.

73. Karl Rahner, "What Is a Dogmatic Statement?" in *Theological Investigations,* vol. 4 (trans. Karl-H. Kruger; Baltimore: Helicon Press, 1966), 5.

74. Karl Rahner, "Yesterday's History of Dogma and Theology for Tomorrow," in *Theological Investigations,* vol. 18 (trans. Edward Quinn; New York: Crossroad, 1983), 10. For more on "amalgams" and the context/content distinction in Rahner, see Thomas Guarino, "Rahner, Popper, and Kuhn: A Note on Some Critical Parallels in Science and Theology," *Philosophy and Theology* 8 (1993): 83–89.

75. Rahner, "Yesterday's History of Dogma and Theology," 13.

76. Pannenberg, *Systematic Theology*, 1:11.

77. Karl Rahner, "Natural Science and Reasonable Faith," in *Theological Investigations*, vol. 21 (trans. Hugh Riley; New York: Crossroad, 1988), 21–22.

78. It is no doubt because of Rahner's insistence on the importance of a metaphysical anthropology that he found Heidegger's thought deficient. See his comment on Heidegger's construal of philosophy in *Karl Rahner in Dialogue* (trans. ed. Harvey Egan; New York: Crossroad, 1986), ch. 2, no. 117.

79. William Hill, *The Three-Personed God* (Washington, D.C.: Catholic University of America Press, 1982), 245. One may legitimately argue that the caution exhibited by Hill and Rahner represents the legitimate concern behind *Fides et ratio*'s hesitation about this distinction. At the same time, it is my judgment that the encyclical was too cautious and failed to state matters as boldly as Vatican II itself had.

80. Hill, *Three-Personed God*, 246.

81. Avery Dulles, *The Craft of Theology* (New York: Crossroad, 1992), 108.

82. Ibid., 108.

83. I hope it is already clear from earlier chapters that I am not claiming that dogmatic teachings, in their abiding truth, are the final words on a particular matter. Chapters five and six, of course, argue that Christian teachings may be reconceptualized, that new points of view may be brought to bear, that new perspectives may be uncovered, that reproductive hermeneutics have a chiaroscuro effect. In this sense, then, one may say that Christian affirmations, even dogmatic teachings, are always, to a certain extent, "inadequate."

84. Blaise Pascal, *Pensées* (Paris: Charpentier, 1861), 388–89.

85. Gadamer, *Truth and Method*, 376. There is, then, no "view from nowhere" as Thomas Nagel's title has it. See Nagel, *The View from Nowhere* (New York: Oxford University Press, 1986).

86. I am in full agreement, then, with Vanhoozer's claim, which, in fact, echoes the thesis not only of this chapter, but of the entire book: "A Christian theological account of hermeneutics, as of anything else, must discipline notions of meaning and interpretation achieved in abstraction from distinctly Christian beliefs." Kevin Vanhoozer, *Is There a Meaning in This Text?* (Grand Rapids: Zondervan, 1998), 198. At the same time, such an approach cannot lead to immobilism but must involve a properly conceived correlation between Christian beliefs and "secular" wisdom. This theme will be treated in chapter ten.

87. Robert Jenson, *Systematic Theology*, vol. 1 (New York: Oxford University Press, 1997), 20.

CHAPTER 7

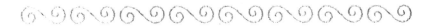

Christian Doctrine and Theological Language

Christian doctrine needs a certain view of philosophy, not for the sake of its ultimacy, of course, which is guaranteed by God alone, but for the sake of its logical explication; that doctrine needs a certain notion of truth if the cognitive status of theological statements is to be truly mediative, allowing for ostensive and "representational" elements; and, such affirmations also need a particular interpretative theory if Christian teaching is to claim coherently that there are certain perduring beliefs, normative from epoch to epoch, from culture to culture.

This chapter will examine the notion of theological language that is most congruent with the affirmations of Christian faith and doctrine. I will argue that the kind of language needed is one suited to balance several forces. On the one hand, theology attempts to mediate and explain Christian revelation, the fact that God has spoken and manifested to us something of his own inner life. Such manifestation is, of course, inherent in the very meaning of the term *apocalypsis*. On the other hand, there is within biblical and theological history a decided emphasis on the hidden and incomprehensible nature of God, on the *Deus Absconditus*. This God is hidden, as Scripture and tradition attest, both because of his own transcendence to created reality, as well as because of the cognitive limitations of the finite intellect. This chapter will examine how the traditional notion of analogy seeks to balance this dyadic oscillation between presence and absence; the criticisms made of such attempts; the current retrievals of analogical language; and how such retrievals may be further supplemented by contemporary postmodern "forms."

Introduction

Of course, under the influence of certain postmodern thinkers, Christianity is frequently characterized as a baroque metanarrative, one of the *grands récits* of history offering definitive and authoritative answers to questions about the origin, meaning, and goal of human life. The cognitive hubris of Christian faith is such that, even in this fragmented era, it speaks confidently not only about human action and destiny but about the very nature of God as well. As this chapter will make clear, although Christianity does have a certain confidence about "revelation," about its ability to grasp the *locutio Dei*—the salvific narrative between God and his creatures—this confidence is strictly tempered by an epistemological humility recognizing both the limits of the created intellect as well as the inability of human concepts to fully mediate divine life. In our own day, such inability is intensified by the indefeasible dimensions of historicity and sociocultural specificity, thereby further accenting language's partiality and inadequacy. Any fair reading of history will recognize that the entire theological and spiritual tradition of the church exhibits a conscious concern to avoid the kind of positivism that fails to recognize the limitedness of the human intellect or the full breadth of mystery and transcendence proper to God's own life. The cognitive asceticism of "negative theology" is an impressive witness to just such Christian reserve.

Before moving on to a more systematic examination of the nature of theological language, it is worth reviewing some significant historical mileposts regarding the kind of truth expressed by Christian doctrine and the role of language in just such mediation.

Selected Church Documents

Certain official ecclesial documents are pointed in their awareness of the dialectic between theological knowledge and nescience. Most important in this regard is the statement of Lateran IV, held in 1215. As asserted by the council, the declaration reads: Between Creator and creature no similitude may be expressed without indicating a greater dissimilitude ("Inter creatorem et creaturam non potest tanta similitudo notari, quin inter eos maior sit dissimilitudo notanda," DH 806). The context of this statement is the attribution of "perfection" to God and creatures, as this is reflected in the translation of Matthew 5:48: "You must be perfect as your heavenly

Father is perfect." Such perfection, the council observes, subsists on entirely different levels, divine and created; no similarity between creatures and Creator may be noted without insisting on a greater dissimilarity between them. It is no accident that this assertion of Lateran IV has received a great deal of attention over the course of Christian history. Recently, it has been cited approvingly by the encyclical *Fides et ratio* as well as by the *Catechism of the Catholic Church*.[1] In the encyclical, for example, this statement is adduced within a general section devoted to how language both mediates revelation and yet stands unknowing before it. The papal letter claims, "Faith clearly presupposes that human language is capable of expressing divine and transcendent reality in a universal way—analogically, it is true, but no less meaningfully for that." Were this not the case, the encyclical continues, "the word of God, which is always a divine word in human language, would be incapable of saying anything about God" (no. 84). With a clear but implicit reference to recent postmodern and Derridean trends, the encyclical continues, "The interpretation of this word [of God] cannot merely keep referring us to one interpretation after another, without ever leading to a statement which is simply true; otherwise, there would be no Revelation of God, but only the expression of human notions about God" (no. 84). Two issues are at stake here. In the first place, the encyclical wants to rebut the hermeneutical and veridical claim that one only has interpretations apart from ostensive reference, that what is "given" is only continuing context and iterability, never with an actual referent. Secondly, the document wishes to make clear that while doctrine is able to mediate something of divine truth, this truth is only known analogically, never comprehensively or completely. This dual approach reflects both the encyclical's commitment to the doctrinal mediation of knowledge about God together with the recognition that the Godhead is transcendent and so ultimately beyond human understanding.

Vatican I

Although Vatican I, held in 1869–1870, is known primarily as the body that issued the claim that, under very restricted conditions, the papal magisterium may teach certain elements of the Christian faith as infallibly true, that council also had some important things to say about theological language. The *mise en scène* for such statements, of course, is the rise of philosophical and theological rationalism in the nineteenth century. This "other" dogmatic constitution of the council, *Dei Filius*, was an attempt by the Roman Catholic Church to offer some response to such leveling, instrumentalist trends. While the aforementioned statement of

Lateran IV is well known, few are aware of the equally important apophatic assertions of Vatican I. The latter council, then, should be seen neither as solely sustaining the unyielding presence of "infallibility" nor as advocating an exhaustive grasp of revelation's inner intelligibility. Vatican I also recognized the dimensions of mystery and absence surrounding the human understanding of divine reality. Central here is this defining paragraph: "The divine mysteries, by their very nature, so excel the created intellect that even when they are handed on by revelation and received by faith, these mysteries remain covered by the veil of faith itself and, as it were, shrouded in darkness, as long as in this mortal life 'we are away from the Lord for we walk by faith and not by sight'" (2 Cor 5:6–7) (DH 3016).

What is striking about this sentence is its very intense apophatic tone. Even when revelation is received by the church in faith and believed by grace, it remains shrouded in obscurity. What gave birth to such an ardent claim? The antecedent for this paragraph comes from a letter of Pius IX to the archbishop of Munich, written in 1862. The letter expresses concern over the allegedly rationalist principles of Jakob Frohschammer, who, it is claimed, holds that certain fundamental teachings of the Christian faith, such as the incarnation, belong within the province of philosophical reasoning. One may reach certitude even about the mysteries of faith through natural human principles. Frohschammer seemed to argue not that one can deduce the mysteries of faith a priori, but that once the truths of revelation were grasped in faith, they were then capable of being exhaustively understood, even demonstrated by reason.

In J. B. Franzelin's *votum*, a long, carefully argued opinion submitted to the theological commission prior to Vatican I, the profound accent on the church's inability to know fully the mysteries of faith was vigorously argued.[2] So, for example, Franzelin cites the words of St. Jerome: "Concerning the mystery of the Trinity, the proper confession is lack of knowledge" (Patrologia Latina 24, col. 651). And the early Christian writers teach this nescience, Franzelin contends, not only of knowledge exercised *extra fidem* but also of *etiam fide supposita*. Certain truths of Christian doctrine are like the Trinity itself, which, as Fulgentius of Ruspe teaches, "exceeds all that we are able to think or know just as it surpasses all we are" (PL 65, col. 245).

Franzelin worries that certain thinkers hope to deduce the mysteries of faith from philosophical principles, thereby conforming and molding revealed truths to their own systems. Franzelin compares this method to that of the ancient Eunomians who held for the perfect comprehensibility of the divine essence. On the contrary, Franzelin asserts, both Gregory of Nyssa in his writings against the Eunomians and Gregory Nazienzen in his *Theological Orations* defended the "suprarationality" of the mysteries of faith "even supposing revelation and faith." It is true, Franzelin concedes, that when enlightened by faith, reason has a place in searching out the divine mysteries. However, revelation proposes "mysteries properly called" that are fundamentally beyond reason's ken. Despite the concern of some bishops that the council endorsed a hyper-apophaticism, the central text, as written first by Pius IX, and then cited by Franzelin, was ultimately approved. The council thereby forcefully asserted the "negative" element in our knowledge of God; the divine mysteries, even when they are revealed and accepted in grace and faith, remain partially hidden from us. Insofar as these mysteries do not constitute the proper object of the created intellect, human beings can never claim to exhaust their intelligibility.

Although Vatican I is sometimes characterized solely as an ultramontane council, with an abiding interest in the dogmatic hypostatization of Christian truth, it is clear that the council was more nuanced than has sometimes been supposed. The conciliar distrust of excessive anthropomorphism, theological Cartesianism, and epistemological arrogance sounds surprisingly contemporary when juxtaposed with the current postmodern critique of Enlightenment excesses. Of course Vatican I, with its clear affirmation of the truth of Christian dogmatics, was anything but postmodern—premodern is perhaps more apt—but it cannot be overlooked that by accenting the lethic, the apophatic, and the transcendent dimension of the divine mysteries, as well as the finitude of creatures, Vatican I practiced a theological and intellectual asceticism that was a logical precursor to Vatican II's emphasis on legitimate theological pluralism.[3]

Perhaps one reason the more recondite, even anagogical dimensions of Vatican I have not been properly accented was the imposition of neo-Scholasticism by *Aeterni Patris* within a decade of the council's close. It may reasonably be argued that the imposition of *one* system as adequately mediating the truth of revelation was in contradiction to the very point that the council had been making. Even as the council stressed the transcendence of revelation to any human understanding of it, the encyclical sanctioned a conceptually monistic approach to the divine mysteries. In Roman Catholicism, it was only with the rise of the *nouvelle théologie* at mid-twentieth century that the church, relying at least partially on the transcendence of revelation to any conceptual system, recovered a true plurality of theological approaches without compromising the epistemological realism that is central to the entire ecclesial tradition.

Augustine's insight, then, that when the soul tries to grasp God, it becomes aware of how much it does not know about him, is a thought not entirely foreign to Vatican I.[4] In fact, a rereading of sections of that council as antirationalist, antitotalizing admonitions, resonant with themes dear to postmodernism, is probably in order precisely because the council wanted to make clear that the intelligibility of the existing real (a theme central to both the medieval thinkers and moderns) also required for Christians a significant place for God's hiddenness and incomprehensibility.

Modernism

The Modernist crisis in Roman Catholicism, which took place around the turn of the twentieth century, marked a significant moment for the issue of theological language. The "Modernists," with their decided root-edness in neo-Kantian thought, claimed that cognitive penetration into the mysteries of revelation was severely limited by the very structure of human reason. Of course, at first blush, this positive intellectual asceticism sounds similar to that of Vatican I. The difficulty was that the Modernists gradually came to place the central accent of revelation on human, spiritual experience; the articulation of such experience, however, was decidedly less significant. Doctrinal formulations were often nothing more than a convenient husk, linguistically mediating spiritual experiences for a particular generation, but with no lasting cognitive, noetic, or representational value. Each generation needed to reformulate, in the intelligible terms and concepts available to it, the continuing "prophetic" experience of God's truth. Prior terms and expressions, and even prior content, were not to be understood as constraining or delimiting. What emerged from Modernist writers was an extremely fluid understanding of faith and its cognitive yield. Revelation-as-religious-experience was perennial. Expressions, forms, and creeds were mutable in form and content.

It is no surprise that the Roman Catholic Church reacted quickly to this kind of unvarnished doctrinal mutability. In a series of proscribed propositions contained in the document *Lamentabili* (July 3, 1907), the church declared that revelation was not a human construct but was the gracious gift from God to humanity. Further, dogmas were not to be understood along the lines of practical reason, as prudential, temporary, entirely revisable norms of conduct; on the contrary, they were normative statements of Christian belief requiring the assent of faith. The anti-Modernist accent was markedly on the cognitive validity of doctrine as opposed to what was taken as the Modernists' excessive claims about religious experience and doctrinal fluidity, which, in the eyes of the magisterium, amounted to little more than philosophical agnosticism.

While some answer to Modernism was essential, it is likely the case that the crisis had many deleterious effects on Roman Catholic theology, among which were the strengthening of the conceptual monism of neo-Scholasticism, the odor of suspicion attached to the term "religious experience," and an emphasis on dogmatic "presence" uncomplemented by a similar accent on "absence" in the matter of theological knowing.

Vatican II and *Mysterium Ecclesiae*

Vatican II was called, at least to a certain extent, in order to offset some of the baneful influences deriving from the Modernist controversy. The council was to bear much fruit in areas such as theological pluralism and ecumenism. The issue of theological language, however, was not a central concern of Vatican II. The deeply apophatic sentences of *Dei Filius*, for example, did not find a parallel at the council. Perhaps the closest the council came to affirming the transcendence of the mysteries to human reason is *Dei Verbum*'s citation of another passage from Vatican I: The divine treasures "totally transcend the understanding of the human mind" (*DV* no. 6, citing DS 3005). Vatican II's silence on this issue is not surprising, since the council did not have as its principal raison d'etre a restatement of the hiddenness of God or the mystery surrounding divine revelation. In fact, Vatican II was not particularly concerned with the kind of semirationalism that countenanced an illegitimate deductive probing of the mysteries of faith. On the contrary, the most recent council was exceedingly preoccupied with the kind of rationalism that issued forth in an autonomous human subject seemingly indifferent to the God question. The antidote was not once again to stress the "strict mysteries of faith," an accent that could, if misunderstood, lead to a revelatory and doctrinal heteronomy playing into the hands of Enlightenment rationalism (as the strict natural/supernatural distinction had done previously). Such severe apophasis, if misunderstood, could degenerate into theological extrinsicism, with the mysteries of faith allegedly unrelated to contemporary life.

By way of corrective, then, Vatican II's twin themes of *aggiornamento* and *ressourcement* sought to recover and intensify the seemingly opposite (nonheteronomous) but in fact highly complementary "restless heart," immanent tradition, thereby accentuating the correlation between the deepest desires of men and women and the church's own faith. This council, then, intended not to highlight primarily God's hiddenness, but rather his immanent presence to his own creation.

Unlike Vatican II, the 1973 declaration of the Congregation for the Doctrine of the Faith, *Mysterium ecclesiae*, did adduce the relevantly apophatic passage from Vatican I—ultimately for the sake of conceptually buttressing the theological pluralism called for by Vatican II. That declaration says, "The transmission of divine Revelation in the Church incurs difficulties of various kinds. These occur because the hidden mysteries of God 'by their nature so exceed the intellect that, even when communicated by revelation and received by faith, they reamin covered by the veil of faith and shrouded as if by darkness.' Difficulties also occur because of the historical condition affecting the expression of Revelation."[5]

This document, discussed in the last chapter for its hermeneutical ramifications, here conjoins noematic and noetic apophaticism.[6] The former, with its citation from Vatican I, is reflective of traditional conciliar and patristic theology—that is, God and the divine mysteries are unknowable because of the transcendence and incomprehensibility of the divine nature.[7] By also emphasizing the apophaticism of intentional, cognitive acts, the document concedes that various horizons, such as historical embeddedness and human finitude, necessarily affect the formulation and understanding of revealed truth.

Mysterium ecclesiae, while clearly taking the position that Christian doctrine actually (even if not exhaustively) mediates divine truth, both repeats the tradition and makes an advance upon it. The traditional quidditative-noematic apophaticism is now complemented with a more profound (historically driven) noetic-anthropological apophaticism. The importance of the historical and sociocultural horizons that ineluctably determine all knowing is here intensified.

International Theological Commission

The International Theological Commission of the Roman Catholic Church issued a significant document in 1989, "On the Interpretation of Dogmas," a statement discussed earlier in this work. It, too, in its wide-ranging comments on the nature of doctrine, has something to say about theological language. In line with much of the tradition, the document says that "to be sure we now recognize truth only as in a mirror and in vague contours; only eschatologically will we see God face to face, as God is. . . . Thus, also our knowledge of truth exists in the tension between the 'already' and the 'not yet'" (B.I.1). The clear affirmation, of course, is that Christian faith truly knows something about God, even if not comprehensively so. The document goes on to affirm, in a statement resonant with the earlier tradition and entirely germane to our considerations, "Dogmas, *like every human statement about God*, are to be understood analogically; namely, however great the similarity, there is a greater dissimilarity (citing Lateran IV, DS 806)." Analogy "protects against an objectivist, reified and ultimately mysteryless understanding of faith and dogma." At the same time, analogy "protects as well against an overly negative theology, which regards dogmas as mere ciphers of an ultimately inconceivable Transcendence and consequently, fails to recognize the historical concreteness of the Christian mystery of salvation" (B.III.4.).

What this dyadic balance, avoiding both a wooden understanding of doctrine and an entirely negative theology, is meant to protect is the proper calibration between the *Deus revelatus* and the *Deus absconditus*, between the revealing and the hidden God. Insofar as God has begun a dialogue with his creatures, has involved them in a salvific narrative of creation and redemption, then God has manifested something of his own life. At the same time, the ITC wants to make clear that there are delineated limitations on the kind of understanding yielded by doctrinal language, a restriction duly noted when it says that the "interpretation of the truth of revelation" shares in "the historicity and limitation of all human speech" (B.II.4.). Analogy rebuts any Modernist, equivocal conception of dogma, for not only does analogy prevent the reductionist understanding of doctrine as a simple "cipher" for transcendence, it also, as the statement continues, allows for dogma "to be distinguished from a falsely understood symbolic conception of dogma in the sense that dogma would be a subsequent objectification, whether this be of an existential religious experience or of a determined social or ecclesial praxis" (B.III.4.). If taken in this latter sense, Christian doctrine would be evacuated of any mediating truth-status and would, instead, stand solely as a factitious artifact of religious or particular sociocultural experience. The document insists, rather, that in dogma, "God's own salvific truth" reaches us. Dogma is the "doctrinal form whose content is God's own word and truth."

The ITC document places analogy and the analogical way in which dogmas are to be understood within a wider conspectus of Christian doctrine. The statement insists, for example, that dogmas have an anamnetic character, reminding us always of the "great deeds of God" achieved on our behalf. In this sense, dogmas must be related to Scripture and tradition, interpreted within the overall context of the Bible and "in accordance with the analogy of faith" (citing *Dei Verbum*, 12). Dogmas, then, speak of acts not only in the past but in the present, that is, they "seek to proclaim and make salvation present here and now." Finally, dogmas have an eschatological dimension, that is, they are witnesses to eschatological truth and reality. In a certain sense, "they must be understood as doxology" (B.III.2.).

Summary

This brief review of selected ecclesial documents has shown that a traditional Christian theme is the double-edged nature of theological language, both revealing and obscuring God, both mediating and concealing revelation, both predicating attributes of the Godhead while recognizing the severe limits of such predication.

Given these dual horizons, the question becomes: How can one adequately explain the fact that Christian doctrine actually says something about God while simultaneously recognizing that this "something" is highly delimited by both the nature of God and the nature of humanity. Traditionally, of course, one way of conceiving this dialectic between the kataphatic and apophatic approaches was through the agency of analogical language which, it was claimed, mediated something of God's inner life to us while recognizing that the divine life was, for a variety of reasons, beyond our cognitive grasp. But the use of analogy (especially insofar as analogical language is predicated on a prior analogy of being) as a way of understanding the cognitive yield of theological and doctrinal statements has been under fire for a very long time, both from those who think it represents a theological betrayal as well as from those who find it philosophically unintelligible. Let us now turn to these critics of analogy.

Traditional Opponents of Analogy

A significant source of theological discontent about the analogy of being as the explicatory foundation for the predication of names to God is traceable to Karl Barth. The great Reformed theologian's indictment of analogy continues to resonate in all discussions about the nature of theological language. In addition, his work on the metaphysical roots of analogical predication serves to point to a fault line that continues (although the chasm is continually narrowing) to divide Protestant and Roman Catholic theologians on the question of nature and grace. It is worth reviewing the important discussion that enjoined the profound thinkers, Barth and Balthasar, on the nature of analogy and theological language before moving forward to some contemporary questions. Even with the rise of investigations into symbolic and metaphorical language, the issue of properly predicating names to God, of naming God formally and substantially, always comes back, either openly or covertly, to some variation of the *analogia entis*.[8]

Karl Barth

In Barth's famous manifesto, written in 1932 as the foreword to the first volume of his *Church Dogmatics* and repeated by commentators endlessly, he says, "I regard the *analogia entis* as the invention of the Antichrist, and think that because of it one cannot become Catholic."[9] The wider context for Barth's statement is his intention to avoid the trajectory of Protestant thought that seems to justify theology by way of existential philosophy. This is the Schleiermacher-Ritschl-Hermann line, and leads inexorably to the destruction of solid, biblically based, Protestant theology. Equally destructive is the Roman Catholic *analogia entis*, a mode of thought that is legitimate only on the grounds of the so-called "natural knowledge of God in the sense of the *Vaticanum*."

These unwarranted attempts to justify theology by philosophical means must be unalterably opposed. Barth tenaciously insists that an "explicit account of the special path of knowledge to be trodden by dogmatics, must, to be authoritative, be an inner necessity, *grounded in the thing itself*" (33, emphasis added). One cannot look for some ground, some prolegomenon for faith "outside" of faith, such as one finds in existential philosophy or in the natural knowledge of God which, Barth believes, provides the logical structure and foundation for the *analogia entis*.

Since the time of the Enlightenment, he continues, the path toward dogmatic prolegomena involves "a comprehensively explicated self-interpretation of man's existence" that serves as a "preliminary understanding of an existence in the Church" and so as "a preliminary understanding and criterion of theological knowledge" (39). The concern here, of course, is that dogmatic prolegomena have taken the path of establishing a general philosophy into which faith, at just the proper point, reinserts itself. Barth's legitimate fear is that faith now becomes secondary to a previously elaborated general philosophy. Dogmatics becomes a particular point of view sublated within a "higher" *Weltanschauung*. It is precisely for this reason that Barth takes to task the Heideggerian-Bultmannian approach whereby human existence is analyzed "prior to faith"—that is, there is an attempt to look for "the ontologically existential possibility of the existential occurrence of faith, and by means of its analysis to gain a 'preliminary understanding' of Christian language and Christian theology" (39). On the basis of this conception, dogmatic prolegomena consist in developing a general ontology or anthropology, then showing that there is room for this "ontic" element, for faith, "that man's existence is also realizable as believing existence" (40).[10] Barth rejects this possibility and goes straight to the heart of the problem: One cannot first develop a general anthropology, only secondarily making room for believing existence. As he says, the issue is "whether there really is an essence-context superior to the essence of the church and so a scientific problem-context superior to dogmatics. . . . Is there an existential onto-logical prius to this ontic existential thing?" (40).

Further passages in support of this point could easily be adduced, but there is hardly need for them. Barth's fundamental claim is well known: Dogmatic prolegomena often constitute one part of a larger philosophical project. And this is intrinsically antagonistic to the normative, biblical claims of Christianity. Barth thinks that it is precisely the comprehensive epistemology proposed by Vatican I, especially the claim that sinful men and women can know God apart from faith and grace, by 'unaided reason,' that is the ultimate, and ultimately mistaken, ground on which any notion of analogy rests. So, Barth says, Roman Catholicism "affirms an *analogia entis*, the actuality of a likeness in the creature to God even in a fallen world and therewith the possibility of applying the profane 'es gibt' (there is) even to God and divine things" (44). Barth strings together quotations from Augustine's *Confessions*, Aquinas's *Summa contra gentiles*, Lateran IV, and Erich Przywara testifying to such a belief. But despite the impressive array of witnesses, he remains entirely unconvinced. Such similarity and likeness implies a transformation whereby God's action, although initial, is ultimately secondary; what stands at the fore is human transformation, of "grace here becom[ing] nature, of God's action dissolv[ing] into the action of man visited by grace" (43–44). For Barth, the action of the church can never be a "continuously present relation," which is what Catholicism assumes in its entire dogmatic and analogical system. This is why the Reformed theologian can say, in words that strongly attest to the absoluteness of divine transcendence, "Alike in its investigations and in its findings, [dogmatics] must keep in view that God is in heaven, but itself upon earth, that as compared with any human language and so even with that of the best dogmatics God, his revelation, and faith continue to live their own free life" (96).[11] This is very much like Barth's earlier claim that in Catholicism grace dissolves into nature because Catholicism takes for granted that Jesus Christ is "no longer the free Lord of their existence, but bound up with the existence of the church[,] . . . finally limited and conditioned by definite concrete formulations of man's understanding of His revelation and of the faith that grasps it" (43). Barth concludes that we must dismiss ourselves as "unprofitable servants," recognizing that we are not "masters of the subject-matter."

There is, for Barth, a dissonance between the church (humanity) and God, one that Catholicism illegitimately tries to bridge in many ways—for example, the conjoining of grace with nature, the linking of Christ with the church, the *successor Petri* as the *vicarius Christi*, and the analogy of being. All, ultimately, seek to impose a human construct, a doctrinal law, upon the freedom of faith. Barth concedes, of course, that "even Roman Catholic dogmatics is . . . aware that the Lordship of Christ is a lordship not only in His Church but over His Church" (109). But, he asks, where can this lordship be concretized when "a complete transfer of power to the Church has already taken place"(109)? The Barthian concern is with a collapse of revelation, of God's grace, into the "natural," into human "control." This ecclesial pretension to human control of God's own life constitutes the backbone of Barth's objections to the analogy of being.

From an anthropological point of view, Barth wants to make clear that we cannot understand humanity as *esse capax verbi dei* because this establishes a possibility proper to human beings, independent of God: "Man becomes an independent and . . . independently interesting realization of this experience [of the Word of God] and thereby [he becomes] also the thing that makes it [such experience] possible" (243). In a passage that makes transparently clear the Barthian incapacity of human nature, while also serving as a witness to the charge of "occasionalism," Barth states, "Real acknowledgment of the Word of God by no means rests upon a possibility imparted to man and now inherent in him, immanent in him, but upon the Word of God itself which man can in no sense anticipate" (256).

As these passages indicate, Barth has little use for the traditional notion of humanity as *potentia oboedientialis*, much less for the active sense in which someone like Karl Rahner uses this term (although with the Rahnerian proviso that such *potentia* is always already in the sphere of transcendental revelation/grace). The attempt to establish such potency, of humanity as *capax Dei*, represents the aggressions of fallen nature over and against the grace of God. It is why, of course, Barth turned the full brunt of his wrath against Brunner's defense of an anthropological *Offenbarungsmächtigkeit*, a possibility for revelation.

It is precisely because of the aggressive claims of fallen nature that Barth warns against the analogy of being as the "invention of the Antichrist." This is not simply theological polemic or literary hyperbole. One must take Barth at his word: Analogy is another example of fallen nature seeking to compromise and minimize the gratuitous gifts of God. This is why Barth can say, against the *homo capax verbi Dei*, not simply the traditional Reformed rejoinder *finitum non capax infiniti*, but the more theologically precise *homo peccator non capax verbi Domini* (252). The point, of course, is that God is the generator of every capacity of humanity, and this capacity is never immanent in human nature; it never really "belongs" to men and women, but is graciously bestowed, as Barth says, "lent" to us. As he makes clear, "The possibility of faith as it is given to man in the reality of faith can only be regarded as one lent to man by God and lent exclusively for use. The moment we wanted to regard it as in any sense one belonging to man, the . . . statement about man's incapacity [*finitum non capax finiti*] would have to come back into force" (272).

The capacity in men and women for faith as "lent" by God indicates that Barth will by no means tolerate any "natural" congruity between God and human beings. In his polemic against Brunner, Barth says, "We cannot possibly, with E. Brunner, mean by that [the image of God of Gen 1:27] the humanity and personality of sinful man." This simply cannot signify conformity with God or a "point of contact" with the Word of God. "In this sense, as a possibility for God proper to man *qua* creature the 'image of God' is not only, as we say, with the exception of some remnants ruined, but annihilated. . . . Man's capacity for God . . . has really been lost" (273). It cannot be ascribed to him even *potentialiter*.

It is enough to say, even after this brief review of some of the central points of Barth's polemic against analogy, that his argument possesses a sterling logic and clarity. If fallen man is not, by his nature, even a potential hearer of the word of God, if the "image of God" has been annihilated, how then can one establish an *analogia entis*, an analogy of being, between God and creatures? Even after some of Barth's confusions about analogy are cleared away, it remains certain that Barth differs from one foundational element in any traditional understanding of the *analogia entis*: The metaphysical roots of analogy require the notion of a similitude between Creator and creature, a similitude borne from creation (a creation which is always a gratuitous and so graced gift) and, at least for a significant part of the tradition, witnessed in Genesis with the claim that humanity is made in the image and likeness of God. Philosophically, this was ultimately titled under the rubrics of efficient and exemplar causality; in so doing, it became one way for ancient and medieval thinkers to explain how human beings were made in the *imago Dei*. But with such a notion of similitude Barth could never agree. Even when his later interlocutors would explain that analogy was not and could not be a preconceived, a priori, Procrustean bed into which the Christian faith was then fitted and molded, even when they pointed out the misunderstandings of analogical predication that infiltrated his thought, the fact remains that analogy, even as an a posteriori explanation of speech about God, makes certain anthropological assertions, offers certain interpretations of the *imago Dei*, that Barth refuses to accept on the grounds that they appear unbiblical, compromising both the absolute gratuity of God's grace and the abject fallenness of humanity.

At the same time, as Barth recognizes, his own notion of the *analogia fidei* puts him "into hairbreadth proximity to the Catholic doctrine of the *analogia entis*." This is the position, of course, that the possibility for knowledge of God is not given with nature, is not an immanent possession of human beings but is given, rather, with the image of God "awakened through Christ from real death to life and so 'restored' the newly created *rectitudo*, now real as man's possibility for the Word of God" (273).

Barth's understanding of analogy will be discussed further later. But what is certainly central to his entire theological corpus is the relentless Anselmianism that must remain at the heart of Christian faith and thought—that is, that one must begin with the word of God, with revelation itself, only later asking what is ontologically, hermeneutically, veridically, linguistically, and correlationally acceptable. This is Barth's enduring legacy and one that Christian theology is mandated to follow.[12]

The Response to Barth

Does theology need the notion of analogy in order to explicate logically its dogmatic claims about God and Christ, in order to explain intelligibly the nature of theological language? As Pannenberg has indicated, it seems likely the case that some understanding of analogy is necessary if theology is to continue to maintain the distinction between God's presence and absence, between the unveiledness and hiddenness inherent in revelation. No other theory has presented itself as an adequate defender of the entire tradition affirming both God's essential incomprehensibility and the church's confidence in its creedal and dogmatic statements.

In the following sections, I intend to outline the renewed notion of analogy that has emerged during the last decades, which has received impetus from Balthasar's examination of Barth's objections to analogy as well as his own creative response. Balthasar's work, along with that of several others, has allowed the theory of analogy to renew itself at the headwaters of the tradition, while concomitantly taking account of at least some of Barth's most trenchant objections.

Henri Bouillard and Hans Urs von Balthasar were two early Roman Catholic interlocutors with Barth's theology. Both were sympathetic to his fundamental project of establishing the primacy of revelation, of overcoming monistic attempts to "ground" theological language outside of faith. In some regards, then, Barth, Bouillard, and Balthasar were companions in a joint project seeking to overcome the rationalism bequeathed to them by aspects of an earlier, modern, theological approach. Indeed, both Roman Catholic authors were highly appreciative of Barth's labors exposing the latent, and even at times overt, rationalism in many neo-Scholastic discussions of "nature" and "analogy."

At the same time, both Bouillard and Balthasar were concerned to correct some of Barth's misconstruals about the nature of the analogy of being, conclusions deemed misconstruals when judged against the actual Thomistic tradition. These theologians argued that the *analogia entis*, a construct used to explain the nature of theological language, was never intended to be a grounding philosophical idea, a fully elaborated general ontology, now serving as a logical foundation for Christian faith. On the contrary, analogy is a structure disengaged from *within* the logic of the faith. It is an attempt to understand, *precisely given the priority of revelation and the church's faith*, the claim that Christian doctrine truly tells us something about God and Christ. Consequently, both Bouillard and Balthasar are in firm agreement with Barth when he insists that one cannot posit a prius, that is, an existential-ontological foundation outside of faith. It is never a matter of starting a priori, with an understanding of being bequeathed by philosophy, then tailoring revelation and faith to these pre-existing contours and anticipatory determinations.[13] On the contrary, their argument runs, in Catholic theology one does not and cannot discern a general epistemological project and then try to determine the place of what Heidegger called the "ontic" discipline of faith. (Recall once again Heidegger's attempt to dragoon Luther and the Reformation for his own "ontological" project.) In fact, it is precisely this notion—that there could be some category "broader" or "deeper" than faith, to use spatial metaphors—which the tradition rejects. Rather, the traditional methodology is precisely the Anselmian *fides quaerens intellectum*, with its dual movement of *auditus fidei* and *intellectus fidei*. And it is only in light of *this* movement—that is, the attempt to understand and explore faith's claims—that one finds some place for the notion of analogy.

Both Bouillard and Balthasar make interesting cases, but here I shall limit myself to an examination solely of Balthasar's position.[14] Even though now over fifty years old, Balthasar's work still very helpfully illuminates the central issues not only of theological language but also of the subtle intertwining of nature and grace.

Balthasar on Barth and Analogy

What is Balthasar's fundamental argument regarding Barth and the nature of analogy? Balthasar observes that Barth accuses Catholicism of possessing an overarching systematic principle that is merely an abstract statement about being rather than a frank assertion that Christ is Lord: "This means that God's revelation in Jesus Christ seems to be but the fulfillment of an already existing knowledge and reality." Indeed, "Christ's place as the fulfillment of salvation history is still reserved 'in advance'; in an ontology that exists prior to the order of revelation and cannot be shattered by it."[15] Balthasar, however, disputes this indictment from several points of view. In fact, this response constitutes the bulk of his work. Almost immediately, he distances himself from the position that the analogy of being is the "key" to Catholicism, an idea Barth took from Erich Przywara.[16] On the contrary, Balthasar rejoins, there is no "single" Catholic approach to the issue of analogy (39–40).

What quickly becomes limpidly clear is that Balthasar is willing to concede to Barth every possible point about the priority of grace over nature, Barth's central concern. Again and again, in a virtual drumbeat throughout the book, Balthasar champions the *unicus ordo supernaturalis*. There is one and only one supernatural order. Catholic neo-Scholasticism often advanced a bifurcated dualism of nature and grace, a dichotomy that seemingly allowed for a purely "natural" order, outside the realm of grace. Balthasar is quick to argue, however, that there is no such entity as pure nature. There is only a human nature existing within the one and only order of grace.[17]

In support of his position, Balthasar adduces research that had been gaining ground during the first half of the twentieth century: Aquinas, in continuity with early Christian writers, recognizes only the existing supernatural order; he attributes only one, supernatural end to created spirits, as Henri de Lubac had definitively shown (267).[18] As created beings, men and women have no goal other than the vision of God, the *desiderium naturale visionis*. This is why Balthasar can boldly claim, "The whole patristic tradition right up to the high Middle Ages—including Thomas for the most part—conceive the issue [i.e., the use of Greek philosophical categories, such as analogy itself] within the *unicus ordo realis supernaturalis*— and thus within the analogy of faith, which nestles within itself the analogy of being as a subordinate moment" (261). Balthasar's intention here is twofold: to overcome the notion of pure nature advanced by several Catholic neo-Scholastics and to demonstrate to Barth that the notion of nature in the earlier tradition is clearly inscribed within the compass of grace. This is why Balthasar again and again makes clear that we are always, *ab ovo*, in the supernatural order. On this point, then, Barth is entirely correct: It is only within the estate of grace and faith that human beings—and a fortiori, analogical language—can be properly understood.

But if, on the one hand, Balthasar argues against neo-Scholasticism that nature cannot be surgically extracted from the supernatural order, on the other, he challenges what he sees as Barth's total collapse of nature into grace. It is precisely to strike a via media between these positions, to elaborate a concept of the *relative autonomy* of nature always embedded within the supernatural order, that Balthasar ultimately intends. Balthasar sees his work as both a concession and a challenge to Barth: *Within this one order of prevenient grace*, there exists some intrinsic relation between God and creatures.

Of course, any intrinsic relation between God and humanity is diametrically opposed to the Barthian claim that the analogy between God and creatures must always be an "extrinsic analogy of attribution." Why extrinsic? Because, as Barth has made clear, "the relationship that grace establishes between God's Word and the creature is not intrinsic or inherent (*proprie*)" (110). On the contrary, such relationship must always be freely given, indeed "lent," and never be regarded as "proper" to the creature. But this extrinsicism troubles Balthasar. Even after all of his concessions to Barth about the priority of grace and the existence of only one graced order, he nonetheless insists that if "the 'authentic' truth of the creature resides in God, then it is indeed *God's* truth, created and established by God. This being so, this truth must be, not extrinsic, but intrinsic" (110).

Balthasar wants Barth to admit that within the one order of grace there exists a relative autonomy of the order of nature, that is, God has graciously established the creature and creation in truth and goodness. This is the reason that Balthasar pursues the claim that Barth, even when he speaks of the extrinsic analogy of attribution, admits that creation is "thoroughly good and positive in itself, that is, in its very being it is not-God." For the first time, Balthasar concludes, Barth takes seriously the concept of the creature: "No longer need creatureliness be done away with, as it was in 1919, to make room for revelation and God's own life" (110). Barth is now free, Balthasar concludes, to "say that *creation itself* is blameless in its freedom, its self-awareness, its relatedness to God" (111). He clinches his argument with the comment, "In other words, the existence of a reality distinct from God cannot be a source of embarrassment solely because of its distinctness from God" (111).

One sees here the essential point: Balthasar thinks that even in Barth there is an instinct, reserved and not yet fully surfaced, that allows for the relative autonomy of creation: relative, because it always exists within the one and only estate of God's graciousness; autonomous, because it possesses a certain freedom, a certain "nature" in and of itself, in its distinctness from God. This is why Balthasar can say that the goodness of creation, inasmuch as it is always and everywhere God's handiwork, need not lead ineluctably to the notion of justification by works. Recognizing the goodness of creation, of nature, is always primarily the recognition of God's gracious action.

Of course, intrinsic to Balthasar's own argument, and essential given his desire to push Barth in this direction, is the recognition that nature is always a *theological* concept, never a purely philosophical one: "If the beatific vision of God is made the goal of the creature and thus if its whole being is directed and equipped for this goal, then it can indeed be expressed with the dynamic Aristotelian concept of nature. . . . But it must be clear that this application is only *analogically valid*" (275). Nature, then, is a concept drawn from the one and only supernatural order, and it is, rather than a purely Aristotelian or Stoic concept, essentially oriented toward the beatific vision.[19] One must, therefore, look to grace and revelation, and not merely to philosophy, in order to know how one speaks properly of human nature.

This is why Balthasar says that grace presupposes nature, at least logically, but a nature already transformed: "Nature exists concretely in the transformed, exalted 'mode' of being graced" (281). The existing subject so transformed is none other (*non aliter*) than that of nature, even if it has become something different (*aliter*). The human person, then, is the *aliter non aliter*, possessing of a human nature in the exalted, transforming realm of grace. Human nature exists in a new formality, the *novus ordo* of grace. It is true, Balthasar avers, that grace is free in its relationship to nature, but this admission does not allow making pure nature a governing concept. Nature, rather, is the

> *minimum* that must be present in every possible situation where God wants to reveal himself to a creature. And this minimum is expressed by the term *analogia entis*. . . . [Revelation] can only proceed from God to the creature—to a creature that precisely as a creature does *not* include revelation in its conceptual range. The "nature" that grace supposes is createdness as such. (285).

It is precisely this createdness as such that constitutes, for Balthasar, the formal concept of nature. Nature, then, must be understood, logically, as the baseline presupposition to grace. It is that which allows God to reveal himself fully to creatures. It is entirely true that creation itself is a gift and grace of God, the presupposition for revelation. But this creation must take the form of an existing created nature. Balthasar can argue, "Created being must be . . . relative and non-divine but *as* something created, it cannot be

utterly dissimilar to its Creator. And if this creature is a spiritual and intellectual being . . . [its] nature must bear some relation to its Creator" (285).[20]

But while nature may be a formal presupposition to grace, Balthasar
adds a telling comment, ensuring that no understanding of nature
emerges purely from the "natural" order: "This same formal nature, on a
higher plane, has for *its* presupposition the Son's willingness to make this
descent into creation"(287). In other words, while, in one sense, the presupposition of the incarnation is human nature, if one continues to question "back," it is the eternal willingness and obedience of the Son that
exists as the presupposition of nature itself.

Here again, one witnesses Balthasar's single-minded desire to bring
the concept of nature entirely within the estate of grace, while simultaneously preserving nature's *relative* autonomy. He says that no element of
nature escapes the penetration of grace, since grace "irradiates" and "transforms" nature (287). This is why nature is best thought of as a "kind of
'servant concept' to help protect the concept of grace" (290).

Further Reflections on Nature/Grace

Nature, for Balthasar, is a thoroughly theological concept, drawn from the
supernatural order. It is disengaged as a logical structure, an essential element if revelation is to be fully intelligible and properly explicated.
Balthasar does not want a collapse of nature into grace, in which creation
would become invisible, but seeks a sublation of nature by grace, so that
nature, while not losing its identity, is thereby integrated into a more comprehensive theological synthesis.[21]

Where then does Balthasar stand on Barth's original question: Is the
potentia oboedientialis in the order of nature or grace? Balthasar tries to
defang the question, arguing it should not be directed in so stark a manner. There exists, rather, a continuing tension: Nature on its own has no
access to the world of grace even though nature was created because of
grace and for grace and cannot be understood without grace. One will
remain mired in something of a false problem, Balthasar claims, if one
insists on speaking of "unassisted" human nature or of God's overweening
grace.[22] There is no order of "pure" nature apart from grace; neither is there
an order of grace alone, apart from a relatively autonomous human nature.

If placed within its proper context, allowing for the continuing tension
between nature and grace, the Barthian polemic against natural theology
and the analogy of being is, Balthasar thinks, rendered "superfluous"
(302). Both "sides" agree that the order of grace takes absolute priority
over the order of nature in the sphere of intentionality, while the created

order takes relative priority over the order of grace in terms of executing the divine plan (i.e., nature is a relative condition for grace). Therefore, we can only examine the order of nature within the sphere of revelation and faith. This is why Balthasar can say that the whole order of reason is embedded in the estate of faith just as the whole order of creation is embedded within graced existence (325). All knowledge of God, then, occurs, de facto, within the conditions of the supernatural order, since the spiritual and intellectual life of men and women is always already existent within this formal dimension of grace. Reason and nature are not lifeless abstractions but are, instead, invariably implanted within an "elevated" supernatural formality.[23]

Given this anthropology, Balthasar is convinced that Barth's attacks on the analogy of being are unjustified, even if Balthasar's own work testifies that Roman Catholic authors have provided Barth with ample ammunition, speaking of nature, at times, as if it were materially separable from the order of grace. Balthasar is convinced, however, that "Barth was forced to ground Catholicism on the systematic concept of the analogy of being. But his version of this concept was extremely simplistic—in fact, it was downright fraudulent. So his first task was to set up a straw man" (382).

Balthasar credits himself with having "dismantled this illusory battlefield. It is not formulas that are battling against one another (*analogia fidei* vs. *analogia entis*) but two ways of understanding the one revelation of God" (382). And these two ways can be harmonized without forced syncretism. What Balthasar is conceding, of course, is that Barth is entirely right that any talk of the analogy of being must always be nestled within the order of revelation and grace. The analogy of faith is the de facto supernatural order of revelation within which the analogy of being serves as a useful and important construct helping to explicate the nature of theological language. The analogy of being is not and can never be an a priori *Grundprinzip*, a frozen, nonperformative "form" adopted apart from revelation. It is, instead, a matter of an intelligible structure that explains how one may formally and substantially predicate names of God within the order of revelation and grace.

One must acknowledge, then, that nature and reason have a relative autonomy and legitimacy. This includes the openness of humanity or the *potentia oboedientialis*. This potency enables human beings, once the order of grace is opened up, to explore the inner meaning and content of revelation (383). This is certainly not to set up nature in opposition to grace, once again moving in the direction of stark opposites. It is, however, to recognize that nature, while moving from and toward grace, does not lose its own formality. This is why Balthasar pleads for the conjunction rather than the bifurcation of nature and grace. Grace, he says, is the vine, the principle of all fruitfulness, while nature, like the branch, bears fruit only when united to the vine. Catholics traditionally stress one element, while Protestants accent the other. But neither should be neglected. Christ says that "you shall bear much fruit," but he also says "without me you can do nothing" (387).

The Analogia Entis *Disciplined by Revelation*

Balthasar sees the great contribution of Barth, especially when judged within the context of Catholic neo-Scholasticism, as having called theology away from universal concepts and abstractions and back to the one concrete order of salvation.[24] This is not to extirpate the legitimacy of the concept of nature, but to place it within the horizon of the concrete salvific order.[25] So Balthasar can say, essentially summing up the theme of his book, "This *concretissimum* [of the incarnation and the order of salvation] is also the fullest and richest of realities. . . . [It] is the source of all the meaning in existence and nature, justifying and fulfilling them. And within the various interpretations of this event . . . we find room for the use of universal concepts, categories, properties and finally of Being itself" (384). What Balthasar is asserting here is that the *analogia entis* is hardly meant as a prior foundation for theology; its use, rather, is for the sake of theologically explicating the faith within the concrete order of salvation. Even Barth himself recognized that this way of saying things, of using the notion of being and the categories associated with it, "is the opposite of trying to force the revelatory truth of Jesus Christ and of the salvation history that leads up to him into philosophical categories that would drain history of its most characteristic properties" (384). In fact, Barth recognized the possibility, even the necessity, of using some notion of being in theology's doctrine of God, always, of course, firmly disciplined by faith: "We must not yield to a revulsion against the idea of being as such" (*CD* II/1, 260).[26]

In Roman Catholic theology, Balthasar argues, the work of Joseph Maréchal and Erich Przywara provides legitimate examples of this kind of disciplined, performative use of being-language. If we do as they have done, there is little danger of tying down the preambles of the faith to a frozen philosophical system, as Barth once feared. Both of these thinkers "recognize the relativity and finitude of our conceptual schemes" but "they also avoid any taint of modern skepticism and relativism, for they judge these schemes by God's own concrete dealings with history" (385).

Balthasar wishes to make clear, then, that the analogy of being is not intrinsic to Catholic teaching inasmuch as doctrines "do not have their meaning and justification on the grounds of some philosophy, still less from a synthesis of a particular philosophy with Christian theology." On the contrary, these doctrines "come from revelation exclusively" (386).[27] The use of analogy is intended to illuminate Christian teaching; it is meant to help understand how we may speak of God in human terms and concepts. But the *analogia entis* should not be the church-dividing issue that Barth has made of it with his original manifesto about the Antichrist. The same objection holds true for Barth's claim that the "the great sham doctrine of the analogy of being" is the "foundational schema" of Catholic thought and doctrine (254). The church hardly possesses a rigidly enclosed metaphysics. In fact, conceptual pluralism is essential to Christian theology.[28]

Summary of Balthasar
In his afterword of 1961, ten years after the completion of his initial examination of Barth, and after Barth had produced several more volumes of his *Church Dogmatics*, Balthasar affirmed that his original work would not be much different were he to have written the book later. Balthasar notes that Barth's primal inspiration remains intact, namely, no form of philosophy can possess a reflective understanding of the human spirit as a whole; revelation necessarily remains the primary and central narrative. Of course, with this aspect of Barth's thought Balthasar is in firm agreement.

Nonetheless, some Balthasarian reservations about Barth remain. He continues to complain, for example, about Barth's "narrowing" or "constricting" approach. By this he means that Barth appears to "reject philosophy because it works only from material drawn from within this world" while "all truths about man and the world have to be drawn from the Christology that presupposes them" (393). What Balthasar resists here—and this is the basis for his referring to Barth's "narrowing" (*Engführung*)—is not Barth's legitimate accent on the primacy of grace, faith, and revelation, but that such emphasis appears to marginalize the limited autonomy that should be afforded to nature and reason. At times, one senses a collapse of the natural order into the supernatural one, of creation into salvation, so that even the relative autonomy of nature and reason is thereby compromised.[29] So when Balthasar complains about Barth's placing all of creation within a christological Procrustean bed, one should see this as an indictment of Barth's failure to recognize the relative autonomy of cre-

ation—and so of nature—within the graced order (242). This is why
Balthasar declares that "revelation does not annul creation's own proper
and original meaning" (242). One may be entirely theocentric and christocentric without thereby denying nature's own sphere. Barth is not
wrong in recognizing the gift of grace given to us, but he cannot clearly
recognize that this gift is now *ours*.[30]

Is the Barthian accent so marked on the supernatural order, Balthasar
wonders, that man cannot now respond to God "with his own word"
(393)? Is the human response truly a *verbum hominis*? Balthasar buttresses
his case by adducing Barth's own example wherein the latter had compared creation to the "reflector lights on an automobile. They reflect back
to the motorist but only when he is shining his own headlights" (393). In
other words, the creature responds to God, but it is not really his own
word. This critique is simply a reiteration of Balthasar's original claim that
Barth fails to recognize the relative autonomy of nature and reason—of
being and so of the analogy of being—as important elements within the
one supernatural order. Balthasar ultimately charges Barth with talking so
much about Christ as *the* true human being that other human beings
appear to be "mere epiphenomena" (243).

This is the reason Balthasar is at pains to defend an authentic and
integral philosophical act that has a legitimate autonomy, that of nature,
even though this autonomy is never absolute.[31] As Balthasar asks, "Is
Barth's challenge justified, or does the analogy of grace not possess in its
inner pre-supposition an analogous (and by no means identical!) analogy
in the order of creation and even in the order of sin?" (396). The point
here is that some notion of nature is needed as the logical presupposition
for grace—not that the analogies of faith and of being are on the same
level. Balthasar is insistent that there is only an analogous relationship
between them, just as there is an analogous relationship between the God
of the philosophers and the living God of Abraham and Jesus. One sees
here a kind of turning of the tables on Barth. The Procrustean bed, the
nonperformative, frozen notion is not the properly (revelationally) disciplined and chastised analogy of being; it is just as easily the (Barthian)
theo- or christopanism that collapses truly human action into the supernatural order.

Of course, the discussion between Barth and Balthasar is—after all the
concessions about the absolute priority of revelation, grace, and faith are
finally tallied—really about metaphysics and the kind of metaphysics necessary if one is to explicate properly the truth of revelation. Balthasar is
arguing that there is a metaphysical structure to reality, to created being—

that the analogy of being, that is, the relationship between God and creature given with creation (which is always graced!) ultimately founds the possibility of the dialectic of veiling and unveiling in theological language.[32] Balthasar's argument, then, is that one need not turn against the analogy of being—as if concrete, existing human nature were not already in the realm of grace. Even though grace is "contingent" in the sense of being entirely gratuitous, it forms the ultimate ground and foundation for revelation. The analogy of being, as with any philosophy, must finally be understood within the orbit of the "contingency" of grace itself.

What is offered here finally is a metaphysics chastened and disciplined by revelation. Classical Protestant concerns about the priority of grace are protected, but not without also seeing the analogy of being as a logical—indeed, metaphysical—moment abstracted from the existing, graced order. It is just this analogy of being upon which an intelligible theory of analogical predication of names to God, formally and substantially, can be established.

Concluding Reflections

Balthasar offers, then, a twofold "reparative" narrative about nature and grace that seeks, simultaneously, to move Catholicism away from the rationalistic notion of *natura pura* that took hold in the sixteenth century while displaying to Barthian thought that the priority and prevenience of grace need not subvert the relative autonomy of the created, natural order. Balthasar argues that both neo-Scholastic rationalism and Barthian supernaturalism need finer calibration. Legitimate Barthian concerns need to be conjoined with the tradition's accent on nature and reason, thereby avoiding a forced syncretism and achieving an authentic synthesis. Consequently, the analogy of being must be thought within the analogy of faith; the former is simply a child of the Anselmian *fides quaerens intellectum*.[33]

One may perhaps legitimately conclude that Balthasar would have little difficulty with Stanley Hauerwas's recently delivered Gifford Lectures, published as *With the Grain of the Universe*. Barth is clearly the protagonist of Hauerwas's work, as is the Barthian claim that a Christian must begin his or her theology proper, not from the natural theology mandated by Lord Gifford's will, but from an explicitly christological context. At the same time, Hauerwas asserts that Etienne Gilson, for example, has much to teach us by his use of Aquinas's metaphysics. Hauerwas only cautions against metaphysics when it, rather than revelation, is extended a theologically foundational primacy.[34] But this, of course, is precisely the point

Balthasar makes with his repeated references to the concrete order of revelation as the theoretical norm for the *analogia entis*, for metaphysics, indeed, for all philosophy.

This debate between Barth and Balthasar, with its lively and in many ways unsurpassed claims about the relationship between the analogy of being and the life of faith, now draws us more deeply toward the headwaters of the tradition of analogical language. We now turn to these headwaters with the hope that a cold draft from them will serve to clarify the nature of theological language.

Notes

1. In its commentary on the Nicene-Constantinopolitan Creed, the catechism cites this passage in conjunction with the important statement of Aquinas from *Summa contra gentiles*, I, 30. See *Catechism of the Catholic Church* (Vatican City: Libreria Editrice Vaticana, 1994), no. 43.

2. Franzelin's *votum* was first published in the work of Hermann-Josef Pottmeyer, *Der Glaube vor dem Anspruch der Wissenschaft* (Freiburg: Herder, 1968).

3. In fact, even though Vatican I was limited to emphasizing the *quod* (or the excess of intelligibility in the Godhead), nonetheless this still provided one argument for a healthy, commensurable diversity of *Begrifflichkeiten*. I am not, of course, suggesting that Vatican I encouraged theological pluralism. I am only saying that its proper emphasis on the caliginous character of revealed truth allows such an argument to be made.

4. *De ordine* II, 16, 44; and II, 18, 47 (PL 32 1015/1017); cited in Etienne Gilson, *The Christian Philosophy of St. Augustine* (trans. L. E. M. Lynch; New York: Random House, 1960), 352.

5. Congregation for the Doctrine of the Faith, *Acta apostolicae sedis* 65 (1973): 402.

6. The terms "noematic" and "noetic" are used here to refer to intentional acts and their contents.

7. This approach is also found in the *Professio fidei* of Paul VI of 1968. He describes God as *super omne nomen, superque omnes res et intelligentias creatas*. Similarly, when explaining the mystery of the Trinity, the pope says, "infinite omne id superat, quod nos modo humano intelligere possumus." Paul VI here cites DS 3016 even though the exact words of *Dei Filius* are not used.

8. The limits of this book will not allow a sufficient investigation into the symbolic nature of religious language. Nonetheless, I wish to state that a theology of the symbol need not contradict the analogical nature of theological language. There is a legitimate sense in which one may speak of the symbolic nature of Christian doctrine without opposing the positions outlined here. For a good argument along these lines, see Avery Dulles, *Models of Revelation* (Garden City, N.Y.: Doubleday, 1983), 133–34, 141–43, 160–62.

9. Karl Barth, *Church Dogmatics* I/1 (trans. G. T. Thomson; Edinburgh: T&T Clark, 1949), x. Further citations will be from this volume, unless noted.

10. This is why Barth would find Heidegger's interpretation of Luther, which reduces Christianity to one discrete area of being—one "ontic" dimension subsumed under a general, philosophically imperialistic "ontological" study—absolutely unthinkable. It would allow for a general ontology, Heidegger's own, prior to a further specification by faith. Barth is here much closer to the traditional understanding whereby philosophy must ultimately conform to revelation. This theme is treated at greater length in chapters nine and ten.

11. One finds here resonances of Luther's claim that "there is no analogy between the word of mortal man and the Word of the eternal and almighty God." Luther, *Sermons on the Gospel of John* (vol. 22 of *Luther's Works*; ed. J. Pelikan and H. Lehmann [St. Louis: Concordia, 1955–1986]), chs. 1–4, 9.

12. R. Jenson, W. Pannenberg, and E. Jüngel take their starting points from Barth's original polemic against analogy. Perhaps a word from Pannenberg on this matter will show that the Barthian critique is alive, although it has taken a slightly different form. Pannenberg recognizes, with the entire tradition, that one must balance God's hiddenness and transcendence with the fact of his unveiling, of his entering into a dialogue of salvation with his creatures. He says that "any intelligent talk about God . . . must begin and end with confession of the inconceivable majesty of God which transcends our concepts." Nonetheless, "it does not follow that we do better to be silent about God than to speak about him, or that nothing definite is conceivable in our talk about God." Pannenberg, *Systematic Theology*, vol. 1 (trans. Geoffrey Bromiley; Grand Rapids: Eerdmans, 1991), 337. He avers that Aquinas insisted on the incomprehensibility of the divine essence (344) and agrees that "only by analogy can we attribute positive descriptions of God to the divine essence." This, Pannenberg says, is the element of truth, "notwithstanding all the objections that can be brought against his idea of analogous predication." One objection, in particular, is that the notion of causality, the ontological ground of analogy, can be too easily predicated of the relationship between God and creatures. And even if there is an analogical notion of causality at work, does *this* analogical relationship properly explicate the idea of analogical language? Pannenberg seems to see here a *petitio principi*, explaining one analogical principle by another. Pannenberg, *Basic Questions in Theology*, vol. 1 (trans. George Kehm; London: SCM Press, 1970), 223, no. 20.

   In his *Systematic Theology*, Pannenberg revives Scotus's claim that all analogous predication demands and presupposes a univocal basis (1:344, no. 14). This objection "has not yet been answered." For Scotus, concepts are univocal. His logic is as follows: Precisely because we have no concept of God in his distinctive essence we are forced to use general concepts, such as that of being, to embrace both the creaturely and the divine, so that on this basis we may distinguish between the infinite being of God and everything finite (345). William Hill, taking a Thomist viewpoint, has noted that if one abstracts entirely from the modes of actualization, the resulting concept would, indeed, be univocal, not analogical. But the traditional notion of analogy demands not a common idea but an analogical *ratio* predicated *per prius et posterius*, with differing modes of subsistence. See William Hill, *Knowing the Unknown God* (New York: Philosophical Library, 1971), 142.

13. This is not to say, of course, that some notion of the analogy of being cannot be achieved philosophically. It is to say that any such notion, as Bouillard and Balthasar argued, must be performatively disciplined by revelation. But this is simply to recognize that the truth of revelation will always stimulate philosophy itself to more incisive insights.

14. For Henri Bouillard's insights, see his magisterial work, *Karl Barth*, 2 vols. (Paris: Aubier, 1957). His evaluation of Barth on analogy is summarized in Thomas Guarino, *Fundamental Theology and the Natural Knowledge of God in the Writings of Henri Bouillard* (Ann Arbor, Mich.: University Microfilms, 1984).

15. Hans Urs von Balthasar, *The Theology of Karl Barth* (trans. Edward Oakes; San Francisco: Ignatius, 1992), 37. The original text appeared as *Karl Barth: Darstellung und Deutung Seiner Theologie* (Cologne: Jakob Hegner, 1951). The Oakes translation is of the unabridged original German text. A useful but abridged English translation by John Drury appeared in 1971 (New York: Holt, Rinehart & Winston). All citations in the text will be from the Oakes translation unless otherwise noted. For Barth's well-known plaudits of Balthasar's study, see *Church Dogmatics*, IV/1 (trans. Geoffrey W. Bromiley; Edinburgh: T&T Clark, 1956), 768.

16. Przywara advanced analogy as a central theme in Catholicism largely in response to Barth's early championing of dialectical approaches. For a recent analysis of Przywara's work, see Thomas O'Meara, *Erich Przywara, S.J.: His Theology and His World* (Notre Dame, Ind.: University of Notre Dame Press, 2002).

17. For more details, see Rodney Howsare, "A Trojan Horse in the Catholic Church: On Balthasar's Interpretation of Barth," *Fides Quaerens Intellectum* 1 (2001): 275–316. As Howsare has pointed out, Balthasar is wielding a double-edged sword, striking out against both Barth and the neo-Scholastic, Cartesian-influenced tradition of autonomous pure nature, all the time hoping to promote the ecumenical cause.

18. De Lubac had argued that the entire Christian tradition, up to and beyond Aquinas, witnesses to the fact that intelligent creatures have only one possible supernatural end for which they were created. This does not, de Lubac asserted, destroy the traditional notion of "double" gratuity, that is, that there exists a grace of both creation and of elevation to a supernatural end, as the neo-Scholastics had argued. It merely recognizes that the two are entirely intertwined. See Henri de Lubac, *Surnaturel: etudes historiques* (Paris: Aubier, 1946). Given de Lubac's own research on later, sixteenth and seventeenth-century developments, one can understand how Barth may have concluded that Catholicism defended a pure nature outside of grace.

19. Balthasar, again relying on de Lubac, makes clear that the notion of "nature," in a purely philosophical sense, made its appearance in theological discourse only as a direct response to Baius in the sixteenth century. He agrees with de Lubac that the very notion of "pure nature" is a theological absurdity. Balthasar claims that Karl Rahner's notion of nature as a *Restbegriff* or remainder concept accords with his own terminology of nature as a "formal, servant concept" only logically disengaged from the order of grace (298).

20. Balthasar here draws attention to the metaphysical roots of analogy that are so disputed by Barth: "It is quite right to say . . . that being *God* and being *creature* [*Gott*sein and *Geschöpf*sein] are utterly dissimilar. . . . But even here we are already talking about *being* God and *being* a creature. So we have already introduced some kind of similarity of the creature with the ever dissimilar God" (286).

21. To this end, Balthasar warns philosophers and theologians that the problem with the concept of nature is that the more we inject into the formal, minimum concept (as belonging to nature per se) the more we expropriate elements that have already been affected by nature's de facto ordering toward our supernatural destiny. Not taking account of this difficulty is often the problem with natural law theory. In a recent book, Russell Hittinger tries to place natural law more securely in its original theological context. See Hittinger, *The First Grace* (Wilmington, Del.: ISI Books, 2003).

22. As Howsare observes, Balthasar was convinced that disputants were asking the wrong question: "What can unassisted human nature do to prepare for grace?" See Howsare, "Trojan Horse in the Catholic Church," 312.

23. This is why, Balthasar notes, Barth has little use for defining "man" as *animal rationale*; one must first look at the concrete situation, that is, the human being before God. Similarly, Balthasar says that one cannot reason "as if man's nature was indifferent to its final determination in God" (192). Once again, Balthasar agrees with Barth's affirmation about the one supernatural order and uses this, with Maréchal and de Lubac, against an uncritical notion of *natura pura*.

24. Balthasar can say that while Scholasticism concentrates on "natures" and "essences"—and its slogan is *operari sequitur esse*—the opposite is the case with Barth, who makes the fullest concrete realization the standard, invoking the *esse sequitur operari* (191). Barth's theology, then, is always a *scientia de singularis*, focusing on the one concrete event of salvation.

25. As de Lubac had said, "The history of salvation contained within itself the realm of nature." Cited in Howsare, "Trojan Horse in the Catholic Church," 282 n. 21.

26. In the 1961 afterword to his book, Balthasar added that Barth ultimately buried the hatchet on the analogy of being (394). Pannenberg, similarly, observes that the increasing emphasis on God's creative action (i.e., the realm of grace) "which grounds analogy both ontologically and noetically from God's side . . . has led Karl Barth to suspend his criticism of the analogy of being." Wolfhart Pannenberg, "Analogy and Doxology," in *Basic Questions in Theology*, vol. 1 (London: SCM Press, 1970), 214 n. 3. (citing *CD* II/1, 81ff.)

27. This is why Balthasar can affirm, when speaking of the analogy of being, that "every concrete philosophy must answer to the order of Revelation" rather than a preexisting ontology (257).

28. Balthasar argues that Przywara himself holds that "there must be no philosophy as a rigid, formal framework into which the content of theology would be poured" (257). Balthasar continues, "Nothing whatever can be found [in Przywara] of that ogre that Barth has made of the analogy of being" (257).

29. Przywara had claimed that Barth's early thought was a "theopanism," that is, a collapsing of everything into God. As Balthasar rephrases it, Barth's actualism "with its constant relentless reduction of all activity to God the *actus purus* leaves no room for any center of activity outside of God" (105).

30. Bruce McCormack confirms this when he says that for Barth, "the being of the subject is not altered through the experience of faith's knowledge of revelation. The 'analogy of faith' never passes to human control. It is effected moment by moment by the sovereign action of the divine freedom." One can hardly argue here, then, for any notion of *potentia oboedientalis* in the traditional sense. See McCormack, *Karl Barth's Critically Realistic Dialectical Theology* (Oxford: Oxford University Press, 1995), 16.

31. One hears these same echoes in the recent encyclical of John Paul II, *Fides et ratio*. The primacy of revelation is affirmed concomitantly with the relative autonomy of philosophy, an autonomy, it should be clearly noted, that is distinguished from a "self-sufficiency."

32. As Stephen Wigley concludes, for Balthasar, "only an understanding of Being, interpreted through the framework of analogy, can do justice to God's revelation in creation and covenant, to the Word of God which is also the Word made flesh, Jesus Christ." Wigley, "The Von Balthasar Thesis: A Re-examination of Von Balthasar's Study of Barth in the Light of Bruce McCormack," *Scottish Journal of Theology* 56 (2003): 345–59.

33. Of course, one part of Balthasar's argument is that one should not rely too heavily on Barth's polemical comments found in the prolegomena to the *Church Dogmatics* because the later volumes "correct or move beyond the positions adopted in the Prolegomena" (61). Balthasar argues that, over time, Barth increasingly moves away from "dialectic" and toward "analogy." So, for example, Barth came "to sing the praises of the goodness of creatureliness as such" (112). Citing several passages from Barth's works, Balthasar concludes, "However much . . . creation may be dependent ontically and noetically on God's revelation in Christ, it is just as true that we can glimpse *in* this revelation a *presupposition* lying at its foundations that makes revelation possible in the first place" (112). Barth even speaks of man as fundamentally related to God as a constant constituent of his essence (126)—even if this is known, of course, only on the de facto basis of revelation. But such an admission has "tremendous implications" for Barth's earlier position. "Man is not in any way now an immanent being closed off and without hope in the world whose dialectical encounter with an utterly alien grace shatters his whole being" (127). This is why Barth can later say, "If God has created man to abide in his Word and thus to become a partner in his covenant, then we must assume God has created a being who can *sense* [*vernehmen*] him."

Balthasar argues that the legitimate implication of this shift in Barth's thought is that nature should no longer be seen merely as an assertion of willful human autonomy over against grace, a kind of extension of a works-righteousness mentality. Rather, Barth himself is groping to explain humanity's unique position, both denying humanity any "natural" capacity for God and simultaneously granting it. For Barth, Balthasar approvingly notes, this capacity is denied if man tries to draw it out of himself alone, but affirmed when man's potential knows that it has been created for revelation (155). Balthasar's clear inference is that Barth's own theological anthropology moves inexorably toward accepting the *analogia entis*, but only, as Balthasar himself counsels, as a function of the *analogia fidei*. In this context, Barth says, even the well-known phrase of Aquinas may be accepted: "gratia non tollit sed perficit naturam" (167).

Not long ago, Bruce McCormack challenged Balthasar's reading of Barth by arguing against the Balthasarian claim that there was an *Umbruch*, or "radical change," in Barth's thought, that is, a shift from dialectic to analogy. McCormack urges the abandonment of Balthasar's thesis that this turn is the predominant *Denkform* of Barth's theology. McCormack argues, rather, that dialectic forms the core of Barth's work and is never abandoned; even the *analogia fidei* is a dialectical concept: "In truth, the *Realdialektik* of veiling and unveiling is the motor driving Barth's doctrine of analogy." McCormack, *Karl Barth's Critically Realistic Dialectical Theology*, 16–18.

It is not my intention to enter into the marrow of the debates about continuities and discontinuities in Barth's theology. While Balthasar would have little difficulty with McCormack's dyadic emphasis on "veiling and unveiling" in analogical language, and while he endorses the theology of God's sovereign freedom, he certainly did have difficulty, as seen above, with the notion that the gift once given in creation—the capacity for God—cannot now truly become a *human* capacity. This, Balthasar argued, was Barth's fatal flaw—the collapse of the relative autonomy of nature into grace—despite all of his other merits. In any case, McCormack's interpretation of Barth would not in any way touch the primary goal envisaged here: Balthasar's attempt to show that the intelligibility of the analogy of being, and thus the intelligibility of theological language, ultimately exists within the one supernatural order. For a recent attempt to defend Balthasar's thesis against McCormack, see Wigley, "The Von Balthasar Thesis."

34. Stanley Hauerwas, *With the Grain of the Universe* (London: SCM Press, 2002). For his positive comments on the important role of metaphysics in theology, see p. 37. Curiously, however, metaphysics plays a small role in Hauerwas's work as compared with, for example, the thought of Wittgenstein.

CHAPTER 8

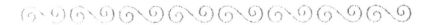

Analogy and Its Supplements

Aquinas on Analogy

In his dialogue with Barth, Balthasar's entire point has been that a defense of the analogy of being can only take place *within* the analogy of faith, that is, within the one supernatural order of grace. At several critical junctures, Balthasar adduces Aquinas as one who is in full accord with just this point of view. Given that Aquinas is the figure most clearly identified with the *analogia entis* and, therefore, with the use of analogy as the logical explication for formally predicable theological language, it is worth reexamining his thought on this question. In particular, this chapter will show that Aquinas's understanding of analogical language, if allowed to bypass the misunderstandings of Cajetan and Suarez (which themselves helped give rise to varying Barthian and Roman Catholic misconstruals) avoids the establishment of a preexisting and determinate philosophical horizon apart from disciplining biblical and performative motifs.

At root here, of course, is the very nature of Christian doctrine. Aquinas was convinced, as was the tradition before and after him, that revelation, and a fortiori Christian doctrine, allows a certain cognitive penetration into the Godhead, that is, it allows us to say something formally and substantially about God while concomitantly recognizing the inadequacies of all conceptual formulations. An unyielding contention of

Christian faith is that God has manifested something of his inner life through the history of Israel and, uniquely, through the person of Jesus of Nazareth. But such divine unveiling lives together with significant elements of mystery, unknowing, otherness, and nescience, a profound hiddenness rooted in both the finitude of the knower and the infinity of the known. As a consequence, Aquinas's thought is always an oscillating, dyadic movement between these two poles of presence and absence, of knowing and unknowing.

Aquinas's understanding of the analogical predication of names to God, and its role within theology, is such that the discourse and rhetoric of analogy never tries to "encompass" God, to enclose him within a totalizing, univocal narrative. On the contrary, Aquinas is proleptically sensitive to the postmodern admonition of Jean-Luc Marion that when one deals with God one deals primordially with the "Other." Aquinas's understanding of the kind of truth mediated by theological and doctrinal language clearly reflects such caution. At the same time, of course, Aquinas is acutely cognizant of the fact that revelation is about God's manifestation, about his decision to enter into a salvific dialogue with his creatures, thereby requiring some understanding of how this "presence" is actively and actually mediated to us.[1]

How does Aquinas balance the essential task of thinking about both absence and presence inherent in revelation? How are "otherness" and "sameness" dyadically related in his theory of theological language? How can names be predicated of God formally and substantially, that is, in more that simply "improper" metaphorical fashion (e.g., God is a fortress, a rock, or a lion) without compromising the essential incomprehensibility of the Godhead? Proper predication, of course, Aquinas takes to be the invariable message delivered by both Scripture and the tradition of the church. The one God may be found in three divine persons; God is revealed to us in the person of Jesus of Nazareth, the eternally generated Word incarnate; God possesses attributes clearly attested by the Scriptures such that he is love, goodness, and wisdom. Can such intelligible elements be maintained while simultaneously protecting God's otherness and transcendence?

Aquinas's profoundly apophatic passages, his constant attestation that God remains hidden from us, are well known. Among these is his iron assertion that "in this life, we cannot grasp what God is, but what he is not and how we are related to him" (*SCG*, I, 30). He comments elsewhere, "No such likeness [of an abstracted concept] will enable us to know the divine essence because God surpasses every created form."[2] In yet another context, Aquinas first cites Dionysius's *Mystical Theology*: "We are united with God as to one unknown." He then continues, "This is the case, for while we know what God is not, what he is remains utterly unknown" (*quid vero sit penitus manet ignotum*; *SCG*, III, 49). Our ignorance of this sublime knowledge of God is illustrated by Moses who, Exodus 20 teaches, "went to the dark cloud wherein God was" (*quod accessit ad caliginem in qua est Deus*).[3] Aquinas holds, in other words, that we reach the peak of our knowledge of God when we know him as an unknown, when we recognize that his essence surpasses anything we know in this life. What God truly is remains unknown to us.[4]

In the *De potentia Dei*, questions disputed in Rome between 1266 and 1268, Aquinas quotes John Damascene's claim, "That God is, is manifest to us, but what he is in substance is entirely unknown to us" (q. 7, a. 2, obj. 1). In his reply, Aquinas asserts that when Damascene uses "is" he means here only that God's existence is manifest to us, that the phrase "God exists" is a true, constative proposition. His existence, however, insofar as it is identical with his essence, remains entirely unknown to us (*De pot.*, 7, 2, ad 1). The same point is made a bit later when Aquinas avers that "the divine essence surpasses our intelligence and is unknown to us: wherefore man reaches the ultimate point of his knowledge about God when he knows that he knows him not, inasmuch as he knows that that which is God transcends whatsoever he conceives of him" (*De pot.* 7, 5, ad 14).[5]

Even when the human understanding is aided in its attempts to understand God by the light of faith and grace, "the human intellect remains incapable of achieving knowledge of the divine essence."[6] Neither faith, then, nor infused gifts of grace grant us comprehensive knowledge of God in this life. As Aquinas makes clear in the *Summa theologiae*: "By the revelation of grace we do not know what God is and so are joined to him as to an unknown" (*ST* I, q. 12, a. 13 ad 1).[7] In other words, God's essence eludes human cognitive capacities even when they are illumined by grace and faith. This profound sense of God's hiddenness, then, at least in one sense, places Aquinas in full accord with the Barthian dictum: God is known—essentially and quidditatively known—only through God alone.

Given these passages clearly endorsing divine otherness, one can hardly accuse Aquinas, as Jean-Luc Marion did in his early work, of an idolic consciousness, of an enveloping horizon of being. On the contrary, Aquinas could hardly emphasize more strongly the "difference" and "transcendence" of God vis-à-vis human creatures. At the same time, of course, as earlier noted, Aquinas wants to defend the claim that we have some enduring knowledge of God, otherwise the very notion of revelation would be called into question. Our language of God would become, Aquinas fears, entirely equivocal in nature.[8] It is to forestall just such a mistaken move that Aquinas, at several points in his work, criticizes Moses Maimonides for placing severe restrictions on our knowledge of God: "Some have maintained, and Rabbi Moses most emphatically, that these names [e.g., goodness or wisdom] do not signify the divine essence" (*De pot.*, 7, 5, c.). Such names do not *formaliter et per se* signify the divine essence because Maimonides takes these names to mean only that (1) God is wise not because wisdom resides in him but because in his effects, he acts like a wise man, or (2) we may only proceed by way of negation, that is, when we say God is "living" we mean only that he is not inanimate, not that "life" is of his very essence (*De pot.*, 7, 5, c.). But if Aquinas clearly rejects Maimonides' strictures, how does he proceed then to balance the two elements of the *Deus absconditus et revelatus*?

Aquinas first addresses the metaphysical roots of analogy, stipulating that every agent produces something like itself.[9] Even though God surpasses every created form, there is some kind of necessary similitude between Creator and creature. Any form present in an effect will exist in God in a higher and, of course, more eminent way. For Aquinas, the heart of the analogy of being is the act of existence or *actus essendi*. This act of existing is shared by all beings and is ultimately traceable back to a common source, who is the very fullness of existence and act, *Ipsum Esse Subsistens*.[10] This act of existence is not simply a static stasis; it is rather, as Norris Clarke has called it, an "intensive inner act of presence."[11] And this act of existence is, for Aquinas, the positive core of all other perfections. Clarke adds that it is precisely this existentialist, participationist metaphysics that "provides the ground for our ability to speak meaningfully about God in analogical language drawn from the perfections we find in creatures."[12]

Wherever there is a sharing of a real perfection, then this perfection is traceable back to a common source.[13] All others participate in the perfection, each in his or her own way. So what is true of existence or being is necessarily true of the other perfections such as wisdom, love, and goodness. What is the foundation for the claim that a perfection may be found differently but proportionately in God and creatures? It is, once again going to the roots of analogy, causal participation, with all of its implications: "If God were not the ultimate causal Source of all the perfections . . . we would have no way of talking meaningfully about him at all. It is the causal bond which grounds all analogous predication about God."[14]

There is, then, an ontological bond of similitude that derives from causal participation—from which men and women reason from effect to cause, and, ultimately, predicate perfections to God—with the realization, of course, that such names subsist in the Godhead in very different ways than they subsist in creatures.[15] If there were no ontological bond between God and creatures, then ideas apparently having something in common would be, in fact, entirely equivocal; conversely, if the ontological bond were misunderstood, then God would no longer be transcendent and names would be predicated univocally.[16]

But surely one may object, as Luther did with Dionysius, that the kind of participationist metaphysics on which Aquinas relies is more Plato than Christ, more the academy than the cross.[17] Of course, it is just this claim that we have some relationship to God—that there is a spine between God and creatures that is "prior" to revelation, that exists as an immanent possession of human beings—that Barth firmly rejected as a deformity of the biblical theology of grace.

Aquinas, however, thinks that such a relationship is sanctioned by Scripture itself. Important for Aquinas at several points is the Pauline claim that "the invisible things of God are understood by the things that are made" (Rom 1:20). This, for Aquinas, implies some kind of relationship, ontological and noetic, between God and creation. Otherwise, how could the philosophers know many things about God, as Aquinas is convinced they do (*ST* I, 13, 5, c)? Further, Aquinas is fond of citing Genesis: "Let us make man in our own image and likeness" (*ST* I, 13, obj. 2). Even though this citation is found in an objection, Aquinas will answer that there is a resemblance between God and creatures—which he clearly understands as biblically sanctioned—but this resemblance is not proportionate, for God and creatures share no common genus.[18] Even more basic, of course, is Aquinas's belief that God is the creator of the world. Creation has already established a bond between humanity and God, one that is already a relationship of grace. We do well here to remember Montagnes' caution that causality is not simply, for Aquinas, the resemblance of a copy to a model, but a relationship of dependence, of one being vis-à-vis another who produced it. God, Being in act, causes new beings to exist in act, each existing according to its own mode or manner, but with the effects having this act in common with the cause.[19]

Analogical Language

It is precisely this ontological similitude between God and creatures, which is always a greater dissimilitude, that explains Aquinas's rejection of equivocal language. This limited resemblance allows us to understand how one says something formally and substantially about God, while at the same time insisting that comprehensive knowledge of God's essence is ultimately precluded. Aquinas argues that we may attribute pure perfections to God, such as wisdom and goodness, while concomitantly observing that these attributes are deficient in their mode of attribution, or what Aquinas calls the *modus significandi*. By this he means that we can only express these perfections according to our own, limited, human mode of knowledge. Aquinas here invokes Dionysius, who had claimed that pure perfections must be both affirmed and denied of God, now giving Dionysius his own singular twist. Yes, attributes must be affirmed of God with regard to their *ratio*—that is, the thing signified—but they must also be denied because the formality or perfection is always attributed according to a human, creaturely mode of signifying. The perfections, then—such as goodness, love, and being—really exist in God, but in a way or mode that is beyond human comprehension.[20] This is why Aquinas can say, in a paragraph cited earlier, that at

> the ultimate and most perfect height of our knowledge in this life, as Dionysius says in *Mystical Theology*, "we are united with God as to an Unknown." This is indeed the case for although we know of God what he is not, what he is remains utterly unknown [*penitus manet ignotum*]. And to manifest his ignorance of this sublime knowledge, it is said of Moses that "he went to the dark cloud wherein God was (Exodus 20.21)." (*SCG*, III, 49)

Again in *De potentia Dei*, q. 7, a. 5, Aquinas makes several of the same points about the predication of names to God (and therefore about theological language) that he earlier indicated, namely, that attributes signify the divine essence not comprehensively but imperfectly: "Names signify what the divine substance is, but they do not signify it perfectly, as it is, but how it is understood by us." One cannot, it is clear, have a quidditative knowledge of God.[21] Those perfections that are attributed to God are truly ascribed to him; however, as regards the creaturely *modus significandi*, they must be denied of God. Aquinas continues to claim that he follows Dionysius, but, once again, with a unique twist: Perfections may be both affirmed and denied of God, but not, as with Dionysius, entirely so. Rather, perfections are legitimately affirmed with regard to the *ratio* or perfection, denied with regard to the creaturely *modus* or way of signifying. This allows Aquinas to say, "Absolutely speaking the perfections can be denied of God, because they are not predicated of him in the way signified." And as he reaffirms a bit later, "We cannot give God a name that defines or includes or equals his essence: since we do not know to that extent what God is" (*De pot.*, q. 7, a.5, ad 6).

Aquinas repeats here his earlier argument that names signify the divine substance, but in a deficient fashion. This is possible, once again, because every agent produces something like itself; the form of an effect must bear some resemblance to the cause. Because the human intellect derives its knowledge from created things, and because these forms cannot be adequate to the divine essence, our knowledge of these attributes must be imperfect as regards God's essence.

Finally, let us glance at the *Summa theologiae*, written only slightly later than the disputed questions in *De potentia Dei*. Aquinas again asks if names may be predicated of God formally and substantially. And again he rejects the view, attributed to Maimonides, that when we say, for example, that God is "living" we mean only that God has a mode of being different from inanimate things (*ST* I, 13, 2, c). He rejects the position as well that when we say God is "good," we mean only that he is the cause of goodness in others. Both of these solutions, for Aquinas, remain on a level of predication decidedly agnostic about God's own life. His own conclusion, expectedly by now, is that names truly signify the divine substance and are predicated of God substantially, even though these names represent him deficiently: "Names signify the Divine essence and are substantially predicated of God but they are deficient in their representation of Him." When one calls God "good," therefore, the name signifies something that God really is; the perfection of goodness preexists in God in a higher way (*ST* I, 13, 2, c). John of Damascene is right, therefore, to say that words used of God signify not what he is but what he is not because no name expresses completely God's essence; rather, the names signify him imperfectly (*ST* I, 13, 2, ad 1).

After showing that the predication of names is possible, that they tell us something actually but deficiently about the Godhead, Aquinas insists that one never uses names about God in the same sense as one uses them of creatures. There is a "proportion" between how a particular *ratio* is predicated of God and creatures. Not only, then, must one deny the creaturely *modus significandi*, but even the *res*, the thing signified, must be attributed only analogically because we are unsure of how the perfection exists in God. One may apply the concept to God, but one may affirm it only in a "tendential" manner, recognizing that how the *ratio* is actually realized in him is beyond human understanding.[22]

Summary of Aquinas

Two points, then, are essential to Aquinas's theory of analogy. In the first place, Aquinas uses the analogy of being in order to explicate the traditional affirmations of Christian faith and doctrine. The *analogia entis* is far from being an a priori, fully finished Procrustean bed into which Christian truth is squeezed and trimmed. It is a theory intended to explain how revelation truly mediates God's presence, to understand more completely the scriptural predications of God as love, wisdom, and goodness. As such, the theory of analogy is planted firmly within the tradition of *fides quaerens intellectum*. One observes that Aquinas resisted, in a carefully qualified way, the Platonic/Proclean notion that God is above being because he saw in this position both an enervation of the existing real as well as a failure to provide a proper explanation for the intelligible mediation provided by theological language. God was not beyond being, but was, of course, Being itself. This insight, that God is the pure intensive act of existing, without a trace of potency or imperfection, is not arrived at purely philosophically but is, for Aquinas, God's very identity as revealed in Exodus.[23] At the same time, Aquinas was well aware that even such scriptural affirmations about God's love, wisdom, and being fell well short of fully comprehending or defining the mystery of the sovereign and transcendent Godhead. This brings us to the second point: Even though analogy helps to explain how names can signify the divine substance, it teaches us as well that such signification is imperfect, involving a profoundly lethic dimension. This is why Aquinas can say confidently, "While we know of God what he is not, what he is remains utterly unknown" (*SCG*, III, 49). For Aquinas, the "essence of God is being itself, which is *supra intellectum*," above understanding. To conclude, as some have done, that Aquinas simply thinks of God within the horizon of an a priori notion of Being, or that he succumbs to an encompassing or totalizing understanding of God, is entirely unsupported by the texts. Our understanding of God is, ultimately, always a *docta ignorantia*. As William Hill properly says, "Metaphysical theology . . . does not, as it were, lift the veil on the divinity. Rather it clarifies the way in which language can be used of a God beyond our reach."[24]

There is even a sense in which Aquinas can say with Barth that God is known through God alone, that is, God can only be known quidditatively through himself alone and not through any human intellective powers in this life, not even those elevated by grace and faith. Revelation does not offer us quidditative knowledge of God because, inasmuch as revelation is expressed in human language, it presupposes concepts derived from sense experience. But the forms delivered by sense experience, even when seen within the light of faith and grace, cannot offer defining knowledge of God.[25]

Are we to conclude that Aquinas here is simply relying on his own gnoseological theory, that his noetic reserve is not based on Scripture and the subsequent theological tradition? This would be a hasty conclusion. Aquinas's reservations are based on the transcendence of God to creation, a truth delivered by the entire prior tradition of Jewish and Christian (and even Islamic, insofar as Aquinas was familiar with the work of Averroes) thought. Further, the (alleged) apostolic authority of Dionysius, as well as the cognitive humility of Augustine and Damascene, all contributed to Aquinas's claim that the "sublime knowledge" granted to Moses on Sinai was, in fact, the knowledge of ignorance. One must hesitate, therefore, before attributing Aquinas's reserve simply to Aristotelian epistemological presuppositions.

At the same time, Aquinas was convinced, again with the prior tradition, that through revelation, God has manifested to us something of his inner life. Augustine himself had said, "In God, to be is to be mighty or wise; such is the [divine] simplicity that whatsoever you may say of him is his essence" (*De pot.* 7, 5, c., citing *De trinitate*, viii, 7).[26] While any comprehensive and defining knowledge of God necessarily escapes us, even when we are illumined by grace and faith, we do have some imperfect and deficient but nonetheless proper knowledge of who God really is. The message of Scripture and Christian doctrine is unmistakable in this regard: God has revealed himself uniquely in the history of Israel; Jesus of Nazareth is the Logos incarnate, consubstantial with the Father; the Holy Spirit, worshiped together with the Father and the Son, sanctifies us and leads the church into the fullness of truth. So while the divine transcendence is fully respected, so also is the constant faith of the Christian church: that there has been a true *locutio Dei*, that God has entered into a dialogue with his creatures. God's action and word in history, then, is never simply an unknown; this gift is itself subject to intelligible exploration.

The intent of Aquinas is certainly not reductive rationality, an algorithmic mapping of God and the universe. His intent, rather, is to affirm the full intelligibility of the existing real, including the actuality of revelation—indeed, the reality of God himself—the most intelligible, even if beyond our finite ken. Aquinas, then, can easily agree with Marion's language about "non-reductive saturating phenomena" designating those unique moments that transgress our delimiting, ordinary, unimaginative horizons. Aquinas is hardly condoning predeterminative notions intent on shaving phenomena until they are locked into an a priori "frozen" notion of being or Kantian-like transcendentals. He is affirming, however, that every appearance, that all moments, whether they are Marion's "saturating phenomena" or Tracy's "fragments," have dimensions of intelligible existence and so fall within being's purview.[27]

The point of this chapter is certainly not to defend Aquinas as the last word on theological language.[28] The major claim, rather, is that if the discipline of theology is to explicate intelligibly its assertion that theological language, the language of Christian creeds and doctrines, tells us something of God's inner Trinitarian life, then some theory is needed that can properly illuminate this position. One may argue, of course, that the veracity of theological language is assured by an act of grace, that positing an ontological bond, such as the analogy of being, is at best unnecessary and at worst heretical because it obscures God's own initiative in revelation. But while the emphasis on grace is welcome (and essential, if rightly placed), does its mere assertion truly solve the abiding systematic problems? How does one avoid the twin shoals of univocity and equivocity? How is theological language not reduced to metaphor or doxology?[29] Most importantly, if the response to these questions is "By God's action," then does this not, perhaps once again, fall prey to that lack of the *relative* autonomy of nature that would seem to belong to humanity by the very fact of (graced) creation?

Aquinas had offered his understanding of the analogy of being, and so the analogical predication of names to God, within, as Balthasar pointed out, an anthropology constituted prior to any radical natural/supernatural distinction. It was offered within the horizon of faith delivered by Scripture and the prior tradition, within the *unicus ordo supernaturalis* established by revelation. His theory is anything but a Procrustean bed; its purpose, rather, is to buttress and explicate the affirmations of the existing Christian tradition of faith. In order that Aquinas's understanding of being as disciplined by revelation, as performative of Christian truth (and in qualified opposition to that line of thought claiming "being-language" constitutes a reductive horizon) may be more clearly visible, I have listed below some important elements in Aquinas's understanding of analogical predication of names to God. Many of these themes have only been brought clearly to the fore within the last fifty years. Perhaps reviewing them will help to obviate future misunderstandings.

Aquinas's Strategies: Disciplining the Analogy of Being by Faith

The following constitutes a list of the essential elements in Aquinas's understanding of the analogical predication of names to God. Such elements are illustrative of the claim that Aquinas did not simply adopt a preexisting horizon for understanding of analogy, thereby opening himself to the charge of thinking about revelation within the preexisting mold of a frozen, Parmenidean concept of Being.[30] Rather, at every cardinal theological point, Aquinas indicates the way in which language of being must be rethought given the actuality of God's revelation.

The list indicates the manner in which the notion of analogy avoids the totalizing discourse that postmodernism and Barth, in different ways, both feared. The latter turned to dialectic, although the debate continues about the extent of the dialectical moment in Barth's theology, while the former regards any "being-language" and a fortiori the analogy of being, as an unwarranted attempt to enclose the ungraspable and ultimately "impossible" reality of God. A thorough examination of Aquinas's apophatic and delimiting strategies, however, shows his awareness of these concerns. The list is as follows:

1. *The essential unknowability of God.* As indicated above, Aquinas holds that human beings do not and cannot possess comprehensive knowledge of God; God's essence remains unknowable to us. While Aquinas reads Exodus 3:14 as teaching that God is "Qui est," and while he takes this "sublime truth" as the message delivered to Moses by the Lord, even such divine revelation does not yield knowledge of God's essence. No determinate perfection can circumscribe God's being; he remains quidditatively unknown. This remains the case even when the believer is elevated by the light of faith and the infused gifts of the Holy Spirit. The essential thought that Aquinas repeats, in one form or another, remains constant: "The essence of God is beyond all that may be apprehended in this life and so what God is remains unknown."[31]

2. *The* res significata/modus significandi *distinction.* This distinction offers significant explanatory power by allowing one to predicate names of God—thereby saving theological and dogmatic language from equivocity—while at the same time making clear, in accord with the prior tradition, that God's essence remains unknown to us. Aquinas is certain that perfections may be formally attributed of God. As St. John says straightforwardly, "God is love"; further, the entire Bible witnesses to God's goodness, mercy, wisdom, and power. But precisely *how* or *in what manner* attributed perfections subsist on the transcendental level remains beyond human ken. Our knowledge is limited to created, finite forms that, while analogically predicable of the divine essence, cannot encompass it.[32] For this reason, the creaturely mode of signification must always be denied. One may, therefore, affirm perfections of God, even while, in a manner similar to but not identical with Dionysius, negating them (as regards their mode

of predication).

Even the name (i.e., the *res* or *ratio*) can only be predicated analogically, never univocally. So while we must, for example, deny the creaturely mode when we say "God is love," we must equally recognize that this attribute exists in God in a way that is beyond human understanding. So, although we say, with Scripture, that "God is love," we do not know how love subsists in God because such subsistence is only analogically related to our creaturely understanding.

3. *The* per prius *predication of perfections to God*. When discussing the names of God in the *De potentia* q. 7, a. 5, ad 8, Aquinas observes, by way of example, that while other bodies may be heated, fire is hot by nature: *proprie et eminentius* (as compared to other bodies) *et per prius*. Similarly, although creatures exhibit certain perfections, such as being, life, intelligence, wisdom, and so on, these attributes are ascribed properly and primarily to God: "They are properly said of God, indeed primarily of him and more eminently than of creatures." In other words, Aquinas was well aware that perfections belonged primarily and properly to God and were found only imperfectly in creatures. He reiterates this point in the *Summa theologiae* q. 13, a. 6: Perfections belong *per prius et proprie* to God. It may be true that in the *order of discovery* names are predicated *per prius* of creatures and only *per posterius* to God. But, in the ontological order, perfections such as love and wisdom belong first to God and only secondarily to creatures. So Aquinas can say, "The perfections which are in creatures many and various pre-exist in God as one" (*ST* I, 13, 5, c). One sees here that the divine essence is hardly made subject to finite concepts, to human horizons. Just the opposite is the case. A particular *ratio* or perfection belongs to God *per essentiam* and to creatures only *per participationem*.

4. *God is truly beyond being, properly understood*. For Aquinas, God is always beyond *ens* or any finite notion of being. In this sense, then, one can properly say that God is beyond being, for God is always *supra ens*, beyond common being. God is, however, not beyond *esse*, since he is pure act, *Actus purus*, the pure intensive act of existing, *Ipsum esse subsistens*.[33] (As a trinity of divine persons, God is also the purely intensive act of relationality). One may never confuse God, then, with a Heideggerian *Vorhandenheit*, ready-to-hand notion of being. Aquinas completely rejects just such a notion of common being, *ens commune*, as inapplicable to the divine essence. Further, it should be said that the creaturely understanding of being is hardly the last word, since God's *esse* subsists in way that we can never fully understand.

5. *The rejection of the* plura ad unum *notion of analogy*. Aquinas clearly

repudiates at several points a position that Barth and others had accused him of advancing, namely, of holding that "being" constitutes a category in which both God and creatures participate and, therefore, of defending a category logically "more comprehensive" than God himself.[34] In fact, Aquinas deals with just this objection in several places.[35] He argues that there are two kinds of analogy. The first involves a word used of two things, because "each of them has an order or relation to a third thing" (known as the *plura ad unum* type of analogy). The second type of analogy involves one thing having a relationship to another (the *unus ad alterum* kind of analogy). In the first case, "Being" would be the third thing, a *tertium quid*, to which both God and creatures have some kind of relationship; it would be an attribute in which God and creatures participate each in their own way. But Aquinas firmly rejects this kind of analogy because it seems to indicate that God and creatures participate in a perfection that assumes a certain primacy over God himself.[36] God, in this first instance, becomes subordinated to one of the transcendentals. But Aquinas argues that we are unable to abstract a notion, such as that of being, by which we denominate created and uncreated modes of realization.[37] In the second case, Being is perfectly realized in God, while creatures participate in this perfection only in a limited way. God is nothing by participation. Insofar as he is Pure Act, he "is" by virtue of his essence, never as a participant in some perfection. Created beings, on the other hand, are more or less perfect insofar as they participate in that *esse* or act which belongs *per essentiam* to God. Once again, Aquinas makes transparently clear the transcendence of God to creation and to participated perfections. At the same time, it is an affirmation of faith that God does exist, even if one cannot understand comprehensively how existence subsists in him.[38]

Conclusion

One sees in the ontological and linguistic strategies developed by Aquinas a strong desire to protect the otherness of God, avoiding in the process the invocation of any delimiting horizons and creaturely predeterminations. Jean-Luc Marion very badly missed this point in his original manifesto, *God without Being*. While Marion's thought continues to undergo modifications, his original suspicions about the use of "being-language" when speaking about God still inform a good deal of his work. What remains without doubt is that one can only tendentiously hold that Aquinas tried to "enclose" or "encompass" God within a predetermined Procrustean bed of being.[39] This is why Aquinas introduces multiple performative hedges around such language in order to relativize any unrefined theological discourse. Such performative hedges are meant precisely to overcome and stand guard against *Vorhandenheit*, idolic, reified, and objectivist thinking in the matter of God-language. When we speak of God, we speak—as Levinas and Marion consistently remind us—of the Other. Aquinas is well aware of this. His whole notion of being is already predetermined by the concrete order of salvation; the language of being is salubriously chastised by his prior faith in revelation. It is likely because of his adherence to the truth of revelation, as Gilson points out, that Aquinas is able to move beyond Aristotelian substance-based thinking (thereby advancing beyond the prior philosophical tradition, of being as "form"), making the center of his philosophy and theology the notion of being as intensive, dynamic, existential act, of *esse*.[40]

Not only has Marion missed the manner in which Aquinas lets revelation norm his understanding of being, and therefore his understanding of theological language, Heidegger has as well. Heidegger's claim that one cannot dance or pray before the *causa sui*, with its overt implication that the Christian tradition merely expropriated Aristotelian thought, poorly describes the God defended by Aquinas or the best of the prior tradition.[41] "Being" is not a determinative language now philosophically applied to God. When Marion argues that in the question of God we must be without anticipatory horizons altogether—in order to allow the Gift to appear without limits—Aquinas would largely agree. He would, however, insist that even this transcendent and sovereign Gift truly "is" and so exists—and is intelligible—even if ultimately beyond our understanding. Even in the act of faith, God remains *incognitus*. God's transcendence is such that there is no proper conceptual representation of him; we cannot possess defining knowledge about him. It would be difficult, it seems, to stress the element of nescience inscribed within theological language any more clearly than this.

But while denying that concepts can offer comprehensive knowledge of God, Aquinas insists they have some role in designating him. There is a limited intelligibility afforded by the "pure" perfections such as goodness, wisdom, and love. Such intelligibility is demanded by the very belief in God's manifestation to us, by the faith of the church in the mediating role of creedal and doctrinal statements. Such statements must have intelligible content if Christian doctrine is to be anything more than a mere cipher of God's existence. Aquinas engages analogy, then, precisely as a "form" to aid in the intelligibility of the impossible gift of revelation. It is not a totalizing form; it clearly respects the balance between presence and absence that is essential to Scripture, the creeds, and Christian doctrine. It need not even be the only or exclusive form, but it is perhaps the best form for intelligibly explaining the dyad of manifestation and hiddenness inherent in revelation itself.

The preceding discussion of Barth, Balthasar, and Aquinas has, I hope, addressed the central issue of theological language: how Christian doctrine speaks meaningfully about God and the history of salvation. At this point, given our discussion of Aquinas's performative disciplining of analogical language in the light of revelation, with its decided accents on nescience and hiddenness, it is worth examining, at least briefly, the strong resonances of negative theology found in Luther's work and in contemporary postmodern thought. Both of these streams provide helpful supplements to the more traditional forms of thinking about the nature of theological language.

Theological Language: Supplements to the Analogical Tradition

If analogy and analogical language provide one significant way or "form" that is able to explicate both the positive content of revelation and Christian doctrine while avoiding theological positivism, then, one may ask, can there be supplements to the analogical tradition that would further enhance the intelligibility of theological language? Of course, the strong streak of negative theology characteristic of the tradition has been well documented.[42] By the time of the Reformation, however, Martin Luther, in his reflections on the hiddenness of God, added a new dimension to negative theology, one that had not been fully examined before him. Rather than the neoplatonic fertilization of Christian principles that had dominated previous explorations into the nature of language, Luther firmly planted his "negative theology" on the cross alone and the revelation of God apprehended therein.

Luther

Luther found the apophatic tradition of the *theologia negativa* that preceded him to be severely wanting because, although it clearly defended the transcendence of God, it did so prescinding from the cross of Christ, from the *theologia crucis*. The primary salvo launched by Luther against Dionysian thought is that it is philosophically rather than biblically inspired; it owes more to Plato than to the Bible. Theologians, Luther counsels, should spend less time on Dionysius and more on "Jesus Christ and him crucified." It is Christ who is the way, the truth, and the life; only in Christ's cross does one learn something of the true God.[43] Luther's primary argument is that the centrality of Christian *faith* must supplant other theoretical concerns; as he says in his commentary on Genesis: "Nowhere does he [Dionysius] have a single word about faith or any useful instruction from the Holy Scriptures." Dionysian "negative theology" then is at least insufficient, if not entirely wrongheaded. Luther, on the contrary, "insisted on a radically different understanding of apophatic theology. He might use the same term, but what is meant by it was not a matter of affirmations and negations in general" (293–94). In his commentary on Psalm 90, for example, Luther makes clear that negative theology is not, as Dionysius has it, about saying "God is being" and "God is nonbeing." Rather, "we should say that it [negative theology] is the holy cross." The cross is the definitive standard for negative theology, not an unending Dionysian series of affirmations and denials. *Crux probat omnia*: One only properly speaks of God while remaining focused on the life and suffering of Christ himself.[44]

Luther's christological critique of negative theology continued in his 1519–1520 *Operationes* on the Psalms. Commenting on the soul entering into darkness and the cloud, Luther says, "This leading the mystical theologians call going into the darkness, ascending beyond being and non-being." Luther opposes to this a stern christocentric challenge: "The cross alone is our theology." Rorem concludes: "Here [as in his comment on Ps. 90] . . . Luther contrasts the negative theology of the mystical theologians, the Dionysian and Platonic methodology regarding negations and affirmations in the abstract (God as being and non-being), with his 'negative' theology of the cross" (297).[45]

Rorem further observes that Luther found the anonymous spiritual work *Theologica Germanica* to his liking, suspecting that the work had been written by J. Tauler. Such suspicion was founded on the fact that Tauler had "added an emphasis on Christ crucified to the more abstract theology of Meister Eckhart" (299). Luther's generous words about Tauler are one indication that he did not see his own accent on the crucified Lord as entirely unique but as rooted in an earlier strand of the tradition. Both Bernard and Bonaventure are examples of those taking the incarnation and cross, rather than Platonic philosophy, as theologically central. Given their emphasis on the cross, and thus their christocentrism, how do these earlier authors regard the Dionysian corpus? Do they presage something of Luther's own attitude?

While Bernard showed no interest in Dionysian theology,

Bonaventure was seriously attracted to the Areopagite. In the *Itinerarium*, for example, he did not hesitate to cite Dionysius, while concomitantly emphasizing the centrality of Christ crucified. Such duality, Rorem points out, constitutes an important extension of the prior tradition. Bonaventure "supplement[ed] the Areopagite precisely where Luther aimed his critique. Neither darkness nor negative theology are ever linked to the cross of Christ in the Dionysian corpus" (300). This is not to say, at least with any finality, that Bonaventure was the source of Luther's own christocentric criticisms of Dionysius. Nonetheless, he remains one significant predecessor on this score.[46] But while a few spare precursors had "found the Areopagite lacking regarding a linkage between the apophatic method and the incarnation" (302), Luther, on the other hand, and with particular force, insisted that negative theology be rooted not in Platonic dialectic, but primarily in the passion and cross of Christ.

Luther's steadfast emphasis on Christ's death as the foundation for negative theology, and therefore for theological language, need not necessarily stand in opposition to a simultaneous accent on analogy. After all, both aim at the same telos, balancing the *Deus revelatus* with the *Deus absconditus*. While analogy takes for granted the incarnation, passion, and death of Christ as the essential horizon for the dialectic of God hidden and revealed (seeing in these salvific acts the concentrated work of God already begun in creation), Luther's approach places the christological element at the forefront, salutarily reminding theologians that such dialectic must be firmly rooted in the actuality of redemptive history.[47]

One may regard Luther's thought then as a salubrious corrective to certain exaggerations within the Christian tradition. The Reformer's stinging critique of a philosophically inspired negative theology developed apart from the cross—of a metaphysics that, despite demurring *obiter dicta*, has not been sufficiently formed and disciplined by the biblical narrative—remains fully in force. At the same time, one need not necessarily see the interest of Aquinas in Dionysius (and of course his own singular appropriation of Dionysian themes) and Luther's assertion of the cross's centrality as indefeasibly antipodal. Aquinas surely had no doubt about the pivotal role of the incarnation and the crucifixion as ultimate paths to knowing the triune God. But he was looking for a way to explicate intelligibly *how it is the case*, in the created structure of reality itself, that finite creatures are able to predicate names of the transcendent God—not apart from grace or the cross but precisely as a logical structure within the realm of the salvific narrative of grace begun with creation.

Even given this intention, however, it remains the case that one of the primary fruits of Luther's thought, and indeed of the Reformation itself, was to recenter speculative theology in the revelation of Christ, to salutarily shock a narrative back to its biblical roots, to recall theologically Jesus' own words: "No one comes to the Father but by me" (John 14:6). Luther's work serves the purpose, then, of explicitly reinscribing the analogical tradition within the more foundational dialogue of revelation itself.

Theological Language and Contemporary Themes: David Tracy

One contemporary speculative theologian who has attempted to recover Luther's stress on God's hiddenness, and therefore his importance for theological language, is David Tracy.[48] In particular, Tracy adduces Luther's biblical understanding of the *via negativa* as one significant theological bulwark against the totalizing tendencies of Enlightenment modernity. Tracy, along with Marion and others, is trying to develop a reparative counternarrative to the algorithmic tendencies of modernity, which is frequently guilty of marginalizing religious discourse. Tracy's interest in Luther, therefore, constitutes part of his larger project of developing the notion of "fragment" as a form of thought mediating legitimate theological insights while, simultaneously, challenging the comprehending embrace of rationalism. Of specific concern here is the extent to which "postmodern" challenges to modernity, such as that mounted by Tracy, have ramifications for theological language.[49]

In a 1999 lecture, Tracy accented two classical fragmenting forms as highly significant for, even if unfortunately neglected by, contemporary theology: the apophatic and the apocalyptic.[50] Tracy argues that these two forms have been marginalized within the recent tradition but are once again attracting attention. Both are important because both are profoundly resistant to systems of totality and closure, thereby challenging Enlightenment and even earlier classical forms of thought.

Systems demand closure or finitude, leading inexorably, Tracy argues, to a univocal reductionism, an unimaginative predetermination, a sameness ignoring otherness and difference. This is the dreary "more of the same" that Caputo has similarly lamented in his reflections on the nature of certain forms of religious thought. It is the danger of allowing an enclosing totality, a comprehending omneity, to envelop and encompass the polysemy and pluriformity of religious living and thinking. Levinas and Marion, for example, have asserted that the thought of "being" has courted, and in fact has actualized, just such an encompassing danger.

To the contrary, Tracy argues; the notion of "fragment" serves as a protest against enclosing totalities and systemizations, against the transcendental conditions of the possible beloved by modernity. The fragment is a harbinger not of the foreseen and predetermined possible but precisely of the impossible (i.e., God)—and thus of the "impossibility," the unpredetermined, which is religion.[51] In his quest for those champions of fragments, Tracy nods to Kierkegaard, one of the first to use the notion of the Impossible against the totalizing pretenses of modernity and one of the first, along with F. Rosenzweig, to develop the notion of "fragments" and "postscripts" against an all-encompassing and reductive rationalism: "[Kierkegaard] invented form after [fragmentary] form to render present the one content modernity denied—the reality of the Impossible—grace, Christ, God" (72). Tracy also nods to Marion, who has pointed to religion as one of the saturating phenomena of life and who has argued, against Derrida, that the Impossible cannot simply be linked to the absent, the *khora*, but may be nonreductively present as well. He similarly lauds Rosenzweig, who in his *Star of Redemption* seeks an image, in this case the Star of David, that will shatter any all-encompassing totality system devised by modernity. These thinkers resist the Enlightenment colonization and mastery of religion, in the process celebrating its unassimilability. One sees, of course, what Tracy is asserting here: that religion is the "other" *par excellence*, the countertotality that resists the domination of rationalist, reductive, transcendentally determined modernity. One also discerns in his comments something of the postmodern fear of the *grand récit*, the rationalist metanarrative, and the attempt to "abstract" from the pulsating and fissiparous notion of human existence. Tracy strenuously resists the danger of idolically reifying and conceptualizing either humanity or God's own divine life.

But Tracy's is not merely a lament. He is not only rejecting improper forms but also proposing apposite ones for the Unassimilable and the Impossible, and he thinks that the notion of "fragment" provides it. So, he argues, what is needed is a recovery of the pre-Augustianian stress on apocalyptic and the apophatic. What is needed is a renewed emphasis in Christian thought on the "radically apocalyptic strand of Mark, Paul and the Book of Revelation," thereby recovering, in the process, the symbol of the second coming (76). Conjoining the "two great fragmenting forms [of] . . . the apocalyptic and the apophatic" with the incarnation, passion, and resurrection will ultimately allow for a full Christian naming of God.

With his emphasis on the "fragmentary" knowledge yielded by specific tropes, Tracy is seeking to advance appropriate "forms" that are capable of mediating faith's recognition that pure presence is not available to us and equally capable of resisting totalities without thereby becoming enmeshed in total ignorance. As with Luther's dyadic stress on the knowledge/ hiddenness of God apprehended in the cross, Tracy too is seeking biblical "forms" or vessels that abjure enclosing totalities while simultaneously avoiding an abyss of unknowing. The symbols of the second coming and Christian apocalyptic serve to "make present" the absent horizons within which (religious) life is lived and thought. Apocalyptic, hiddenness, and the apophatic are forms that resist the direct discourse of revelation and presence; they escape, therefore, the dangers of a rationalizing, reductive, encompassing narrative. Positively, they make manifest the vibrant horizons of the nonpresent absent. Ultimately, Tracy's point is that the Christian naming of God must remain fragmentary if it is to be true to its own profound tradition of understanding God as the hidden and incomprehensible One. Even the "gathering of the fragments" yields not reductive totalizing, but the recognition of God's transcendence and, indeed, "impossibility."[52]

Tracy's recent work, then, offers a contemporary retrieval and advance of the hidden God/apophatic tradition. By seeking appropriate "forms" for the Christian naming of God—and by offering the "fragment" as one such vessel—Tracy hopes to offer a counternarrative to the totalizing and algorithmic modes of thinking characteristic of modernity. As with Luther's stress on the hiddenness/knowledge of God revealed through the cross, Tracy's marked emphasis on fragment as a way of mediating God's presence/absence need not be at antipodes with the tradition of analogical language discussed earlier. It is true, of course, that Tracy appears to have serious reservations about the continued viability of metaphysics. At the same time, it may be argued that Tracy's stress on fragments, like Luther's emphasis on hiddenness, serves as a salutary caution, reminding metaphysics that it cannot simply present itself as an overarching narrative undisciplined by the "performance" of revelation and biblical truth. If one theme of this chapter has been that the best of the tradition is clearly cognizant of the need for metaphysics to be chastised by revelation (rather than acting as an anticipatory determination of it), then Tracy's insistence on speaking of fragments, of apocalyptic, of the eschatological, and of the second coming can certainly be incorporated into a wider analogical approach that seeks to explicate the nature of theological language. Neither analogy nor "fragment" is unfamiliar with the Augustinian dictum that resounds throughout the tradition: "Si comprehenderis, non est Deus" (Sermones, 117, 3, 5; PL 38, 663).

Conclusion

I have argued here that if theology is to explain intelligibly the nature of

Christian doctrine, it requires not only a certain notion of metaphysics, a particular understanding of truth, and an appropriate hermeneutical theory; it requires as well a specific idea of theological language, one that can explicate the dyadic interplay between presence and absence, between God's manifestation and hiddenness.

The notion of analogy, properly understood—that is, as developed within the sphere of grace (thus coming close to Barth's overarching *analogia fidei*)—provides a legitimate and highly useful way of explaining just how finite terms may be predicated of God *formaliter et substantialiter*. Luther's emphasis on the cross as the ultimate gateway to knowledge of God serves to salutarily reinscribe the analogical tradition within the concrete events of salvation history, while certain "postmodern" concerns, such as those advanced by David Tracy, remind analogy that significant Christian symbols, and so Christian truth itself, are resistant to fully encompassing forms.

In its best sense, theology offers a counternarrative and not a counter-totality, if "totality" necessarily implies an enveloping comprehension of reality. It is true, of course, that the Christian story contains certain elements of an organic system—and not simply "elements" or "fragments"; it offers a protological-eschatological narrative, indeed, a *grand récit* from creation until the consummation of the world. At the same time, the entire tradition harbors a very strong reserve, as we have seen in Aquinas, about defining knowledge of God and, therefore (one cannot understate this) about the actual formal object of the discipline itself. In fact, analogical language, properly understood, constitutes a countertotality system when one considers the performative "hedges" that have been built around it. Analogy is meant to allow the Impossible to appear, *without abandoning what is essential to revelation and doctrine itself*. The Impossible has indeed appeared, even fleshly and concretely, and so linguistic articulations are possible, indeed necessary, even if they must remain moderate and restrained. The language of being may subsist in the horizon of presence, but it recognizes that the subsisting One to whom we are conjoined is an "Unknown." The Other, the Unknown, the Impossible, and the Unassimilable are all recognized as proper names of God, modified, of course, by precisely what the Other has freely manifested of himself. It must be equally clear, then, that the unknown God is not the Void or the Abyss. He is the One both present and appearing.

It is certainly true that theology is *not* a totalizing narrative, especially if such is identified with one definition of ontotheology, namely, an absolute equation of God with being so that the human notion of being now becomes determinative of God's existence.[53] On the contrary, the entire point of this chapter has been that knowledge about God may only be partial, never defining; theological language is about the Other, not the same. Insofar as it engages the infinite and eternal God, theology can never deal simply in direct, representative, rationalist, discourse. It seeks, as Tracy says, forms proper to its unassimilable "object."

Two things must be avoided in understanding theological language. The first is attempts to marginalize speech about God; the temptation of modernity is that, having borrowed the classical and medieval emphasis on the intelligibility of the existing real, it has attempted, on the basis of largely empiricist presuppositions, to marginalize the very source of that real. The second, conversely, is those attempts, more endemic to Christian thinking, either of reducing God to *Vorhandenheit* reification or of asserting, in a legitimate desire to avoid such objectification, that theological language is largely evanescent and so names cannot be formally predicated of the Godhead.[54] Analogy is one form or trope that avoids these dangers, simultaneously balancing the dyadic dimensions of divine presence and absence, explaining the cognitive penetration of the language of Christian doctrine without adopting any pretense of complete presence.[55]

Tracy, Marion, and Levinas should be applauded for seeking some approach other than that sanctioned by the Enlightenment, wherein religion is necessarily discarded as an unassimilable reality best thought of as publicly unredeemable and so unworthy of inclusion in public conversation and the free exchange of ideas. Tropes such as "fragment," "apocalyptic," and "nonreductive saturating phenomena" may indeed be sanctioned; they should be sublated, however, into the wider narrative of God's continuous and enduring presence to his people. Fragments are surely not all that is available to us. Apophaticism and hiddenness cannot be intensified to the point that one concludes the church cannot speak with a certain surety about the gifts given in creation and redemption. It remains fundamentally true that God has entered into a dialogue of salvation with his creatures. It is a narrative of manifestation that is uniquely concentrated in the person of Jesus of Nazareth and is borne in the church from age to age. The language about God found in Christian doctrine continues, then, to reliably, if cautiously, display and mediate this divine presence. Analogy, aided and even chastised by the supplements discussed above, is an important way of understanding precisely how such mediation is possible.

Having examined why theology needs, in order to explicate intelligibly Christian doctrine, a particular notion of metaphysics, a certain understanding of truth and hermeneutics, and a specific approach to theological language, we now turn to the question, adumbrated in the preceding chapters, of the relationship of theology to the "disciplines," that is, the kind of correlation that should exist between a discipline normed by faith and revelation and those that offer "secular" wisdom.

Notes

1. Gerald McCool, then, is entirely right when he says that "the analogy of being enables the finite mind to know the Creator imperfectly and indirectly through deficient concepts contained in its affirmations." There concepts can "never be more than approximations to infinite pure truth since conceptual representations can never encompass the unlimited fullness of reality." McCool, *From Unity to Pluralism* (New York: Fordham University Press, 1992), 218.

2. Thomas Aquinas, *Expositio super librum Boethii de Trinitate* (ed. Bruno Decker; Leiden: Brill, 1959), 65:14–20; cited in John Wippel's highly informative essay, "Quidditative Knowledge of God," *Metaphysical Themes in Thomas Aquinas* (Washington, D.C.: Catholic University of America, 1984), 217.

3. *SCG* III, 49. For more on this passage and its importance, see the excellent study of Anton Pegis, "Penitus Manet Ignotum," *Medieval Studies* 27 (1965): 212–26.

4. Aquinas, *Expositio super librum Boethii*, 67:2–6; cited in Wippel, *Metaphysical Themes in Thomas Aquinas*, 219.

5. For a fine exposition on the meaning of this "ultimate unknowing," see William Hoye, "Die Unerkennbarkeit Gottes als die letzte Erkenntnis nach Thomas von Aquin," in *Thomas von Aquin* (vol. 19 of *Miscellanea Mediaevalia*; ed. A. Zimmermann; Berlin: Walter de Gruyter, 1988), 117–39.

6. Aquinas, *Expositio super librum Boethii*, 66:18–67:1; cited in Wippel, *Metaphysical Themes in Thomas Aquinas*, 219.

7. This strongly apophatic passage was cited by Bishop Peter Ferrè during the debates at Vatican I for the purpose of making clear that not even with the light of faith is one elevated to the contemplation of the divine essence, thereby refuting the kind of theological rationalism associated with Frohschammer and others. For Ferrè's intervention, see Giovan-Domenico Mansi, *Sacrorum conciliorum nova et amplissima collectio*, vol. 50 (II) cols. 200–204.

8. As Pegis says, "That God is, in St. Thomas' sense, *omnino* or *penitus ignotum* is itself a radical doctrine. . . . Yet the aim of the doctrine was not to say that we have no positive knowledge of God; the aim was rather to remain faithful to the divine transcendence." Pegis, "Penitus Manet Ignotum," 225.

9. *SCG* I, 29. The best book I have found on the metaphysical roots of analogy, which traces the development of Aquinas's thought throughout his entire corpus, is Bernard Montagnes, *La doctrine de l'analogie de l'être d'après saint Thomas d'Aquin* (Louvain: Nauwelaerts, 1963).

10. Balthasar similarly argues, "Created being is relative and non-divine but as something created it cannot be utterly dissimilar to its Creator." Hans Urs von Balthasar, *The Theology of Karl Barth* (trans. Edward Oakes; San Francisco: Ignatius, 1992), 285. He reminds us that Gott*sein* and Geschöpf*sein* have some similarity, although always, of course, within a greater dissimilarity.

11. W. Norris Clarke, *The Philosophical Approach to God* (Winston-Salem, N.C.: Wake Forest University, 1979) 40.

12. Ibid., 37–38.

13. Clarke asserts that one finds in Aquinas, as in the Platonic tradition, an inter-weaving of the metaphysical and the mystical, a drive for the full intelligibility of the real with the quest, obscurely sensed, of the One at the center of the universe.

14. Clarke, *Philosophical Approach to God*, 35 and 54. Of course, it is essential to reiter-ate that this causal bond is ultimately in the order of *grace*, belonging as it does to the gra-tuitous gift of creation. It is in this sense, then, that Balthasar can claim that the analogy of being always and necessarily moves within the prior analogy of faith.

This bond of causal participation that is effected by creation undergirds Clarke's refusal to subscribe to the description of God as "totally other," even though understand-ing what is intended by such a term. He thinks it more accurate to say that God is "infi-nitely Higher" because if "total otherness" were taken literally, it would sever entirely the "bond of community, of connatural affinity, between ourselves and God" (55). Clarke here echoes Przywara's original assertion that Kierkegaard's claims about the absolute otherness of God leads inexorably to equivocity—and perhaps even despair—while Kierkegaard's antagonist, Hegel, allows such a strongly univocal moment between finite and infinite Spirit that pantheism is hardly avoided. Clarke continues: "Total hetereogeneity would allow of no meaningful union [between God and creature]. Cut this bond of causal par-ticipation between creature and Creator, and all bonds of ontological similarity vanish into the mists and with it all meaningful analogical language about God." Of course, it is just the claim of some theologians that sin has abolished this community between God and humanity, which can be restored not by the metaphysics of creation, but only by a singu-lar act of God's grace. Clarke, on the contrary, holds that once this causal bond is severed, there can be "no alternative for speaking about God, save poetic, metaphorical, symbolic language" (55). Of course, one can claim, as Barth does, that God allows for such language purely as the result of grace and apart from any causal, metaphysical relationship. But it should also be noted that causal participation, too, is founded ultimately by the grace and gift of creation rather than by efficient causality alone, taken in the sense of "separated phi-losophy." What is surely true is Clarke's claim that the bond of causal participation helps to explain analogy, how one can speak of God. But one should likely explicitly add that one remains more faithful to Scripture and tradition by emphasizing that creation itself is a grace, so any later philosophical reflection on causality and participation, and therefore analogy, is itself within the horizon of grace and not exclusively and without remainder a metaphysical principle.

Clarke's useful insight, of course, is that one need not downgrade the order of creation in order to uphold the order of redemption, although the estate of creation must be defended while recognizing, as Clarke finally does explicitly (55), that creation and causal participation exist already within the formality of grace. Inscribing the philosophi-cal moment within the theological one is precisely representative of the "relative auton-omy" that Balthasar championed.

15. Of course, it is precisely this ontological character of the analogy of being that Barth contests, claiming that there is no natural capacity in man for understanding being in general, now serving, presumably, as a prolegomenon to revelation. Rather, the capacity to know God is "lent" to humanity; only by the gift of grace does humanity discover a similarity to the Word. So, in Barth's formulation, it is only in the profession of faith that God's Word becomes a human thought and a human word (*KD* I/1, 254; cited by Balthasar, *Theology of Karl Barth*, 108). Any "similarity" between God and human persons is based on faith, not on efficient and exemplar causalities, even when these are understood within the horizon of graced creation.

16. Montagnes, *La doctrine de l'analogie*, 53. Pannenberg avers that Aquinas relies

heavily on causality as the ontological root of analogy. He wonders, however, if the causal relationship itself—derived, of course, from human experience—can be "uncritically transferred to the relationship between God and creatures." Is God a cause in the same way as we are causes? And if causality is already an analogical relationship, can this analogy serve as the ground of analogical language? Wolfhart Pannenberg, *Basic Questions in Theology*, vol. 1 (trans. George Kehm; London: SCM Press, 1970), 223 n. 20. Of course, one might respond to Pannenberg that predicamental and transcendental causality is certainly analogical, just as the intensive act of being subsisting in God and creatures is always already analogical. No attribute can ever be univocally predicated of God and creatures. But this does not necessarily undermine causality, inscribed within the formality of grace, as a metaphysical ground of analogy; it serves only to underscore the indubitability of God's transcendence.

17. As Luther said of Dionysius, "He is downright dangerous, for he is more of a Platonist than a Christian." Cited in Paul Rorem, "Martin Luther's Christocentric Critique of Pseudo-Dionysian Spirituality," *Lutheran Quarterly* 11 (1997): 291.

18. Clarke confirms this point: "The core of such causal participationist metaphysics is already contained in germ, in fact, in the inexhaustibly rich phrase of Genesis, which has nourished so deeply the contemplation and reflection of so many medieval—and modern—mystics and metaphysicians: 'Let us *make* man to *our own image* and *likeness*'" (55). Aquinas could bring together the biblical assertion and Platonic philosophy in phrases such as this: "The created image is an imperfect and inadequate representation of the divine exemplar." (*Sentences* I, d. 22, q. 1, a. 2).

19. Montagnes, *La doctrine de l'analogie*, 91.

20. Worth observing in this regard is the point that Anton Pegis makes when discussing how Aquinas, in his commentary on the *Liber de Causis*, clearly distinguished himself from the Platonism informing Proclus's *Elements of Theology*, especially its claim that the first cause transcends being. Aquinas, outlining the Platonist position, says, "According to the Platonists, the first cause is above being insofar as the essence of goodness and unity, which is the first cause, transcends separate being itself." Aquinas responds to this position with his own philosophy even while hoping to save the Platonic insight into God's uniqueness: "The first cause is above being (*ens*) insofar as it is infinite being itself (*ipsum esse infinitum*). That is called 'a being' (*ens*) which participates in 'being' (esse) in a finite way; and it is this that is proportioned to our intellect whose object is "what a thing is," as said in the *De Anima*, III." Then Aquinas adds the final but essential point: "Therefore, only that is graspable by our intellect which has a quiddity that participates in being (*esse*); but the quiddity of God is being itself (*ipsum esse*), and hence He is above the intellect." Cited in Pegis, "Penitus Manet Ignotum," 224. God is not above being or, in Marion's words, "sans être." God, rather, is Pure Intensive Act, the fullness of Being, and so, as unparticipated, beyond understanding by finite creatures.

21. As Maritain had said in the *Degrees of Knowledge*, there is no "quidditatively quidditative" knowledge of God. This phrase, perhaps seemingly wordplay, is, in fact, a very fine compression of Aquinas's argument that we do not know what God is, but only that he is and how he is related to us, without denying his simultaneous assertion that God can be called "love" and "wisdom" both formally and substantially.

22. For the development of this point, see William Hill, *Knowing the Unknown God* (New York: Philosophical Library, 1971), ch. 4.

23. All are aware, of course, of the different exegetical opinions about Exodus 3:14, but there is no doubt that Aquinas, using the translation of the Latin Vulgate, sees this interpretation as taught, in the first place, by revelation itself. See Etienne Gilson, "L'être et Dieu," *Revue thomiste* 62 (1962): 185–202.

24. William J. Hill, *The Three-Personed God* (Washington, D.C.: Catholic University

of America Press, 1982), 65.

25. See Wippel, *Metaphysical Themes in Thomas Aquinas*, 221.

26. Slightly later, in defending the notion that names may be properly predicated of the divine essence, Aquinas cites Augustine's claim that "inquantum bonus est, sumus" (insofar as God is good, we are). (*De doctrina christiana*, I, 32). Even Dionysius and Damascene, with their more profound accent on negative theology, are understood by Aquinas not as countenancing radical apophaticism, but instead, a healthy reserve regarding the capacities of finite intelligence before infinite mystery.

27. At times, contemporary antitotalizing rhetoric appears less concerned with protecting the divine transcendence from the limiting encroachments of finite concepts—or of recognizing, with Luther, that the transcendent God is primarily known in the hiddenness of the cross of Christ—than in protecting Kantian strictures against metaphysical discourse. Perhaps Milbank is right in saying that even Barth, who sees Kant as a salutary figure in the history of thought, now freeing theology to be theological, makes a faux pas in failing to recognize the deleterious effect of severing the link between God and humanity and so the inner intelligibility of the cosmos.

28. While Thomism is still a highly significant theological/philosophical system, and while its contributions regarding the nature of theological language continue to be, in my judgment, some of the most important, I believe the encyclical *Fides et ratio* is entirely right in contextualizing Thomas as a preeminent model for Christian thought without simply endorsing his work as essential for contemporary theology.

29. Pannenberg, for example, fully concurs that the biblical writers attribute names to God that have been established in other contexts. Consequently, one finds claims about God's mercy, grace, justice, and so on. "Such statements describe the reality of God by analogy with a human act." But, Pannenberg demurs, such words should not be understood as descriptive but as "doxological," that is, they simply express adoration of God on the "basis of his works." Pannenberg, *Basic Questions in Theology*, 1:215. While one can agree with Pannenberg that all scriptural language about God is ultimately doxological in character, it does not at all clearly follow that this is necessarily at antipodes with analogical predication as well. This earlier position of Pannenberg appears to be abandoned in his later *Systematic Theology* (see ch. 7, note 12, above).

30. Fergus Kerr calls this narrative of a Parmenidean, "frozen" notion of being imposed a priori on the Christian theological tradition part of a Barthian-Oxonian narrative, but unrepresentative of Aquinas's thought. Kerr concedes that Barth has some Roman Catholic aid in this matter—for example, Rahner (especially in his work on the Trinity) and at times Balthasar. See Fergus Kerr, "Thomas Aquinas: Conflicting Interpretations in Anglophone Literature," *Aquinas as Authority* (ed. Paul van Geest et al.; Leuven: Peeters, 2002), 167–68. See also Kerr, *After Aquinas* (Oxford: Blackwell, 2002) 181–82.

31. *De Trinitate*, q. 1, a. 1 and 2. In this regard, Aquinas favorably cites, in *SCG* I, 8, Hilary of Poitiers' *De Trinitate*, II, 10 (PL 10, 58–59): "For though he who pursues the infinite with reverence will never finally reach the end, yet he will always progress by pressing onward. But do not intrude yourself into the divine secret, do not, presuming to comprehend the sum total of intelligence, plunge yourself into the mystery of the unending nativity; rather, understand that these things are incomprehensible." *De Trinitate* q. 1, a. 2, ad4.

32. For an excellent article detailing how this distinction is operative in Aquinas, see Gregory Rocca, "The Distinction between *Res Significata* and *Modus Significandi* in Aquinas' Theological Epistemology," *Thomist* 55 (1991): 173–97. Rocca has recently consolidated his work on Aquinas's epistemology in *Speaking the Incomprehensible God* (Washington, D.C.: Catholic University of America Press, 2004).

33. Fergus Kerr's discussion of God as event rather than entity is worth noting here (see

After Aquinas, 187–91). Thinking of the persons of the Trinity as verbs, pure interrelated acts, is also a central theme of Thomas Weinandy, *Does God Suffer?* (Notre Dame, Ind.: University of Notre Dame Press, 2000), ch. 6.

34. Barth is here concerned that both God and creatures have already been wedged into a neutral, a priori category of philosophical ontology: "being as such." In some ways, Barth's objection is quite similar to that of Heidegger's, namely, that being is a *Vorhandenheit* concept, something, as Balthasar says, that "one more or less finds lying about," thereby obscuring the relationship between God and creature. Balthasar, *Theology of Karl Barth*, 161. Against this, Barth insists, of course, that all knowledge of God must be derived from some foregoing revelation, from God's prior condescension, and so from grace rather than from nature. But, as Balthasar and others have argued, the whole question of the analogy of being belongs within the overarching analogy of grace. Inasmuch as creation itself is gratuitous it constitutes a part of salvation history.

35. Among the most important passages are *ST* I, q. 13, a. 5, c; *SCG* I, 43; and *De pot.* q. 7, a. 7.

36. A centerpiece of John Milbank's recent arguments is that it is Scotus who, by making Being a univocal term, laid the groundwork for its status as an abstraction separable from theology, an ontology unconstrained by theology, thereby leading ultimately to secularism, that is, to a thinking of "being" totally apart from God.

37. As Montagnes says, Aquinas formally excludes all analogies *duorum ad tertium* because the *ratio deitatis* (if we may be so permitted to speak) remains in inviolable transcendence. See Montagnes, *La doctrine de l'analogie*, 103.

38. In fairness to Barth and to other critics of Aquinas on this point, an acute interpreter of Aquinas like Montagnes shows the extent to which Thomists like Cajetan and Th. Penido gave the impression that one could speak of a particular perfection or *ratio* stripped of all modes and disengaged of all limits that would be common to God and creatures. This was the disguised univocity against which Barth and the later Thomist tradition reacted. See Montagnes, *La doctrine de l'analogie*, 99–100.

39. Marion seems to have mistaken metaphysics—even in the "performative" hands of Aquinas—as irreducibly totalizing and so unable to serve as a reparative counternarrative to modernity. On this point, the influence of Levinas on Marion cannot be overestimated; one must remember, however, that Levinas's fears about the language of being stem from his concerns about Heidegger's overarching ontology. For an excellent analysis of Levinas, see Robyn Horner, *Rethinking God as Gift* (New York: Fordham University Press, 2001).

40. In Barth's theology, "act" replaces "being" as having the central role but, as Balthasar asked, insofar as Aquinas understands God as *actus purus*, should these terms be placed in dialectical juxtaposition? See Balthasar, *Theology of Karl Barth*, 394.

41. Martin Heidegger, *Identity and Difference* (trans. Joan Stambaugh; New York: Harper & Row, 1957), 72.

42. D. Carabine, "*Apophasis* East and West," *Recherches de théologie ancienne et médiévale* 55 (1988): 5–29. Also see Fran O'Rourke, *Pseudo-Dionysius and the Metaphysics of Aquinas* (Leiden: Brill, 1992).

43. I am reliant in much of what follows on the excellent article by Paul Rorem, "Martin Luther's Christocentric Critique of Pseudo-Dionysian Spirituality," *Lutheran Quarterly* 11 (1997): 291–307. Page numbers in the text refer to this article. Rorem shows that Luther's hesitancy about Dionysius did find some modest support in an earlier strain of Christian thought, including Bonaventure, Maximus the Confessor, and John of Scythopolis.

44. Rorem argues that even in his very early work on the Psalms (1513–1516), Luther, while showing respect for the Dionysian ascent to God by way of denials, juxtaposes his

own christological interpretation of God's hiddenness.

45. Luther's polemic against Dionysius was taken up recently by Colin Gunton in *Act and Being* (Grand Rapids: Eerdmans, 2002), especially 14–18. Gunton's central point, like Luther's, is that the names the Aeropagite attributes to God have a pedigree that "is essentially Neo-Platonic rather than Biblical." Gunton also condemns Dionysius's reliance on metaphysical causality as a structuring dimension of the cosmos (and so of God's relationship with humanity) rather than the "temporally and economically structured biblical characterizations of God's action in the world" (15–16). The congruence with Barth's critique of a "prior ontological relationship" is striking. Of course, Balthasar's critique of Barth would also be equally relevant here.

46. Rorem also discusses Maximus the Confessor, who similarly conjoins Dionysian negative theology with a more concentrated christological focus.

47. As Balthasar has pointed out, Luther provides an antidote to the possible confusion of the form of the cross with the form of exuberant creation. Luther rightly protested against an "analogizing semi-Pelagianism." Balthasar, *Glory of the Lord*, vol. 1 (trans. E. Leiva-Merikakis; San Francisco: Ignatius, 1982), 48. This confusion of the two forms, Balthasar says, "regards the whole cosmos as liturgical worship; [but] often the showy splendour of such cosmic and mystical piety leads to a forgetting of Christ, and the world of beauty overshadows the world of biblical glory, and one must wait for Luther . . . to bring the sharpness of the crisis to consciousness." Balthasar, *The Glory of the Lord*, vol. 4 (trans. Brian McNeil et al.; San Francisco: Ignatius, 1989), 320.

48. David Tracy, "The Hidden God: The Divine Other of Liberation," *Cross Currents* 46 (Spring 1996): 5–16; and Tracy, "The Hermeneutics of Naming God," *Irish Theological Quarterly* 57 (1991): 253–64.

49. It is useful to recall here that postmodernism is not a word embraced by all to whom it is ascribed. Derrida, it is reported, steadfastly avoided the word, preferring to think of his own work as presaging a new, chastised Enlightenment. See John Caputo and Michael Scanlon, "Introduction" in *God, the Gift, and Postmodernism* (ed. John Caputo and Michael Scanlon; Bloomington: Indiana University Press, 1999), 1–2.

50. David Tracy, "The Hidden and Incomprehensible God," *Reflections* (Center of Theological Inquiry) 3 (Autumn 2000): 62–88.

51. In a response to a paper Tracy delivered on fragments, Derrida argues that the notion of fragment is an insufficient form to mediate the "impossible" because the very idea of "fragment" still appears to be connected, at least nostalgically, to a totality system. For Derrida's comments, along with Tracy's vigorous response, see "Derrida's Response to David Tracy" in Caputo and Scanlon, *God, the Gift, and Postmodernism*, 181–84.

52. Of course, Tracy has "gathered the fragments" several times before, most notably in *The Analogical Imagination* (New York: Crossroad, 1981). This title refers to seeing similarities in the cosmos, creeds, biblical, and secular traditions (as opposed to dialectical, discontinuous readings). It does not refer to analogy in the concentrated, metaphysical sense discussed earlier. In fact, as regards the traditional, metaphysical sense of analogy, at least some comments by Tracy indicate that, like Marion, he regards metaphysics as a totality system. On the other hand, he endorses Aquinas's *Summa*, along with Calvin's *Institutes* and Schleiermacher's *Glaubenslehre* as classical nontotalizing theologies. See Tracy, "Hidden and Incomprehensible God," 78. In the last analysis, Tracy's "analogical imagination" may not differ widely from Przywara's classic insight that the "basic Catholic form" is an "all-comprehensive 'yes' to revelation—for everything in creaturely thought that can and has been redeemed." Balthasar, *Theology of Karl Barth*, 257.

53. Some opponents of ontotheology (a slippery term, indeed) legitimately reject an

attempt by metaphysics to achieve conceptual mastery over reality by simply conjoining being and God. I have argued that such an attempt is already rejected on theology's own grounds, as witnessed by much of the Christian tradition. On the other hand, some writers, with their rejection of ontotheology, are actually demanding the exclusion of any being-language at all in theology. At times this stems from a mistaken understanding of how the tradition has performatively disciplined being-language. At other times, however, it consists in a misunderstanding of those elements necessary for intelligibly explicating Christian doctrine's own assertions.

54. If theological language is not simply evanescent, and if metaphor is invoked, it appears that metaphor must be either reduced to extrinsic denomination (the attribute not now truly existing in the Godhead) or suppose a covert ontological bond. Or, in a Barthian way, it must reject any ontological bond established by the grace of creation for the sake of a bond "lent" to humanity by grace.

55. A solid contemporary application of analogy may be found in Gérard Remy, "L'analogie et l'image: De leur bon usage in théologie," *Recherches de Science Religieuse* 92 (2004): 383–427.

CHAPTER 9

Correlation and the Tradition

Christian doctrine, for the sake of its logical explication and enhanced intelligibility, needs a certain view of metaphysics, a particular notion of truth, a specific kind of hermeneutics, and a unique understanding of theological language. In the present chapter I will argue that Christian doctrine, precisely because of the truth-claims it asserts, also demands a singular notion of the relationship that properly exists between theology and other disciplines, between the claims of the Christian *Weltanschauung* and other generalized worldviews.

The proper nature of this correlation is one of the central themes of fundamental theology. Christian doctrine and theology need an understanding of that relationship which is essentially a recovery of the "spoils from Egypt" trope that characterized the work of so many early Christian writers. Insofar as God had created the world, had communicated himself to humanity by a primordial act of grace and love inscribed in creation itself, wisdom and truth could be found in many places. All such wisdom, however, the traditional spoils metaphor insists, must ultimately be disciplined by, and incorporated into, the revelatory narrative. Athens, whatever its own insights into truth, must ultimately be chastened by Jerusalem. It is not just a matter, however, of incorporating any facet of "Athenian" thought; indeed, it could be claimed that every theologian has used some aspect of philosophy in order to illuminate Christian faith. Theology must use, and concomitantly chasten, those philosophies that are able to support doctrine's universal, selfsame, and perduring claims. What is envisaged, then, is the use of some first philosophy, capable of offering theoretical support to the church's understanding of the transcultural and transgenerational nature of Christian truth.

Historical Remarks

Recall Tertullian's famous question: What does Athens have to do with Jerusalem, the academy with the church? Recall as well Tertullian's legendary sentiment summarized in the *credo quia absurdum*.[1] The North African's trepidations about the pretensions of reason even lead him to speak of "wretched Aristotle," a sentiment echoed by Luther some 1200 years later.[2] The strand of Christian thought represented by such convictions wishes to make clear that, with the advent of Jewish and Christian revelation, philosophy has been demoted, even demolished, as an illuminating path of thought. Revelation represents the "true philosophy," as so many early writers called it, thereby marginalizing the ultimacy and normativity of the Greek thought that had been bequeathed to the Western world. Of course, if the early Christians had been aware of philosophies emanating from the Far East, their remarks would have remained unchanged. For the revelation of God in the history of Israel and in Jesus Christ definitively surpassed any other system of thought no matter its antiquity or the distinction of its lineage.

At the same time, most of the early Christian thinkers did not wish simply to dispense with the philosophical heritage of the ancient world. They sought, rather, to incorporate the best theoretical insights for the precise purpose of further explaining the faith, of making it more intelligible. In some matters, certainly, they saw contradictions with Christian truth—and in these instances the philosophical approaches were to be quickly jettisoned. In other matters, however, they saw a confluence and coherence between faith and reason, with the latter expressing incompletely what revelation had fulfilled. In such cases, philosophy could further illuminate what faith knew by the light of grace; the confluence was deep enough so as to allow one to speak of a true *preparatio evangelii*.

Of course, as Christianity moved from its Palestinian matrix into the world of Hellenistic thought and culture, many of its early converts were philosophically trained. Justin Martyr, for example, a Greek thinker living in the middle of the second century, had been deeply schooled in Platonic philosophy. It is no surprise, then, that in his explicitly Christian works, he uses Plato's dialogues, such as the *Timaeus* and the *Phaedo*, at great length. Justin argues that Plato can teach us much that is true, gradually leading us to the greater truth—indeed, the fulfillment of philosophy—which is found in revelation. Insofar as it is the fullness of wisdom, Christianity is rightly called the "true philosophy." While Hellenic philosophers each possess a portion of the *logos*, Christians are in possession of the Logos incarnate, Christ himself (*Apology* II, 13, 3). Justin states that if being a philosopher is to live in accordance with reason, then Christians are indeed philosophers, since they live in conformity with the law of the divine Logos (*Apology* I, 46, 1–4).

Greek philosophy receives a positive valuation from Justin on the grounds that all rational beings share in the universal Logos or Reason who is Christ. Abraham and Socrates are properly called "Christians before Christ" (*Apology* I, 46); indeed, insofar as all people are created in God's image and likeness, they have their share of the *logos spermatikos*, the seed of truth that enlightens all men and women (*Apology* II, 8, 1–3). A proper correlation between Christianity and secular wisdom is allowable for Justin on the grounds that creation itself bestows a certain participation in the personified wisdom of God, Jesus of Nazareth.

Despite this positive assessment of pagan *sapientia*, Justin is careful not to trim Christianity to the parameters of philosophical thought. As Henry Chadwick observes, "Whereas Socrates confessed an acute difficulty in finding God and speaking about him, Christ actually revealed God."[3] Further, Justin's adjudicatory norm of wisdom is not Platonism or Stoicism, but biblical truth: "What is central in his thought is the way in which the Biblical doctrine of God and his relation to the world provides him with a criterion of judgment, in the light of which he evaluates the great names in the history of Greek philosophy."[4] Justin's method is not to diminish or obscure the claims of Christian faith, but to show the extent to which philosophy serves as a legitimate preparation and prolegomenon to them.

With Clement of Alexandria, Justin's marriage between faith and reason continues to be championed. Writing in the late second and early third century, Clement argues that both the Old Testament and Greek philosophy lead us to Christ; they are twin streams flowing toward the river of Christian faith (*Stromateis* 1, 29). Indeed, philosophy, properly understood, is a gift of God's providence, within which the Logos is at work (*Stromateis* 1, 28; 37). Clement resolutely opposes, then, an "illiberal Christian appeal" to the Pauline claim that the wisdom of this world is foolishness. Paul's *monitum*, Clement argues, is not directed against philosophy at large, but against a human sapience that opposes Christian truth.[5] His fundamental principle is that one judges the truth of a matter not according to its author, but according to the value of the claim itself (*Stromateis* 6, 66). At the same time, however, as with Justin, Clement insists that Christianity is the true philosophy because it alone embodies the fullness of the revelation of the divine Logos.[6]

While Justin and Clement clearly sanction elements of philosophical wisdom as coherent with Christian truth, it is Origen of Alexandria who is the preeminent thinker on the matter of properly correlating faith and philosophy. In his *Letter to Gregory*, for example, he endorses a certain confluence between Scripture and Hellenic wisdom: "I wish to ask you to extract from the philosophy of the Greeks what may serve as a course of study or a preparation for Christianity, and from geometry and astronomy what will serve to explain the sacred scriptures." In his treatise against the Roman Celsus, Origen adds, "We are careful not to raise objections to any good teachings, even if their authors are outside the faith, nor to seek an occasion for a dispute with them, nor to find a way of overthrowing statements which are sound" (*Contra Celsum* VII, 46).

Origen then offers a theological accounting for this procedure:

Perhaps something of this kind is shadowed forth in what is written in Exodus . . . that the children of Israel were commanded to ask from their neighbors and those who dwelt with them, vessels of silver and gold . . . in order that, by spoiling the Egyptians, they might have material for the preparation of things which pertained to the service of God. . . . With the spoils taken from the Egyptians by the sons of Israel were made the movable Holy of Holies, the arc with its cover, the Cherubim, the propitiatory, the vessel of gold to hold the manna, the food of angels. These objects were truly made from the most beautiful gold of Egypt.[7]

Under Origen's influence, "spoils from Egypt" gradually became the major biblical image sanctioning the use of philosophy or "secular wisdom" in Christian theology. At the same time, like his predecessors, Origen's appropriation of Greek philosophy is far from uncritical. He urges caution, aware that a lack of care may lead to abuses. He reminds Gregory:

Holy Scripture knows, however, the unhappiness of certain ones who have left the land of Israel in order to descend into Egypt . . . i.e., in the sciences [knowledge] of the world after having been nourished by the law of God. And I tell you from my experience, rare are the men who have taken from Egypt only the useful, and go away and use it for the service of God. . . . There are those who have profited from their Greek studies, in order to produce heretical notions and set them up, like the golden calf, in Bethel.[8]

Origen then offers a dual approach, sanctioning the use of secular philosophy even while remaining cautious about its appropriation.[9] Athens and Jerusalem need not be at antipodes, since Athens may be a legitimate source of wisdom and truth. Two important provisos, however, are always operative: (1) Athens serves as a source of wisdom only because all of humanity is created in the image and likeness of God; and (2) the knowledge emanating from Athens must ultimately be disciplined by the revelational narrative of Jerusalem. The truth of the Jewish and Christian Scriptures remains normative and cannot be compromised.[10]

One interpreter of Origen's *Letter to Gregory* points out, "The main principle arising from this document is that, although Origen allows for the use of nonscriptural and non-Christian learning, he firmly places it in the service of Scripture and particularly what is best for the service of God."[11] Henri de Lubac observes much the same intention when he says that the Alexandrian believes "one can never utilize the doctrines of the time without having purified them, without having abolished in them all that is sterile and dead."[12] For Origen, the reciprocity between secular wisdom and the gospel is symbolized in the relationship between Abimelech and Isaac (Gen 26). They are sometimes at peace, sometimes at war: "For philosophy is neither opposed to everything in the Law of God nor in harmony with everything."[13] In the final analysis, it is the Christian faith that must verify and judge all that is received from philosophy.[14] Origen's own words cause de Lubac, among others, to reject the occasional suggestion that Origen was primarily interested in philosophical wisdom, that he ultimately sought a Platonic gnosis, finally abandoning the cross of Christ to tyros and recent initiates. But the claim that Origen forced the gospel into the Procrustean bed of Hellenism is difficult to sustain; on the contrary, he, along with other early Christian thinkers, was deeply cognizant of proper and improper uses of human wisdom vis-à-vis the revealed truth of Scripture.[15]

Writing more than a century after Origen, Augustine repeats, in *De doctrina christiana*, the Alexandrian's simultaneous endorsement and *monitum* about the uses of philosophy.[16] Although Augustine was deeply influenced by Cicero, Virgil, and Plotinus, although, like Origen, he used the arguments of ancient philosophers against their contemporary disciples (as found, for example, in *The City of God*, chapters one through four), and although he fused elements of neoplatonic philosophy with his Christian faith, Augustine's actual claims about the successful possibility of such fusion are very cautious. So, for example, in a well-known passage, he states:

> If those who are called philosophers, and especially the Platonists, have said anything that is true and in harmony with our faith, we are not only not to shrink from it, but to claim it for our own use from those who have unlawful possession of it. For as the Egyptians had not only the idols and heavy burdens which the people of Israel hated and fled from, but also vessels and ornaments of gold and silver . . . which the same people . . . appropriated to themselves, designing them for a better use . . . by the command of God. (*De Doctrina Christiana*, II, 40).

Augustine continues: "In the same way, all branches of learning have not only false teaching . . . but they contain also liberal instruction which is better adapted to the use of truth . . . and some truths in regard even to the worship of the one God are found among them."[17]

Augustine benignly cites his predecessors for availing themselves of such instruction:

> And what else have many good and faithful men among our brethren done? Do we not see with what a quantity of gold and silver and garments Cyprian . . . was loaded when he came out of Egypt? How much Lactantius brought with him? And Victorinus, Optatus and Hilary, not to speak of living men. How much Greeks out of number have borrowed! . . . For what was done at the time of the Exodus was no doubt a type prefiguring what happens now. [*De Doctrina Christiana*, II, 40, 60]

As one commentator has pointed out, Augustine is the one who brought Origen's image of "spoils from Egypt" to the Western church. Precisely because of his influence, this image became a leading one among medieval theologians. However, Augustine, like Origen, was extremely cautious about the value of the pagan classics. The only way to deal with the treasures from Greco-Roman culture was to subordinate them to the divine wisdom of Scripture itself.[18] Along the same lines, John Rist states that Augustine's attraction to the Latin text of Isaiah (7, 9), *Nisi credideritis, non intellegetis*, implied that the solution of the Greek philosophers to particular problems was, as Origen himself had argued against Celsus, incomplete because it finally lacked the guidance offered by Christ, the Scriptures, and the church.[19] Scripture is always to be the touchstone of truth; philosophical theories may be applied to Scripture, as long as they do not conflict with its claims.[20] In general, then, one may legitimately conclude that Augustine was quite close to Origen regarding the use of the spoils from Egypt metaphor.

The Cappadocian writers also treated the correlation between Christianity and secular wisdom at great length.[21] There is little doubt that Basil of Caesarea, for example, knew well the most important writers who preceded him. One finds in his letters references to Herodotus, Thucydides, Plutarch, Aristotle, and, of course, the favorite philosopher of early Christian thinkers, Plato. Basil's argument is clear enough: We must recognize that we are in a contest for eternal life: "In preparation for it, [we] must strive to the best of our power and must associate with poets and writers of prose and orators and with all men from whom there is any prospect of benefit with reference to the care of our soul."[22] After all, Basil argues, even Moses "first trained his mind in the learning of the Egyptians, and then proceeded to the contemplation of Him who is" (III, 3, 387).

Basil says, for example, that there are some accounts of the poets that his listeners should emulate; others, however, should cause them to stop their ears like Odysseus. Similarly, he notes, "almost all the writers who have some reputation for wisdom have . . . each to the best of his power, discoursed in their works in praise of virtue. To these men we must listen and . . . show forth their words in our lives" (IV, 1, 399). Basil lists several philosophers who, to their enemies and oppressors, did not return evil for evil, moving him to remark that "these examples tend to nearly the same end as our own [Christian] precepts" (VII, 2–8, 403–5). Basil makes clear, of course, with the tradition both before and after him, that caution is the order of the day: "We ought not to take everything without exception, but only such matter as is useful." After all, "a pilot does not heedlessly give over his ship to the winds, but steers it to harbor" (VIII, 1–2, 407). One image adduced by Basil, which may serve as well for the entire tradition, is the metaphor of the bees: Just as they neither approach all plants nor attempt to carry with them the entire flower but only the honey, so we too should take what is suitable from pagan writers, while passing over the rest (IV, 7–8).

Basil, along with the other Cappadocian writers, had a profound but critical devotion to Hellenistic culture and language; he and they remained mindful of the fact that their own rhetoric was always a matter of *logoi* at the service of the eternal Logos.[23]

Summary

What is offered here, of course, is only the briefest summary of the relationship between philosophy and theology in the ancient Christian world and certainly does not claim to be more than a sketch of the most significant points. It is obvious that many early Christian writers, reflecting on the relationship between revelation and the pagan thought that preceded them, did not simply posit a diametrical opposition between Christian faith and philosophical reason. On the contrary, they saw in writers such as Plato and Aristotle, Homer and Thucydides, Virgil and Plutarch, actual truth and wisdom—but a truth and wisdom at times admixed with error and, often enough, given their ignorance of Jewish and Christian Scriptures, yielding a truncated understanding of God and the world. While Greek and Roman thinkers offered elements of truth, Christianity was the "true philosophy" without remainder, the divine wisdom accorded the world by Christ.

Given this position, it is unsurprising that Christians did not merely appropriate the vocabulary of the ancient world. On the contrary, in order to explain their Trinitarian faith, they were required to develop new coinages. Words such as *ousia* and *hypostasis*, for example, surely had a Greek heritage, but were now filled with the new wine of Christian revelation.[24] As Balthasar says, "The Greek concepts themselves had to be widened in a way that comes close to a new coining (e.g., hypostasis) in order to be made suitable for the new content."[25] Joseph Ratzinger amplifies Balthasar's claim, applying it to a particular instance of Christian anthropology. Ratzinger points out, for example, that in certain sectors of theology, it has become fashionable to speak of the triumph of a Hellenistically inspired body-soul dualism, with the language of the "immortal soul" representing just such a dichotomy. But, Ratzinger argues, Plato left no anthropological schema just lying by the roadside for "any interested passerby to pick up."[26] In fact, the current "textbook schematization of 'Greek thought'" is nowhere to be found in Plato, Aristotle, or Plotinus, each of whom defends a highly individuated and distinctive understanding of the soul-body relationship. One may legitimately assert, Ratzinger says, that "the frequently encountered notion of an Hellenic-Platonic dualism of soul and body, with its corollary in the idea of the soul's immortality, is something of a theologian's fantasy."[27]

In his commentary on the Song of Songs, for example, Origen himself discusses the variety of reigning opinions about the nature of the soul,
its composition, its origin, and its relationship to the body, clearly indicating that there was no one paradigmatically conceived "Greek" view
that had been handed down to the early church.[28] On the contrary,
Ratzinger asserts,

> the doctrine of immortality in the early Church . . . was deter-
> mined by the Christological center, whence the indestructibility of
> the life gained through faith was guaranteed. . . . The Christian
> faith itself made certain demands upon anthropology and these
> demands were not met by any of the pre-existing ways of under-
> standing what it is to be human. Nevertheless the conceptual tools
> of such earlier anthropologies could and must be placed in the
> service of the Gospel by way of an appropriate transformation.[29]

Of course, the issue of the "hellenization" of the Christian faith is
important here. Was the Christian message corrupted by its transplanta-
tion from Palestine to the Mediterranean basin, with that region's own
tradition of philosophizing and conceptual thought? In the first place, the
early Christian writers themselves were aware that the philosophical
thought bequeathed to them was tainted, containing error as well as
insight, thereby giving rise to the spoils typology. Secondly, these early
writers constantly opposed the "true philosophy" or "our philosophy" to
the traditions of the ancient world. As Jean Leclercq has shown, under the
influence of the earlier tradition, the life of Christian monasticism continued to be designated by the term *philosophia* well into the Middle
Ages.[30] This evidence leads Pierre Hadot to conclude that while there is
certainly some cross-fertilization between Christianity and philosophy,
"let us be clear . . . [that] there can be no question of denying the incom-
parable originality of Christianity. . . . Moreover, the tendency to assimilation was confined within strict historical limits, and always linked more
or less closely to the tradition of the Apologists and of Origen."[31] Thirdly,
whether historic Christianity itself should, for the sake of its own universal faith and doctrinal structure, subscribe to a particular kind of philosophical architecture in an attempt to enhance its own intelligibility is a
question that has been discussed throughout this book. The answer one
gives to this question will largely determine the extent to which one
ascribes a "contamination" to Christianity given its adoption of *certain
delimited* dimensions of Greek thought. The option taken throughout the

history of Christian reflection involves the endorsement of certain theoretical facets of Hellenism not as illegitimate contamination but as providential illumination, meaning by this that when remolded and transformed, certain Greek concepts and ideas properly serve as useful vessels for Christian truth. This trajectory, with strong roots in the early church, continued to develop in Christian history.

Middle Ages

The medieval Franciscan friar Jacopone da Todi gave new voice to Tertullian's ancient suspicion about marrying faith and reason: "Mal vedemo Parigi che ne ha destrutto Assisi!" With Paris now substituting for Athens and Assisi for Jerusalem, the friar's lament is clear enough: One cannot look kindly on Paris because it has destroyed Francis's city; critical analysis has undermined Christian spirituality. Well known as it is, Jacopone's protest was a relatively isolated one in the Middle Ages. By and large, the spoils trope inherited from the patristic world continued to exert significant and enduring influence. Of course, it was precisely in the Middle Ages that the issue of the theology-philosophy-arts relationship came more intensely to the fore because of the rise of universities at Paris, Oxford, and Bologna. With this upwelling of medieval schools, philosophy in particular began to assert itself as an autonomous discipline unconstrained or bridled by theology or doctrine.[32]

Among the medieval theology masters, both Bonaventure and Albert, for example, strictly adhered to the spoils typology.[33] Thomas Aquinas, too, clearly witnessed to the dual approach countenanced earlier by Origen and Augustine. On the basis of man's creation in God's image and likeness, Aquinas was convinced of the synthetic unity of faith and reason, concisely exemplified in his axiom that grace does not destroy nature but perfects it.[34] Human cognitive activities are held in such high regard that the process of knowing can itself serve as one of the *vestigia Trinitatis* (imitating and developing Augustine's insights in the *De Trinitate*), offering an intellective anthropological trace of the generation of the eternal Word.[35] This inner confluence between intelligence and faith is clearly evident, for example, in the *Summa contra gentiles* where Aquinas discusses the coinherence of faith and reason:

Although the truth of the Christian faith . . . surpasses the capacity of reason, nevertheless, that truth that human reason is naturally endowed to know cannot be opposed to the truth of the Christian faith. For that with which the human reason is naturally endowed is clearly most true; so much so that it is impossible for us to think of such truths as false. Nor is it permissible to believe as false that which we hold by faith, since this is confirmed in a way that is so clearly divine. . . . Hence it is impossible that the truth of faith should be opposed to those principles that the human reason knows naturally.[36]

This abundant confidence in the congruency of faith and reason allows Aquinas to pursue unabashedly philosophical "spoils," using at length the insights of both Plato (especially on the issue of participated being) and Aristotle. Already in his earlier work, the *Commentary on Boethius's "De Trinitate"* (1256–1259), Aquinas had offered a justification for such borrowing from pagan authors. Following usual medieval procedure, Aquinas first adduces the arguments of his opponents. He notes, for example, the hesitations of Scripture: "It seems that in regard to those truths that are of faith, it is not right to employ the rational arguments of the natural philosophers, for, according to I Cor 1:17 'Christ sent me not to baptize, but to preach the gospel: not in wisdom of speech'; that is, 'in the doctrine of the philosophers,' as the gloss says."[37] Aquinas further cites, as a neo-Pauline warning against the use of philosophers, Jerome's famous letter to Eustochium, wherein the irascible scholar claims that he was beaten, according to divine justice, because he was overly fond of the books of Cicero (q. 2, a. 3, obj. 4).

In his reply to these objections, Aquinas counters that even the Bible allows the use of pagan writers, with Paul himself quoting Epimenides and Menander (in Titus 1:12 and 1 Cor 15:33). Given such scriptural warrants, Aquinas asserts, "it is therefore licit for other doctors of divine Scripture also to make use of the arguments of the philosophers" (q. 2, a. 3, *sed contra*). In a retortive argument, Aquinas cites Jerome against himself, noting that, in his letter to Magnus, the Scripture scholar had admitted that the Cappadocians "have so intermingled in their books the teachings and the sayings of the philosophers that one knows not which to admire first in them, their secular erudition or their knowledge of the Scriptures" (Jerome, Letter LXX). But while this may have been no more than one of Jerome's legendary backhanded compliments, Aquinas also adduces Jerome's more straightforward account of a proper Christian use of pagan philosophy: "If you have become enamored of the captive woman, secular wisdom, and captivated by her beauty, cut her hair and her finger nails, cut away the enticement of her tresses . . . and lying with her say: 'His left hand under my head, and his right hand shall embrace me' (Song of Songs, 8, 3) and many children will the captive woman give to you, and from the Moabite, Israelites will be born to you."[38] Aquinas briefly concludes, "Therefore with fruitful results some make use of secular wisdom" (q. 2, a. 3, *sed contra*).

Speaking now in his own voice, Aquinas argues that "the gifts of grace are added to those of nature in such a way that they do not destroy the latter, but rather perfect them; in such wise, the light of faith, which is gratuitously infused into our minds, does not destroy the natural light of cognition, which is in us by nature" (q. 2, a. 3, c). His point, of course, is that those truths manifested to us by faith are not contrary to those manifested by natural wisdom, "since both kinds of truth are from God." Augustine himself "employed many comparisons taken from the teachings of the philosophers to aid in the understanding of the Trinity" (q. 2, a. 3, c.). Aquinas is quick to add, however, that "if anything is found in the teachings of philosophers contrary to faith, this error does not properly belong to philosophy, but is due to an abuse of philosophy owing to the insufficiency of reason." Further, in continuity with the entire spoils metaphor handed down by Christian antiquity, he asserts that one can be in error employing philosophy if one "includes under the estate of philosophy truths of faith, as if one should be willing to believe nothing except what could be held by philosophical reasoning; when, on the contrary *philosophy should be subject to the measure of faith*, according to the saying of the Apostle (II Cor. 10.5), 'Bringing into captivity every thought unto the obedience of Christ'" (q. 2, a. 3, c; emphasis added).[39]

Aquinas makes clear that "philosophical doctrine ought not to be used as if it had primacy of place, as if on account of it one believed by faith" (q. 2, a. 3, ad 1). Paul's statement, "I will destroy the wisdom of the wise" (1 Cor 1:19), should not be understood as rendering philosophy entirely illegitimate, but as a reproof of those who trust in their own erudition (q. 2, a. 3, ad 2). Summing up several points, Aquinas advances a suggestive and important biblical image, further justifying the spoils trope: "Those who use philosophical doctrines in sacred Scripture in such a way as to subject them to the service of faith, do not mix water with wine, but change water into wine" (q. 2, a. 3, ad 5). There is little doubt, therefore, that Aquinas thought that the works of the philosophers could be appropriately used in order to explicate and illuminate the truth of faith, with the proviso, clearly stated, that it was faith itself which determined, disciplined, and molded philosophical arguments, rather than vice versa.[40]

With the continuing translation of Aristotle's works into Latin by William of Moerbeke, Aquinas had the philosopher's insights at his disposal and, needless to add, made ample use of them. Aquinas employed the dyadic categories of form and matter and of substance and accident in order to explain the mysteries of Christian faith, doing so in such a way, however, that the preexisting philosophical categories conformed to theological judgments, rather than placing Christian teachings in an Aristotelian-Procrustean bed. Fernand van Steenberghen and John Wippel have shown at length how Aquinas differed from some of his contemporaries—Siger of Brabant, for example—who clearly followed an unmodified, radical Aristotelianism, endorsing teachings such as monopsychism (one world-soul) and the eternity of matter, positions traditionally at odds with Christian faith and doctrine.[41] Aquinas, on the other hand, when confronted with a choice between Aristotle and the Christian faith, always modified Aristotle's thought, often cleverly drawing out unseen implications, thereby bringing the ancient philosopher into conformity with Christian revelation.[42] Further, as Etienne Gilson has endlessly argued, Aquinas's primary metaphysical insight—the identification of being as dynamic, intensive act, as the *actus essendi*, rather than as form—was a judgment delivered not from Aristotle, who never offered this philosophical observation, but from Aquinas's reading of the Vulgate's translation of Exodus 3:14. Aquinas's claim that being is the fully intensive act of existing, which in God is the act of subsistent existence unlimited by any admixture of potency or composition, was, primarily, a theological insight subsequently utilized in the course of his philosophical theology.[43] Aquinas's understanding of "being" as act, as *esse*, is not the mere adoption of "Greek" notions; it is the appropriation of a classical legacy now rethought and transformed in the light of Christian faith.[44] As Gilson has said, "What deeply alters the Aristotelian notion of metaphysics in Aquinas is the presence, above natural theology, of a higher theology, which is the science of God known through revelation."[45] Similarly, Robert Jenson says that Aquinas did not so much "adopt" Aristotelianism as converse with Aristotle and that "in the conversation was stimulated and helped to his own metaphysical positions, the key items of which could hardly be less Aristotelian."[46]

For Aquinas, philosophical concepts that had been hitherto unknown to Christian language and thought were properly introduced into theological discourse provided they were explicitly disciplined by faith. Take, for example, the concept of "transubstantiation," often used to explain the presence of Christ in the Eucharist, which was unknown in the West before the twelfth century. For Aquinas, however, the use, and transformation, of the conceptual apparatus of substance and accident can suitably elucidate the central assertion of the Christian liturgy: Christ himself is actually and entirely present to us in the Eucharist, even though only bread and wine are evident to our senses.

The same idea is present when Aquinas, and later, the Council of Trent, speaks about the efficacy of God's grace. Both Aquinas and Trent use the language of formal, final, and efficient causality in order to explain the justifying grace that freely comes to us through Christ. This kind of language, of course, is foreign to the evocative, more biblical (and, at times, Platonically inspired) language employed by early Christian writers (and later by Reformation thinkers). It reflects both the conceptual precision of those who were Schoolmen, as well as the ancient conviction that true knowledge was ultimately traceable to discernable causes. But it was certainly not the intention of the medieval theologians to deviate from the path of Holy Scripture or the one laid out by the early church. On the contrary, medieval and Tridentine thinkers saw themselves as preserving precisely the biblical and patristic Christian faith, while adding a dimension of intelligibility and precision only fully available at a later time. Further, they saw the conceptual apparatus of "causality" as a trope useful for the purposes of explication, not as a determinative grid molding, and misshaping, Christian truth.

Despite such intentions, it is unsurprising nonetheless that the introduction of Aristotelian terminology into Christian thought and theology, a hitherto unknown theological paradigm, was met with strong opposition. Such obvious paradigm change engendered profound concern about the continued purity of faith and doctrine. In response to such apprehensions, the statutes for the University of Paris, written in 1215, prohibited the teaching of certain books of Aristotle, such as the *Metaphysics*.[47] Pope Gregory IX, in a well-known letter to the Parisian theology masters in 1228, warned against an overreliance on philosophical writings.[48] Ultimately, of course, the fear of an unchecked radical Aristotelianism, with its incipient rationalism and philosophical imperialism, led to the condemnations by Etienne Tempier, the bishop of Paris, of 219 propositions in 1277.[49] Despite such measures, what appears to be beyond question is that for Aquinas, the use of a new conceptual system was hardly an abandonment of the *depositum fidei* but was instead a further protection and elucidation of it.[50] Ancient, classical thought was to be placed at the service of revelation—useful for its service as an *ancilla theologiae* but hardly claiming for itself revelation's unique veridical status.[51]

This very brief *tour d'horizon* of the Middle Ages is intended to show that for medieval Christian thought the ancient notion of taking "spoils from Egypt" remained the dominant motif for understanding the relationship between theology and the disciplines. The issue becomes a bit more complicated as we move toward the Reformation and the advent of modernity.

The Reformation and Modernity

In its fundamental thrust, the Reformation was a passionate cry for the Christian church to return to its biblical roots, to its essential wellsprings in the inspired word of God. The commanding concern of Martin Luther was that late medieval Christianity as well as Christian theologiasters had inextricably entangled the straightforward gospel of sin and grace in a web of philosophical concepts and Aristotelian notions that served not to illuminate but only to obfuscate biblical truth. Of course, Luther's accent on *sola scriptura* was intended neither to obviate the legitimate role of reason in explicating the sacred text, nor to reject a proper understanding of the correlation between philosophy and faith. What was intended, however, was to call the church back from a theologizing that had become so enamored of Scholastic, philosophical distinctions that fundamental elements of the gospel message could no longer be clearly heard. This is the basis, then, for Luther's attacks on Aristotle, on Scholasticism, and on philosophy at large. They obscure the gospel of grace, trading the word of God for the magniloquent but ultimately vacuous discourse of pagan thought. This absolute primacy of the gospel explains Luther's oft-quoted epithets aimed at "heathen philosophy," at Aristotle as a "heathen philosopher," and at reason itself as "Dame Witch."[52] Of course, given Luther's reputation as a master rhetorician given to hyperbole, such citations can hardly be taken simply at face value.

When more carefully considering the relationship between philosophy and theology, Luther rightly observes that philosophy considers humanity in immanent categories whereas theology considers men and women insofar as they are related to God and Christ. He can conclude, therefore, that as compared with theology, philosophy knows little about human existence because it misses both life's origin and its ultimate telos.[53] Philosophy, then, cannot ultimately explain to us the fundamental essence and nature of humanity; only theology can do this, and it can accomplish this task only on the basis of the scriptural word of God (34, 138).[54] Philosophical reasoning has its place, but, compared to the rich texture of the Bible, it remains flat, formal, and ineffective.

Luther argues, for example, that reason is "blind and mad" because it can never begin to understand the Trinity, nor can it fathom that God's Son, the incarnate Word, "assumed human nature and became flesh and blood with man" (22, 76). Later, disputing against the Zwinglian interpretation of the Eucharist, Luther asserts that "whoever wants to be Christian and apprehend the articles of the Christian faith must not consult reason . . . and whether it [faith] is consistent with reason" (24, 78). If one tries to make the articles of faith "conform to reason, all is lost in advance and we are doomed" (24, 79). During an argument about the Eucharist, Luther exclaims, "Not a single article of faith would remain if I followed the rancor of reason" (37, 53). For the Reformer, reason is impotent before the affirmations of faith, impotent before what is powerfully attested in Scripture. Whatever reason's accomplishments, the fact remains that "Christian life does not consist in things comprehended by reason" (22, 302–3), nor are we "saved through reason" (22, 319). This is why he can say, in an important passage, "Whoever wants to be a Christian must be intent on silencing the voice of reason. . . . To the judgment of reason they [the articles of Christian faith] appear so far from the truth that it is impossible to believe them."[55]

At the same time, it should not be ignored that Luther, in *The Disputation Concerning Man* (1536) says, "It is certainly true that reason is the most important and the highest in rank among all things and, in comparison with other things of this life, the best and something divine" (34, 137). In matters of faith, however, reason can easily become misguided. The Reformer speaks of Origen as one "who embittered and corrupted the Scriptures with philosophy and reason, as the universities have hitherto done among us." And he takes the University of Paris as having "incorrectly defined that truth is the same in philosophy and theology" (38, 239).[56] What Luther wants us to see is the danger of a rationalizing use of philosophy: "God is not subject to reason and syllogisms but to the word of God and faith" (38, 244). This does not mean that reason is always wrong; as Luther avers, "We have to admit that philosophy and reason is not against us but for Christ" (38, 250). But we must keep in mind that "philosophy deals with matters that are understood by human reason. Theology deals with matters of belief, that is, matters that are apprehended by faith" (38, 262). In a strange way, Luther himself sounds, at times, as a proponent of the double-truth theory: Philosophy and theology are so different as regards formalities that they should be kept at arm's length. But this rhetorical strategy is ultimately meant to remind Christians that those elements that are at the heart of the gospel—the incarnation and justification—"are above and beyond reason and philosophy" (38, 264). Faith and the understanding of faith supersede anything taught by mere natural, philosophical reasoning.[57] This is why Luther can say, commenting on 1 Timothy 6:20-21, "The apostle condemns what the universities teach because he demands that everything not from

Christ must be avoided. So every man must confess that Aristotle, the highest master of all universities, not only fails to teach anything concerning Christ, but that what he teaches is idle nonsense." Even Plato and Cicero "who belong to the better state" are not to be trusted; instead, "let us learn true wisdom is in Holy Scripture and in the Word of God" (2, 124–25).

Of course, what is offered here are simply some brief and occasional examples of Luther's thought. Nonetheless, it is perhaps true to say that insofar as Luther was engaged in calling the church back to the headwaters of the gospel, he did not so much reject the spoils from Egypt typology, the proper correlation that has characterized the tradition, as assertively remind the church (much like the early Christian theologians themselves) that such a typology could only be successful if, indeed, it was the Christian faith in its fullness that was norming philosophical thought, rather than the other way around.[58] The decline into a Renaissance naturalism, more influenced by classical thought than by the gospel, threatened to subordinate the word of God to alien and inimical influences. If it is true that Augustine could not reconcile himself to a Christian thinker comfortable within society, it is precisely a retrieval of such discomfort, of unease because of the gospel's challenging and alien character, that is characteristic of Luther's thought.[59]

The Reformer's insights, then, serve as a perennial warning to the church that unless Christianity is firmly rooted in Scripture, it can easily be led astray by the academic tastes of particular times, thereby subordinating the gospel to temporary, and ultimately idolatrous, philosophical fashions, to *au courant* fanfaronade. Luther's demand for a return to Scripture has its proper theological roots in the tradition's concern about reason's autonomy absent the illumination provided by Christ and revelation. In the last analysis, one may say that Luther echoes, surely with his unique accents, a comment of Aquinas that is largely representative of the earlier tradition: "In divine matters natural reason is greatly deficient."[60]

After the Reformation, both Catholic and Protestant thinkers continued to use philosophy in order to explicate Christian doctrine and belief. It would be too elongated a process to follow this attempt at "spoils" throughout theological history. Consequently, only a few attempts, mainly Roman Catholic, will be outlined below.

John Henry Newman

In the middle of the nineteenth century, John Henry Newman sought to repristinate and revivify Origen's ancient spoils paradigm. Newman was particularly concerned about charges, largely from rationalist quarters, that the gospels represented a farraginous stew of superstitious elements emanating from other religions, such as angels and demons, now piously commingled with stories about Jesus of Nazareth. To the claim that Christianity was simply a syncretistic mélange drawn from a wide variety of Eastern and Greek sources, Newman responded with two images, both replicating the spoils typology.

In the first place, Newman does not deny that the church ingurgitates ideas from many sources; he argues, rather, that the church is a "treasure house . . . casting the gold of fresh tributaries into her refiner's fire, stamping upon her own as time required it, a deeper impress of her Master's image."[61] The church, then, properly uses wisdom and truth wherever it may be found, but it does so by first casting any "spoils" into a cauterizing blaze, thereby purging it of interlacing dross, then stamping the molten, newly purified substance with the image of Christ, in the process claiming and subordinating all wisdom for and to the ultimate truth of the gospel.

In a second moment, Newman adduces the image of Aaron's rod, as found in the book of Exodus, as a proper trope for the Christian use of alien wellsprings. In a stirring response to the charge that Christianity, and particularly Catholicism, had gorged itself on the philosophical fruits of the ancient world with baneful results, Newman responds:

> They cast off all that they find in Pharisee or heathen; we conceive that the Church, like Aaron's rod, devours the serpents of the magicians. They [his opponents] are ever hunting for a fabulous primitive simplicity; we repose in Catholic fullness. . . . They are driven to maintain, on their part, that the Church's doctrine was never pure; we say that it can never be corrupt.[62]

Newman's reference here is to Exodus 7:9ff., where Aaron's rod swallows the serpents of Pharaoh's sorcerers. Like Origen's "Egyptian spoils," Newman's "Aaronic rod" is a suggestive metaphor for the relationship between theology and other disciplines or systems of thought. Christianity does not simply reject, expel, or jettison different narratives; it does not simply repress the "other." Rather, it refines, purifies, and deepens truth wherever it may be found. The reciprocity or correlation between the gospel and worldly wisdom is such that the church simultaneously uses and transforms such wisdom, placing it at the service of Christ.

Ironically, even as Newman was seeking to retrieve the patristic notion of "spoils," and so endorsing the casting of a wide theological net, the magisterium of the Roman Catholic Church was concerned about various nineteenth-century attempts to reconceptualize Christian doctrine that employed dimensions of Kant's thought. In reaction to certain of these theological undertakings, including those of L. Bautain, G. Hermes, and J. Frohschammer, Pope Leo XIII asserted the unique position of Aquinas as the preeminent master of Catholic theology. In his 1879 encyclical *Aeterni Patris*, the pope mandated Aquinas as the theological *doctor communis* for the entire Roman Catholic Church. All Catholic universities, colleges, and seminaries were to teach the thought of Aquinas as a sure bulwark against contemporary philosophical errors. The pope argued that Aquinas had understood the proper balance between faith and reason, striking a careful equilibrium between the two and thereby precluding the likelihood of succumbing to the twin theological dangers of rationalism and fideism.

From 1880 to 1962, intensive study of Aquinas's work bore excellent historical and speculative fruit. Theologians such as Chenu, Congar, Grabmann, Rahner, and Lonergan, and philosophers such as Gilson and Maritain, were profoundly influenced by Aquinas's thought. But the palpable danger of *Aeterni Patris* was that, by its imposition of only one conceptual system as adequately mediating Christian faith, it unduly limited the universal scope characteristic of the spoils from Egypt tradition. The encyclical gave the very strong impression that legitimate theological speculation had ended with Aquinas's appropriation of Plato, Aristotle, and the Stoics. Roman Catholic theologians, and therefore the Catholic Church at large, were no longer encouraged to drink at every source, to continue the process, as Newman says, of purging new ideas of their dross while impressing upon them the image of Christ. While the metaphysics of Aquinas undoubtedly provided useful philosophical linchpins for the explication of Christian truth, was the church now limited to this one, medieval formulation?

This unilateral endorsement of Thomism by nineteenth-century papal mandate was further strengthened by the Catholic Modernist crisis at the dawn of the twentieth century. The Modernists, while they raised important issues, seemed to relativize the cognitive status of doctrinal statements by arguing that Christian doctrine was nothing more than historically conditioned reflection on religious experience. Experience was the cardinal locus of revelation; doctrine was simply a time-bound and ultimately dispensable carapace. Not surprisingly, in a series of documents, such as the encyclical *Pascendi* of 1903, the magisterium severely denounced Modernist philosophical errors, without always carefully examining the legitimate questions the Modernists raised.[63] Most significantly for our purposes, Thomism, once again, was proposed as the only conceptual system effectively safeguarding the truth of Christian faith and doctrine. Only the metaphysics of Aquinas provided a suitably explicative "foundation" for the claims of Christian belief. The spoils from Egypt trope, encouraging theology to dialogue with every form of thought, appeared to have been banished, at least temporarily, from Roman Catholic theology.[64]

La nouvelle théologie

At the same time this intense but exclusive Thomistic renewal was underway, there emerged yet another attempt to revive the spoils typology. This movement, called pejoratively by its opponents *la nouvelle théologie*, sought to reinvigorate the ancient ideal of appropriating all human wisdom in service to Christian faith. Aquinas, its proponents conceded, was a unique theological master, but we are called to do today what Aquinas did fearlessly in his own time: integrate the breadth of human learning with the word of God. The names associated with this movement, such as Henri de Lubac and Hans Urs von Balthasar, were ultimately to give impetus to some of the great theological themes of Vatican II.

In his programmatic work of 1938, *Catholicism*, the patristic historian de Lubac tacitly criticizes the conceptual hegemony of neo-Scholasticism by assuming the mantle of Origen: "There is nothing good which Catholicism cannot claim for its own. . . . Nothing authentically human, whatever its origin, can be alien to [the church]." Cyril of Alexandria, then, was on the right track with his use of Plato, similarly Ambrose with Seneca, Aquinas with Aristotle, and Matteo Ricci with Confucius. If the salt of Christianity is to maintain its tang, then there must be an unending process of appropriation, assimilation, and creative imagination. The dynamism of the gospel demands that we incorporate new ideas and develop theological styles suitable for our own times.[65]

In a later work, de Lubac adds, somewhat more daringly, that even thinkers who at first blush appear unalterably opposed to the gospel have much to offer: "Many ideas of a more or less Marxist, Nietzschean, or Positivist stamp may even find a place in some blueprint for a new synthesis, and neither its orthodoxy nor its value will be called into question on that account. In the Church, the work of assimilation never ceases, and it is never too soon to undertake it!"[66]

De Lubac applauds, for example, the spiritual experiences that animate the religions of the world, asking rhetorically, "Must everything be jettisoned to give place to the Gospel?" Answering with a resounding No, he states that there is a real truth to be found in the "beliefs and consciences" of non-Christians. At the same time, it remains "the Church's mission to purify and give fresh life to each of them, to deepen them and bring them to a successful issue."[67]

Of course, this transformation and creative appropriation of "secular" wisdom must also be a preservation. Issuing cautions reminiscent of Origen's invocation of the "golden calf at Bethel," de Lubac says, "The wisdom of Christ will always be madness in the eyes of the world. . . . It would be reprehensible—and futile—to wish to 'adapt' dogma to accommodate the whims and caprices of intellectual fashion."[68] He later adds that, even given the necessity of creative assimilation, any theological development is also a recognition of the "profound union" with our predecessors "in the same dogma by which they lived as we live today, *in eadem doctrina eademque sententia.*"[69]

The entire theological corpus of de Lubac bears witness to his retrieval of the patristic notion of reciprocity and correlation. Truth may be found virtually anywhere; the church's process of appropriation and analogy extends to every realm of thought. The only boundary of the assimilative and analogical imagination is Christ himself, since all truth is subject to further refinement and purification in him. Ultimately, de Lubac and his colleagues wished to free Catholicism from the binding strictures of neo-Scholasticism, from the assertion that only Thomism could adequately mediate the Christian faith, and from the apparent claim that other systems of thought had nothing to offer the church in its task of explicating the gospel message. If the salt of Christianity were to maintain its tang, then the church could never become wedded simply to one theological style. The dynamism of the gospel demanded an unending process of creative imagination and bold appropriation:

> Just to imitate primitive Christianity or the Middle Ages will not be enough. We can revive the Fathers' all-embracing humanism and recover [their] spirit . . . only by an assimilation which is at the same time a transformation. For although the Church rests on eternal foundations, it is in a continual state of rebuilding, and since the Fathers' time it has undergone many changes in style.[70]

De Lubac and others were calling for a new dialogue with the vibrant existentialism, phenomenology, and even Marxism that was sweeping Europe. At the same time, it would always be the gospel shaping human wisdom, not vice versa. To illustrate the relationship between theology and other disciplines, de Lubac liked to cite what Augustine had said in another context: *Non in te me mutabis sed tu mutaberis in me*—"I will not change in you, but you will change in me."[71]

De Lubac's voice was joined by that of Hans Urs von Balthasar in a remarkable essay written in 1946, at the height of the *nouvelle théologie* crisis. Balthasar offers a passionate *cri du coeur*, calling for a widening of the spoils from Egypt approach beyond the achievements of Scholasticism: "Why did Aquinas devote himself to Arabic and Aristotelian philosophy? Why did Möhler avail himself of Hegel, Newman, of Locke and Hume? In all cases, they did so as to transpose natural philosophy to the supernatural order."[72]

Pleading for a new openness to all human wisdom, Balthasar asks, "Why should it be forbidden to the present and the future to enrich the kingdom of thought in a genuine and completely original manner?" Aquinas had made full use of Plato, Aristotle, and the Stoics, and surely, "if he had known Buddha and Lao-Tse, there is no doubt that he would have drawn them too into the *summa* of what can be thought and would have given them the place appropriate to them" (158–59).

Why is it possible to use all currents of thought, even those seemingly at odds with Christianity? Balthasar replies: "A fragment or stone . . . may come from the bed . . . of a pagan or heretical stream, but [the Christian thinker] knows how to cleanse it and to polish it until that radiance shines forth which shows that it is a fragment of the total glorification of God" (159).

As with past thinkers, we too must labor for the successful enrichment of the church's treasury of thought. The *philosophia perennis*, to renew itself properly, must absorb "the quintessence of all that is living, whether one finds this in Leibniz or Kant or Hegel, in Kierkegaard or Scheler or Heidegger" (164). Offering a mid-twentieth century example of a new and successful *spoliatio Aegyptiorum*, one that preserves the realistic epistemological tradition essential to Christian theology even while recognizing that the noetically constitutive dimension of subjectivity can no longer be ignored, Balthasar states, "The methodology carried out by Joseph Maréchal can be adduced as the most perfect example of a clarifying transposition in the present age. Kant has never been understood more deeply and thoroughly by a Catholic philosopher—understood and at the same time applied and overcome" (161).[73] To those opposing the kind of spoils from Egypt methodology that Balthasar sanctions, he impatiently adds:

Indeed, it would be evidence of the worst kind of backwoods mentality if Catholic philosophers were to wish to bypass the evident
progress and enrichments of the modern period to hold rigidly fast
to a medieval *status quo*. . . . This would mean handing on the letter of the great scholastic theologians while abandoning their inner
spirit, which was a spirit of astonishing openness to their own age
and of the most audacious progressiveness. (172)

A few years later Balthasar published his important study of Karl
Barth, sounding many of the same themes developed in the 1946 essay
but now complementing them with a defense of the Christian use of
"spoils" against the original Barthian claim that neo-Scholasticism (and
the *analogia entis*) was an a priori mold into which the gospel had been illegitimately poured. Portending his later work *The Glory of the Lord*,
Balthasar resists the reduction of the transcendentals to a monistic, univocal philosophizing: Truth, goodness, and beauty can be expressed in a variety of styles; the Logos manifests himself in a variety of *logoi*. Against
Barth's charge that Catholicism forces revelation into the Procrustean bed
of Scholasticism, thereby holding the word of God hostage to a particular
conceptual system, Balthasar responds: Philosophy is not a "rigid, formal
framework into which the content of theology would be poured." Every
concrete philosophy, rather, must be measured in terms of its Yes and No
to the supernatural order of revelation and to the one God in Christ.[74]
Balthasar is in complete concordance with Barth: The church can
never tie down revelation to a frozen philosophical system, no matter its
antiquity or lineage. Doing so would be to ignore the limits of human
conceptualities vis-à-vis the dynamism of the word of God. Throughout
his career, then, while always defending the legitimacy of the spoils trope,
Balthasar equally insisted that God is not subject to philosophical
Aufhebungen; such attempts constitute little more than the assertion of
Promethean human pride. It is unsurprising, then, that early on Balthasar
opposed the unchallenged hegemony of neo-Scholasticism almost as
strongly as Barth himself, while, somewhat later, Balthasar saw the
"anthropological method" as a distorted attempt to make transcendental
philosophy the ultimate yardstick for divine revelation. In the latter case,
the *conatus* of the human spirit is in danger of becoming a measure of the
revelatum itself.[75] The "glory" of the Lord could never be revealed if the
human spirit were taken as the measure of its gratuitous and unforeseen
appearance. If neo-Scholasticism could pose a legitimate danger to the
absolute gratuity and narrative supremacy of revelation, German idealism

certainly could as well. The sovereign and free God is simply assigned a post within Hegel's *Geist*, Schopenhauer's *Wille* and Schelling's *intellektuelle Anschauung*.[76] But revelation cannot subject itself to systems that vaunt themselves as absolute truth. Instead, it must demolish them; in the words of Mary's Magnificat, *deposuit potentes de sede*.[77] Ultimately, revelation must employ philosophical systems for its own ends. Such use cannot be limited to classical thought or to neo-Scholasticism: "Revelation can come to terms with every form of genuine philosophy that seeks to plumb the difference between the world's ground and existence whether such philosophy comes from the Mediterranean, the Far East or Africa."[78]

Unfortunately, this plea in Roman Catholic circles for a renewed relationship between theology and other disciplines, led by de Lubac and Balthasar, was brought to a sudden halt by the 1950 encyclical of Pius XII, *Humani generis*. The encyclical rightly warned theologians not to be seduced by the latest in academic fashion, expressing concern that a theology indulging *au courant* intellectual tastes would quickly become outdated and superficial, no longer of use to the church. At the same time, the document seemed to bring an end to the renascent spoils from Egypt methodology by strongly recommending the traditional terminology "built up by great theologians over the course of centuries" and by directing harsh words at the attempts to utilize currents of thought, such as existentialism and Marxism, flourishing in the mid-twentieth century.[79]

Within twenty years, Vatican II would largely endorse the positions of de Lubac and Balthasar by claiming that the Roman Catholic expression of the Christian faith is not necessarily tied to Aristotelian-influenced Scholasticism.[80] Vatican II encouraged a plurality of philosophies, conceptual systems, and notional schemas, with the concomitant demand, of course, that these preserve the *depositum fidei*.[81] Before turning to more recent trends, however, it is important to examine the great Protestant contemporary of de Lubac and Balthasar, Karl Barth.

Karl Barth

Writing at roughly the same time as the *nouveaux théologiens* was the indomitable Reformed thinker Karl Barth. Taking account of his thought on the spoils trope is significant since Barth, of course, has been the paladin of those eschewing all attempts at imposing prior philosophical determinations on the gospel of Christ. His theological fire was directed at the Schleiermacher-Hermann-Ritschl axis of thought (which appeared to impose existential-experiential determinations), against Bultmannian-Heideggerian encroachments (which appeared to import ontological-existential preliminaries), and against the Roman Catholic use of the *analogia entis* (which seemed to establish an ontological relationship between God and humanity prior to and outside of the gospel of grace).[82] Barth goes so far as to see the Schleiermacher-Ritschl approach, that is, the path of liberal Protestantism, as leading to "the plain destruction of Protestant theology and the Protestant Church," while the Catholic attempt, as noted in the last chapter, remains for Barth the "invention of the Antichrist." What is clearly needed is a "Protestant theology self-nourished at its own source, standing upon its own feet, and finally liberated from such secular misery."[83]

But even given Barth's legitimate concern that philosophy neither trespass upon the word of God nor trim the gospel to its own preconceived dimensions, this hardly means that he found any notion of reciprocity or correlation to be out of the question. One finds, for example, in his discussion of the relationship between *eros* and *agape* these remarkable comments:

Is it a mere accident that the Gospel of Jesus Christ, this seed of Israel, took root in the perishing world of Hellenism? Has it been a misfortune that this origin has haunted its whole subsequent career? Is it merely in culpable self-will that we seek in soul the land of the Greeks, and cannot refrain from doing so even today, when we see so clearly that the necessary reformation of the Church cannot be the same thing as a renaissance of Greek antiquity? Is there not here something that is obligatory, and which it is better to see and accept than to ignore and deny, if we are ready and anxious to understand the Gospel of Jesus Christ in the full range of its contents?[84]

A bit later Barth adds, "The violence displayed against Hellenism in recent theology is not a good thing. . . . The Greeks with their *eros* . . . grasped the fact that the being of man is free[,] . . . joyful, cheerful and gregarious." While Paul's theology of Christian love is not derived from Greek philosophy but from divine revelation, "when he portrays the Christian living in this love, he never uses barbarian or Israelite colors and contours but he undoubtedly makes use of Greek, thus betraying the fact that he both saw and took note of the Greeks and their *eros*."[85] Barth here sounds very much like Newman and de Lubac. It is not a matter of simply importing into theology unalloyed notions that will not themselves be purified and transformed by theology's cognitive content. The chief point for all of them is that philosophical affirmations must finally be redeemed in the light of God's word.

Similar passages in Barth may be adduced. He observes, for example, when speaking about causality, a central concept in medieval theology: "The concept of cause does not stem from the Bible. However, that does not mean that its introduction into the thesaurus of theology's vocabulary was an error. It can be of real service to theology in its task of unfolding and applying the message of the Bible for today. . . ." He also states, in what may seem to be a softening of his earlier position but which is, in fact, entirely consistent with his thought: "We must not yield to a revulsion against the idea of being as such."[86] In fact, in his celebrated study of Anselm's method, Barth offers a very clear affirmation of the role of being-language in theology.[87] Gerhard Sauter points out, in just this regard, that Barth does not reject making discoveries from many sources; theology can learn from other disciplines, movements, and insights, "but it cannot learn from these sources how to do theology."[88] Sauter himself thinks that one may cast the difference between the *use* of other disciplines and the adjudicatory *norm* of theology as the well-known distinction between the context of discovery and that of justification. One may be open to the former in all its multifarious and polysemic readings, but it is the latter, with its strictly theological criteria, that must be finally invoked. Such correlation is especially possible, Sauter notes, when Barth is not facing a time of ideological struggle, of a *status confessionis*.[89] Robert Jenson, taking a slightly different approach, points out that the *Church Dogmatics* is meant to read all of reality in the light of Christ. Philosophers, often enough, seek to develop a general understanding of reality *remoto Christo/sola ratione*, and it is just this position that Barth rejects. Nonetheless, while never dependent on philosophers, he was "in conversation with them when that seemed likely to help."[90]

Of singular interest is that Barth adduces the same passage Newman cited when dealing with the relationship between theology and philosophy, namely, Exodus 7:9–12. Using it to a different purpose, Barth makes a very similar point. He claims that the theologian among philosophers is something like Aaron before Pharaoh, casting down his rod and watching it metamorphose into a serpent. The sorcerers of Egypt are summoned and they perform a similar feat. Barth avers that such a story shows the difficulty of the theologian distinguishing himself from the philosopher. After all, both reflect on human existence—and are similarly bound by thinking and human language: "Good for him [the theologian] if in the shroud of the completely similar, he speaks of the completely dissimilar." If he can do this, he can rightly claim the title of theologian; by showing the "absolutely extraordinary reality . . . which only God can speak," he fulfills what is written in Exodus: "But Aaron's rod swallowed up their rods."[91]

For Barth, theology must always be on its guard not to become mere philosophy; theologians must clearly manifest their discipline's uniqueness: "It [theology] continues to affirm its intention of having nothing but God's Word as the origin and object of its strivings" ("Fate and Idea in Theology," 31). The actual danger posed by the alleged convertibility of philosophy and theology is displayed by Barth's question: "Might it not seem improper for Aaron—who after all really couldn't do any more than Pharaoh's magicians—to remain Aaron rather than finally becoming an Egyptian magician himself?" But Barth will respond that whatever the temptations of Egypt, theology must always be on the *qui vive*, carefully guarding against a reduction of the discipline to mere human understanding. Theology is indeed very close to philosophy, "a nearness as necessary as it is perilous" in that both disciplines speak and think about human existence. But theology has a "watchfulness incumbent upon it" that can never be abandoned.[92] Barth, then, defends the use of philosophy; indeed, he claims that theology is necessarily related to it while simultaneously sounding the Origenist tocsin that one cannot build the golden calf at Bethel. Aaron can never become one of Pharaoh's sorcerers; with Scripture and Newman, Barth insists that Aaron's rod must ultimately devour the serpents of the magicians.[93]

After this brief tour of some of the thinkers involved in the appropriation of "secular" ideas for theological use, it will be helpful to review several ecclesial documents concerned with the legitimacy and dangers of the spoils trope. From there, we shall pass to contemporary questions.

Selected Church Documents

We have already observed that a thirteenth-century letter from Pope Gregory IX warned the theology masters at Paris not to rely too heavily on philosophical writings. In passing, we have reviewed some papal encyclicals wherein the Roman Catholic magisterium reasserted the continuing authority of Aquinas over and against theological strains of rationalism, idealism, and Modernism. Vatican II modified this trend by contextualizing Aquinas and sanctioning a variety of theological methods, encouraging, in the process, dialogue with a wide range of sources and thinkers.[94] The council was hardly arguing that theology need no longer seek philosophical warrants for its universal and perduring claims. It was arguing, however, that such seeking need no longer be limited simply to Thomism or neo-Scholasticism. One was no longer forced to claim, as

Aidan Nichols remarks, that "other theologies [or philosophies] are permitted to exist until Thomism has absorbed their better insights (whereupon, like the Marxist State, they can wither away)."[95] A lively dialogue with personalism, existentialism, and phenomenology was now officially sanctioned.

In 1990, the Congregation for the Doctrine of the Faith issued a statement entitled "Instruction on the Ecclesial Vocation of the Theologian." As the title indicates, the primary point of this document is that the theologian, along with being a critical member of an academic guild, is first and foremost a member of the church of Christ. The proper relationship between theology and secular wisdom, therefore, is at stake in determining the theologian's vocation: "It is the theologian's task . . . to draw from the surrounding culture those elements which will allow him or her to better illumine one or other aspect of the mysteries of faith. This is certainly an arduous task that has its risks, but is legitimate in itself and should be encouraged."[96] The statement continues: "Here it is important to emphasize that when theology employs the elements and conceptual tools of philosophy or other disciplines, discernment is needed. The ultimate normative principle for such discernment is revealed doctrine which itself must furnish the criteria for the evaluation of these elements and conceptual tools, not vice-versa."[97] One sees in this document, unsurprisingly, a clear endorsement of the spoils trope, with a reprise of both the encouragement and the caution associated with it.

More recently, in the encyclical *Fides et ratio*, a document of greater significance than other such statements, John Paul II addressed the "spoils" question with some range and deftness. Strikingly, the encyclical opens not with the words of Christ, but with the famous inscription from the portal of the temple at Delphi: "Know thyself" (1).[98] The basic questions of life, it is asserted, are asked not only by the sacred texts of Israel but also in the Veda and Avesta, in the writings of Confucius and Lao-tzu, in the preaching of Buddha, and in the dramatic productions of Euripides and Sophocles. Right at the outset, then, the pope is at least affirming other sacred and secular writings as, collectively, a *preparatio evangelii*; they are reflective of the universal human desire for God.

Such universal desire is understandable since human reason is ultimately conjoined to faith.[99] They are "like two wings on which the human spirit rises to the contemplation of truth" (62). The pope makes clear that these dyadic elements of human knowing, properly understood, cannot be opposed. He says, for example, that the truths of faith and reason are "deeply related" and that there is a "profound and indissoluble unity" between the knowledge of reason and that of faith (16). This is so much the case that the truth "which God reveals to us in Jesus Christ, is not opposed to the truths which philosophy perceives. On the contrary, the two modes of knowledge lead to truth in all its fullness" (34).

Given this position, it is hardly surprising that at significant points in the document the pope adduces Aquinas's statements from the *Summa contra gentiles* with its firm assertion that faith and reason, coequally gifts from God, cannot be opposed (43), as well as Aquinas's claim that grace does not destroy nature but perfects it and brings it to fulfillment (44). In endorsing Aquinas's points, the pope clearly does not think they are simply representative of one thirteenth-century thinker (who, while celebrated by the encyclical, is also clearly contextualized by it) but are, in fact, emblematic of virtually the entire Christian tradition.[100]

This fundamental correlation between faith and reason, then, serves as the theoretical linchpin for the spoils trope, which is warmly endorsed by the rest of the document. The pope makes clear, however, that such endorsement is not born of naïveté regarding the fall's effects. Reason, in fact, has been severely wounded, so that the path to truth has become "strewn with obstacles" and human reasoning "distorted and inclined to falsehood" (22). In fact, insofar as reason has become "more and more a prisoner to itself" (22), "the Christian's relationship to philosophy requires thorough-going discernment" (23). Paul himself reminds us of the profound weakness of our reasoning capacity. Recalling the Apostle's words that "God chose what is foolish in the world to shame the wise" (1 Cor 1:27), the pope argues Christ's death on the cross dooms every attempt to reduce God's plan to mere human logic (23).

But such significant warnings are not intended to undermine the faith-reason synthesis. The encyclical holds, rather, that the "wisdom of the Cross" challenges reason to transcend itself, to break free of its cultural particularities and limitations; the cross, in the very catholicity of its meaning, insists upon "an openness to the universality of the truth which it bears" (23). Faith and reason, then, rather than being antagonists, "mutually support each other," since "they offer to each other a purifying critique and a stimulus to pursue the search for deeper understanding" (100). To say this, however, is not to affirm a mutuality of equals. At several points in the document, John Paul insists upon the primacy and hegemony of revealed truth. For example, he points out that "Christian revelation is the true lodestar of men and women" (15). "Revelation . . . introduces into our history a universal and ultimate truth" (14); in fact, revelation is the "absolute truth" (15). The encyclical endorses Irenaeus and Tertullian (to whose names we may surely add Luther's) who, following the Pauline warning that "no one take you captive through philosophy and empty deceit" (Col 2:8), sound the alarm when confronted with a perspective seeking "to subordinate the truth of Revelation to the interpretation of the philosophers" (37). It is only with this caution in mind, that reason labors under the burden of sin and fragility, that one may sanction the utilization of secular wisdom.

Scripture itself, the encyclical observes, clearly made use of pagan culture: "The Acts of the Apostles provides evidence that Christian proclamation was engaged from the very first with the philosophical currents of the time" (Acts 17:18) (36). Paul and others could not refer simply to Moses and the prophets when speaking to "pagans"; they needed to appeal to the "natural knowledge of God and the voice of conscience in every human being" (36). Similarly, the fathers of the church "fully welcomed reason which was open to the absolute, and they infused it with the richness drawn from Revelation" (41). Indeed, early Christian writers "entered into fruitful dialogue with ancient philosophy, which offered new ways of proclaiming and understanding the God of Jesus Christ" (36). Justin Martyr is invoked as one who positively engaged philosophy, although always with "cautious discernment" (38), while Clement of Alexandria is similarly lauded for calling the gospel "the true philosophy" and for noting that while Greek philosophy does not strengthen truth, it is rightly called "the hedge and protective wall around the vineyard" (38).[101]

Origen too is cited by *Fides et ratio* as outstanding in his judicious use of philosophical thought. The encyclical notes that the Alexandrian, in countering the attacks of Celsus, "adopts Platonic philosophy to shape his argument and mount his reply" (39). However, that Platonism "once adopted by theology underwent profound changes especially with regard to concepts such as the immortality of the soul, the divinization of man and the origin of evil" (39). The process of disciplining Hellenic theory in light of faith, of subordinating and transforming it, is discernible throughout the patristic tradition (40). One must conclude, therefore, that the ancient Christian writers did not identify "the content of their message with the systems to which they referred" (41).

Tertullian's famous question about Athens and Jerusalem, the academy and the church, should not be taken, therefore, as a reproach to a proper understanding of correlation, but as an indication of the "critical consciousness" with which Christian thinkers first confronted ancient philosophy (41). From the beginning, such thinkers "were not afraid to acknowledge those elements in them [particular theories] that were consonant with Revelation and those that were not" (41).

One finds in the Middle Ages a similarly judicious appropriation of ancient thought. Anselm, for example, was a conspicuous representative of reason at the service of the *intellectus fidei*. For Anselm, the priority of faith is never in competition with the legitimate goals of reason; rather, reason's task is "to find meaning, to discover explanations which might allow everyone to come to a certain understanding of the contents of faith." Of course, philosophy is never asked to pass judgment on the Christian faith, "something of which it would be incapable" (42). Aquinas too borrowed not only from Aristotle but also from the Arab and Jewish thinkers of his time (43). He recognized that reason, properly illumined by faith, "could contribute to the understanding of divine Revelation." Aquinas's bold assertion, "Whatever its source, truth is of the Holy Spirit" (*omne verum a quocumque dicatur a Spiritu Sancto est*) is indicative of his entire theological method (*ST* I-II, q. 109, a. 1 ad 1).

In the late Middle Ages and afterward, the document continues, one sees an "exaggerated rationalism," with reason now moving further away from the tutelage of faith, a deformation coming to full bloom in idealism, atheism, positivism, and nihilism. Nonetheless, the encyclical notes, sounding very much like de Lubac and Balthasar, "even in the philosophical thinking of those who helped drive faith and reason apart there are found at times precious and seminal insights which . . . can lead to the discovery of truth's way" (48). Spoils may indeed be found everywhere, even in those ostensible enemies of Christian faith and doctrine.[102] At the same time, *Fides et ratio* does not fail to note that "deprived of what revelation offers, reason has taken side-tracks which expose it to the danger of losing sight of its final goal" (48).

The endorsement of the spoils trope is not limited to historical examples; the process continues today. So the encyclical asserts that "in preaching the Gospel, Christianity first encountered Greek philosophy, but this does not mean at all that other approaches are precluded. . . . As the Gospel gradually comes into contact with cultural worlds which once lay beyond Christian influence, there are new tasks of inculturation" (72). For example, "in India, in particular, it is the duty of Christians now to draw from this rich heritage the elements compatible with the faith, in order to enrich Christian thought" (72). And "what has been said here of India is no less true for the heritage of the great cultures of China, Japan and the other countries of Asia, as also for the riches of the traditional culture of Africa"(72).

However, the encyclical, even while widening its compass beyond traditional Hellenistic insights, calls not just for the use of any philosophy, for any kind of spoils; rather, the pope argues that a certain *type* of philosophy is ultimately necessary for the intelligibility of Christian faith and doctrine. The document insists that any philosophy that is of decisive use to Christian faith and doctrine must have a "genuinely metaphysical range" (83). In fact, any "philosophy which shuns metaphysics would be radically unsuited to the task of mediation in the understanding of Revelation" (83). Only philosophies of this type are able "to confirm the intelligibility and universal truth of its [theology's] claims" (77). What is clear from such statements is that even though theology gleans wisdom and insight from many sources, the fact remains that only philosophies that can offer theoretical support for the universal, perduring, transcultural, and transgenerational claims of Christian doctrine, for what the encyclical calls the "universal validity" of the contents of faith (84), are useful in a broader and wider sense—to use spatial metaphors—since these add a further dimension of intelligibility to faith's claims.

Fides et ratio, then, clearly stands in the tradition of both endorsing "spoils" and chastising them by Christian faith and teaching. But does such an approach, by affirming the hegemony of revelation over philosophical wisdom, fully protect the autonomy of philosophy? And if philosophy's sovereignty is protected, can the priority of faith—and thus the traditional spoils metaphor—be honestly defended?

The encyclical pointedly insists that philosophy is an autonomous discipline (77) with its own methods of which it is "rightly jealous" (13). And the document boldly states that "the content of revelation can never debase [*comprimere*] the legitimate autonomy of reason" (79).[103] Philosophy's "independence" remains unimpaired when theology calls upon it, even if it is undeniably true that philosophy must undergo a "profound transformation" when at the service of the Christian faith (77). While philosophy has been traditionally called the *ancilla theologiae*, the encyclical insists that this term should not be used to call into question the discipline's autonomy (77). Insofar as "philosophy must obey its own rules and be based upon its own principles" (79), the pope seems to be endorsing the older axiom invoking philosophy as *ancilla theologiae sed non ancilla nisi libera*.

Given this very strong endorsement of philosophy's self-governance, one may legitimately wonder if the pope is now abandoning the hegemony of revelation that had heretofore been a major theme of the encyclical. Such, however, is hardly the case. The document says, for example, that "revealed truth offers the fullness of light and will therefore illumine the path of philosophical inquiry" (80). The encyclical also makes a distinction between the "valid autonomy" of philosophy and its "self-sufficiency." While the former remains always true, the latter is illicit because it refuses the "truth offered by divine Revelation" (75). Truth is one and undivided; consequently, philosophy can never be "separated" or "absolutely independent of the contents of faith" (45). Indeed, "when philosophy heeds the summons of the Gospel's truth, its autonomy is in no way impaired" (108). One can hardly conclude, then, that the encyclical has fallen into a kind of semirationalism. The pope is proceeding confidently from the position, reminiscent of Aquinas in the *Summa contra gentiles* (I, 7), that faith and reason can never ultimately conflict. Since truth is one, the "liberty" of philosophy, properly practiced, will only confirm the intelligibility of faith's normative and universal claims.[104] Reason, then, possesses a legitimate independence—but it only proceeds properly when it heeds the truth offered by revelation.

Having examined both theologians and official statements from the Christian tradition, I would now like to address the issue of spoils as this is envisioned in two major models of contemporary thought. Both of these approaches may be characterized as nonfoundationalist in kind. My contention is that these positions, while contributing something to our understanding of the spoils typology, misconstrue, because of their rejection of a *prima philosophia*, the proper balance between faith and reason that the spoils trope ultimately seeks to establish.

Notes

1. For *quid ergo Athenis et Hierosolymis?*, see Tertullian *De praescriptione haereticorum* VII, 9. For the phrase *certum est, quia impossibile est*, see Tertullian, *De carne Christi*, 5. Of course, Tertullian also speaks of the *anima naturaliter christiana*, so there is more than one trajectory in his thought. Henry Chadwick says that Tertullian's Athens/Jerusalem dichotomy (traditionally encapsulated in the *credo quia absurdum*) seeks only to preserve the distinctiveness of faith—to prevent the absorption of grace by nature. Chadwick, *Early Christian Thought and the Classical Tradition* (Oxford: Clarendon, 1966), 1–3. This, of course, in many ways anticipates Luther's reaction to the rebirth of classical learning during the Renaissance and hence his fear that the truth of the gospel would be eclipsed by created beauty.

2. Tertullian, *De praescriptione haereticorum* VII. Tertullian also notes the simplicity of truth as opposed to the "subtlety and vain deceit of philosophy." Tertullian, *Adversus Marcion* V, 19.

3. Chadwick, *Early Christian Thought and the Classical Tradition*, 17.

4. Ibid., 20.

5. Ibid., 43.

6. Pierre Hadot, *Philosophy as a Way of Life* (trans. Michael Chase; Oxford: Blackwell, 1995), 141 n. 15, citing *Stromateis* I, 13, 57.

7. Origen, "Letter to Gregory," in *The Ante-Nicene Fathers*, vol. 4 (Grand Rapids: Eerdmans, 1956), 393–94.

8. Ibid., 394.

9. Other texts wherein Origen comments on the "spoils" issue are his *Homilies on Exodus* XI, 6; *Homilies on Leviticus* VII, 6; and throughout the *Contra Celsum*.

10. Origen's use of ancient philosophy within the *fides quaerens intellectum* has been well documented. Useful texts include: Henri de Lubac, *Histoire et Esprit: L'intelligence de l'Écriture d'après Origène* (Paris: Aubier, 1950); John C. Smith, *The Ancient Wisdom of Origen* (London: Associated University Presses, 1992); and Henri Crouzel, *Origen* (trans. A. S. Worrall; San Francisco: Harper & Row, 1989). A recent defender of Origen's orthodoxy vis-à-vis his appropriation of Hellenism is Mark J. Edwards, *Origen against Plato* (Aldershot: Ashgate, 2002).

11. Smith, *Ancient Wisdom of Origen*, 143.

12. De Lubac, *Histoire et Esprit*, 79.

13. See Origin, Homily XIV, 3, in *Homilies on Genesis and Exodus* (trans. R. Heine; Washington, D.C.: Catholic University of America Press, 1982), 199.

14. Against Celsus's demand that Christianity justify itself by "Greek teaching" or philosophy, Origen argues that the truth of the Christian faith is not subject to alien warrants since the "gospel has a proof which is peculiar to itself and which is more divine than a Greek proof based on dialectical arguments." Origen, *Contra Celsum* I, 2; cited in Robert Wilken, "Serving the One True God," in *Either/Or* (ed. Carl Braaten and Robert Jenson; Grand Rapids: Eerdmans, 1995), 54.

15. Of course, Adolf von Harnack is the classic representative of the view that the emergence of Christian doctrine represented an unwarranted hybrid of *gnosis* and *pistis*. Harnack took Christianity's shift from its Palestinian matrix to the Mediterranean basin as a fateful and degenerative step resulting in a dogmatism that inexorably destroyed the spirit of the gospel. As he says, the dogmatic tradition is "in its conception and development a work of the Greek spirit on the soil of the Gospel." Harnack, *History of Dogma*, vol. 1 (trans. N. Buchanan; Boston: Roberts Brothers, 1895), 17. Later Harnack says, "Every dogmatic formula is suspicious because it is fitted to wound the spirit of religion." *History of Dogma*, 1:71. Of course, Harnack defended himself by saying that "the foolishness of identifying dogma and Greek philosophy never entered my mind." Further, he does not look upon "the development of the history of dogma as a pathological process within the history of the Gospel." However, he continues, this does not mean justifying the continuing permanent significance of dogma, which "has once been formed under definite historical conditions." *History of Dogma*, 1:22–23.

16. Despite its age, one good summary of the attitude of Augustine and other early Christians in the West toward pagan literature and learning may be found in P. De Labriolle, *Histoire de la littérature latine chrétienne* (Paris: Societé d'Editions, 1924), esp. 15–39.

17. Augustine, *De doctrina christiana* II, 40. One important text dealing with Augustine's use of Plato is Endre von Ivanka, *Plato Christianus* (trans. E. Kessler; Paris: Presses Universitaires de France, 1990).

18. Lawrence Frizzell, "'Spoils from Egypt' between Jews and Gnostics," in *Hellenization Revisited* (ed. Wendy Helleman; Lanham, Md.: University Press of America, 1994), 383–94.

19. John Rist, *Augustine: Ancient Thought Baptized* (Cambridge: Cambridge University Press, 1994), 13.

20. Ibid., 300. However, Rist observes that sometime after 400, after reading Porphyry's pamphlet *Against the Christians*, Augustine came to identify Porphyry as the epitome of a blasphemous element in philosophy, forcing Augustine, in the process, to a more sober estimate of both the strengths and weaknesses of the Platonists. For more on Porphyry and the Christian reaction, see Robert Wilken, *The Christians as the Romans Saw Them* (New Haven, Conn.: Yale University Press, 1984), 126–63.

21. Very helpful in this regard are the Gifford Lectures of Jaroslav Pelikan, published as *Christianity and Classical Culture* (New Haven, Conn.: Yale University Press, 1993).

22. Basil, *Ad adolescentes de legendis libris gentilium*. The translation used here is "Address to Young Men on Reading Greek Literature," in *The Letters*, vol. 4 (trans. Roy Deferrari and Martin McGuire; Cambridge, Mass.: Harvard University Press, 1934), 365ff. All of the following in-text citations are from this translation.

23. Pelikan, *Christianity and Classical Culture*, 15.

24. The International Theological Commission of the Roman Catholic Church has rightly said, "The Church has not just adopted already given conceptual systems. Rather, it has subjected pre-existing concepts, deriving for the most part from sophisticated discourse of the day, to a process of purification as well as of redefinition and new definition thus creating a speech which suits its message." "On the Interpretation of Dogmas," *Origins* 20 (1990): 12 (C.III.3).

25. Hans Urs von Balthasar, *Truth Is Symphonic* (trans. G. Harrison; San Francisco: Ignatius, 1987), 55.

26. Joseph Ratzinger, *Eschatology* (trans. Michael Waldstein; Washington, D.C.: Catholic University of America Press, 1988), 143–44.

27. Ibid., 145. Of course, Ratzinger is arguing here against the assertion that Christianity simply adopted preexisting philosophical forms, allowing them to shape the gospel to their own ends. Ratzinger claims that such is hardly the case, sounding here very similar to Pannenberg, who notes that the reception of Greek thought by Christian antiquity was an important presupposition for the acceptance by Gentiles of the God of Israel. "For how were non-Jews to believe in the God of Israel as the one God without themselves becoming Jews?" Wolfhart Pannenberg, *Systematic Theology*, vol. 1 (Grand Rapids: Eerdmans, 1991), 100.

28. Origen, *Commentary on the Song of Songs*, Book X (PG XIII, 126b–127a).

29. Ratzinger, *Eschatology*, 146–47. To this end, Ratzinger argues that Aquinas's definition of the soul as the *anima forma corporis*, the form of the body, was intended to protect the Christian certainty that human life united to Christ cannot be destroyed by death, in the process entirely reinterpreting Aristotle's prior understanding wherein the soul is entirely bonded to matter, similar to organic life at large. Aristotle's position, of course, could not finally protect the Christian claim that union with Christ overcomes death, leading Anton Pegis to remark, "The Thomistic doctrine of an intellectual substance as the substantial form of matter must be seen as a moment in history when an Aristotelian formula was deliberately used to express in philosophical terms a view of man that the world and tradition of Aristotelianism considered a metaphysical impossibility." Pegis, "Some Reflections on the *Summa contra Gentiles*, II, 56," in *An Etienne Gilson Tribute* (Milwaukee: Bruce, 1959), 177.

30. Jean Leclercq, "Pour l'histoire de l'expression 'philosophie chrétienne,'" *Mélanges de Science Religieuse* 9 (1952): 221–26; cited in Hadot, *Philosophy as a Way of Life*, 129.

31. Hadot, *Philosophy as a Way of Life*, 129.

32. One sees such assertion, for example, in the philosophy of Siger of Brabant and in the rise of "radical Aristotelianism," or, as it is sometimes called, "Latin Averroism." For Siger's philosophy, see Fernand van Steenberghen, *Thomas Aquinas and Radical Aristotelianism* (Washington, D.C.: Catholic University of America Press, 1980); and John Wippel, "Siger of Brabant," in *Routledge Encyclopedia of Philosophy*, vol. 8 (ed. E. Craig; London: Routledge, 1998), 764–68.

33. Zachary Hayes, for example, says that Bonaventure "cannot accept the categories of Greek metaphysics in an uncritical way for every form of philosophical metaphysics is open to correction and completion in light of the New Testament." Hayes, "Christology

and Metaphysics in the Thought of Bonaventure," *Journal of Religion*, supplement to vol. 58 (1975): 82–96. (I owe this reference to the kindness of Kevin Hughes of Villanova University). John Wippel further points out that Bonaventure, in his conferences of 1267, entitled *Collationes de decem praeceptis*, railed against the improper use of philosophical investigation in certain matters such as the eternity of the world and the unicity of the intellect. For Bonaventure, "radical Aristotelianism" indicated a wanton use of philosophical reasoning no longer theologically controlled. Wippel, *Mediaeval Reactions to the Encounter between Faith and Reason* (The Aquinas Lecture of 1995; Milwaukee: Marquette University Press, 1995), 79 n. 27. For Albert on this issue, see Fernand van Steenberghen, *La philosophie au XIIIe siècle* (2nd ed.; Louvain-Paris, 1991), 245–75.

34. *ST* I, q. 1, a. 8.

35. *ST* I, q. 27, a. 1.

36. *SCG* I, 7. A recent book by Charles Murray, *Human Accomplishment: The Pursuit of Excellence in the Arts and Sciences, 800 B.C. to 1950* (New York: HarperCollins, 2003), goes so far as to say that the cultural, scientific, and humanistic hegemony of Europe between the thirteenth and mid-nineteenth centuries was likely occasioned by Aquinas's claim that human reason, no less than faith, is a gift from God, meant to penetrate the intelligibility of creation. While Aquinas was certainly a significant purveyor of this point of view, it is certainly not true that he was alone in this enterprise. Further, it is clear that here, as in so many areas, Aquinas was developing and enhancing a tradition that had been firmly rooted in Christian thought.

37. Thomas Aquinas, "Commentary on the 'De Trinitate,'" in *The Trinity and the Unicity of the Intellect* (trans. Sister Rose Brennan; St. Louis: Herder, 1946), question 2, article 3, p. 56. Citations in the text come from largely this commentary, although I have occasionally altered the translations.

38. The "comely captive," a somewhat frequent image of secular wisdom in the early Christian writers, is taken from Deuteronomy 21:10–14. For more on the "comely captive" trope, see Frizzell, "Spoils from Egypt," 391. Also see Henri de Lubac, *Exégèse médiévale*, vol. 1 (Paris: Aubier, 1959), 290–92.

39. Aquinas was well aware of the limitations of fallen reason. Even while he praises the *lumen naturale*, he makes clear that the light of faith must always discipline reason since the natural light is subject to sin and thus easily led astray. Alfred Freddoso is entirely right when he says that medieval theologians saw themselves as the successors of those ancient philosophers who had initiated the search for wisdom "but had been incapable of bringing [it] to fulfillment in the absence of Christian revelation. . . . Indeed, this commonly shared perception of themselves as the intellectual heirs of the classical philosophers helps explain the naturalness with which the Catholic medievals carried out their interestingly diverse attempts to assimilate . . . a wide variety of non-Christian philosophical traditions." Freddoso, "Ockham on Faith and Reason," in *The Cambridge Companion to Ockham* (ed. Paul Vincent Spade; Cambridge: Cambridge University Press, 1999), 328.

40. Of course, Aquinas was convinced that reason itself, properly used, could go a long way toward disarming philosophical errors. Further, given the coinherence of faith and reason, one could not advance a specious form of the "double truth" theory, holding one principle by reason and another by faith. Aquinas firmly adheres to two theses: (1) Faith and reason cannot ultimately contradict each other, since both are gifts of God, and (2) faith always has priority over philosophical insights, which explains, as John Wippel observes, his passion against that anonymous defender of the unicity of the intellect who claimed, "By reason I conclude that the intellect is numerically one; nevertheless, I firmly hold to the opposite by faith." Wippel, *Mediaeval Reactions to the Encounter*, 31. To this kind of rationalist approach, Aquinas responds, "He judges that faith is concerned with

doctrines the contrary of which can be concluded 'of necessity.' Since, however, what I conclude of necessity can only be what is necessarily true . . . it follows that faith must be demanded in what is false and impossible: a thing that not even God could do. But the ears of men who have faith cannot endure such words." Aquinas, "On the Unicity of the Intellect," in Brennan, *Trinity and the Unicity of the Intellect*, chapter 7, 276.

41. See Steenberghen, *Thomas Aquinas and Radical Aristotelianism*; and Wippel, "Siger of Brabant."

42. Aquinas, for example, subtly worked his way around Aristotle on the issue of monopsychism, showing why individuated human souls are necessary as the "form" of the body and why monopsychism is untenable.

43. See Etienne Gilson, *Being and Some Philosophers* (Toronto: Pontifical Medieval Institute, 1952).

44. While Robert Jenson is entirely right in saying that "the concept of being is incurably theological," the major issue is how that concept, a child of Athens, is ultimately disciplined by Christian faith. Needless to add, Jenson is entirely cognizant of this point, with much of his theology revolving around just such recognition. See Jenson, *Systematic Theology* (New York: Oxford University Press, 1997), 1:208.

45. Etienne Gilson, *Being and Some Philosophers*, 157; cited in Rodney Howsare, "A Trojan Horse in the Catholic Church: On Balthasar's Interpretation of Barth," *Fides Quaerens Intellectum* 1 (2001): 282 n. 19.

46. Jenson, *Systematic Theology*, 1:21, 212–14.

47. Wippel, *Mediaeval Reactions to the Encounter*, 11.

48. See *Enchiridion symbolorum definitionum et declarationum de rebus fidei et morum* (ed. Peter Hünermann; Freiburg: Herder, 1991), DH 824.

49. John Wippel thoroughly examines the condemnations of Aristotelianism in theology by Tempier in Wippel, "The Condemnations of 1270 and 1277," *Journal of Medieval and Renaissance Studies* 7 (1977): 169–201. See also Wippel, *Mediaeval Reactions to the Encounter*, 14–28.

50. To say this, of course, is not to ignore that several of Aquinas's positions were themselves touched by the condemnations of 1277, as Mandonnet, Gilson, Wippel, and many others have argued.

51. In just this regard, Stanley Hauerwas has recently observed that Aquinas, at the very outset of the *Summa theologiae*, makes clear that the spoils trope is operative, assuming the subservience of the disciplines to theology: "For whatever is encountered in the other sciences which is incompatible with its [theology's] truth should be completely condemned as false: accordingly the second epistle to the Corinthians alludes to the pulling down of ramparts, destroying counsels, and every height that rears itself against the knowledge of God (II Cor. 10, 4–5)." See Hauerwas, *With the Grain of the Universe* (Grand Rapids: Brazos Press, 2001), 23. For this very reason Hauerwas, despite the very little emphasis he gives to first philosophy throughout his work, registers his approval of metaphysics early on in his Gifford Lectures, saying that it is helpful for "displaying the truthfulness of theological claims." Hauerwas, *With the Grain of the Universe*, 37. But while Hauerwas is convinced that a metaphysical approach properly subordinating philosophy to faith is entirely legitimate, he does not see, perhaps because of an overweening Barthianism married to his fondness for contemporary nonfoundationalist thought, that some *prima philosophia* is, in fact, necessary if theology is not to fall into fideistic assertion, lacking the further intelligibility provided by the philosophical order.

52. For more on Luther's relationship to Aristotle, see the comprehensive work of Theodor Dieter, *Der junge Luther and Aristoteles* (Berlin: Walter de Gruyter, 2001). Dieter indicates not only those aspects of Aristotle rejected by Luther but also those elements in

the philosopher's thought (such as the notion of act/potency) that Luther used to show the processive nature of Christian life. See also W. Eckermann, "Die Aristoteleskritik Luthers: Ihre Bedeutung für seine Theologie," *Catholica* 32 (1978): 114–30. For reason as "Dame Witch," see *Luther's Works* (ed. J. Pelikan and H. Lehmann; St. Louis: Concordia, 1955–1986), 24:91. For Aristotle as a "heathen philosopher" see *Luther's Works*, 52:165; for "heathen philosophy," see *Luther's Works*, 2:302.

53. *Luther's Works*, 34:137ff. All citations in the text refer to this English edition of Luther's works.

54. "Philosophers and Aristotle are not able to understand or define what the theological man is, but by the grace of God we are able to do it, because we have the Bible" (*Luther's Works* 34:142).

55. *Luther's Works*, 24:99. I thank Steve Webb of Wabash College for bringing this passage to my attention.

56. Luther sees the Scholastic thesis that truth is the same in philosophy and theology as absurd since philosophy cannot begin to grasp such matters as the nature of the incarnate Word. He may not fully realize, however, that this thesis, which Aquinas defended against the "double truth theory," was propounded precisely in order to protect the hegemony of the Christian faith against the radical Aristotelians at Paris in the thirteenth century. Lateran V's condemnation of P. Pomponazzi (without mentioning him) in 1513 was also intended to prevent the development of an imperialist philosophy (essentially an Averroes-inspired neo-Aristotelianism) entirely independent of faith's truths. Luther opposes to the claim that "truth is the same in philosophy and theology" the Pauline claim (which he takes to be its antithesis) that "all thought is to be taken captive to the obedience of Christ." He fails to see that it is just this Pauline dictum that ultimately inspired both Aquinas and Lateran V (whatever this council's other limitations).

57. As Graham White notes, Luther's intention was to define clear boundaries between theology on the one hand, and natural science and philosophy on the other. White, *Luther as Nominalist* (Helsinki: Luther-Agricola Society, 1994), 31.

58. It is worth mentioning here that the letter of Pope Gregory IX to the Parisian masters of July, 1228, cautioning theologians to expound their theology according to the approved tradition of the saints and not with "carnal weapons" since "in the power of God is destroyed every obstacle to the knowledge of God," is not really so far from Luther's thought. Of course, Luther's anthropology vis-à-vis original sin would also have to be considered in any fuller treatment of this issue.

59. For Augustine, see Rist, *Augustine*, 291.

60. *ST* II-II, q. 2, a. 4; cited in Freddoso, "Ockham on Faith and Reason," 328–29. Freddoso goes on to observe that sometimes Ockham is unfavorably contrasted with Aquinas, with the latter portrayed as a defender of standards of natural rationality while the former as emphasizing the limitations of "unaided" reason. However, "such a portrayal obscures the firmness with which *all* the important Catholic medieval thinkers held to the conviction that divine revelation is absolutely necessary for us to flourish as human beings and that, as far as ultimate metaphysical and moral questions are concerned, we remain in an utterly perilous state of ignorance without it." Freddoso, "Ockham on Faith and Reason," 330.

61. John Henry Newman, *Development of Christian Doctrine* (London: Longmans, Green & Co., 1894), 382.

62. Ibid., 382.

63. Even Gilson, hardly a man with Modernist sympathies, admitted that the suppression of Modernism was conducted by unreasonable men. See *Lettres de monsieur Étienne Gilson au père de Lubac* (Paris: Cerf, 1986), 76.

64. Of course, one may also argue that in this continual reversion to Aquinas, the magisterium sought to keep the gospel and Christian faith far from the entanglements of an ultimately anti-Christian Kantianism. In this sense, then, even though unduly restrictive, the magisterium was defending the proper understanding of faith's hegemony vis-à-vis philosophy.

65. Henri de Lubac, *Catholicism* (trans. L. Sheppard; New York: Longmans, Green & Co., 1950), 149–53.

66. Henri de Lubac, *The Drama of Atheist Humanism* (trans. E. Riley; London: Sheed & Ward, 1949), vi.

67. De Lubac, *Catholicism*, 144, 116, 152.

68. Henri de Lubac, *Theological Fragments* (trans. R. H. Balinski; San Francisco: Ignatius, 1989), 96. The citation is from de Lubac's article, "Apologétique et théologie," *La nouvelle revue théologique* 57 (1930): 361–78.

69. De Lubac, *Catholicism*, 172. For the role Vincent of Lerins's "second rule" (*in eodem sensu eademque sententia*) has played in Roman Catholic theology, see Thomas Guarino, "Vincent of Lerins and the Hermeneutical Question," *Gregorianum* 75 (1994): 491–523.

70. De Lubac, *Catholicism*, 172.

71. Henri de Lubac, *A Brief Catechesis on Nature and Grace* (trans. R. Arnandez; San Francisco: Ignatius, 1984), 69; citing Augustine, *Confessions*, VII, 16.

72. Hans Urs von Balthasar, "On the Tasks of Catholic Philosophy in Our Time," *Communio* 20 (1993): 155. Page numbers in the text refer to this article.

73. Of course, despite the glowing comments here, it did not take long for Balthasar to sour on the achievements of transcendental philosophy and theology. Since Balthasar was soon to come under the more pronounced influence of Barth's thought, one wonders if it was precisely Barth, with his animus against philosophical predeterminations of the gospel (real and perceived), that led to Balthasar's change of heart.

74. Hans Urs von Balthasar, *The Theology of Karl Barth* (trans. Edward Oakes; San Francisco: Ignatius, 1992), 257. It is precisely because revelation must discipline the natural order that Balthasar can say, "*Spolia Aegyptiorum*: the famous image so much discussed by the Fathers, expresses the essential: the investment of the rightful heir with the goods of an earlier culture." But Balthasar is equally clear that such "spoils" can only *portend* the glory of God, not substitute for it. See Balthasar, *The Glory of the Lord*, vol. 4 (trans. Brian McNeil et al.; San Francisco: Ignatius, 1989), 320.

75. See John Riches, "Balthasar and the Analysis of Faith," in *The Analogy of Beauty* (ed. John Riches; Edinburgh: T&T Clark, 1986), 53.

76. Hans Urs von Balthasar, *Love Alone* (trans. A. Dru; New York: Herder & Herder, 1969), 34.

77. Balthasar, *Truth is Symphonic*, 54.

78. Ibid., 62. I find ultimately unconvincing the intent behind Roger Haight's rhetorical question, "What would have been the result [in Christology] if Christianity had spread toward the East?" The implication here, given earlier considerations in his work, is that concepts such as the "hypostatization of the Logos and a pattern of objectivist thinking" would have been unknown and therefore given rise to a very different understanding of Christ's identity. While it is certainly true that there would have been different concepts and formulations in use, and no doubt different perspectives would have been brought to light, is it not also true that fundamental affirmations regarding the divinity of Christ and the Trinity would be essentially changed? See Roger Haight, *Jesus, Symbol of God* (Maryknoll, N.Y.: Orbis, 2000), 270–71.

79. The encyclical clearly exaggerates the positions of several of the best thinkers (no individual was named by the document) when it says that "the bolder spirits" hope to

reconceptualize dogmatic statements, statements in which the truth is approximated "but at the same time is necessarily deformed" (DH 3882). To reformulate Christian teaching was certainly one goal of these theologians; however, it was never a matter of understanding Christian doctrine in a way that would betray a teaching's original intention.

80. For an examination of Pope John XXIII's comments prior to the council and of the council's nuanced endorsement of conceptual pluralism, see Thomas Guarino, *Revelation and Truth* (Scranton, Pa.: University of Scranton Press, 1993), appendix.

81. I have examined at some length, from a study of the *Acta synodalia*, the kind of theological pluralism sanctioned by Vatican II. See Guarino, *Revelation and Truth*, 166–79.

82. For Barth's comments on these streams of thought, see *Church Dogmatics*, I/1 (trans. G. T. Thomson; Edinburgh: T&T Clark, 1960), x–40.

83. Ibid., x.

84. Karl Barth, *Church Dogmatics*, III/2 (ed. G. W. Bromiley and T. F. Torrance; Edinburgh: T&T Clark, 1960), 282–83.

85. Ibid., 283–84.

86. Karl Barth, *Church Dogmatics*, II/1 (ed. G. W. Bromiley and T. F. Torrance; Edinburgh: T&T Clark, 1957), 260.

87. As Balthasar says, Barth recognized that the concept of being cannot be avoided in theology's doctrine of God, even if Barth rightly cautions against allowing the philosophical notion of being to predetermine the contents of Christian faith and doctrine. See Balthasar, *Theology of Karl Barth* (trans. Edward Oakes; San Francisco: Ignatius, 1992), 164.

88. Gerhard Sauter, *Eschatological Rationality* (Grand Rapids: Baker Books, 1996), 122, citing *CD* IV/3. Sauter further discusses this issue in *Gateways to Dogmatics* (Grand Rapids: Eerdmans, 2003), 257–59.

89. Sauter comments that Barth's thought on this subject is often difficult to ascertain precisely because he rarely made his own method the object of reflection.

90. Jenson, *Systematic Theology*, 1:21. While agreeing with Barth that one should not understand reality *remoto Christo*, one may nevertheless ask if his application of this principle did not lead to exaggerations in interpretation. Barth's well-known claim, for example, that the ontological argument in Anselm's *Proslogion* is not substantially philosophical or apologetic in character seems contrary to all the available evidence. Henri Bouillard offers a very sympathetic portrayal of Barth's claim (insisting, against Gilson, that one cannot a priori claim that Anselm's work is not theological) while simultaneously arguing that Anselm, elaborating his proof within the horizon of faith, intended that it have a rational validity independent of faith. See Barth, *Anselm: Fides Quaerens Intellectum* (trans. Ian Robertson; Richmond: John Knox Press, 1960), 36–43. Bouillard treated Barth's argument in several places. One of the best is "La preuve de Dieu dans le 'Proslogion' et son interprétation par Karl Barth," in *Spicilegium Beccense* (Paris: J. Vrin, 1959), 191–207. See also M. J. Charlesworth, *St. Anselm's Proslogion* (Oxford: Clarendon, 1965), 40–46.

91. Karl Barth, "Fate and Idea in Theology," in *The Way of Theology in Karl Barth* (ed. H. Martin Rumscheidt; trans. George Hunsinger; Allison Park, Pa.: Pickwick Publications, 1986), 29.

92. Barth thinks Aquinas's notion of analogy comes perilously close to philosophy because it means that "even at its lowest level human existence participates in the *lumen divinum* of the highest level." Barth argues that the twin pillars of Aquinas's thought— *gratia non destruit sed supponit et perficit naturam* and the *analogia entis*—indicate that human beings participate in the *similitudo Dei* even apart from grace. Barth, "Fate and Idea in Theology," 38–39. This is of a piece with Barth's idea that metaphysics—or any *prima*

philosophia—even if salubriously disciplined and chastened by Christian belief, represents not a further explication and philosophical aid to faith but a rationalist competitor to faith's primacy.

93. A good analysis of Barth's 1929 essay, "Fate and Idea," may be found in A. Katherine Grieb, "Pharaoh's Magicians at the Holy of Holies? Appraising an Early Debate between Tillich and Barth on the Relationship between Philosophy and Theology," *Scottish Journal of Theology* 56 (2003): 360–80.

94. The conciliar *loci classici* here are *Gaudium et spes*, 62, and *Unitatis redintegratio*, 4, 6, and 17.

95. Aidan Nichols, "Thomism and the *Nouvelle Théologie*," *Thomist* 64 (2000): 19.

96. Congregation for the Doctrine of the Faith, "Instruction on the Ecclesial Vocation of the Theologian," *Origins* 20 (1990).

97. A very similar sentiment was earlier expressed by the Congregation for the Doctrine of the Faith in its 1984 statement on liberation theology: "The use of philosophical positions or of human sciences by the theologian has a value which might be called instrumental, but yet must undergo a critical study from a theological perspective. In other words, the ultimate and decisive criterion for truth can only be a criterion which is itself theological. It is only in the light of faith and what faith teaches us about the truth of humankind and the ultimate meaning of human destiny that one can judge the validity or degree of validity of what other disciplines propose, often rather conjecturally, as being the truth about humankind, its history and its destiny." "Instruction on Certain Aspects of the 'Theology of Liberation,'" *Acta apostolicae sedis* 76 (1984): 892–93.

98. John Paul II, "Fides et ratio," *Acta apostolicae sedis* 91 (1999): 5–88. An English translation may be found in *Origins* 28 (October 22, 1998): 317–47. The encyclical is dated September 14, 1998. Numbers in parentheses indicate paragraphs in the encyclical.

99. The document prescinds from the question of the possibility of revelation outside of the Judeo-Christian tradition. John Paul II had treated this issue more fully in his earlier encyclical *Redemptoris Missio*, where the notion of "participated mediation" plays a larger role.

100. For example, on the same points, see the encyclical's citation of the Cappadocians, Dionysius, Augustine (40), Anselm (42), and its explanation of Tertullian's famous Athens/Jerusalem dichotomy (41).

101. The encyclical cites here the *Stromata* I, 20; and *Sources chrétiennes* 30, 124. It should be noted that "hedge" and "wall" in this sense do not mean that philosophy is a necessary bulwark for an otherwise helpless faith. Clement says, rather, that philosophy is useful for rendering sophistry impotent and disarming those who betray truth. The encyclical, then, is careful to note Clement's christological focus: "The teaching of the Saviour is perfect in itself and has no need of support, because it is the strength and wisdom of God" (38).

102. The encyclical then goes on at some length to argue that the proper spoils typology, with the sublation of philosophy into theology, at times demands the intervention of the Roman magisterium to ensure that philosophy does not improperly contort theology to its own image. The encyclical explains that the "magisterium's interventions are intended above all to prompt, promote and encourage philosophical inquiry" (51). It points out that many streams of thought have needed to be rebuked because they were "erroneous and negative." On the other hand, in commenting on just this passage, Walter Kasper asks whether, in the case of Antonio Rosmini, an Italian philosopher, the magisterium's interventions "were influenced by other passions than the love of truth." Kasper, "Magisterium's Interventions in Philosophical Matters," *L'Osservatore Romano* (English edition), April 28, 1999, 5–6.

103. John Paul II made a similar point in his statement on the Galileo case: "It is a duty for theologians to keep themselves regularly informed of scientific advances in order to examine, if such be necessary, whether or not there are reasons for taking them into account in their reflections or for introducing changes in their teaching." "Lessons of the Galileo Case," *Origins* 22 (November 12, 1992): 372. What the pope here says about the physical sciences must surely be the case, *mutatis mutandis,* for the human sciences as well.

104. On the nature of philosophy's autonomy according to *Fides et ratio,* see Avery Dulles, "Can Philosophy Be Christian?" *First Things,* no. 102 (April 2000): 24–29.

CHAPTER 10

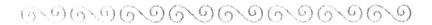

Correlation and Contemporary Models

Contemporary Models of Correlation

The great recent classics on the issue of correlation remain those of H. Richard Niebuhr and Paul Tillich. While a full study cannot be granted to them here, it is enough to say that Niebuhr treated the historical, paradigmatic issues, without necessarily taking full account of all of the vital philosophical questions lurking at the base of his various models.[1] Tillich, on the other hand, while certainly aware of the theoretical issues, and while clearly endorsing the spoils typology, had little interest in exploring the extent to which philosophy can offer further intelligibility to the universal and enduring claims of Christian faith and doctrine. On the contrary, his work has the more explicitly apologetical intent of displaying how questions arising from philosophy and the contemporary cultural "situation" constitute a "first moment" ultimately issuing forth in a theology charged with establishing an intrinsic correlation between the "existential" pole and the pole constituted by Christian faith itself.[2] Consequently, while Tillich's method of correlation remains important (especially as regards the extent to which Christian and existential claims may be related), it is not entirely germane to the questions of philosophy and doctrine discussed here.

Instead, I will move to two important contemporary models for the relationship between theology and the disciplines, known respectively as postliberalism and revisionist thought. These approaches are entirely relevant to the issues discussed throughout this work. I will argue that while both theological positions have significant merit, both insufficiently recognize how the historical use of the spoils trope provides useful guidance for contemporary thought.

Background

Of particular interest today is how the typology of "despoiling the Egyptians" has changed in light of the widespread theological turn toward contemporary nonfoundationalist philosophy.[3] Nonfoundationalism, used here not simply as an antonym for evidential empiricism but in the wider sense discussed previously, essentially accepts the criticisms of the Western philosophical tradition leveled preeminently by Heidegger and Wittgenstein. The former claimed that Western thought, in both its classical metaphysical and modern transcendental versions, had fallen victim to the ontotheological tradition, with its identification of God and being and with its twin foundationalist shoals of substance and subject. In a similar vein, the later Wittgenstein argued that philosophy, as encapsulated in the Augustinian-Cartesian tradition of ostensive definition, moved ineluctably toward a calculating and manipulative understanding of reality that ignored the swarming and irreducible forms of life and linguistic communities constituting the *Lebenswelt*. Both thinkers resist traditional attempts at universalizing thought as characteristic of an outdated and ontologically inappropriate metaphysics, *prima philosophia*, or *Ursprungsphilosphie*. On the contrary, they seek to expose the overarching horizons of historicity and temporality that totally saturate and suffuse human life and thought. Traditional attempts at understanding the nature of being and truth are properly subject to deconstruction because they fail to account for the newly presenced life-world and are, therefore, philosophically inappropriate.

For this kind of nonfoundationalism, prior recognition must be accorded not to universalizing thought but to the cultural-linguistic determinacy of forms of life and to the encompassing horizons of human finitude. Claims to truth are not here disallowed; such claims, however, must take full account of our postmetaphysical, posttranscendental, postmodern situation. Ontologically *appropriate* notions of truth must acknowledge the fissiparous and fragmented nature of human existence, the decentered subject and the enveloping presence of *lēthē* and *différ(a)nce*.

The two schools to be examined, widely known as postliberalism and revisionism, usually associated with Yale and Chicago, are taken as prime exemplars. These schools of thought are often perceived as being opposed, or as taking very different approaches to theology. I will argue that insofar as each of them relies heavily on nonfoundationalist positions, the difference between them is much less than is sometimes supposed.[4]

Postliberalism

The term "postliberalism" has been widely associated with the work of George Lindbeck and, with nuances, various other thinkers.[5] Strongly influenced by the notions of incommensurability, historicity, and sociocultural particularity pulsating through the work of Wittgenstein, Quine, Sellars, Kuhn, and Geertz, postliberal thinkers are united in their distaste for universalizing or metaphysical thought. Having placed these "defenders of difference" in their collective pantheon, Lindbeck and other postliberals logically avoid speaking about "universals" of any kind, whether it is a matter of universal religious experience or universal standards of rationality. Such encompassing speech indicates a severe epistemic misunderstanding of the radical flux and difference penetrating all levels of thought and regulative forms of life. It is precisely their illegitimate claim to universality that causes Lindbeck to reject both the cognitive-propositionalist and experiential-expressivist models dominant in some theological quarters.[6]

Postliberal thinkers argue, rather, that if one gives proper weight to the finite, the particular, and the local, then one speaks not of universal experiences and standards, but of enveloping cultural-linguistic systems, of encircling networks and webs of belief, of the incommensurability informing various conceptual frameworks. Human thinking, acting, and judging are deeply rooted in the forms of life from which they emerge. And Christianity is not exempt from this determinacy. It too has its own forms of rationality and justification; its truth-warrants and criteria are to be found in the Christian community itself, not in universal standards imported or imposed from elsewhere.[7] Truth-claims should not be measured, therefore, against external, universally accessible norms. Such an approach is ontologically inappropriate, resurrecting classical and Enlightenment modes of thought that the newly presenced horizons of nonfoundationalism have discredited and superseded. Truth is to be found, rather, in the standards, warrants, and rules proper to the uniquely Christian form of life.

Criteria and canons, then, used to judge one community are necessarily inapplicable to another. This is precisely the reason we have moved past rationalist modernity to postliberal postmodernity. The overarching circumscription by sociolinguistic worlds demands that postliberalism reject the claims of transcendental thinkers (even if they are truly historicized metaphysicians) such as Lonergan and Rahner, as well as those advanced by Schleiermacher and all "experiential" reactions to neo-Kantianism. These very different brands of universalism are both philosophically and theologically inappropriate.

One major reason postliberals resist this kind of universal metaphysical or transcendental thought is because they see it as a secular Archimedean level, a purely philosophical warrant by which some thinkers, even those entirely unconnected with the house of faith, seek to judge Christian belief. The gospel of grace now becomes secondary to some prior unity, some prior "foundation," some epistemological or metaphysical standard to which the Christian message must submit its truth-claims.[8] But cultural-linguistic systems are incommunicable; modes of verification and justification are proper and unique to specific forms of life. Christian theology, therefore, is under no obligation to offer public warrants for its claims or to defer to any kind of extrabiblical adjudication.

Questions that quickly arose about postliberal theology remain with us today: Does the avoidance of universal and public standards of truth and rationality limit theology merely to intrasystemic consistency? And does such "intratextual coherence" offer us an adequate notion of truth? It certainly appears that on any "strong" version of the postliberal model, the issue of reference disappears.[9] As Geoffrey Wainwright has said, "[Lindbeck's] theory of truth appears inadequate, at least to the claims Christians have traditionally thought they were making for their message and teaching."[10]

Even if Lindbeck has not been entirely clear on the referential nature of Christian truth-claims, he, along with postliberalism generally, is certainly clear that such assertions do not rely on first principles adduced from philosophical systems outside of faith. Christian theology affirms and substantiates its beliefs on the basis of the gospel alone. One sees in this position a healthy postliberal reprise of the *sola gratia, sola fide* tradition; one espies here as well as a renewed Barthian emphasis on the priority of the evangelical content of faith as opposed to existential/ontological/transcendental predeterminations. Such predeterminations, of course, constitute the "secular misery" that Barth described in his prolegomena, the subjection of the gospel to the alien standards of Protestant liberalism and Roman Catholic neo-Scholasticism.

An enduring question about postliberalism remains, however, with regard to the spoils from Egypt tradition under discussion. One wonders, for example, if postliberalism, in rightly asserting the priority of gospel claims over and against particular philosophical approaches (thereby rejecting the determinative nature of extrinsic warrants), does not move too severely in the direction of a faith/reason dichotomy, failing to search for a philosophy that is ontologically appropriate, that is, one helping to illuminate postliberalism's own assertions about Christian faith and doctrine. It is one thing to hold that Christianity submits its claims for public validation by alien warrants only at its peril. Postliberalism rightly argues that this would constitute, in fact, an illegitimate capitulation to secular, extrabiblical norms now inappropriately adjudicating doctrinal teaching. It is another matter altogether, however, to argue that Christian faith cannot use some kind of metaphysics to explicate philosophically its universal assertions. For this reason postliberalism has surrounding it something of the scent of fideism, meaning that assertions are made without necessarily showing how such claims are also philosophically intelligible.[11] Again, this is not a matter of making philosophy an alien, predetermining norm of the Christian faith; it is matter of showing the extent to which Christian faith and philosophy, properly understood, conjunctively cohere.[12] It is perhaps here that the salubriously chastising aspect of the *sola fide, sola gratia* perspective takes an unfortunate turn, driving an unnecessary Tertullianesque stake between faith and reason. The assertion of Christian truth is combined with a rejection of overarching philosophies because the latter systems are perceived less as *ancillae (atque liberae)* and more as competitors.[13]

Postliberalism, then, rightly understands one essential aspect of the spoils from Egypt typology, namely, that Christian faith and doctrine must always be hegemonic, that philosophy and the other disciplines are ultimately at the service of the claims of Christian faith. This is the meaning of Lindbeck's claim that we must once again take up "the ancient practice of absorbing the universe into the biblical world."[14] However, postliberalism also seems to think that in order to legitimize this option for Christian faith, one must not only show the real inadequacies of Enlightenment modernity (a legitimate goal) but also, concomitantly, accept in its entirety the postpositivist, nonfoundationalist philosophical accent on historicity and cultural-linguistic specificity. The acceptance of the latter, some argue, deconstructs rationalist Enlightenment pretensions, opening the way to "foundations" other than those purveyed by modernity. However, a truer appropriation of the spoils typology would indicate that there are philosophies available that can support and further explain precisely how the claims of Christian doctrine (intelligible in themselves) and the material identity of Christian faith through the ages (including a certain dimension of meaning-invariance, to once again invoke the hermeneutical issue) may receive philosophical support as well. One need not neglect these supportive philosophies in order to allow the splendor of divine revelation—in its foundational priority and form—to appear. It is this aspect of the typology, however, that Lindbeck and postliberalism, perhaps overly reliant on a particular *sola gratia* interpretation, with nature and grace at antipodes, neglect.[15]

It is precisely this neglectful aspect that "revisionist" theology seeks to rectify.

Revisionist Theology

Seemingly opposed to postliberalism, with its unabashed assertion of Christian belief and doctrine, is revisionist theology, a label widely associated with David Tracy and others. Unlike postliberalism, revisionist theology is concerned with defending and adjudicating theological truth-claims by means of publicly warrantable criteria.[16] Revisionist thought fears that postliberalism, with its accent on the cultural-linguistic embeddedness of the Christian form of life, taken together with its claim that adjudicatory criteria are theory-specific, is inordinately preoccupied with mere internal coherency, thereby courting the possibility that theology will become locked in a closed circle, excluded from the larger world of scholarly and humane discourse.[17]

This quest to establish public criteria for the redemption of Christian truth-claims has led to the postliberal countercharge that the revisionist position reverts to untenable universalist and Enlightenment standards of rationality. On closer inspection, however, the revisionist stance, despite its emphasis on publicly redeemable warrants, is, in many ways, quite close to postliberalism. Both methodologies are deeply indebted to Heidegger, Wittgenstein, and contemporary nonfoundationalist philosophy in general. Like postliberalism, then, revisionist theology accepts the ontological priority of temporality and historical embeddedness and the consequent illusion of searching out first principles or Archimedean points whether metaphysical, transcendental, or phenomenological. Any attempt to use such principles would be to illegitimately ignore the deconstruction of *prima philosophia* wrought by contemporary nonfoundationalist thought.[18]

On the other hand, the revisionist theological trajectory does seek to develop some philosophical justification for its assertions. Unlike postliberalism, revisionist thought holds that all validity claims, including theological ones, must have public attestation; in Habermasian terms, truth-claims must be redeemed by publicly available warrants rather than by authoritarian assertion. Such an approach is ultimately fueled by the desire to justify theology in the educational and political marketplace, to establish the discipline as a legitimate academic, and therefore public, enterprise. This task becomes especially urgent when thinkers such as Habermas argue that theology must be excised from the public forum because its assertions are not open to domination-free discussion.

What must be clearly understood is that the public redemption of truth-claims that revisionist thought defends must be on decidedly non-foundationalist grounds. Something of the Enlightenment concern for universality is retrievable, but this retrieval must be in accordance with the encompassing horizons of historicity and sociocultural specificity.[19] The revisionist concern, then, for universality and publicness should not be confused with notions of truth and rationality interested in enforcing transcultural or metaphysical absolutes. On the contrary, revisionism holds that one must avoid the univocal Enlightenment notion of rationality that led to manipulatable domination and, in a backlash, to the contemporary rage against reason reflected in certain radical strands of postmodern thought. It is not a matter, then, of seeking unshakable foundations or principles, but of pursuing notions of truth and rationality neither bound by the metaphysical *epistēmē* nor locked into a (postliberal) noncommunicative cultural system. Revisionists, therefore, explore ideas of truth and rationality emerging from Peirce's community of inquirers, James's consistent, ethical pragmatism, Habermas's ideal-speech situation, and Gadamer's rehabilitation of Aristotelian *phronēsis*. Thinkers such as Tracy continue to grope for appropriate notions of truth that do not require the metaphysical or transcendental supports (even if such supports are adduced a posteriori in light of the demands of Christian faith and doctrine) associated with more traditional referential theories.[20] This move allows a certain dimension of universality to be reclaimed, but without adhering to the standards of universality found in classical or Enlightenment construals of human rationality. Revisionists argue, then, that we are all gathered in the "rocking hull" of contingencies and none of us, even those on the ship of faith, has a secure and privileged position amidst the roiling tides of historicity.

This embrace of nonfoundationalist thought, coupled with an accent on the justification of Christian truth-claims by publicly warrantable criteria, causes revisionist theology to introduce into the traditional spoils from Egypt typology a deeply lethic sense. One now cannot take the assertions of Christian faith and doctrine to be normative a priori as tra-

ditionally understood by the *fides quaerens intellectum*. It is less a matter
of Christianity taking "spoils from Egypt" as it is a mutually critical
despoiling in which the criteria for the adequacy for such despoiling must
be redeemed in the public square.[21] To the claim that it has abandoned the
purity of Christianity for the golden calf of mutuality and public redemption, revisionist theology responds that the mere assertion of
Christianity's truth ghettoizes the faith, excluding it from the larger world
of scholarly and humane discourse.

In some ways, of course, the revisionist school is echoing classical
Christian, particularly Roman Catholic, themes.[22] Its concern with "publicness," for example, with the idea that some evidence for faith is available to all reasonable inquirers, strikes a deeply resonant chord in the
Christian tradition. The endorsement of true interchange between theology and the disciplines is firmly rooted in the Catholic understanding of
the relationship between faith and reason, grace and nature. In seeking a
common language of discourse between Christianity and other narratives,
revisionist thought avoids a complete privatization of faith antithetical to
the deepest instincts of a well-wrought theology.

On the other hand, the reflections of revisionist thought raise significant questions: To what extent can Christianity justify its truth-claims
publicly, apart from faith? If revelation and its a priori authority are
eschewed, or if it can only be redeemed by the community of inquirers, by
what criteria are theological claims now authenticated? By liberative
praxis? Emancipatory transformation? Reception by the community?
Continuing claim? Consensus? While one might rightly insist that there
is an important and legitimate place for each of these criteria, can any of
them be taken as an ultimately justifying warrant? If we cannot stipulate
that the faith that seeks understanding extends a certain priority to
revealed truth and its linguistic formulation as doctrine, can we ever make
any final determinations about Christianity's ultimate content and message?[23] Or is there only a mutually critical correlation between texts from
which, on the basis of publicly warrantable and redeemable criteria, a consensus regarding truth-claims emerges?

Evaluation
In the final analysis, revisionism, like postliberalism, only inadequately
replicates the traditional spoils from Egypt typology bequeathed to us by
early medieval and even several modern Christian thinkers. One reason
that neither position can successfully conduct a reprise of this ancient
trope is because of their embrace of nonfoundationalist thought.

Postliberalism satisfies only one dimension of the spoils methodology by adhering to the uniqueness of revelation and the methodological priority of the *fides quaerens intellectum*. But postliberalism also embraces non-foundationalist philosophy, not, or at least not primarily, to agree with all of its assertions, but because nonfoundationalist thought *makes theoretical room for the foundational assertion of the Christian faith.* The logic appears to be this: If all statements are culturally conditioned and paradigm bound, beholden to no other criteria than those internally developed, then Christianity is similarly bound and need hardly seek warrants alien to its unique content. Unfortunately, many postliberals do not see that some appropriation by the tradition of first philosophy (whether that proposed by classical and medieval thought, [Christian] transcendental or phenomenological realism) helps to provide another dimension of intelligibility precisely for the perduring claims of faith that many postliberals seek to defend. This leaves them with an enduring assertion of the universality and continuity of Christian truth that is inappropriately wedded to a philosophy uninterested in defending such positions. It is perhaps because of a misunderstanding of the nature-grace relationship (with all of the cautions adduced in chapter seven in this regard) that postliberal theology is possibly subject to the charge of fideism.

Revisionism, on the other hand, also inadequately reprises the spoils typology, but its inadequacy stems from a different problem than that afflicting postliberalism. As noted above, revisionist thought also embraces nonfoundationalist philosophy, but not for the purpose, as with postliberalism, of opening space for a neo-Barthian assertion of the foundational character of Christian faith and doctrine. On the contrary, this must be avoided, since theology's own integrity requires public attestation for Christian claims. But this embrace of nonfoundationalist thought, even if taken in a different direction, means that, once again, only one element of the spoils from Egypt typology is satisfied, namely, the possibility of using other forms of thought for the further explication of Christian faith and doctrine. But at what price is this exchange between theology and nonfoundationalism made? How is the selfsame identity and perduring universality of Christian faith and doctrine protected in the revisionist model? By embracing the profound sociocultural and linguistic determinacy stemming from Wittgenstein, along with the pronounced accent on temporality characteristic of Heidegger, and by simultaneously renouncing the bare assertion of Christian truth (à la postliberalism), revisionist thought loses any theoretical basis for protecting and undergirding the material identity of Christian faith and doctrine in and through history. There exists now no *ontological* basis for such continuity.[24] Insofar as truth must be inextricably interlaced with its historical, cultural, and epiphanic form, one cannot legitimately speak of a universal, perduring, and continuous assertion of Christian belief.[25] Once the metaphysical grounds are expunged, then one has no basis for arguing for the fundamental identity of meaning of Christianity throughout history, unless, of course, it is simply a matter of pure assertion, which tends toward a faith/reason dichotomy. A selfsame and universal content existing within a variety of interpretative forms is now philosophically unsustainable.[26] Because historicity and sociocultural determinacy is now invoked as the most basic philosophical category, it is only with difficulty that one can speak of a universal and enduring identity of Christian faith and doctrine. For example, the truth about "who Christ is" is "given" in one way to the ancient world and is "given" another way to us today. One cannot simply take one fundamental meaning as normative, as if the conciliar definitions of Nicea and Chalcedon could act as ultimate criteria for adjudicating contemporary christological proposals. Such an approach would be ontologically inappropriate, profoundly underestimating the significant cognitive impact, the lethic effects, of history and culture. What survives from age to age, then, is not an identity of faith and doctrine. What survives, rather, are various interpretations, some of which continue to make a claim on us, continue to be liberative and transformative. Since the truth proper to theology is primarily epiphanic, perdurance and continuity are not necessarily inherent to it. Rather than defending the universality and fundamental meaning-invariance of the Christian message, theology is left to defend only the formal and historical continuity of reflection on the Christ event.[27] But this decided turn toward nonfoundationalism leads, at least seemingly, to significant dimensions of meaning-variance and "undecideability" that militates against the very notion of God's self-manifestation, of the truth which the church grasps in faith, of the unity of the *depositum fidei* (*parathēkē*, 1 Tim 6:20; 2 Tim 1:4).

There is, then, clearly a notion of "spoils" operative in revisionist thought, but one must acknowledge that this understanding moves in a quite different direction from the one sanctioned by the tradition, which did not think that the truth of ecumenical councils or of formal creedal statements is subject to the mutable and even reversible truth of historical flux.

Toward a New Typology of Spoils from Egypt

In distinction from both postliberalism and revisionism, I would like to offer a third understanding of correlation. In my judgment, this position represents a contemporary reprise of the traditional spoils typology while endorsing an important place for significant elements of a first philosophy. With the neo-Barthian postliberals, this approach rejects the secular foundationalism that seeks to provide a universally available option outside of faith now serving as a norm for faith's claims. Lindbeck is quite right in saying that Christianity cannot endorse a profane Archimedean touchstone that judges its truth-claims and acts as an epistemological standard to which Christian faith must adhere. If pushed too far, the notion of "mutually critical correlation" becomes pernicious, since the gospel cannot be understood as simply one tradition within a farrago of narratives, nor can the primacy of Christian truth be ultimately subject to publicly verifiable warrants.

At the same time, revisionist thought rightly criticizes a certain species of postliberal theology that can quickly degenerate into assertive fideism divorced from any attempt at providing philosophical warrants for universal Christian claims. By championing the notion of critical correlation, the revisionists creatively develop and advance the classical interpenetration and cross-fertilization of faith and reason, of theology and the disciplines. By resisting a simple formal assertion of Christianity's truth-claims, they recognize that such assertions, if not supplemented by public warrants, can possibly lapse into fundamentalism and ideological authoritarianism.

Both schools, then, offer significant theological insights. However, in their highly qualified typological reprise of Kierkegaard and Hegel, with, to continue Origen's analogy, one group not venturing sufficiently into Egypt while the other lingering a bit too long, they both miss, because of their largely antimetaphysical presuppositions, the third option largely operative within the Christian tradition. A certain critical correlation between Christian faith and "secular" wisdom, based on the integrity of nature, even wounded and graced nature, has been classically sanctioned in the Christian tradition. Theological history itself witnesses to this understanding of intertextual mutuality that, at the same time, is always also a symbolic "despoiling of the Egyptians." Secular narratives may, therefore, sharpen, illumine, or help explicate some aspect of Christian truth; however, the tradition has always insisted that such illumination and explication must necessarily proceed from the a priori truth of Christian faith itself. There cannot be a capitulation, by way of example, to the Habermasian demands of discourse ethics, thereby implying a complete equality among narratives and an entirely publicly warranted redemption of truth-claims. This approach violates the primacy of faith and the uniqueness of knowledge yielded by it.[28]

In this third understanding of correlation, theology is not captive to Enlightenment modernity, neither in its traditional form nor in its contemporary metamorphosis as communicative rationality. Nor is theology bound to assert the truth-claims of Christian faith and doctrine absent the benefit of further philosophical, even metaphysical (taken in a broad sense) support. With postliberalism, the normativity of the gospel message is proclaimed. However, this evangelical primacy does not need to result in a dichotomous either/or, so that a proper correlation between theology and the disciplines, especially in the form of some first philosophy, is repudiated. With revisionist thought, then, the importance of correlation is championed. However, there is an option in the act of faith such that sheer interpenetrative mutuality between theology and the disciplines is excluded. While always seeking some further elements of truth in new methods, this third option, perhaps best called, for lack of a better name, the "renewed spoils typology," recognizes the ascendancy of the revelatory narrative. And if revelation, for its further intelligibility, requires some form of metaphysics or first philosophy for the sake of protecting and explicating the unity, continuity, and material identity of the gospel message, then this too must be defended, always within the limits of the spoils methodology.[29] This third form of envisioning the proper relationship between theology and the disciplines supersedes the positions of postliberalism and revisionism by recognizing both the primacy of the gospel and the importance of mutual fertilization. At the same time, it calls into question the accepted ontological presuppositions informing the thought of both Lindbeck and Tracy as, in the last analysis, theologically inappropriate.

The goal of the renewed spoils typology is to maintain the material identity of Christian faith and doctrine while taking account of contemporary philosophical currents, of using truth wherever it may be found. It is a matter of developing a theologically appropriate notion of correlation, just as it has been a matter, throughout this work, of developing theologically apposite understandings of truth, hermeneutics, and theological language. And by theologically appropriate, I mean understandings that are able to mediate the body of Christian faith and doctrine, the *depositum fidei* that has been bequeathed to Christians today from the church of the ages. It is, in all cases, a matter of using the proper form for the body of Christian faith and life.

If theology, then, needs some notion of first philosophy, whether a classical or renewed metaphysics or a transcendental gnoseology or a realistic phenomenology in order to explicate philosophically the truth of its transgenerational and transcultural doctrinal assertions, this is not because of some a priori philosophical commitment to a particular ontology, but because such a commitment to a *prima philosophia* appears to be demanded for the sake of the intelligibility of revelation itself. Within Roman Catholicism, the epistemological achievement of Vatican II was to demonstrate that the defense of the material identity of Christianity does not require a commitment to one particular philosophical system, namely, Christianized Aristotelianism. A true pluralism of philosophies and theologies was endorsed and affirmed. However, the council endorsed only the kind of pluralism that can sustain an understanding of revelation that includes the historical identity and universal normativity of Christian faith and doctrine. "Spoils" may indeed be found everywhere; however, this absorption, correlation, and utilization of human wisdom is always normed and disciplined by the gospel's own claims. The encyclical by John Paul II, *Fides et ratio*, renews this tradition, rightly calling for both a renewed metaphysics (as essential for philosophically undergirding the claims of Christian truth) while at the same time recognizing that the church is not bound to the particular formulations of Aquinas or any other individual theologian. What is needed is precisely a *renewed* and continually dialogical search for a more adequate mediation of the deposit of faith.

Within Roman Catholicism, Bernard Lonergan and Karl Rahner represent two thinkers who understood well the need for seeking out some first philosophy in order to offer further intelligibility to the universal and perduring claims of Christian faith, while concomitantly insisting that such philosophy needs to be chastened by faith itself. Since their thought has been discussed in other chapters, there is no need to repeat it here. It is enough to say that both Lonergan and Rahner, following Joseph Maréchal, rejected Kant's claim that knowledge of God must be closeted in the realm of the noumena. More to the point, transcendental Thomism intended to show that modern philosophy, with its emphasis on universal structures of subjectivity, could, when properly elucidated, serve to confirm both the logical intelligibility of Christianity's perduring claims as well as the realistic principles essential to Christian faith and doctrine. Of course, this contemporary appropriation (and clear transformation) of modern philosophy was meant as a development of the theological tradition, not simply a repetition of it. However, even in this appropriation/transformation, two issues were never in doubt: (1) Christian faith and doctrine, revelation itself, was always the hegemonic narrative in the correlation between theology and philosophy, and (2) some philosophy was needed that was congruent with the universal and perduring claims of Christian doctrine to ensure faith's intelligibility in the philosophical order.[30]

Such principles are clearly at work in Rahner's 1977 essay in which he states that in the formulation of Christian dogma, while new *Denkstile* and conceptual forms will always be found, and while some older forms will necessarily be abandoned (e.g., the Aristotelian notion of substance vis-à-vis the Eucharistic presence of Christ), one

> must of course make simultaneously clear that the sameness of dogma in the old sense is assured and the effort to do this must not be regarded in principle as dubious, as a feeble and cowardly compromise between holding on verbally to a traditional doctrine and its formulations on the one hand, and a new perception on the other which, if expressed honestly, would presumably be bound to exclude the previous teaching as erroneous.[31]

It is clear from this citation that Rahner recognizes that various philosophies and conceptual systems will serve Christian faith for a certain period of time, but are hardly essential in and of themselves. It is Christian faith that ultimately determines what is usable and what can be jettisoned.[32] At the same time, Rahner's own philosophical commitments (he never abandoned his transcendental position even while always taking further account of its interlacing with historicity) make clear that he thought some species of universal philosophy was necessary that could further explicate Christian faith's enduring and encompassing claims. Without some such philosophy, the material identity of doctrine would either be swallowed by the maw of particularity, or be asserted without confirming warrants from the philosophical order.

A similar procedure is to be found in Lonergan's work. For example, in defending a realist understanding of truth, Lonergan baldly avers, "Realism consists in this, that the truth that is acknowledged in the mind corresponds to reality."[33] Lonergan claims that Isaiah, Paul, and Athanasius were not fully aware of the relationship between the knowing subject and the truth to which the human mind corresponds. But, he asserts, "we are saying that these men had minds, that they knew the word of God and that they lived according to the reality that they came to know through God's true word" (129).

Having established this preliminarily, Lonergan asks if it is just to say that Nicea embraced a "Hellenistic ontology." His answer is that the dogmatic realism of Nicea is anything but the importation of an alien system. Indeed, the Nicene defense of the *homoousion* is contained implicitly in the realism of the word of God. One can hardly speak, then, of an alien ontology: "The more carefully one examines the brands of Hellenistic ontology that were actually available at the time, the more obviously superfluous does any such hypothesis appear" (131). So, Lonergan argues, Tertullian's brand of Hellenism (fundamentally a form of Stoicism) does not allow him to affirm consubstantiality, while Origen's Platonism, with its subordinationist emanationism, is at "even greater remove than Tertullian from the doctrine of Nicea" (131).[34]

Lonergan's point is clear enough: "We do not mean to suggest that dogmatic realism, contained implicitly in the word of God, became an explicit realism without any contributory influence of Hellenistic culture" (131). On the contrary, Lonergan fully admits such influence. But always with the traditional spoils proviso, it is a matter of Greek metaphysics serving the affirmations of the word of God rather than bending them to their own image. Only certain philosophies are congruent with the demands of revelation. As Lonergan says, "From the beginning the word of God contained within it an implicit epistemology and ontology" (133). For him, this is a realistic epistemology, rooted ultimately in human judgment and a metaphysics that is capable of defending the universality and continuity of faith's claims. It is unsurprising then that much of Lonergan's career was devoted to explaining what he called the invariant cognitive structure of human subjectivity. It explains his claim that classical culture rightly understood that there was a universal human nature; it misunderstood the extent to which this nature was open.[35]

What is important to see in the work of Rahner and Lonergan (and one need hardly agree with their theologies, nor with their methodological approaches *in actu*) is that it is a matter of maintaining a careful balance between the priority of faith and the intelligibility required in the philosophical order for the sake of illuminating faith's claims. Theologians use and sanction particular philosophies (and will develop others in the future) because they find such systems of thought useful for explicating the church's faith, that is, the material identity, continuity, and perpetuity of the salvific narrative between God and his creatures. One sees this procedure clearly in the works of Origen, Basil, Clement, and Augustine. Aquinas bears exemplary witness to it, even as he rejects the radical Aristotelianism of those masters who would mold the faith in the image of philosophy. The Reformers recognized the necessity of it, even if they were primarily (and legitimately) concerned about the hegemony of the gospel over mere philosophizing. More recently, in Roman Catholicism alone, the process is in full evidence in the conative immanentism of Blondel, the phenomenological personalism of Marcel and Scheler, and the critical realism of Maréchal and Rahner.

Because of this intrinsic relationship between the theological and philosophical orders, one must, I think, reject Jean-Luc Marion's claim in *God without Being*: "The Gxd who reveals himself has nothing in common . . . with the 'God' of the philosophers, of the learned and, eventually, of the poet." He comes very close here to positing a complete chasm between nature and grace. But is this disjunction needed to protect God's otherness and sovereignty?[36] Does it not come very close to a retrieval of Harnack's thesis: Hellenic versus Palestinian? And does it not fail to recognize the importance for theology of confirming warrants from the "natural order?"[37] The revival of the "dehellenization" theme, of which Marion is only one representative, while rightly recognizing the possibility of reconceptualization (one is not bound to use the concepts of a particular culture, only their equivalent meanings) fails to take account of the importance of the philosophical—indeed, metaphysical—warrants for the explication of Christian faith and doctrine, and tends, ultimately, toward either a fideistic abjuration of such warrants or an untenable embrace of historicism.[38] These twin shoals constitute the foremost dangers to an understanding of faith and doctrine which is materially continuous and perduring (and, of course, in organic development) and which holds that revelation is the *locutio Dei*, the disclosure and unveiling of the living God in Jesus Christ.

Conclusion

I have argued in this chapter that the spoils trope, broadly conceived, has been operative throughout the history of Christian theology. More specifically, I have argued that some type of first philosophy is needed in order to illuminate and further substantiate theology's doctrinal claims. Only some *prima philosophia*, theologically controlled, can explicate, in its own order of intelligibility, the universal, perduring, materially continuous claims of Christian faith and thought. It is not surprising, then, that in the encyclical *Fides et ratio* John Paul II argues that "theology needs philosophy as a partner in dialogue in order to confirm the intelligibility and universal truth of its claims" (77), and that what is needed is a "renewed metaphysics."[39] Theology and the revelatory narrative evaluate philosophies (again, with the spoils trope operative) as to their suitability for serving theology's own claims. It is assuredly not a matter of philosophy trimming theology to the contours of a preconceived Procrustean bed (Barth's legitimate worry); such, of course, entirely violates the parameters of the traditional understanding of the dyadic movement of theology (*auditus fidei, intellectus fidei*) as well as the entire intentionality of the spoils trope. In every case, then, it is a matter of allowing the content of Christianity to determine the particular form; philosophy must be judged and disciplined as to its suitability as a proper vessel.[40]

What remains of particular concern today is the theological move toward nonfoundationalist, antimetaphysical thought. It is certainly true that the insights which Heidegger, Wittgenstein, Gadamer, Habermas, Kuhn, and Geertz have brought to light must continually be incorporated into a first philosophy. These include the finitude of the subject, the horizons of temporality and historicity, the sociocultural specificity of thought, the hidden presence of ideological interests, the linguistic embeddedness of reason, the theory-laden status of the inquirer, the incommensurability of frameworks, and so forth. What is essential to the renewed spoils typology is the constant interlacing of historicity and facticity with the metaphysical dimension that theology clearly needs. It is not a matter of asserting an ahistorical metaphysics hermetically sealed in a radically historical world. It is a matter of claiming that there are perduring and constitutive structures, eidetic elements, which persist precisely in and through history. If duration constitutes one element of appearance, then the actuality of eidetic duration within history is exactly what metaphysics is asserting.

What must be avoided, on the one hand, is a historicized understanding of Christian truth that inadequately appropriates the spoils typology because it imbibes philosophical presuppositions inimical to the perduring unity and material identity of Christian faith and doctrine; on the other hand, equally to be avoided is the position that so insists on the hegemony of the Christian narrative that further warrants from reason and philosophy, especially when they take the form of overarching first principles, are looked upon with suspicion. Neither position is theologically congruent with the traditional appropriation of spoils.

What the spoils trope clearly indicates is that Christianity's relationship to culture is only appropriate insofar as the church does not allow a prevailing culture to mold faith into the image of an alien philosophy. Of course, this was the charge leveled by Harnack: Has not the simple gospel been transplanted to a foreign, Hellenic soil, with dyslogistic effects? More recently, John Caputo, in the service of contemporary postmodern questions, expressed similar concerns, even resurrecting Leslie Dewart's

long forgotten treatise on the "dehellenization of Christian doctrine" from
its extended slumber.[41] Dewart's thesis, an early protest against a certain
form of ontotheology, was that theology had become so enamored of the
language of being, and of the correspondence notion of truth, that it had
lost its original kerygmatic power and, in the process, had imbibed Greek
rather than biblical-Hebraic-historical forms of thought. Dewart's claim
then was the familiar one that the philosophical spoils ingurgitated by
early Christian writers served to corrupt rather than to illuminate.

Precisely in answer to Dewart's charge, Joseph Owens, the redoubtable
historian of Aristotelianism, responded: "But where was there hellenization, in any historical sense? Did not the Greek fathers, expressing
Christian notions in forms of their own thought, successfully clear the
concepts of anything opposed to creation, to divine omnipotence, to
God's freedom in dealing with the world?"[42] Echoing the original claim
by W. Elert that the church's teaching, far from engaging in hellenization,
erected a wall "against an alien metaphysic," Owens continues:

> And where in Greek philosophy do you find the *notions* of person,
> essence or subsistence? Even when Greek concepts such as sub-
> stance, accident, word and nature were used, were they not
> painfully hammered into a new shape to convey Christian con-
> tent? Take a quick journey through pagan Greek philosophy and
> religion. Compare them with traditional Christian belief. Do you
> need anything more to apply here than the observation of Galen
> that the doctrine of Moses differs from that of Plato and all right
> thinking Greeks?[43]

Owens's point is clear enough: New forms were needed for the new wine
of performative Christian faith and doctrine. Older currencies were still
available, but these needed to be recast and reforged in order to serve as
useful vessels for the new teaching. Spoils were taken, of course, but not
without, as Newman said, being cast into the refiner's fire and stamped
with a deeper impress of the Master's image. It should be clear, then,
that the church did not unthinkingly adopt a preexisting ontology or
epistemology. The tocsin sounded by Origen, against building the
golden calf at Bethel, generally resounded in the ears of the later tradition.[44] The dictates of history itself testify as to why such a position has
been largely discredited.

Robert Jenson is entirely correct, then, when he says, "If theological
prolegomena lay down *conceptual conditions* of Christian teaching that are
not themselves Christian teaching, that are more than a formal demand

for coherence and argumentative responsibility . . . the prolegomena sooner or later turn against the *legomena*."[45] It can never be a matter of the content of theology toadying to preconceived ontological and epistemological foundations, of an apriority of some universal canon of reason. On the contrary, it is a matter of the church using certain philosophies in order to better express, illumine, and explicate its faith and teaching.[46] Ultimately, Athens and Jerusalem are not in entirely different spheres; both reason and faith are gifts from God. But reason must always be placed at the service of the revelatory narrative, even as it helps to confirm the fundamental claims of faith. It has been the argument here that it is difficult to claim that the church's faith has been deeply molded by Hellenistic or secular philosophical thought. At virtually every point in history—the Fathers, the councils, the Scholastics, the Reformers, and into the modern period—the church has generally resisted simply accepting an a priori philosophical approach.

At the same time, the Christian employment of the spoils typology is never a surgically precise, arithmetically exact procedure. It is always true that theologians, in their reconceptualization and reformulation of the Christian tradition, have a transformative as well as a preservative task. A renewed spoils typology fully recognizes that there is no positivistic method for defining the exact parameters of the *depositum fidei*.[47] Even if, as is necessarily the case, one takes Christianity as normative for other narratives, the attempt to refine, adapt, and incorporate new insights will always, at least for a period of time, yield loose ends and anomalous formulations. The history of theology bears witness to the difficulties encountered when trying to determine exactly what belongs to the "substance" of Christianity and what is merely "accidental."[48] It will not always be immediately and entirely clear, then, if a new attempt at incorporating "spoils" truly protects Christian faith and doctrine.

In conclusion, only a particular notion of spoils is appropriate for Christian theology. It is a notion that recognizes the ultimacy of Christian faith and doctrine, as well as those universal philosophical elements needed to explicate it more fully. It has a preservative as well as a transformative dimension, always open to new ideas and new points of view that will further illumine the deposit of faith, even while maintaining the material continuity and abiding nature of Christian truth.

Notes

1. H. Richard Niebuhr, *Christ and Culture* (New York: Harper, 1951).
2. Tillich treats these issues, in overture-like manner, in *Systematic Theology* (Chicago:

330 Foundations of Systematic Theology

University of Chicago, 1967), 61–65. For a good summary of Tillich on correlation as well as his understanding of ontology, see David Kelsey, "Paul Tillich," in *The Modern Theologians* (2nd ed.; ed. David F. Ford; Oxford: Blackwell, 2001), 87–104.

3. As I made clear in chapter one, I regard nonfoundationalism as not simply the claim that one cannot establish incontrovertible foundations for knowledge, that is, the rejection of certain positivist, empiricist, and evidentialist positions asserting such bedrock epistemological principles. With the widespread nonfoundationalist rejection of such positions, I am in agreement. Further, as I explained in chapter eight, I reject the notion of "foundationalism" if this means importing some foreign epistemic standard now utilized to adjudicate the adequacy of theological statements. Rather, I regard nonfoundationalism in a wider sense, encompassing, as I think is the case with several contemporary thinkers, the attempt to establish any first philosophy whatsoever, even, as is the case with the spoils typology, in an a posteriori way, after the acceptance of the gospel in faith. In this wider sense of nonfoundationalism, the use of any *prima philosophia* or metaphysics at the service of the gospel and Christian doctrine would itself constitute a foundationalist claim. One sees this argued clearly, for example, in Richard Bernstein's criticism of *Fides et ratio*. For Bernstein, the pope's emphasis on first principles at the service of the gospel, as well as his call for a renewed metaphysics, already constitutes a deleterious foundationalist turn. See Richard Bernstein, "Fides et ratio," *Books and Culture* 5 (July/August 1999): 30–32.

4. In his article "The Postpositivist Choice: Tracy or Lindbeck?" *Journal of the American Academy of Religion* 61 (1993): 655–77, Richard Lints points out that both authors clearly reject Enlightenment modernity. This is certainly true. It should be added, however, that for different reasons, both reject the metaphysical and transcendental principles espoused, differently of course, by classical, medieval, and modern thinkers. Lindbeck's rejection is based on his concern that Christianity is now subject to external, philosophical warrants. Tracy rejects this kind of thought because he connects it with a desire to avoid the epistemological impact of history and culture.

5. William Placher identifies several of those associated with postliberalism in "Being Postliberal: A Response to James Gustafson," *Christian Century*, April 7, 1999: 390–91. For similar lists, see William C. Placher, *Unapologetic Theology* (Louisville, Ky.: Westminster/John Knox, 1989), 22 n. 24. Lists of theologians may also be found in Carl Braaten, *No Other Gospel!* (Minneapolis: Fortress, 1992), 19; and Mark Cladis, "Mild-Mannered Pragmatism and Religious Truth," *Journal of the American Academy of Religion* 60 (1992): 24 n. 5. All authors acknowledge that such lists involve painting with a wide brush and ignoring many specific differences. Ronald Thiemann, for example, points out his disagreements with Lindbeck and postliberalism in *Constructing a Public Theology* (Louisville, Ky.: Westminster/John Knox, 1991), 18–25.

6. George Lindbeck, *The Nature of Doctrine* (Philadelphia: Westminster, 1984), 14–17.

7. This determinate element in postliberal thought is aptly described by David Bryant in "Christian Identity and Historical Change: Postliberals and Historicity," *Journal of Religion* 73 (1993): 31–41. Of course, it is precisely the Wittgensteinian claim that norms for truth are inextricably linked to the standards hegemonic within particular communities that gave rise to Kai Nielsen's dyslogistic description: "Wittgensteinian Fideism." See K. Nielsen, "Wittgensteinian Fideism," *Philosophy* 42 (1967), 191–209. It is no surprise then that Bryant thinks postliberalism inconsistently seeks to affirm both cultural-linguistic determinacy and "an enduring and unchanging structure within the Christian tradition that can anchor Christian identity" (35). Such an assertion of unchanging and perduring truth becomes anomalous once the turn to nonfoundationalism is made.

8. Although there are clearly differences between Lindbeck and Stanley Hauerwas,

there are also many convergences in their work. Much of Hauerwas's own political and moral thought is based on an embrace of a neo-Barthianism similar to that of Lindbeck's. Further, Hauerwas, like Lindbeck, is distrustful of universals and is enamored of nonfoundationalist thinkers (with Wittgenstein ranking high). I believe one may legitimately, then, classify Hauerwas under the rubric of postliberalism. Hauerwas does speak well of metaphysics, particularly Gilson's understanding of first philosophy in dialogue with revelation, but his remarks there are brief and undeveloped, making it unclear if Hauerwas realizes that an acceptance of metaphysics (even as an a posteriori system congruent with Christian revelation) would very much change his philosophical theology—and the thinking of those to whom he appears most indebted.

9. In a recent review of essays by Lindbeck entitled *The Church in a Postliberal Age* (ed. James Buckley; Grand Rapids: Eerdmans, 2002) Avery Dulles is convinced that Lindbeck insufficiently handles the question of truth and reference. See Dulles, "Postmodern Ecumenism," *First Things*, no. 136 (October 2003): 57–61. Lindbeck responds to this criticism, affirming his allegiance to the ontological truth of doctrine, in "George Lindbeck Responds to Avery Cardinal Dulles," *First Things*, no. 139 (January 2004): 13–15. William Placher, for his part, has argued that it is not completely clear if Lindbeck adopts a strong version of the cultural-linguistic model. See Placher, "Paul Ricoeur and Postliberal Theology: A Conflict of Interpretations?" *Modern Theology* 4 (1987): 3–52.

10. Geoffrey Wainwright, "Ecumenical Dimensions of George Lindbeck's 'Nature of Doctrine,'" *Modern Theology* 4 (1988): 121–32. Wainwright has recently reiterated his concern with Lindbeck: "It is hard to pin Lindbeck down as to whether such a substratum [of belief] may or must have any substantive content or is rather itself simply a regressive 'rule' which may be treated independently of its truth or falsity." Wainwright, *Is the Reformation Over?* (Milwaukee: Marquette University Press, 2001), 23. Alister McGrath has made similar comments about Lindbeck's palpable hesitancy on the referential character of Christian doctrine. See McGrath, *The Genesis of Doctrine* (Oxford: Blackwell, 1990), 26–32. More recently, McGrath has made similar charges in *A Scientific Theology*, vol. 2 (Grand Rapids: Eerdmans, 2002), 53. Along the same lines, Brian Hebblethwaite criticizes Lindbeck for following too closely the tradition of Kant's constructivism. See Hebblethwaite, "God and Truth," *Kerygma und Dogma* 40 (1994): 2–19.

11. The claim of "fideism" has been a traditional and at times facile Roman Catholic charge in response to some Protestant theology. However, this term is hardly limited to certain Protestant thinkers. As I argued in chapter one, the Roman Catholic philosopher Jean-Luc Marion, by asserting the claims of the traditional Christian faith (and concomitantly refusing to see, at least for the most part, any universal philosophical correlate to such claims), is perhaps subject to the same charge.

12. Peter Ochs has characterized postliberal thought as a reparative narrative vis-à-vis the Enlightenment, and surely this is correct. But one wonders if this anti-Enlightenment attitude, with its attempt to restore the primacy of the revelatory story, does not mistake a domineering and adjudicatory reason with any attempt at first philosophy, even a theologically controlled one.

13. Lindbeck is certainly not against the spoils trope as such. As he says in a 1986 article, "One may inscribe neo-Platonism within the biblical text as did Augustine, or Aristotelianism as did Aquinas, or late medieval nominalism, as did Luther, or Renaissance humanism, as Calvin did. . . . To the degree they lived in the Bible's strange new world, they wrought better than they knew." Nonetheless, it is a matter here of the *type* of spoils Lindbeck is himself willing to accept. Lindbeck's own alliance with nonfoundationalist thought shows that he regards any *prima philosophia* as ultimately an intrusion on Christian faith rather than an illuminative and congruous support for its claims.

Lindbeck, "Barth and Textuality," *Theology Today* 43 (October 1986): 368.

14. Lindbeck, *Nature of Doctrine*, 135. William Placher, in an article in the *Christian Century* explaining postliberalism (which itself was a response to a question posed by James Gustafson), uses the phrase "absorbing the universe into the biblical world" to explain that postliberals both use biblical categories to illuminate their lives and do not hold views that are incompatible with central biblical claims. Responding to Placher, Gustafson offers some "Troeltschian" questions, asking if other interpretations of reality, from physics or psychology for example, that do not cohere with the "biblical world" are thereby labeled as false or inadequate. Are postliberals against evolutionary theory, Gustafson presses, and if not, doesn't that mean that many other aspects of the biblical world need to corrected or altered? What one sees in this debate is Gustafson essentially claiming that in the postliberal assertion of the epistemic priority of the gospel, the social, historical, and intellectual context within which Christians may ask questions is severely limited. It remains the case, however, that Placher and postliberalism are hardly seeking to limit questions, or insights, from other disciplines. They are asserting the traditional view that Christian faith acts as a norm, a fundamental *Weltanschauung* against which other points of view are ultimately judged. Even here, however, Gustafson is correct on pressing the rights, and even, in a way similar to *Fides et ratio*, the autonomy of reason, in the sense that reason cannot be reduced to a slave but is able to critically challenge faith and theology to rethink its own claims. Aquinas, for example, was clear on this, indicating that no Christian teaching could stand that was, at base, *repugnans ad rationem*. But the traditional understanding of the faith/reason relationship held the conviction, in a way that Gustafson does not, or at least not fully, that reason would ultimately confirm faith's own revealed claims. And the only substantive criterion for this confidence can be faith in the revealing God himself. See Placher, "Being Postliberal: A Reply to James Gustafson," *Christian Century*, April 7, 1999; Gustafson, "Just What Is Postliberal Theology?" *Christian Century*, March 24–31, 1999, and April 14, 1999.

15. Needless to add, the very mention of the nature/grace issue should remind us, as in the Balthasar/Barth dialogue outlined in chapter seven, that nature here is not understood as outside the realm of grace but as, *ab ovo*, within the realm of God's salvific activity.

16. Useful descriptions of revisionist theology and its adherents may be found in Placher, *Unapologetic Theology*, 17–21, 154ff.

17. An astringent critique of the "ghettoizing" tendencies of Wittgensteinian philosophy may be found in the Popperian-influenced analysis of Peter Munz, *Our Knowledge of the Growth of Knowledge* (London: Routledge, 1985).

18. Such a position is clearly reflected in several of Tracy's works: *Plurality and Ambiguity: Hermeneutics, Religion, Hope* (San Francisco: Harper & Row, 1987), 43, 59; and "Beyond Foundationalism and Relativism," in *On Naming the Present* (Maryknoll, N.Y.: Orbis, 1994), 3–26.

19. As Tracy says, "The Enlightenment notion of rationality is in danger of becoming part of the problem, not the solution." Tracy, *Dialogue with the Other* (Louvain: Peeters, 1990), 1. Tracy's comments on Husserl's *Crisis* (*Dialogue with the Other*, 3) further illuminate his evaluation of the modern project.

20. In the past, Tracy has relied rather strongly on the approaches of Gadamer and Habermas for developing criteria of adequacy. His interest more recently has turned toward the phenomenology of Marion, which, I would argue, has stronger resonances with postliberalism (insofar as Marion seems, at least at times, to assert the truth of Christianity, while eschewing attempts to see the metaphysical implications of such assertions). Tracy's recent work on "fragments" bears further witness to his doubts about the enduring revelancy of any metaphysical or transcendental approach.

21. Tracy, for example, has long defended the notion of mutually critical correlation. This was seen at first in *Blessed Rage for Order* (New York: Seabury, 1975), 43–47. (This work was reprinted in 1996 by the University of Chicago Press with a new preface by the author). Tracy clearly explains his own view of correlation, vis-à-vis other approaches, in *The Analogical Imagination* (New York: Crossroad, 1981), 88 n. 44.

Somewhat similar to Tracy's position is that of Roger Haight, who has described the method of correlation as follows: "A method of correlation rests on this necessary fusion of past and present in the reception of revelation. It consists in distinguishing and then bringing together the original revelation as mediated through its traditional symbols and the situation of human consciousness in which it is received at any given time. What are correlated are the meaning of the original revelation and present-day human experience." Haight, *Dynamics of Theology* (New York: Paulist Press, 1990), 191. There is nothing objectionable about this statement as it stands. The crux of the matter will be in the precise way the correlation between "original revelation" and "present-day human experience" is understood. Haight's later work, *Jesus, the Symbol of God*, gives us some indication inasmuch as this Christology relies heavily on Gadamer's hermeneutics and so, by casting into doubt the very ability of the interpreter to engage in reconstructive hermeneutics, necessarily calls into question the adjudicatory priority extended to the creedal formulations of Christian faith. One suspects that Haight would claim that extending such priority to earlier formulations is tantamount to an unfortunate "revelational positivism." See *Dynamics of Theology*, 191–95.

22. It is perhaps, then, unsurprising that revisionist thought has been more popular among Roman Catholics, while postliberalism has been more representative of certain streams of Protestant theology. This is likely related to Habermas's astute comment that while Catholicism has always had a less troubled relationship with the *lumen naturale*, the lurking danger with such correlation is that theology will lose its identity in an alternating series of "takeover" attempts. See Jürgen Habermas, "Transcendence from Within, Transcendence in the World," in *Habermas, Modernity, and Public Theology* (ed. Don S. Browning and Francis Schüssler Fiorenza; New York: Crossroad, 1992), 231.

23. For this reason, I argued in chapter four that an emphasis on *phronēsis* or the *endechomena* (reversible matters) is not ultimately suitable for understanding Christian faith or doctrine.

24. There is no need to repeat the hermeneutical issues adduced in chapters five and six, but without an ontological basis, one cannot now legitimately argue for the separation of a normative Christian content from a historically, culturally, and linguistically conditioned form or context. I argued in those chapters that the form/content distinction, which has borne excellent fruit—for example, in ecumenical dialogues—requires a particular philosophical basis for its very possibility.

25. It must be said clearly, to avoid the introduction of red herrings, that to speak of a universal and continuous assertion of truth is avowedly not to speak of disembodied contents (and precisely this avowal constitutes the truth in the claim that, in one sense, all truth is necessarily linked to its historical, cultural, and linguistic form). However, it certainly is to acknowledge a distinction between a universal truth-claim and the cultural and linguistic milieu in which it was born. This is why I argued in chapter four that despite Gadamer's other merits, his hermeneutical theory ultimately seeks to overthrow any interpretative theory ultimately relying on such a metaphysical basis (and, again, one adduces metaphysics here only in service to the claims of Christian faith, which holds that some kind of context/content distinction is demanded to ensure the material continuity of the faith itself).

26. This is why, as I argued in chapter three, by logical necessity, thinkers strongly

influenced by nonfoundationalism, including revisionist theologians, must turn toward nonreferential or, more likely, pragmatic notions of truth now deemed ontologically consistent with the historical flux and sociocultural norms characterizing human life. If our humanity varies from age to age, then the truths we claim to grasp must themselves be subject to a strong dose of historicity. With the excision of metaphysics or of first philosophy of any kind, the only exercise of reason that is available is one that is entirely subject to the changing tides of temporal and historical embeddedness leading inexorably to a notion of truth completely subject to the delimiting character of these horizons.

27. Of course, to argue for the material identity and continuity of fundamental assertions of Christianity is not to disdain the essential task of reconceptualization (i.e., of making the Christian faith intelligible in each new age and culture), nor is it to underestimate the indubitably productive role of historicity (i.e., how the very grasping of truth in history allows new points of view to be uncovered). The proper theological task will always be preservative but also will be transformative in that new conceptual frameworks and new theological insights will bring to light elements and perspectives formerly unseen.

28. Of course, Habermas would respond that it is precisely this position that gives rise to his claim that religious speech must be excluded from public discourse since such speech cannot adduce publicly available warrants for its claims. Such domestication of religious speech is one element that virtually all those who reject many other aspects of the Enlightenment still appear compelled to defend. Revisionist theologians, such as Tracy, do not accept Habermas's conclusions. My concern, rather, is that by allowing Habermas to establish the rules of discussion, revisionist theologians have already conceded too much ground to communicative theory.

29. Such a position, perhaps, represents a reprise of Adorno's claim: The great Scholastics neither ostracized reason nor absolutized it. But what Adorno says about Scholasticism is better said of the Christian tradition at large. See Theodor Adorno, *Vernunft und Offenbarung*, cited in Matthew Lamb, *Habermas et la théologie* (ed. E. Arens; trans. D. Trierweiler; Paris: Cerf, 1993), 123.

30. Of course, given Rahner's notion of transcendental revelation, of the "supernatural existential" as ontologically constitutive of human nature as such, one cannot speak of the relationship between theology and the disciplines as if the latter were entirely *remoto Christo*. Rahner's entire theology, built upon the interlacing of the ontological and soteriological orders, demands that the interrelationship between the two is highly congruous, even if not finally identical.

31. Karl Rahner, "Yesterday's History of Dogma and Theology for Tomorrow," in *Theological Investigations*, vol. 18 (trans. Edward Quinn; New York: Crossroad, 1983), 13.

32. Of course, this brings up once again the thorny hermeneutical question: What belongs to Christian teaching—and what belongs only to the philosophical concepts used by such teaching? Ultimately, this can only be decided, as Rahner himself said, by conceding that the church is able to determine that which belongs essentially to Christian thought and that which does not. Surely, as pointed out in chapter six, just this procedure was enacted in terms of recent ecumenical agreements between the Roman Catholic Church and non-Chalcedonian churches. Language other than the two-nature formula was found that both protected the fundamental intention of Chalcedon (about Christ as true God and man) and was concomitantly acceptable to the non-Chalcedonian Christians. The recently concluded Joint Declaration on Justification between the Roman Catholic and Lutheran Churches offers another such example.

33. Bernard Lonergan, *The Way to Nicea* (trans. Conn O'Donovan; Philadelphia: Westminster, 1976), 128. Page numbers in the text refer to this work.

34. It goes without saying that one can disagree with or complement Lonergan's philosophical evaluations of Tertullian and Origen without disagreeing with his fundamental point on the relationship between the Christian faith and the use of "spoils."

35. Bernard Lonergan, *Doctrinal Pluralism* (Milwaukee: Marquette University Press, 1971), 8. This is why Lonergan sought to combine a philosophy defending the universal structures of consciousness while concomitantly championing the "openness" of cultural mutability and changing worlds of meaning.

36. Jean-Luc Marion, *God without Being* (trans. Thomas Carlson; Chicago: University of Chicago Press, 1991), 52. Marion's cementing of the nature/grace disjunction is sealed with his benign appraisal of Heidegger's remark that "each concept, in order to appear authentically theological, must measure its essential disparity with the 'pre-Christian' *Dasein.*'" But is an *essential* disparity really necessary? (*God without Being,* 67; citing Heidegger, *Phänomenologie und Theologie,* 63).

37. Of course, a strict and unbridgeable division between the "god of the philosophers" and the God of Abraham, Isaac, and Jacob has rarely been accepted by Roman Catholic theology. To do so would be to sever the link between nature and grace, between reason (even as fallen) and faith. However, we would do well, on just this point, to heed the comments of Balthasar, who, while clearly admitting that the Barthian *analogia fidei* and the philosophical *analogia entis* are only analogously (but really) related (since the analogy of being must always be inscribed within the graced order of faith), so, in the same way, there is an analogous relationship between the living God of Abraham and Jesus and the god of the philosophers, the latter subordinated to, but really related to, the former. See Hans Urs von Balthasar, *The Theology of Karl Barth* (trans. Edward Oakes; San Francisco: Ignatius, 1991), 369.

38.   John Caputo and Michael Scanlon, for example, claim that the "Hellenization" of theology, especially as inherited from the patristic tradition, is causing some sectors of contemporary thought to perform "a Hegelianism in reverse." By this they mean that while Hegel sublated religious symbols into philosophical concepts, contemporary theology is, so to speak, deconceptualizing theology insofar as concepts are recognized as "partial and transitory clarification[s] of the density of the symbolic." It is the first-order symbolic and metaphorical language of faith that is now primary, with concepts, again reversing Hegel, having an important but secondary dimension. Scanlon and Caputo do not develop these suggestive ideas, but, from the standpoint of the spoils trope, one can see its strengths and limitations. The clear strength is that it recognizes the limited dimension of intelligibility afforded by the concept, especially when any human concept is applied analogically to God. Any concept, even one sanctioned by long theological tradition and conciliar warrant, must always be a "partial" clarification of religious faith—and surely a limited clarification of the nature of the Godhead. Further, one may certainly hold that concepts are mutable, even if judgments are not. Concepts may change even if a new, equivalent concept will protect the truth reached in judgment.

The weakest point in their argument, if I understand them correctly, is that concepts canonized by the church's own doctrine are to be considered not only "partial" but "transitory" as well. If what is meant is not simply equivalent reconceptualization (concepts are mutable but dogmatic judgments are not), then this, ironically, would likely be subjecting faith to a new "hellenization"—or what might better be called a "Greco-Germanic" sublation—because, from this point of view, the revelatory narrative of Christian faith and doctrine would be called into question by a certain philosophical understanding of the radical effects of historicity so that even concepts sanctioned by the church as essential to its teaching and doctrine, such as the *homoousion* or the impassibility and immutability of the

Godhead, would, once again ironically, be challenged under the guise of "dehellenization." In fact, the only significant change would be that Hellenic philosophy would now give way to Heideggerian/Derridean thought—a later philosophy substituting for an earlier one. Because metaphysics (again in a wide sense) must be eschewed as ontologically inappropriate, faith's claims must now be differently understood—as epiphanic and transitory rather than definitive and lasting. In such a construal, Christian faith and doctrine would ultimately be stripped of its cognitive claims, or such claims would be regarded as tentative and fallibilistic at best.

Ultimately, what is at stake here is one's faith that the Christian church retains the ability to determine what is "alien" to its faith and what is properly attributable to its faith. Only the church at large can determine if a particular philosophy is or is not congruent with the gospel of grace; only the church can ultimately determine if the "spoils" taken illuminate or contaminate the Christian faith. See John Caputo and Michael Scanlon, introduction to *God, the Gift, and Postmodernism* (ed. J. Caputo and M. Scanlon; Bloomington: Indiana University Press, 1999), 11.

Several other points need to be clarified here: (1) Caputo and Scanlon do not adduce the concept of *ousia* as in need of dehellenization. My use of this term is an extrapolation from their argument; (2) I am not arguing that traditional divine attributes cannot be rethought; indeed, within certain limits they must be. Christian faith and doctrine are not inexorably tied to a particular lexicon or conceptual system. I am arguing, however, that attributes such as the immutability and impassibility of the Godhead, with very strong warrants in the entire patristic, medieval, theological, and liturgical Christian tradition, and, from the Roman Catholic perspective, canonized by several councils (e.g., Lateran IV and Vatican I), can be regarded as "partial" but not simply as "transitory" without eviscerating, and ultimately instrumentalizing, the assertions of Christian doctrine. Claiming that such concepts were "transitory" would be possible if, in fact, one were aiming for a reconceptualization that protected the fundamental meaning of such an attribute. This would mean that while *semantically* incommensurable interpretations may arise, these would be ultimately commensurable with regard to fundamental meaning. This, however, does not seem to be the primary intention of the authors. For reinterpretations of both attributes that seek to preserve their traditional intention, see Thomas Weinandy, *Does God Suffer?* (Notre Dame, Ind.: University of Notre Dame Press, 2000); and Weinandy, *Does God Change?* (Still River, Mass.: St. Bede's Press, 1985). Of course, on this issue of the divine attributes, Protestant and Roman Catholic theology may diverge because of different criteriologies in determining essential dimensions of Christian doctrine. However, the *principle* remains the same in both, namely, the hegemony of the revelatory narrative vis-à-vis philosophical spoils. Christian doctrine makes claims to truth that necessarily remain normative for any philosophical adoptions.

39. The pope's comments here should not be construed to mean that theology does not possess its own intelligibility and universal truth. What is meant is that properly understood, philosophy will offer a further dimension of intelligibility by confirming, in its own sphere, theology's claims.

40. Kevin Vanhoozer rightly says, "A Christian theological account of hermeneutics, as of anything else, must discipline notions of meaning and interpretation achieved in abstraction from distinctly Christian beliefs." Vanhoozer, *Is There a Meaning in This Text?* (Grand Rapids: Zondervan, 1998), 198.

41. John Caputo, "Metanoetics: Elements of a Postmodern Christian Philosophy," in *The Question of Christian Philosophy Today* (ed. Francis J. Ambrosio; New York: Fordham University Press, 1999), 192. For Dewart's original treatise, see Leslie Dewart, *The Future*

of Belief (New York: Herder & Herder, 1966).

42. Joseph Owens, "Dewart's View of Christian Philosophy and Contemporary Man," in *The Future of Belief Debate* (ed. Gregory Baum; New York: Herder & Herder, 1967), 97.

43. Ibid., 97–98. For Elert, see *Der Ausgang der altkirchlichen Christologie* (Berlin: Lutherisches Verlagshaus 1957), 14. For Galen, see Robert Wilken, *The Christians as the Romans Saw Them* (New Haven: Yale University Press, 1984), 68–93.

44. This is certainly not to underestimate the contribution of Luther and the entire dialectical stream of thought. Its essential purpose was always to reawaken the church to the gospel over against the illegitimate encroachments of a philosophy incongruent with the gospel or a culture confusing worldly beauty with transcendent glory.

45. Robert Jenson, *Systematic Theology*, vol. 1 (Oxford: Oxford University Press, 1997), 9 (emphasis added).

46. Jenson properly explains that his foregoing strictures (against conceptual criteria that are not Christian in inspiration) should not be "read as a rejection of Western Christianity's inheritance from pagan antiquity. . . . That the fathers were able to agree with 'the Greeks' as they regularly called their counterparts, that, for example, 'God has a *Logos*,' or that the debate about God's 'being' should be pursued, was constitutive in the missionary history that leads to Western forms of Christianity." Jenson continues: "What must not continue is only the Enlightenment's elevation of the Greek element of our thinking to be the unilateral judge of the whole." To move in this direction, of course, is not simply to argue for a legitimate autonomy extended to philosophy, but to subordinate the revelatory narrative to alien criteria. Jenson, *Systematic Theology*, 1:9.

47. Of course, in determining the precise nature of the Christian faith, theology relies on a variety of dimensions, classically denominated as the *loci theologici*, such as the authority of Scripture, the early Christian writers, creedal statements, the declarations of ecumenical councils, the liturgical life of the church, etc.

48. Need one refer again to the condemnations at Paris in 1270 and 1277 regarding the introduction of Aristotelian terminology? Karl Rahner has spoken with frequency on the difficulty of determining whether a new theological system has, in fact, performed its preservative as well as transformative task. He argues that theology will always generate a certain amount of healthy friction precisely because of this dual goal. See Karl Rahner, "Yesterday's History of Dogma and Theology for Tomorrow," in *Theological Investigations* (vol. 18; trans. E. Quinn; New York: Crossroad, 1983).

CONCLUSION

This book has been largely concerned with Christian doctrine and with those characteristics, such as universality and material identity, classically attributed to it. The argument has been that a Christian theology fully aware of its own doctrinal tradition, of the unity of the faith throughout history, and of the cognitive yield of faith's affirmations needs an appropriate and determinate understanding of philosophy, of truth, of hermeneutics, of theological language, and of correlation in order to illuminate and further substantiate faith's own claims.

Conversely, the book has argued that revelation and Christian faith cannot chain themselves to any philosopher whose thought is essentially nonfoundationalist or who finds metaphysics (in the wide philosophical sense of *prima philosophia* used throughout this book) inappropriate. To cast one's philosophical and theological lots in this direction is to either lose the intelligibility associated with faith's claims or to abandon the material unity and continuity of faith that is essential to Christianity's self-understanding.

Of course, to say this is decidedly not to affirm that theology cannot learn a great deal from Heidegger, Gadamer, nonfoundationalist thought generally, and even from Derrida and the currents of postmodernism. The "spoils" typology discussed earlier demands that theology take every thought captive to Christ—with no exceptions. Postmodernism, for example, demands that theology maintain a sense of openness toward the unfamiliar and the "other," awakening us in the process to the "otherness" of God, thereby rescuing us from latent rationalism, from theological Cartesianism, and from the "naturalism" endemic to human experience. Postmodernism helps us to live with contingencies and differences, correcting a provincial monism and warning us against a lapse into a univocity of thought or language. It cautions us about facile claims regarding divine and natural law; it alerts us to systemic distortions, ideologies, and pathologies.

The enduring genius of Heidegger and Gadamer is that they have forced theology to examine, in a philosophically unparalleled way, the relationship between historicity and truth. If thought and truth are only born within the horizons of temporality and tradition, which is unarguably the case, then to what extent is any claim permanent? And, perhaps more to the point, how is such permanence finally conceived? Right from the outset, Heidegger recognized the epic importance of his insights: Philosophical change could only be initiated by a radical deconstruction of the prior tradition; what was needed was a new "fundamental ontology."[1]

One of the crucial questions of the book is this: Is the deconstruction of any *prima philosophia* and the theoretical turn toward nonfoundationalism—with all of the pulsating implications this has for truth, hermeneutics, and allied questions—theologically and revelationally appropriate? That is to say, can such a philosophical move clarify, sustain, illumine, and explicate the theology of revelation undergirding the doctrinal claims of historic Christianity? Such a philosophical turn is clearly not theologically appropriate in any final and ultimate way if revelation is understood in the classical sense as a *locutio Dei*, that is, as in some substantive manner continuous, perpetual, universal, and selfsame across cultures and generations.[2] At least traditionally, what Christian faith and theology affirm is that there is a material content of belief, classically denominated the *depositum fidei*, that perdures from age to age.[3] This identity, to be sure, is highly nuanced and qualified, allowing for organic growth and development but necessarily displaying significant elements of continuity and duration as well.[4] This is what propels the traditional theological defense of some first philosophy, of truth as correspondence (along with disclosure), of reconstructive hermeneutics (along with reconceptualization), of the possibility of analogy (along with the priority of grace), of the *spolia Aegyptiorum* (along with a *relative* philosophical autonomy). If revelation implies that there has truly been a "material" handing-on (*paradosis*) of the central, selfsame affirmations of Christian faith, then the nonfoundationalist approach is, in the last analysis, unacceptable because it regards this understanding as philosophically untenable.

On the other hand, it is legitimate to invert the question: Does the theological tradition, precisely because of its use of certain philosophical perspectives, provide an ontologically inappropriate understanding of revelation? One particular understanding of revelation—with its deeply interwoven veridical, hermeneutical, linguistic, and correlational corollaries—would need to be abandoned if it were unquestionably proven to be philosophically unsustainable. Surely no view of revelation, however deeply rooted in the tradition, can finally stand if it is repugnant to reason.[5] In his encyclical *Fides et ratio*, John Paul II comes very close to this position when he defends the autonomy of philosophy, making clear that "the content of revelation can never debase the legitimate autonomy of reason" (79), and even obliquely calling into question the traditional role assigned to philosophy (and thus to reason) as the *ancilla theologiae*.[6]

The questions necessarily addressed to the positions defended in this book are these: Is this particular understanding of revelation and doctrine, with its corollaries of truth, hermeneutics, language, and correlation, linked to a now discredited and truncated philosophy? Must not a theology of revelation, too, properly adapt itself to the illuminating work of Heidegger, nonfoundationalism, and even postmodernism? While revelation cannot collapse before philosophies vaunting themselves as absolute truth, must not the Christian understanding of revelation and doctrine be reconceived if the philosophies illuminating them are themselves no longer theoretically tenable? Surely the traditional conjunction of faith and reason, as well as the legitimate "liberty" of philosophy, requires an answer to these questions.

Of course, several theologians, some noted in this book, have already concluded that one must rethink the nature of revelation and doctrine in order to meet this new situation honestly. If the traditional emphasis on a *prima philosophia* and its allied correlates—precisely as illuminative and explicative tools of the material continuity and universal identity of the Christian faith—are philosophically inappropriate, then one must seek a new understanding of revelation, one properly befitting the newly presenced horizons of life and thought. One's understanding of revelation and doctrine cannot be conjoined to an inappropriate, misleading, and ultimately illusory philosophical vessel. To do so would be to mock the very congruency of faith and reason, of grace and nature; it would itself constitute a dégringolade toward fideism of the worst sort.

Further, there is a certain logic in the nonfoundationalist construal of thought, being, and truth—and so in its construal of theology and doctrine. One cannot simply posit a theory of revelation and maintain it at all costs and in the face of all evidence. As Thomas Kuhn, Norwood Hanson, and others showed early on, this kind of theoretical, paradigmatic myopia was fully operative in the scientific tradition. Rather than adapt to evolving evidence and the accumulating weight of facts, scientists frequently complicated older theories in order to avoid entirely new paradigms. Most infamously, of course, were the additions of epicycles to the Ptolemaic model in order to avoid the conclusions of Copernicus. It is legitimate to ask, then, if some theology, as well, remains in this "epicycle" period. Are apodictic and ideology-driven minds still foolishly hoping to protect fanciful interstices of truth not saturated by enveloping change? And is the current admission of the influence upon Christian doctrine of historical limitations, finite perspectives, sociocultural horizons, and ideological conditioning simply another "Ptolemaic" strategy to avoid conceding the triumph of nonfoundationalist and postmodern thought? Is perduring Christian doctrine, as Lord Radnor said to de Tocqueville, simply a haven for tired minds?[7]

Of course, if theology and doctrine are to be rethought along non-foundationalist lines, then the Christian understanding of revelation must be entirely reconceived as epiphanic and even dialectical in kind. Revelation and doctrine must now be understood as highly changeable and protean, not simply in linguistic form (an advance already demanded by history) but even in fundamental content.[8] In this instance, revelation possesses the "givenness" characteristic of Being itself; it is conceived along the Heideggerian lines of event, with its constant oscillation between presence and absence. Even if there are material contradictions from age to age, these should not be understood pejoratively, but as newly revelatory of the elusive character of being and truth. What continues in the church is not the same doctrinal content held from age to age (even as organically developed and nuanced); what survives, rather, is Christian reflection on the same texts and symbols, elements that have been handed down in the community and that continue to make a claim on believers. Interpretations of these texts will vary, even widely, from epoch to epoch. A certain normativity is accorded to the texts themselves, as witnesses to an originary event. But the understanding of them will always be reflective of varying and incommunicable forms of life. Changes in interpretation and meaning will reflect the inexorable tides of historicity and culture characteristic of all humanity, including the Christian community. We do well, in this schema, to recognize that there is no "final" name for being, for truth, or even for revelation. There is, instead, the "play of the sendings," that is the play of varying interpretations which may be validated only by means of variable criteria such as the "claim" and "emancipatory praxis."

But can Christian faith and doctrine actually be so conceived without becoming something entirely different from the tradition that preceded it? Is the cognitive yield of Christian truth so ephemeral, no longer certain of its content? Does philosophy itself bear witness to this kind of nonfoundationalist understanding?

This book has argued that Christian theology, particularly in its explication of doctrine, has rightly become postrationalist, postpositivist, and post-Enlightenment. It has incorporated more fully the principles of historical and ideological sensitivity. It has abandoned a naïve and wooden referentialism, dismissed the phantom of naked conceptualism, accepted the variety of horizons attendant upon the hermeneutical process, and intensified the apophaticism inherent in speaking of the divine. And the best of this theology has perceived these changes not as grudging concessions, but as ontologically productive and enriching developments.

At the same time, questions have been raised: Can Christian and Catholic theology avoid the abiding referentialism traditionally associated with its understanding of the mysteries of faith? Can metaphysics or some species of *prima philosophia*—confirming the logic of realism, presence, universality, and continuity—be thought of dyslogistically? Can theology continue to defend the material continuity and perduring presence of Christian truth without thereby lapsing into a simplistic claim of absolute presence and luminosity? And if such material continuity is defended, must it be thought of as dogmatic intolerance, as an unfortunate, anachronistic, and perhaps reactionary response to a historicized, postmodern world?

The answers to these questions, I have argued, force a clear departure from full-blown nonfoundationalist (and postmodern) thought. Certain parameters are essential if theology is to render service to the church as faith seeking understanding. It is not a matter of endorsing the merely customary; it is a matter of seeking what is eidetically constitutive given the church's own belief. My contention is that the notion of first philosophy, truth, hermeneutics, language, and correlation outlined here are, when taken in broad contours, essential for undergirding and illuminating the profound and enduring claims of Christian faith and doctrine. Such notions provide a further measure of intelligibility to the *depositum fidei* taught by and handed down by the church. Such positions, while often philosophically defensible on their own, belong to the very logic of revelation, to the affirmation that God has manifested himself to us and taken us into profound communion with his own intensive and relational Trinitarian life. Such positions are, indeed, necessary if theology and Christian doctrine are to avoid courting the twin dangers to its claims: a fideism that holds for the continuity of faith while abjuring the philo-sophical implications of such an assertion (and so dichotomizing nature and grace), or a historicism insisting that claims for a materially perdur-ing content of Christian truth are themselves ontologically inappropriate and illusory.

The championing of these positions as an alternative to certain fideist and historicist tendencies is decidedly not simply a return to "ontotheol-ogy," nor an attempt to establish an ahistorical metaphysics (as if such were possible) hermetically sealed from a radically historical world. Nor is it to suggest that doctrine is collapsible to its cognitive content, thereby emptying it of personalist, existentialist, or symbolic elements. It is to suggest, however, that if revelation is understood as God's own self-manifestation, then there must be an irreducible cognitive dimension that is identical, referential, and continuous; the narrative of salvation, precisely as narrative, must exist without radical rupture, reversal, or breach. It is also to recognize that, while all thinking and language come to being within history, from the Christian point of view, history itself, while a constitutive human dimension, is a created reality, not the final or determinative horizon. That horizon, ultimately, is the *creatio ex nihilo* by which an eternal God began a salvific dialogue with his creatures.[9]

The Christian self-understanding is saturated *ab initio* with options for finality and ultimacy. By this I mean that the revelation offered in Jesus Christ has established an unshakeable Archimedean point that is at the heart of the *mysterium fidei*, a point embracing basic dimensions of mate-rial identity, continuity, and presence. The integrity of this *fides*, then, requires certain elements, outlined here, which offer intelligibility and illumination to perduring affirmations of Christian truth. In the final analysis, this approach represents a theological attempt to understand Christian faith and teaching within the broad contours of both the tradi-tion and contemporary thought.

Notes

1. Martin Heidegger, *Being and Time* (trans. John Macquarrie and Edward Robinson; New York: Harper & Row, 1962), 34. Gadamer, penetrating more deeply, rejected the term "fundamental ontology" as still not capturing fully the philosophical revolution that Heidegger had intiated. See Gadamer, *Philosophical Hermeneutics* (trans. David Linge; Berkeley: University of California Press, 1976), 171.

2. The term *locutio Dei* intends to refer to God's speaking in a wide sense, denoting the entire complex of events that comprise revelation. This term should not be reduced, then, as occasionally was the case among the neo-Scholastics, to a doctrinal *summa* virtu-ally independent of the salvific good news of the gospel of Christ.

3. It bears repeating that to affirm such a content is not to engage in a search for some "ahistorical" nugget within the river of historicity. The claim that one is seeking an ephemeral and illusory ahistorical dimension of truth is a convenient but inaccurate shibboleth. See, for example, Edward Farley, *Ecclesial Reflection* (Philadelphia: Fortress, 1982), 96 n. 19, which lodges precisely this charge of an "ahistorical" seeking. On the contrary, affirming the claim that truth comes to light within a historical horizon is to aver that one appearance of being within history is precisely that of duration. And what Christian faith affirms is that the material continuity of fundamental doctrines constitutes just such a historical appearance of abiding truth.

4. From a Roman Catholic perspective, I am affirming this continuity/development with all of the necessary qualifications that must be added—for example, the possibility of errors and reversals by the ordinary magisterium, the epistemological importance of both the hierarchy of truths and the *sensus fidelium*, and the danger of systemic distortions within the church. Further, as I hope is clear by this point, the material continuity of the deposit of faith cannot be confused with the theological mummification properly decried by Rahner as "sacrosanct immobility." See Karl Rahner, "Theology and the Roman Magisterium," in *Theological Investigations*, vol. 22 (trans. J. Donceel; New York: Crossroad, 1991), 176–90.

5. In just this regard, it serves to remember that Aquinas recognized that, while the Trinity is a mystery of faith *stricte dictu*, intelligible explanations of the Trinity must be pursued lest the very foundations of Christian belief be found *repugnans ad rationem*.

6. Of course, the true meaning of the axiom *ancilla theologiae sed non ancilla nisi libera* is meant precisely to accent philosophy's relative autonomy.

7. Alexis de Tocqueville, *Journeys to England and Ireland* (trans. G. Lawrence and K. P. Mayer; London: Faber & Faber, n.d.), 58.

8. It is precisely the alleged mutability of revelation itself that allows Gordon Kaufman to say, "Theological work grounded principally on what is claimed to be authoritative 'revelation' is simply not appropriate today. The concept of revelation is itself a part of the conceptual scheme which has become questionable, and it is the overall scheme, therefore, which now must be carefully examined and possibly reconstructed." Kaufman, *In the Face of Mystery* (Cambridge, Mass.: Harvard University Press, 1993), 21.

9. In my judgment, it is precisely this affirmation, rather than an unseemly Hellenistic residue, that explains the Catholic Church's official resistance to every theological attempt to introduce change and fluctuation into the life of the immutable and passionate Godhead.

elision (70)

lethic (21)

indefeasibly (24)

perduring (58)

ostensive (74)

enervate (147)

elide (169)

cipher (217)

anamnetic (217)

quidditatively (246)

INDEX